RED CARPET

JOSEPH FINDER

RED CARPET

A New Republic Book/Holt, Rinehart and Winston
New York

Published by Holt, Rinehart and Winston, 383 Madison Avenue, New York, New York 10017.
Published simultaneously in Canada by Holt, Rinehart and Winston of Canada, Limited.

Library of Congress Cataloging in Publication Data
Finder, Joseph.
Red carpet.
"A New republic book."
Includes bibliographical references and index.
1. United States—Commerce—Soviet Union. 2. Soviet Union—Commerce—United States. 3. Businessmen—United States—Biography. I. Title.
HF3105.F56 1983 382′.0973′047 [B] 82-18694
ISBN 0-03-060484-2

Portions of this book have previously appeared in *Harper's* magazine.

First Edition

Designer: Robert Bull
Printed in the United States of America
10 9 8 7 6 5 4 3 2 1

Grateful acknowledgment is made for permission to reprint excerpts from the following:

"John Callaway Interviews Armand Hammer," October 8, 1981. John Callaway Interviews from WTTW Chicago (Distributed nationally on PBS). "Bill Moyers' Journal: The World of David Rockefeller," WNET, New York. "The Russian Connection: Dr. Armand Hammer," produced by NBC News. Mike Wallace Collection, George Arents Research Library for Special Collections at Syracuse University. The oral history memoirs of Sir Robert Watson-Watt and of Warren Weaver, © 1980, The Trustees of Columbia University in the City of New York.

ISBN 0-03-060484-2

For
Anne Bernays and Justin Kaplan—
with gratitude

CONTENTS

PART THREE: THE RISE AND FALL OF DÉTENTE

PREFACE

This is a book about how a few very rich and very powerful American businessmen—Cyrus Eaton, Armand Hammer, W. Averell Harriman, Donald Kendall, and David Rockefeller—illustrious capitalists all, have courted and been courted by the leaders of Soviet Communism, and why. It is a story not so much about money as about the behind-the-scenes dealings at the rarefied juncture of international commerce and foreign affairs.

One man, Armand Hammer, overshadows the rest. His extensive involvement with Russia began in 1921 and continues to this day, and so his story comprises about half the book. Much of the information about Hammer is here told for the first time, although a great deal remains to be told.

Each of my subjects (with the exception of the late Cyrus Eaton) consented to be interviewed. Governor Harriman graciously allowed me to research in his voluminous and invaluable personal archives.

A large part of the material in this book was gathered through investigative work, using recently declassified government documents, other documents made available under the Freedom of Information Act, and, most importantly, more than a hundred personal interviews in this country and in the Soviet Union. This undertaking would have been impossible if not for a generous grant from the Fund for Investigative Journalism and the encouragement of the Fund's director, Howard Bray.

My work was made much easier because of E. J. Kahn's brilliant *New Yorker* profiles of Eaton, Harriman, and Rockefeller. I am grateful for the kind assistance of Harold B. Scott and Michael Forrestal of the U.S.-U.S.S.R. Trade and Economic Council; Ambassador Jacob Beam, Paige Bryan, Malcolm Forbes, Dr. Philip S. Gillette, Val Ginter, Sheila Hart, Milton Katz, Flora Lewis, Lev Navrozov, Norman Podhoretz, Katharine Tait; and the outstanding chroniclers of the Soviet Union, Harrison Salisbury, Murray Seeger, Henry Shapiro, and Hedrick Smith.

My advisers at the Harvard Russian Research Center—Professors Marshall Goldman and Adam Ulam—were of enormous help, although they can in no way be blamed for the final outcome. Finally, I am indebted to a few people whose help was indispensable: Edward Jay Epstein, Yuri Handler, and Ronald Steel; Martin Peretz, my editor Marc Granetz, my agent Patricia Berens, Justin Kaplan and Anne Bernays, and, of course, my parents.

RED CARPET

INTRODUCTION

A BANQUET IN THE KREMLIN

THE LINE of sleek black Soviet limousines entering the Kremlin around noon on December 6, 1978, was so long that bystanders thought a delegation of high-level Communists—the Poles, perhaps, or the East Germans—had come to Moscow. But within the chauffeured Chaikas and ZILs were, instead, the heads of some of America's most powerful corporations, coming to a luncheon in the Kremlin's Palace of Congresses.

Not all the Americans arrived by limousine. Some of lesser standing walked from their hotels, most of which were close to Red Square; others took taxis. Altogether there were four hundred businessmen in Moscow for the Sixth Annual Meeting of the Directors and Members of the U.S.-U.S.S.R. Trade and Economic Council, a conference that promised to revive the immense trade the Soviet government had hinted at when Richard Nixon was in office.

This assembly of true-blue capitalists took on the appearance of an official Soviet function. Protocol was strictly observed. The result was all kinds of headaches for the organizers of the meeting.

There was the problem of private jets. In the years since Nixon and Brezhnev had initiated détente, a few Americans who were used to flying around the world in their own planes had managed to acquire such an influence with the Soviets that they were allowed to fly into Moscow, once an unthinkable luxury. The Russians, fearing that an American jet might fly over a sensitive military area, always required that a Soviet pilot board any private craft before it entered Soviet airspace and direct it safely to Moscow's Sheryemetyevo Airport. But there were not enough Soviet pilots around to guide the large number of jets this meeting would attract, so the Soviets told the American organizers to limit the numbers.

As there was no graceful way to permit one chief executive to fly in and not permit another, no private planes were being allowed to fly into Moscow this time. Then the word got out that Armand Hammer, head of Occidental Petroleum, had arranged secretly with one of the leading Soviet trade officials, Dzhermen Gvishiani (Premier Alexei Kosygin's son-in-law), to allow in his Boeing 727, the *Oxy-1*. Hammer had paid handsomely for the privilege (something like thirty thousand dollars) and had also agreed to entertain the Soviet pilots for a week before the flight at a swank hotel in Paris.

The other Americans were outraged. Had it not been agreed there would be no private planes? Publicly, the Soviets claimed that there had been some sort of misunderstanding; privately, they admitted that some very influential Soviet leaders had a soft spot for Hammer. So the rules were now amended to allow anyone who wished to take his own plane into Moscow to do so as long as he paid at the rate Hammer did, and also wined and dined the Soviet pilot at a good Western hotel.

As it turned out, only nine American businessmen took up the offer; David Rockefeller, J. Paul Austin of Coca-Cola, and C. William Verity of Armco Steel, Inc., who was the new chairman of the Trade and Economic Council, were among them. Verity had the privilege of flying to Moscow with the meeting's guest of honor and star attraction, eighty-seven-year-old Averell Harriman.

Accommodations were another problem. Harriman, as an official guest of the Soviet government—he had after all helped save Russia from destruction by the Nazis by negotiating Lend-Lease aid during the Second World War—received the finest lodgings. He, his wife, Pamela, and an aide, Peter Swiers of the State Department, were put up in the Moscow suburb of Lenin Hills in a magnificent villa that had once belonged to a czarist aristocrat. In the villa next door were housed two other guests of the government: Juanita Kreps, Jimmy Carter's Secretary of Commerce, and Kempton Jenkins, who as president of Armco was involved in negotiations for a gigantic, multibillion-dollar steel plant in Russia.

Everyone else got a hotel room; but good hotel rooms in Moscow are always scarce. David Rockefeller, accustomed to the very best a country has to offer, was given the grand, commodious room on the second floor of the National Hotel, where Lenin had lived during March 1918; the Lenin Suite, as it was called, was furnished with exquisite paintings and a grand piano. Donald Kendall, the chairman of PepsiCo, who had helped found the Trade Council and who, as one of Richard Nixon's closest friends, was once enormously influential in Moscow, was also given a suite in the National, though a less grand one. One American did not need a hotel room: Armand Hammer had recently been granted a luxurious private apartment, reputedly almost as elegant as the Moscow apartment of Leonid Brezhnev.

Americans less sophisticated in the ways of Moscow reasoned, mistakenly, that the best rooms would be in the newer hotels, and so requested suites in the "Howard Johnsons" of Russia—the Intourist and the Rossiya. At the Rossiya, where Bill Verity and the Trade Council's president, Michael Forrestal, were lodged, there was an unfortunate and very Soviet difficulty that the businessmen discovered shortly after moving in: none of the elevators was working. This was unpleasant for the Americans, all of whom had rooms between the seventh and fourteenth floors. Returning to their suites after a long day of talks and vodka receptions proved to be a difficulty. Some had grown accustomed to such problems. Stories were told of Edgar F. Kaiser, the late chairman of Kaiser Industries, who had a regular suite in the Intourist equipped with large stores of frozen and canned food as well as a gallon of Liquid Plumber for the times when the bathtub got stopped up.

And then there was the question of limousines. The ZIL, reserved for the twenty highest Soviet leaders, is a handmade vehicle that resembles an elongated Lincoln Continental, with plush interiors, a burnished black exterior, and gray curtains inside to shield its passengers from the stares of ordinary Soviet citizens. The second-echelon limousine, more widely available, is the Chaika, which looks like a Cadillac Fleetwood. Three ZILs were allocated—one each to the U.S. Secretary of the Treasury Michael Blumenthal, Bill Verity, and Averell Harriman. Rockefeller, Hammer, Kendall, and the other important business chiefs got Chaikas.

The limousines entered the Borovitsky Gate of the Kremlin and brought their passengers to the Palace of Congresses, which was normally reserved for such grandiose affairs of state as Party congresses. Long tables covered with white cloths were set up with large, beautiful floral arrangements and place settings for four hundred; each setting included crystal glasses for mineral water, wine, vodka, and cognac. At the head table sat the U.S. Treasury Secretary and the Soviet Deputy Foreign Trade Minister. At their sides were Juanita Kreps, in a white Russian fur hat; Averell Harriman, in a pinstriped suit; and Dzhermen Gvishiani, in an elegant Western-tailored suit and a Dior tie.

Harriman, who had met for ninety minutes before lunch with Leonid Brezhnev, rose to give a speech and announced that no man in the world had a greater desire than Leonid Brezhnev to "do all that he can to prevent nuclear war." Harriman's remarks, though made without notes and somewhat rambling, held everyone in the hall spellbound. For not only did he know Brezhnev, he knew just about everyone of importance in the Soviet government. He reminisced fondly about his old friend Anastas Mikoyan, a longtime Minister of Foreign Trade, whose grave he had visited the day before. He called Joseph Stalin a fine and effective leader but criticized Stalin's "extraordinary brutality." Though the Soviet officials listening betrayed no discomfiture at public criticism of Stalin, the Russian waiters gasped in amazement and flattened themselves against the walls.

Behind the pomp and finery was a clash among American political leaders that approached backbiting. By 1975, in part because of Senator Henry Jackson's successful effort to tie Soviet-American trade to emigration of Soviet Jews, trade had almost halted. When Jimmy Carter became President in 1977, he told business leaders that he wanted to increase trade. The new chairman of the Trade Council, Bill Verity, began to do what he could to hold Carter to his word.

One of the first orders of business was to select as the Council's president a key Carter supporter, Michael Forrestal. A brilliant New York lawyer (and son of James Forrestal, Harry Truman's Secretary of Defense), Forrestal considered the position with reluctance, for it seemed an unpleasant chore. But Verity persuaded Cyrus Vance to call Forrestal and tell him that by taking the job he would be serving his country.

Forrestal and Verity devised a strategy to get Carter and Brezhnev to agree to a list of twenty-eight commercial projects, from steel plants to oil refineries, that American firms wanted to undertake in the Soviet Union. At first Carter, who was preoccupied with the Middle East negotiations at Camp David, refused to meet with them. So in May 1978 they arranged to see Brezhnev, described the plan, and gave him a silver model of a Yankee Clipper ship as a symbol of a new era in trade. Brezhnev, teary-eyed, gave them several copies of his autobiography, *The Little Land,* one of which was for Carter. He also told them he wanted to give a special banquet in the Kremlin for 150 top American businessmen when the Trade Council convened in December.

On October 6, Verity and Forrestal saw Carter in the Oval Office. Carter looked more tired and worn-out than ever before. The Presidency, it seemed, was an enormous strain on him. Nonetheless, he seemed enthusiastic about the proposals—especially the benefits to the United States' balance of payments—and phoned Henry Owen of the National Security Council to instruct that all applications for export licenses over sixty days old (which included the twenty-eight projects) should be released. Zbigniew Brzezinski, Carter's National Security Adviser, had been invited to the meeting but chose instead to remain in his White House basement office. The whole matter struck him as not befitting the participation of a President. When Commerce Secretary Kreps called Carter a few weeks later to ask why she had not yet gotten the export-license files from the National Security Council, Carter did not know what she was talking about.

A full year before the hostages were seized in Teheran, Jimmy Carter's administration was in disarray. Thus Brzezinski, who was able to take a great deal of power into his hands, had refused to release the files despite the President's orders. And when Treasury Secretary Blumenthal went to Moscow, Brzezinski called him in to brief him on the true state of Soviet affairs, warning him against giving speeches in Moscow filled with rosy predictions and joviality as Blumenthal's predecessors had done. He should instead take a harder line and make the Russians aware that the obstacles to trade were large and possibly insurmountable. Brzezinski even decided he would write Blumenthal's speech. In Moscow, Blumenthal delivered Brzezinski's blisteringly negative speeches and delivered similar messages to the Soviet leadership in person. While the Council meetings were in session, Blumenthal received a cable from Brzezinski. "The President wishes," the cable read, that Blumenthal proceed to Rumania after leaving Moscow and, while in Bucharest, give another speech critical of Soviet policy that would help exploit the divisions between the two Communist nations.

This was a peculiar command. It did not come from the President directly yet indicated that Carter had approved it. Blumenthal showed it to Harriman, the old sage who had served every Democratic President since Franklin Roosevelt. Harriman thought it was ridiculous. "Carter probably never saw that," he said. "On something this serious, you take orders only from the

President. If you start taking orders from Brzezinski, you may as well pack your bags."

Blumenthal insisted, however, that it was too difficult to argue about something like this from Moscow. Several days later he went to Bucharest and made the requested speech, which infuriated the Soviets and American business leaders alike.

The evening after Averell Harriman shocked the Russians in the Palace of Congresses, the 150 specially selected American business and political leaders gathered for dinner in one of the oldest and most majestic banquet halls in the Kremlin, the Granovitovaya Palata, or "faceted palace." It was a splendid chamber of warm, red-orange hue, low vaulted ceilings, and massive, ornate chandeliers. The floor was tiled in polished agate jasper; in the center of the room was a great pillar. The walls and ceilings were covered with icons by Andrei Rublyev and a giant fresco of the Last Supper.

In this room six years earlier Richard Nixon, on his first visit to Moscow, had joined Brezhnev for a state dinner. As were the American businessmen at the Trade Council banquet in 1978, Nixon had been taken with the overwhelming religiosity of the room. To him it seemed a peculiar setting for a dinner given by the antireligious Communist leaders of the Soviet Union:

> Sitting next to each other at the head table, Brezhnev and I looked directly across the room at a several-times-life-size mural of Christ and the Apostles at the Last Supper. Brezhnev said, "That was the Politburo of those days." I responded, "That must mean that the General Secretary and the Pope have much in common." Brezhnev laughed and reached over and shook my hand.

When all the Trade Council members had taken their assigned places, Leonid Brezhnev, looking frail, was escorted into the hall. He immediately went up to Armand Hammer and chatted for a few moments, and then did the same with Donald Kendall.

Before dinner Brezhnev gave a toast that went on for thirty-seven minutes. He praised the "network of contacts" the Trade Council had established and urged his friends to lobby the American powers that be long and hard for increased trade. "I am looking around this hall and see that our contacts have really become a system," he exclaimed. "How many familiar faces! I am glad to see my old acquaintances: Mr. Harriman, Mr. Hammer, Mr. Kendall. . . ." Some of the Americans, unaware that Brezhnev would go on at such length, had spread Beluga caviar on chunks of black bread before he got up to speak and were left holding them aloft throughout the speech.

The Granovitovaya Palata had been used for almost five hundred years during czarist times as a reception hall for visiting emperors, kings, and queens. Somehow it was appropriate for this meeting's gracious toasts and opulent cuisine, lavishness to which few if any of the Americans were accustomed.

Among the visiting celebrities there were several clearly discernible stars—men who, by virtue of their extraordinary power or long and faithful friendship, or both, were favored by the Soviet leadership above everyone else. While every person in the room did business with Russia, only a handful were honored with private audiences with the men who ruled the Soviet Union, with invitations to their dachas, and in general with access to the Kremlin exceeding that of any Western statesmen.

One of these luminaries was David Rockefeller, whose mystique was known throughout the world. Soviet propaganda had always held that the Rockefellers, along with a few other families, ran the capitalist world. Propaganda aside, the Soviets knew that David Rockefeller, as head of the Chase Manhattan Bank and unelected chairman of the American establishment, did indeed have great influence; Soviet leaders from Khrushchev on had befriended him. But in his toast Brezhnev did not mention Rockefeller's name. Brezhnev's colleagues privately explained that this was in order not to rile businessmen who were tired of seeing chiefs of state kowtow to the Rockefellers.

Averell Harriman, though, was by now an American legend, a seasoned Democratic statesman, and long an advocate of East-West trade. He had known all of the top Bolsheviks since Trotsky. One did not omit to mention his name.

Donald Kendall, the staunch Republican whose days of great influence passed when Carter entered the White House, was quietly pleased by this special attention from Brezhnev. Others in the room were similarly impressed that Brezhnev appeared to value the friendship of one no longer very useful to him.

Armand Hammer, eighty years old, was perhaps more gratified to be singled out than anyone else in the room. Virtually his entire life he had been involved with the Soviet Union, where he had once spent eleven years. He never tired of reminding people that almost six decades ago he had met with Lenin in the Kremlin.

One American tycoon who would have given anything to be at the dinner was Cyrus Eaton, then ninety-five years old and too ill to make the journey. Throughout the fifties and sixties he had made repeated journeys to Moscow to tout trade and disarmament. He had been so cordially received by Nikita Khrushchev that he came to be disparaged in the United States as "Khrushchev's favorite capitalist." Now the bonhomie for which he had been so scorned was acceptable, but he was not here to enjoy it.

About sixty years earlier, the founder of the Soviet state, a small, fiery-spoken man named Vladimir Ilyich Ulyanov, who called himself Lenin, had laid out a plan for the overthrow of capitalism throughout the world. The capitalists, he said, would sell Russia the rope with which they would be hanged. Lenin, who was never reticent about his methods, had once predicted:

> The capitalists of the world and their governments, in pursuit of conquest of the Soviet market, will close their eyes to the indicated higher reality and thus will turn into *deaf-mute blindmen.* They will extend credits, which will strengthen for us the Communist party in their countries and, giving us the materials and technology we lack, they will restore our military industry, indispensable for our future victorious attack on *our suppliers.* In other words, they will labor for the preparations for their own suicide.

As young Soviet Russia became an established world power, its leaders continued to be amazed by Lenin's prescience. In 1936 Stalin sent his agent, W. G. Krivitsky, to buy weapons in Europe. Krivitsky was astonished that even Nazi Germany, an avowed enemy, was willing to sell munitions. Lev Navrozov, the Russian émigré writer, has pointed out that Western businessmen are a singularly useful group of friends for the Soviets: " . . . businessmen handle unique equipment, patents, weapons, and what not. They can lobby their statesmen amid the complete indifference of the rest of the population." But it is good that they reside in the West and not in Russia, for what Soviet leader would want "a rich, numerous, powerful, subversive, or treacherous group like that in his country?"

To the businessmen in the Granovitovaya Palata on December 6, 1978, Lenin's words, if they knew them, were rhetoric best forgotten. Amid the ringing toasts and inebriated camaraderie, probably none of them—whether Hammer, Kendall, Harriman, Rockefeller, or any of the lesser lights—understood exactly the room's origins.

For there was a peculiar irony in the setting. In 1491 Czar Ivan the Terrible had the Granovitovaya Palata built to celebrate a resounding victory over the Tatars, who had once been Russia's greatest enemies.

PART ONE

And now, in the person of this capitalist shark, we have won a propagandist for trade relations with Soviet Russia.

—VLADIMIR ILYICH LENIN, *December 24, 1920*

THE EARLY YEARS

1

A MISSION TO MOSCOW

IN THE COUNCIL of Ministers building in the Kremlin, Lenin's personal study is preserved exactly as it was on the day he left it for the last time, October 19, 1923. A large, oval chamber with dull tan wallpaper, the study is lined with maps, bookcases, and a portrait of Karl Marx. In the center of the room is a small wooden desk beside a giant potted palm; in front of the desk is a table draped in red cloth fringed with gold. This table holds an odd collection of knickknacks, gifts Lenin received from visiting dignitaries. The most striking of these gifts is a foot-high bronze statue of a monkey sitting on volumes by Charles Darwin and examining a human skull.

The bronze monkey has an intriguing history. Visitors to the Central Lenin Museum in Revolution Square in Moscow, where Lenin's study is replicated to the tiniest of details, are told by the museum guide, "Please look at this bronze. Vladimir Ilyich especially prized this gift because, he said, it depicts what will happen when man destroys himself in the final war. 'Someday,' Lenin said, 'an ape will pick up a human skull and wonder where it came from.'"

"This is a gift from the famous American capitalist Armand Hammer when he visited Lenin in 1922," the guide continues. "Hammer told Vladimir Ilyich, 'I am a capitalist, but I know that we capitalists and you Communists must work together to ensure peace.' Today Armand Hammer is one of the most eminent American businessmen, the head of the Occidental Petroleum Company."

Now that Dr. Armand Hammer is the one industrialist in the world most closely identified with East-West trade, it is convenient for the Central Lenin Museum tour guide to so eulogize the young man who gave Lenin the bronze monkey. But the story, like much of what is known of Armand Hammer, is not quite true. Armand Hammer did *present* the gift to Lenin—on October 22, 1921, not in 1922—but it was an offering to the founder of the world's first Communist state from one of the founders of the American Communist Party, Julius Hammer, Armand's father. At the time, Julius was in Sing Sing Prison; when he was paroled two years later he would join his son and the rest of his family in Moscow. Along with the monkey, Julius sent a personal letter to Lenin. In return Armand asked for Lenin's inscribed photograph. Lenin complied a few days later, sending a dramatic picture of himself against a dark background. It was inscribed in white ink, "To comrade Armand Hammer."

The Hammers were a Russian-Jewish family from Odessa, merchants in this port city legendary for its aggressive Jewish traders. Armand's grandparents, Jacob and Victoria, immigrated to the United States in 1871. Their son, Julius, was born in Russia two years later, and came to this country in 1874 at the age of one—adopted, apparently, by Jacob and Victoria.

The family settled in Bradford, Connecticut, a stronghold of the American socialist movement. Julius was raised to speak Russian and English; as a teenager, he found work in a foundry and, growing disillusioned with the worker's lot, joined the Socialist Labor Party. A few years later the family moved to the Lower East Side of New York, where Julius was apprenticed to a druggist. Eventually he became a registered pharmacist, bought the drugstore, and went on to establish not only a chain of drugstores but also a plant to manufacture pharmaceuticals.

His interest in socialism did not diminish as his life became more prosperous, and he joined the Socialist Labor Party in New York. At one party meeting he met a young widow named Rose Robinson, who had recently emigrated from Russia with her young son, Harry. Julius and Rose were married, and they moved into an apartment over one of his drugstores on the Lower East Side. On May 21, 1898, Rose gave birth to a son, whom they named Armand. Years later Julius told a fellow socialist, Bertram Wolfe, that his son was named for the official emblem of the Socialist Labor Party: a laborer's arm holding a hammer. (Armand has always denied this, insisting that his father named him for Armand, the lover in Dumas's *La Dame aux Camélias.* "My father was very much influenced by Dumas's novel," he says.)

A few months after Armand was born, Julius entered the Columbia College of Physicians and Surgeons, paying for his studies and supporting his family with earnings from his pharmaceutical business. In 1901 another son, Victor, was born; named, more simply, for his grandmother, Victoria. A year later Julius finished medical school and moved his family to a house on Washington Avenue in the Bronx, where he also practiced medicine.

In August 1907 Julius took a leave from his practice to attend the International Socialist Congress in Stuttgart. There, according to several Soviet texts, he made the acquaintance of Lenin, the leader of the Russian Bolshevik Party, who had recently arrived from exile in Finland. The new friendship between Lenin and Julius Hammer became extremely valuable to both of them after the Bolsheviks seized power in Petrograd in 1917. Julius was among those American socialists who exulted at the birth of the world's first socialist state, but unlike most socialists, who merely gave exuberant speeches at rallies, Julius decided to help out the Bolsheviks in a way that only a true capitalist could have done. Soviet Russia, blockaded by the French and the English, badly needed war supplies, medicines, bandages, and other goods. Julius Hammer's pharmaceutical company became the only American firm to circumvent the blockade; through his contacts in the Soviet Communist Party, Julius sold the goods, on credit. Though it was illegal for any American company to export to the Soviet Union, Julius, along with his fellow socialists, considered it a moral imperative to do so.

It was also lucrative. The Hammer family became wealthy from this trade. They moved into an elegantly appointed apartment in the Hotel Ansonia and purchased several cars. As his wealth increased, so did Julius's socialist activity. He became a major benefactor of American Communism.

The Greater New York Left Wing Section of the Socialist Party of the United States held its organizational meeting in a hall of the Rand School of Social Science on February 16, 1919. A City Committee of fifteen was elected to direct the party; they included John Reed, Jim Larkin, Rose Pastor Stokes, Bertram D. Wolfe, Benjamin Gitlow, Jay Lovestone, and Julius Hammer. Hammer was also elected to the Editorial Committee, which was in charge of drafting the party's Manifesto. Later he was chosen chairman of the City Committee.

The Left Wing was the radical extreme of the American socialists, advocating immediate revolution in America using the Bolshevik Revolution as a model. According to Benjamin Gitlow, who wrote about the wing many years after he helped lead it, the party's Manifesto "might just as well have been written by the Man in the Moon." Though the Manifesto's framers sincerely believed they were "preparing a guide for the coming revolution in the United States," it was really little more than excited chatter. "There was plenty of talk. Everybody talked. If talk could make a revolution, the Left Wing would have won in the United States."

Another Left Winger, Bertram Wolfe, has set down his recollections of Julius Hammer. He remembers him as wealthy, dignified, and strangely silent—he participated actively but said almost nothing. Julius, a swarthy, stocky man with a distinguished black Vandyke beard (the emblem of a doctor at the time), dressed immaculately in suits of black or dark blue. "Though he chaired big meetings, ruling discreetly in favor of the faction he favored at the moment, I never knew him to make a speech, or to lose an appeal against his rulings as chairman of turbulent meetings."

Julius's party was controlled and made up largely of Russian Jews like himself. It seems curious that these ardent revolutionaries were, by and large, not oppressed workers but men of means. One explanation for this apparent paradox has been offered by Harvard sociologist Nathan Glazer: "Despite the relatively good economic position of Jews [in the early years of the century], their rapid rise to middle-class status produced certain strains—a sense of discrimination, a feeling of oppression and exploitation, if not its reality." Many of the Russian Jews in the party, who had been hounded from Russia by the czar's anti-Semitic pogroms, looked to the Russian Revolution—which had to a large extent been accomplished by Jews—as a triumph of a new, just world order.

As founder, president, and principal stockholder of his Allied Drug and Chemical Company, Julius profited handsomely from the accession of the Bolsheviks to power; his political convictions had material as well as psychological rewards. When Leon Trotsky came to the United States briefly in 1917, he met Julius and other leaders of American socialism and came away with a feeling of great revulsion. In his memoirs he records nothing but distaste for the rich, smug socialists he encountered on his visit:

> To this day I smile as I recall the leaders of American Socialism . . . successful and semi-successful doctors, lawyers, dentists, engineers, and the like who divide their precious hours of rest between

> concerts by European celebrities and the American Socialist Party. . . .
>
> Since they all have automobiles, they are invariably elected to the important committees, commissions, and delegations of the party. . . . And, properly speaking, they are simply variants of "Babbitt" [in Sinclair Lewis's novel], who supplements his commercial activities with dull Sunday meditations on the future of humanity. These people live in small national clans, in which the solidarity of ideas usually serves as a screen for business connections. Each clan has its own leader, usually the most prosperous of the Babbitts. They tolerate all ideas, provided they do not undermine their traditional authority, and do not threaten—God forbid!—their personal comfort.

Julius Hammer was one of the socialist community's chief Babbitts, the oldest and by far the richest. Jay Lovestone remembers riding around the city, from rally to rally, in Julius's King automobile, thereby enabling Lovestone to address several meetings in one evening, an amazing feat in those days.

The United States steadfastly refused to recognize the Soviet Union diplomatically, but in January 1919 the Soviet government, undaunted, named an ambassador to the United States anyway. He was a friend of Julius's, a Russian-born New Yorker with a German surname: Ludwig C. A. K. Martens.

Martens had spent time in czarist prisons for his radical activities, and had emigrated to the United States in 1916 by way of Germany and Britain. He became a secret member of the U.S. Communist Labor Party. When he was named the official representative of the Soviet government in the United States, he was given two assignments—to press for American diplomatic recognition and to interest American businessmen in trading with Russia. As recognition was difficult to lobby for, Martens concentrated his efforts on drumming up business, something the Communists in Russia needed desperately. Martens chose Dr. Julius Hammer as his commercial attaché. It was a sensible choice; as the businessman the Russians most trusted, Julius had already demonstrated his ability to deliver merchandise; Martens was convinced that Hammer had good connections; and the so-called Soviet bureau, located in the World Tower Building at 110 West 40th Street, had been established with money Hammer donated.

But things went badly from the start. The State Department rejected Martens's credentials as soon as he presented them. The Soviet bureau had to exist in a precarious state of quasi legality, functioning as the purchasing headquarters for a country that the

United States had decided did not exist. This state of affairs went on for one year, at the end of which the State Department shut down the bureau and deported Martens.

In the meantime, however, Martens and Julius went about their business. As commercial attaché, Julius signed the paychecks of the bureau's employees, amounts ranging from an average of thirty-five dollars a week to Martens's salary of one hundred dollars. Julius also regularly contributed money to keep the bureau solvent, contributions often as large as a thousand dollars. Most of the bureau's money, however, came from the Soviet Union, and in peculiar ways. Confiscated Russian jewels were smuggled to the United States and fenced in New York: several Soviet couriers were caught smuggling diamonds to Martens; and one Russian was arrested on his way to New York with sixty diamonds in the hollow heels of his shoes.

Julius also traveled around the country, as far west as San Francisco, in an effort to persuade businessmen that the Soviet Union was a modern-day El Dorado. Most of his efforts, though, were unavailing. American businessmen were terrified of the risks of Soviet confiscation of their merchandise, and the State Department warned businessmen that the United States would not be responsible for anything that happened to them in Russia. Despite the pleadings of the taciturn Dr. Hammer, the Soviet bureau succeeded only in placing orders for pharmaceuticals—Hammer's.

As the year went on, Martens and Julius had the misfortune to become involved in party squabbles. A faction of the Left Wing wanted the Soviet bureau under the control of the American party. Martens, who claimed to be taking orders only from Moscow, seemed too independent, a meddler. His function seemed unclear. As Martens's link to the Left Wing—Martens feared the legal repercussions of becoming officially involved in politics—Julius defended Martens in party arguments and served as his envoy. There was, for instance, a full-membership meeting of the Left Wing Section on April 20, 1919, at which Julius delivered "a message sent to the gathering by Martens, who was unable to attend in person, extending his allegiance and support to the Left Wing movement." Although quiet and diffident, Hammer was unable to stay aloof when the battle over Martens became bitter. He argued that Martens should be permitted to continue his work without answering to American socialists. At a Left Wing executive committee meeting in June, there was a motion that "Comrade Hammer be expelled from the Left Wing." The motion was defeated.

America's first and most widespread Red scare occurred that

year, 1919. The New York State Senate formed a commission, known as the Lusk Committee, to investigate domestic Communist activities. The committee had been on the trail of the members of the Left Wing for some time, waiting to catch them openly committing what might be prosecuted as sedition. "We existed in a state of semi-legality," Benjamin Gitlow recalled, "always expecting to be attacked and arrested."

The Soviet bureau was raided on June 12, 1919, and Martens was forced into hiding. Julius, who helped Martens evade the authorities, took over a larger share of the bureau's responsibilities. He became director of the medical department, which meant simply that he organized the shipment of medical supplies to Russia. He also assisted another employee of the bureau, Abraham A. Heller—another wealthy businessman with socialist leanings—in a drive to raise millions of dollars in relief aid for the Soviet Union.

Throughout the spring and summer of 1920, Hammer's company made a full-scale effort to purchase supplies from other concerns and ship hundreds of cases of codeine, camphor, gauze, morphine, and quinine to Moscow.

But life for Julius became complicated. In July 1919, the wife of a diplomat in the embassy of the Russian Imperial Government had come to him for an abortion. Hammer had consented to perform the curettage, although it was illegal. Five days later the woman died, and Julius was arrested for manslaughter. At the time an epidemic of Spanish influenza plagued the nation, and there were indications that the woman had died of that, not from the abortion itself. Hammer was probably framed. During the long and sensational trial, Tammany Hall, which was determined to put this Communist behind bars, bribed at least one of the jurors to find Hammer guilty. There were counterefforts, presumably supported by the Soviet bureau, to publish propaganda in New York newspapers favorable to the doctor.

Even while his trial dragged on, Hammer continued his involvement in socialist politics. He served on a steering committee to run the First National Conference of the Left Wing in New York during the summer of 1919. In September, at the National Socialist Party Convention in Chicago, the Left Wing was reorganized. Julius, preoccupied with his trial, was unable to attend. John Reed, Ben Gitlow, and Jim Larkin represented the Left Wing, which, by the end of the convention, had been absorbed into the Communist Labor Party. This new party's headquarters were established at 108 East 12th Street in New York, in a house rented and later donated by Dr. Hammer.

When over seven hundred New York police agents, acting on orders from the Lusk Committee, raided the meetings and headquarters of various Communist groups throughout the city during the night of November 8, 1919, two of Julius's comrades in the new Communist Labor Party were arrested and charged with criminal anarchy: Ben Gitlow and Jim Larkin. Bail was set at ten thousand dollars each. Julius came to their aid with twenty thousand dollars in Liberty Bonds.

All of this visible socialist activity did little to aid Julius's cause at his politically charged trial. In the summer of 1920 he was found guilty of manslaughter in the first degree. He was sentenced to three-and-a-half to fifteen years. The judge angrily denounced "the insidious and uncalled-for propaganda which had been conducted in the doctor's behalf." Julius listened without showing emotion.

Julius Hammer entered Sing Sing on September 18, 1920. For many editorial writers around the city, it was a happy day. Calling him "a black sheep in the medical flock," *The New York Times* crowed that the imprisonment of the doctor refuted the charge that "there is one law for the rich and another for the poor—that with money and influence crime can be escaped." The press showed a morbid interest in this inmate, because, according to one account, "the prison inmates and attendants heard Dr. Hammer is 'worth a million dollars.'" Appearing downcast, Julius was fitted with a suit of convict gray and assigned, at first, to work on the coal pile. But it was not long before he established himself as the prison's resident intellectual. He published a newspaper and set up a school. "In Sing Sing," Bertram Wolfe writes, "Julius Hammer did not lose his air of dignity; even in prison garb he carried himself as if he were well dressed. He did the work assigned to him, often helped out in medical matters, and when Jim Larkin and Ben Gitlow were transferred from Dannemora to Sing Sing, they were delighted to find Hammer there to guide them in the mysteries of prison life."

With Julius in jail, there was only one person who could run the company and coordinate operations with the Bolsheviks—Julius's twenty-two-year-old son, Armand, who was in his last year at Columbia medical school.

Armand Hammer was a small, extraordinarily handsome, dark-eyed young man of uncommon self-possession. "Girls would fall all over him," remembered an acquaintance. "He was good-looking, supremely confident, and had a mind like a steel trap." While his father's company expanded, Armand, though in medical school, proved an invaluable and adept manager. By renting out part of his Central Park West apartment to another medical student in exchange for class notes, Armand was able to help his father and, in 1921, graduate at the top of his class.

His ingenuity and extraordinary independence were perhaps fostered by his unusual upbringing. At the age of ten he had been sent by his parents to live with the family of one of Julius's socialist friends in Meriden, Connecticut; he spent five years there. Shortly before the First World War, Armand and his younger brother, Victor, were sent to live for a while with relatives in Paris. Armand returned to the Bronx, graduated from Morris High School, and then spent two years in Columbia University's premedical program.

After the Bolshevik Revolution, Armand became Secretary of the Allied Drug and Chemical Company and helped the company prosper. When his father was imprisoned in 1920, Armand and his half-brother, Harry, took over the company. They had periodic consultation sessions with Julius in the visitors' room at Sing Sing.

As the burdens of running his father's Soviet business mounted, Armand's new medical training fell by the wayside. Friends of his recount that Armand was disillusioned about medicine as a result of his father's ugly criminal trial. Whether or not that is true, in the summer of 1921, twenty-three-year-old Armand Hammer set off on a business mission to the Soviet Union.

All his life Hammer has concealed the reason for his first journey to Russia. He went as a delegate from his father to his father's comrades in Moscow to collect a debt owed the family firm by the Soviet government; also to arrange related transactions; and very likely also to set his family up in a much larger venture on Soviet soil.

But in an autobiography he published in 1932, *Quest of the Romanoff Treasure,* Hammer furnishes an altogether different explanation. He went as a physician, he asserts, "planning field hospital relief work among the famine refugees." He had heard of "revolt and pitiless repression, of madness and despair," but "my family and friends in New York knew better. Through Charles Recht, attorney for the Russian diplomatic mission in New York and through Ludwig Martens, its Chief, we had been in fairly close touch with Russian affairs." While conceding that he was going to Moscow to "make arrangements" for "a chemical concern controlled by my family," he avers that his main motivation was philanthropic and medical. Nowhere in the book does he mention his father.

His passport application is more truthful: "commercial business and pleasure." He brought with him a fifteen-thousand-dollar war-surplus ambulance stocked with sixty thousand dollars' worth of surgical instruments and supplies, equipment the Soviets needed and which would also help strengthen his alibi should he run into trouble.

He did. British intelligence, aware of Julius's politics and Allied Drug and Chemical's activities, detained Hammer when he docked at Southampton, England. The British authorities did not believe his explanation that he planned volunteer work in the Urals, especially since they found among his belongings a motion-picture film of Ludwig Martens's departure from America, which he was conveying to Martens as a gift. J. Edgar Hoover of the U.S. Justice Department had informed Scotland Yard that Armand Hammer was going to Russia "to carry some messages for Martens" and to "bring back some important papers for those interested in the Soviet movement in this country." And, most startling, Hoover also reported that the Hammers' company was half owned by Martens, on behalf of the Soviet government. After a delay of a few days, during which Hammer bought the bronze monkey for Lenin in a London shop, Hammer was released.

He proceeded to Berlin, where he waited for a Soviet visa that was to be received at the U.S.S.R. consulate there. On another shopping expedition, he purchased—somewhat inappropriately for a famine volunteer—a Mercedes-Benz, which he asked the Allied Drug and Chemical representative for Europe, Boris Mishell, to deliver later. Within a few days, Hammer's visa arrived, personally approved by Maxim Litvinov, Deputy Commissar of Foreign Affairs.

In Moscow a powerful group of Soviet officials, all close friends of Julius from the American socialist movement, awaited Armand. There was Martens, now a member of the Presidium of the People's Commissariat for Foreign Trade, which was in charge of rebuilding the country's mining industry. There was also Gregory Weinstein, who had been an adviser to Martens and Julius in the Soviet bureau, and who had been a member of the Left Wing and an editor of its newspaper, *Novy Mir* (The New World). Weinstein, who had been deported from the United States in 1920 together with Martens, Emma Goldman, and others, was in charge of the Anglo-American Department of the Commissariat of Foreign Affairs.

But the most important contact was Boris Reinstein, a Russian-born Jew who came to the United States in the 1890s, became a pharmacist in Buffalo, New York, and was an active member of the Socialist Labor Party. He had accompanied Julius to the International Socialist Congress in Stuttgart in 1907; in fact, he and Julius were the closest of friends. When, in 1917, Reinstein told his comrades in New York that he was returning to his native Russia to help lead the country, Julius gave a speech at a meeting held in his honor. A mustachioed, bespectacled man with thickly accented English, Reinstein helped teach Russian to the Americans who came to Petrograd to join the Revolution. John Reed and Albert Rhys Williams, who were among them, called Reinstein "Daddy." Reed used to "twit Reinstein about the Socialist Labor Party," Williams recalls, since it was a small splinter group of the Socialist Party. But "Reinstein knew Marx and Engels, and did not let us forget that that was more than Reed and I did." He spoke at Reed's funeral in 1920. After the Revolution, Reinstein became one of Lenin's most trusted advisers; his area of expertise was the United States. By the summer of 1921 when Armand arrived, Reinstein was extremely influential in the government as the Comintern official in charge of relations with America.

Equipped with a packing case stuffed with cheese, butter, jam, sardines, bread, and biscuits, Hammer arrived at the Soviet border, thrilled as he had never been in his life, and was whisked through customs by an official who seemed to know all about him. At the railroad station in Moscow he was met by someone from the Foreign Ministry named Wolff, who had been sent by Gregory Weinstein. Wolff piled Hammer's luggage onto a truck and trundled Hammer off to the Foreign Ministry. No one was there, so Wolff took him to the Government Treasury Department to exchange his dollars for food coupons. Hammer was next escorted to his lodgings, a room at the Savoy Hotel, which was a few blocks from the Kremlin. "Never in my life," Hammer wrote later, "have I seen a hotel less worthy of the name 'Savoy' than this was." The place was squalid; there were roaches and bedbugs, rats and mice, and the few furnishings were threadbare.

The diet of sardines and cheese soon made him ill. When he ventured out into the streets in search of better food, dressed in his newly tailored English tweeds, he received stricken stares from the bedraggled Muscovites. During his first few days he met with the Soviet Minister of Health, Dr. N. A. Semashko, who thanked him for the ambulance and supplies, and arranged payment. He probably also met with Reinstein; it is likely that he gave Reinstein a note for Lenin from his father in order to set up an interview. In 1926 Hammer told a correspondent for *Krasnaya Gazeta* (The Red Gazette)—in an interview he may have suspected no American would ever read—"When I departed New York I took with me a private letter to Vladimir Ilyich from my father, Dr. J. J. Hammer, an old party worker in the United States who met with Lenin in 1907 at the International Socialist Congress in Stuttgart." Presumably it was a letter of introduction.

Armand Hammer's arrival in Moscow could not have been better timed. Lenin had just decided upon his New Economic Policy, under which limited capitalism would be permitted and foreign capitalists would be invited to rebuild Russia's industry, which the Revolution and years of civil war had devastated. A few European consortia had hesitantly discussed concessions in oil and minerals, but nothing had been signed. Lenin was especially interested in the American market (which would also, he thought, help bring about diplomatic recognition), and so Reinstein, Weinstein, and Martens were glad to see Julius Hammer's eager and ambitious son in town. Perhaps the Hammer family could take a concession—some industry in the Urals—operate it profitably, and show America the good sense of doing business with the Bolsheviks.

So Reinstein arranged an expedition to the Urals, headed by Martens. Hammer would be joined by Abraham Heller, late of the Soviet bureau, and the suffragette Lucy Branham, who was interested in seeing Russia and delivering speeches of greeting from American comrades. In *Quest of the Romanoff Treasure,* Hammer explains that this trip was "undertaken as a relief from the boredom of Moscow." Seeking to avoid mention of the role of his father's comrades in the Soviet leadership, Hammer constructs an elaborate tale of his serendipitous discovery of a Russian business venture. Thus he describes Lucy Branham, a history instructor at Columbia University and an old friend of the family, as "a plucky little social worker," and the industrialist Abraham Heller as "a writer who sympathized with the new Russian regime." Hammer does not mention, of course, that Heller was one of the two directors of the Allied Drug and Chemical Company, the other being Julius Hammer.

The group set out at the end of August in a train that had once been used to transport high-ranking members of the czar's ministry. At Ekaterinburg, Hammer asked why so many of the factories he saw were not operating, and was told that there was not enough grain to give the workers for their labor. If the workers had enough food, they would work. Hammer then made his first deal with the Soviet government: he offered to trade one million *poods* of surplus American grain (over thirty-six million pounds) for valuables such as furs and precious stones.

On September 25, the party reached the town of Alapayevsk. Here was the asbestos field Martens wished to show to Hammer—huge gray amphitheaters of tiered rock. Narrow-gauge rail cars stood idle. Hammer was intrigued by what he saw and took careful note. Ironically perhaps, Alapayevsk was the scene of one of the Bolsheviks' most hideous assaults on the czarist family. The asbestos mine in which Hammer was interested held the bodies of six Romanovs, murdered by their Bolshevik guards on the night of July 17, 1918. Their confiscated possessions—works of art, jewels, and heirlooms—were to make the Hammers very wealthy ten years later.

Sometime in late September, when Hammer and his party were still inspecting the Urals, Lenin received word that young Hammer was discussing several deals, one for grain and another for an asbestos mine. Lenin was most interested. "We must conclude with *Hammer very soon,*" he told V. V. Kuibyshev, a member of the Presidium of the Supreme Economic Council "and *conclude* the agreement on the concession." If Hammer did not want the asbestos mine, perhaps he could be persuaded to sign the grain contract in the *form* of a concession, so that it could be publicized around the world.

Hammer and company were back in Moscow by the middle of October. Weeks of bargaining over the concession and grain contract began. For some reason the discussions included a session with Leon Trotsky, the Commissar of War. It seems strange that Trotsky wanted to meet with Hammer, son of Babbitt. Hammer explains that the purpose was to discuss, of all things, security for the mine.

Trotsky's office was large, dark, and shrouded in heavy curtains. At the far end of the room, at a desk under a solitary electric light, sat Trotsky, wearing khaki breeches and a plain tunic. "He greeted me quite cordially," Hammer recalls, "but his glance was cold and piercing." The two spoke in German, and discussed, according to Hammer, the willingness of the American business community to invest in Russia. Trotsky assured him that "when the Revolution comes to America," the Hammer holdings would be safe.

By October 13, Reinstein was able to inform Lenin that the

negotiations with Hammer were progressing smoothly. Lenin was so optimistic that he sent a letter the next day to all members of the Central Committee:

> Reinstein informed me that the American millionaire [Julius] *Hammer,* who is Russian-born (is in prison on a charge of illegally procuring an abortion; actually, it is said, in revenge for his communism), is prepared to give the Urals workers *1,000,000 poods of grain* on very easy terms (5 per cent) and to take *Urals valuables* on commission for sale in America.
>
> This Hammer's son (and partner), a doctor, is in Russia, and has brought Semashko $60,000 worth of surgical instruments as a gift. The son has visited the Urals with Martens and has decided to help rehabilitate the Urals industry.
>
> An official report will soon be made by *Martens.*
>
> *Lenin.*

For a time, Lenin was obsessed with the idea that Hammer might provide the answer to all kinds of business difficulties. On October 15, 1921, Lenin asked Martens to find out whether Hammer could prod other Western finance groups to help the development of the Urals. Also, Lenin asked, would Hammer be interested in a scheme to electrify the Urals? (Lenin considered electricity a panacea; "Communism," he once proclaimed, "equals electrification plus Soviet power.") But Hammer was uninterested in so large an undertaking.

Lenin appeared at times doubtful that Hammer was serious; it seemed almost too good to be true that Julius Hammer's son was so interested in doing business. Asking Martens to draw the grain deal up in concession form, for example, Lenin nervously wondered whether "Hammer is in earnest . . . and [whether] the plan is not just so much hot air."

The importance of this first Hammer deal transcended mere economics. Lenin saw it as a way to protect Soviet Russia from Western intervention, for if the capitalist countries, seeing that there was money to be made in Russia, began to compete with each other to trade with the Soviet Union, Soviet power would be made secure. The West would be divided. "Agreements and concessions with the *Americans* are of *exceptional importance* to us," Lenin wrote. "We almost have something with *Hammer.*"

But negotiations reached a deadlock. Reinstein knew that the only solution would be a meeting with the Leader himself, who tended to be persuasive. He called Lenin and arranged an interview for October 22, 1921. This was Hammer's first—and only—

meeting with Lenin. Hammer has recounted it hundreds of times in the six decades since, retelling and embellishing it so that what was really quite a routine conference has attained a legendary quality. Lenin was, Hammer remembers, "smaller than I expected—a stocky little man about five feet three, with a large, dome-shaped head, wearing a dark grey sack suit, white soft collar and black tie. His eyes twinkled with friendly warmth as he shook hands and led me to a seat beside his big flat desk." Hammer says he told this sprightly Soviet leader that he had, upon first arriving in Moscow, made a point of learning one hundred Russian words a day, and had in this manner built up a respectable mastery of the language. "Shall we speak in Russian or English?" Lenin asked Hammer. Hammer preferred English, since Lenin "spoke so perfectly."

Legend has it that Hammer went alone. Lenin's letters, however, show that Hammer was accompanied by Boris Reinstein. Yet Hammer has denied the presence of Reinstein, probably because it is a reminder of his father's role in the whole affair. Once, however, Hammer admitted Reinstein's presence but explained that he was Hammer's "translator." In "The Russian Connection," a 1974 NBC documentary on Hammer's life, Edwin Newman asked Hammer how Lenin knew of him in advance. "Well, he had known, I suppose, before—before I got to see him," Hammer answered falteringly. "He'd had a full report on, on the fact that I had—was running a company while I was studying medicine. . . ."

Hammer, Reinstein, and Lenin spoke animatedly for an hour, during which time, Hammer says, "I was completely absorbed by Lenin's personality." They discussed terms of the asbestos-mine agreement. Lenin was far more lenient than his negotiators had been, going so far as to approve the right of Hammer's employees to travel about Russia at will, and granting them private railroad cars for that purpose. To combat the bureaucracy in supervising the concession, Lenin told Hammer that he was forming a special "Concessions Committee," headed by Felix Dzerzhinsky, the chief of the Soviet secret police. If there were any problems whatsoever, Felix Dzerzhinsky would be the man to solve them.

They discussed sensitive political issues as well. Hammer told *Krasnaya Gazeta* in 1926, "We conversed for an hour and a half. Questions of a personal character (about my father, about my stay in Russia) gave way to questions of political significance. He was especially interested in the recognition of Soviet Russia by the United States."

Hammer came away from the meeting very impressed by the

founder of the Soviet Union. "Lenin has been called ruthless and fanatical, cruel and cold," Hammer writes. "I refuse to believe it. It was his intense human sympathy, his warm personal magnetism and utter lack of self-assertion or self-interest that made him great." More adulatory words could not be found in a Soviet textbook.

Once Lenin had placed his imprimatur upon the Hammer venture, the negotiations proceeded apace. Meanwhile, Hammer was shown an office building—a four-story marble building that was once a bank—that was his for only thirty dollars a month. Hammer said that he did not need all that space, and settled for the first floor of a building, at a more reasonable twelve dollars a month. Curiously enough, this building, at Kuznetsky Most 4, had only recently been occupied by the workshop and display room of the jewelers Karl Fabergé and Company, whose Imperial Easter eggs Hammer would soon be selling in the United States.

On October 27, 1921, Hammer and his assistant Boris Mishell signed the wheat contract. Armand cabled his stepbrother, Harry, in the Bronx, explained the nature of the transaction, and instructed him to charter some ships as soon as possible.

While the negotiations on the asbestos deal continued, Lenin continued to dash off letters stressing its urgency. "There is much indication that it is of great importance for us to have this concession and the contract publicized as widely as possible," Lenin wrote Martens. "Special attention must be given to our thorough *actual* fulfillment of the terms. There must be no reliance on orders! Without a triple check-up our men will spoil everything and will fail to do anything right." Lenin was not exactly confident in the ability of his own bureaucracy. "I believe this contract to be of enormous importance, as marking the beginning of trade," he wrote to his Minister of Foreign Trade, S. I. Radchenko, the same day. ". . . I am sure that *not a damn thing will be done* unless there is *exacting* pressure and supervision."

Lenin wanted to be sure that Hammer was treated regally. "We must make a special effort to *nurse* the concessionaires," he told Martens. "This is of exceptional economic and political importance." Separately, he instructed the Council on the National Economy, "We must *without delay* give him [Hammer] a good apartment."

Hammer was moved out of the rundown Hotel Savoy and given luxurious quarters in the Government Guest House. Called the Sugar King's Palace, it was a mansion that had been confiscated during the Revolution from a Ukrainian merchant who made his fortune in sugar beets. "Suddenly I found myself in a palatial suite with bathroom attached," Hammer recalls. "There were well-trained servants, an excellent cuisine, and if need be, a bottle of old French wine from the well-stocked cellar. . . . Such was the magic of Lenin's name."

At last, on November 2, 1921, the asbestos contract was signed. It was done, Hammer recalls, "with all the ceremony of a peace treaty." The document, signed on the Soviet side by Maxim Litvinov, Vice-Commissar of Foreign Affairs, and P. Bogdanov, President of the Supreme Economic Council, was adorned with a giant red seal the size of a saucer. As the chairman of the Allied Drug and Chemical Company was in jail, his son, Armand, signed in his capacity as vice-president and secretary of the company. Boris Mishell signed as Director of the Foreign Department.

The Hammers were granted mining rights for twenty years; they were required to double the output of asbestos within five. The Soviet government would receive as commission 10 percent of the annual output, in hard currency or in asbestos, as it preferred. Half of the company's mine employees, the contract stated, were to be Russians "in order to avoid turning the concession enterprise into a 'foreign colony.'" The Hammers were required to deposit fifty thousand dollars in gold in the new Soviet State Bank as a security deposit (really a mandatory loan). The Hammer family thus became the bank's first depositors.

Hammer's own account of how he came to deposit gold in the State Bank is "different." "In the winter of '21, after our asbestos concession had been signed," he writes in *Quest of the Romanoff Treasure,* "I went to see Mr. Shineman who had just been appointed to his position as head of the newly formed bank." The two talked for a while.

> Then he said, smiling: "I hear, Doctor Hammer, you are the first American concessionaire in Russia. Don't you think you would like also to be the first depositor in the Soviet State Bank?"
>
> It so happened that I was just beginning to feel the need of Soviet currency, so I produced my letter of credit and opened an account in dollars—I forget how many millions of roubles my first deposit of five thousand dollars was worth—and received a passbook numbered "1."

As part of the agreement, the Hammers were named purchasing agents for American agricultural machinery. They were to help "repair the productivity of consumer goods" by buying such items as Ford tractors.

Although Lenin wanted the concession publicized as widely as possible, there was a problem. The Allied Drug and Chemical Company had a disreputable past (in the eyes of the American business community), with all of its known ties to the Communist movement, and with its chairman behind bars. Hammer decided to return to the United States and reincorporate, entirely dissolving the old firm.

But the Soviets, in their eagerness for publicity, slipped, and made an announcement. A large notice appeared on the front page of *The New York Times*: "SOVIET GIVES AMERICANS ASBESTOS MINING CONCESSION." The name of the firm, though specified by the Soviet government, was withheld pending a federal investigation.

The response was just as Hammer feared. The financial community in America was stunned. An article two days later reported that the Department of Justice had begun an investigation into the Allied Drug and Chemical Company, "of which Dr. Julius Hammer, serving a term in Sing Sing for criminal abortion, was President." When Federal agents called Rose Hammer's apartment in the Hotel Ansonia, "it was said she was out the city," according to the newspaper report. One of the directors of Allied Drug and Chemical, William Hamlin Childs, issued a strong, and probably sincere, denial: "I am certain that nobody has been authorized to acquire such a contract from the Soviet Government. We would not be interested in the working of asbestos mines, because we do not use asbestos in our business. It is unlikely that the corporation would enter such a negotiation with the Soviet Government without my being informed of the matter."

The hapless Childs may well have been kept ignorant of the Hammers' dealings. It made little difference, however, for within a few weeks his company was dissolved. In its stead was created a unique corporation, one owned and operated jointly by the Hammer family and the government of the Soviet Union.

In Moscow, Armand Hammer asked Reinstein to arrange a final interview with Lenin before Hammer left for the United States. Lenin was unable to see him again, but sent an apologetic letter in English on November 3, 1921:

Dear Mr. Armand Hammer:

Comrade Reinstein tells me you are leaving Moscow tonight. I am very sorry I am occupied at the session of the Central Committee of the Party. I am extremely sorry I am unable to see you once more and greet you.

Please be so kind and greet your father, Jim Larkin, Ruthenberg and Ferguson, all best comrades now in American gaols. My best sympathy and best wishes to all them.

Once more best greetings to you and your friends in connection with flour for our workers and your concession. The beginning is extremely important. I hope it will be the beginning of extreme importance.

With best wishes
Yours truly,
Lenin

P.S.: I beg to apologize for my extremely bad English.

In *Quest of the Romanoff Treasure,* Hammer goes to great lengths to conceal the paragraph about his father and the other jailed Communists. While this letter is reproduced there in facsimile, the offensive paragraph is carefully masked by a blank sheet.

A few days after he sent this letter, Lenin sent Hammer the autographed photo Hammer had requested; the photo was dated November 10, 1921. This was the first of a tremendous number of photographs of politicians Hammer was to acquire as office ornaments over the course of his long business career.

The first shipment of American wheat arrived in Russia on November 17, 1921, at Reval. The steamer was unloaded and then filled with Russian wares—sables, minks, hides, decorative metal castings, paintings, and nearly a ton of Russian caviar in fifty-pound wooden kegs. In early December, laden with valuables, the ship cast off.

On board was Dr. Armand Hammer, bound for America.

2

A LETTER TO STALIN

JULIUS HAMMER, in the visitors' room at Sing Sing, was glad to see his son and happy that negotiations with Martens and Reinstein had gone so well. Armand told his father about his meeting with Lenin and about Lenin's greetings. They made plans for the dissolution of the old Allied Drug and Chemical Company and the establishment of a new firm.

Soon after, Armand went to Delaware, the home of swift and cheap incorporation, and filed papers for the Ural-American Refining and Trading Company; his father was listed as chairman. Not long afterward, as the possibilities of enlisting other American companies expanded, he changed the name to the grander-sounding Allied American Corporation, known in short as Alamerico. Its offices were located at 165 Broadway in New York.

One of Alamerico's new employees was an old friend of Julius's, Alexander Gumberg. In *Quest of the Romanoff Treasure,* Hammer makes a passing, disguised reference to him as "Uncle Sasha," a relative who had a Ford agency in southern Russia before the Revolution. There was good reason for Hammer's wishing to conceal the role of Gumberg in the Allied American Corporation.

The son of a rabbi, Alexander Gumberg was born in the Ukraine in 1887; he left Russia in 1902. As did his friends Julius Hammer and Boris Reinstein, he became a pharmacist in America and eventually entered the pharmaceutical business. An astute businessman and a dedicated Communist, he became the business manager of *Novy Mir,* the Russian socialist newspaper.

When the Bolsheviks took power in Russia, Gumberg returned to the old country as an agent for a number of American companies. When Raymond Robins came to the Soviet Union to lead the American Red Cross mission, Gumberg became Robins's interpreter and adviser. He also assisted other Americans who made the pilgrimage to Petrograd, such as John Reed, Louise Bryant, and Albert Rhys Williams. The idealistic Americans quickly came to dislike Gumberg, who was sarcastic and blunt-spoken. Williams recalled that Gumberg enjoyed "looking for another's Achilles' heel and celebrating the discovery in words of mordant wit," a practice from which Gumberg refrained only when it came to Lenin. Such bad blood developed between Gumberg and John Reed that in Reed's book *Ten Days That Shook the World,* Gumberg appears under the name *Trusishka,* Russian for "little coward."

In May 1918, Gumberg decided that he could be of greatest service by returning to the United States and lobbying for recognition and persuading American companies to do business with the Bolsheviks. He came to New York, bearing two manuscripts of Trotsky's, which he sold to publishers. With Raymond Robins's help, Gumberg quickly acquired a powerful set of contacts in American business and political circles. As an American citizen who refused to get involved in socialist politics, he was widely regarded as a respectable, if mysterious, agent of the Soviet government. He dispensed advice to the *Nation* and the *New Republic*; to prominent banks such as the Chase National Bank; and to such reputable law firms as Simpson, Thatcher & Bartlett—all of which were interested in the Soviet Union as a potential market.

Gumberg, whom his biographer described as "the most important bridge linking America and Russia," possessed the eminence and influence that the Hammers needed for Alamerico. One of his contacts was Charles Sorensen, the head of the tractor division of the Ford Motor Company. Early in 1922, Gumberg arranged a meeting in Dearborn, Michigan, of Sorensen, Armand Hammer, and Henry Ford.

Hammer has made much of this meeting. In his 1932 autobiography, and in interviews and speeches years afterward, he has spun a dramatic tale of his conversion of Henry Ford from a frothing anti-Bolshevik into a wise advocate of trade with the Soviet Union. According to his version, Hammer had lunch with Ford and Sorensen at the offices of the *Dearborn Independent,* where he made an eloquent case for the stability and responsibility of Russia's new government. "If you're waiting for a change of regime in Russia," Hammer says he told Ford, "you won't do any business there for a long time." He explained that "in Russia they think you're one of the most wonderful people in America." By the end of the lunch, Hammer claims, Ford had changed his mind about Bolshevism and agreed to send three hundred tractors and—perhaps more significantly—to allow Soviet experts to study mass production at the Ford works in Dearborn. With Henry Ford as one of his customers, Hammer says, he was able to sign up scores of other American companies.

It is true that Ford assumed a public posture as a fierce anti-Communist. For a time it may have been genuine, tied to his well-known anti-Semitism (since so many of the Bolsheviks were Jews). But it was not long after the Revolution that Ford abandoned his ideological opposition in favor of easy profits. And the occasion was not a lunch with Hammer; it was three years earlier.

In March 1919, with Gumberg's help, Ludwig Martens and Abraham Heller traveled to Dearborn and met with Charles Sorensen, according to a report that Martens sent to Moscow that year. Sorensen received them cordially, and became so interested in the idea of exporting the Ford Motor Company's Fordson tractors to Russia that he immediately (in their presence) sent off a letter to the State Department requesting permission to do so. Martens and Heller arranged to purchase four hundred Fordsons and send several Soviet engineers to study the Ford method in Dearborn. In his unpublished memoirs at the Henry Ford Library, Sorensen recorded that from 1919 on, the Soviet government "kept purchasing more tractors annually right through until the year 1927. All their purchases and shipments were handled through an office that they had in New York called the Amtorg Corporation."

Armand Hammer may have met Henry Ford, though it is undocumented. But—if the meeting took place—he claims it was at the offices of the *Independent*. This is a significant detail. If it were a business meeting, it would probably have been held at Ford Motor headquarters. Since it was at the *Independent*, it was probably just a social call. In any case, in their role as Soviet purchasing agents, the Hammers probably purchased an *additional* lot of tractors. Amtorg (an acronym of the Russian for "American trade"), the official Soviet commercial bureau in New York, which is still in operation, was not established until 1924. From 1922 to 1923, the Hammers served Amtorg's function.

Gumberg, who had been so instrumental in bringing the Hammers together with Ford, may also have helped Armand to interest other American companies in doing business with the Soviets. Within a few weeks, Allied American had become the Soviet agent for thirty-seven other firms, including Allis-Chalmers, American Tool Works, National Supply Company, Oliver Farm Equipment, Parker Pen, Underwood Typewriter, and United States Rubber. With this impressive roster, Hammer returned to Moscow, leaving his stepbrother, Harry, to run the New York office. "Fate was now beckoning me on to seek my fortune in this land of promise," Hammer remembers thinking as he settled in at the Sugar King's Palace in late March 1922. He had brought with him the good news that trade with America, if on a small scale, had begun.

Lenin took notice of Hammer's arrival. In a letter to his deputy, Aleksei I. Rykov, he instructed: "Please pay attention to the concession of the American *Hammer,* who, as Reinstein, who knows him personally, has informed me, is now in Russia." Lenin railed against the bureaucratic disorder that was now so bad that even the goods Hammer had received in exchange for wheat had "turned out to be of bad quality." He added, "We must see to it that our obligations under this concession are performed with undeviating strictness and accuracy, and in general we must pay greater attention to the whole business." Apparently Hammer had complained to Reinstein, though he publicly claimed, as an unofficial public-relations agent for the Soviets, that he had made a 150 percent profit on the Soviet goods.

Hammer and Boris Mishell spent the month of April in Moscow setting up their Soviet operations. There was much to coordinate. The Allied American Corporation was a peculiar organization. Apart from its chairman's being a convict, the strangest aspect of the company was that—in violation of Delaware incorporation laws—two members of the board of directors were high-ranking officials in the Soviet government. One Soviet account reveals that "the management of the company included two Soviet directors with the right to protest transactions contrary to the interests of the business." Hammer has always denied this. "I made all the decisions," he insists, "and the Soviet government had nothing to do with the running of the business."

Toward the end of April 1922, Hammer and Mishell traveled around the southern provinces, taking orders for Ford tractors. They went to Kharkov, the Ukraine, Rostov-on-the-Don, the Northern Caucasus, Baku, and Tiflis. In a short time, they had allocated all of the first shipment of Fordson tractors plus a few hundred more. When the first load of tractors arrived at Novorossisk, the port on the Black Sea, Hammer and Mishell were there to greet the ship. Russian mechanics, trained at Dearborn, were also on hand to unpack the crates, assemble the machines, and fill them with gas and oil. Atop the tractors, Hammer and his entourage set out for the center of Novorossisk. A comical overreaction resulted: the citizens thought they were being invaded by some strange type of American tanks, and the local garrison was called out. When the true nature of the invasion was determined, the welcome turned cordial.

The procession continued a hundred miles and a few days north along the Don River to the town of Rostov. There Hammer met several local officials who were to rise to the top of the Soviet government during the next few decades. One was a Red Army commander named Kliment Voroshilov, later one of the most powerful and shadowy members of Stalin's Politburo as the Chairman of the Presidium of the Supreme Soviet. Another was the province's twenty-eight-year-old Party secretary, Anastas Mikoyan, who would become the Politburo's most forceful proponent of trade with the West until his death in 1978.

A hundred miles north of Ekaterinburg, now Sverdlovsk, were the asbestos mines of the Allied American Company. Actually, it was a large hole one thousand feet in diameter with terraced walls that went about a hundred feet below the surface. The operations were abominably inefficient. Everything was done by hand. Chunks of ore were carried on laborers' backs and pounded until the asbestos could be separated.

Hammer revolutionized the process with an array of sophisticated equipment—compressed-air drills, automatic sawmills, and mechanical rock crushers. He had houses built for the workers, as well as schools and a hospital, and supplied the employees with surplus American military uniforms. With such progress under way, Hammer and Mishell returned to Moscow.

Lenin, who had begun the long decline in health that ended with his death a year and a half later, welcomed Hammer back to the capital with a warm letter in flawed English. "Excuse me please," he wrote on May 11, 1922, "I have been very ill; now I am much, much better. Many thanks for your present—a very kind letter from American comrades and friends who are in prison." He wished Hammer "full success of Your first concession: such success would be of great importance also for trade relations between our Republic & United States."

At the same time, Lenin instructed his secretaries to "Make note of *Armand Hammer,* and *in every way help* him on my behalf if he applies." He delivered to Hammer a letter of introduction to Grigory Zinoviev in Petrograd. "I beg you to help the comrade

Armand Hammer," Lenin had written. "It is extremely important for us that his first concession should be a full success." Later in the day, he called Petrograd with another message for Zinoviev, in the event that his written message was not received. "Today I wrote a letter of reference to you and your deputy for the American Comrade *Armand Hammer,*" Lenin said. "His father is a millionaire and a Communist (he is in *prison* in America)." He asked Zinoviev to "see that there is no red tape and that reliable comrades should personally keep an eye on the progress."

What did Lenin's repeated use of the term "comrade" mean when referring to Armand Hammer? Lenin did not bandy the title about loosely. "Comrade" referred to a fellow Communist, but since Armand Hammer was not that, in his case it referred to a Communist's son who was, in Lenin's eyes, helping Communism.

It is significant that Lenin gave "comrade Armand Hammer" an inscribed photograph. A year earlier, an American businessman named Washington Vanderlip, pretending to be one of the Vanderlips who owned the First National City Bank, saw Lenin to discuss leasing the Kamchatka oil fields. As he left, he asked Lenin for an autographed portrait. Lenin recalls:

> I had declined, because when you present a portrait you write, "To Comrade So-and-so," and I could not write, "To Comrade Vanderlip." . . . I did not know what to write. It would have been illogical to give my photograph to an out-and-out imperialist.

This is why no other Western businessman ever received a signed picture of V. I. Lenin. Armand Hammer was not an "out-and-out imperialist"; he was—in Lenin's opinion—at least a Communist sympathizer.

Hammer's position of privilege among the Soviet leaders proved quite handy several times. When a railroad official north of Alapayevsk demanded a bribe, Hammer contacted the Special Concessions Committee, and Felix Dzerzhinsky—whom Hammer fondly remembers as "that remarkable man"—had the official executed. Another time, Hammer had difficulties with an obstinate bureaucrat in Petrograd, and fired off a letter to Reinstein. On May 22, Lenin angrily wrote to Zinoviev:

> Today, Reinstein showed me a letter from *Armand Hammer,* of whom I wrote you (an American, a millionaire's son, one of the first to have taken a concession from us which is *highly profitable* to us).
>
> He says that in spite of my letter, his colleague *Mishell* (Ham-

> mer's colleague) has bitterly complained about "the *rudeness* and *red tape* on the part of *Begge,* who received him in Petrograd."
>
> I am going to complain about Begge's behavior to the Central Committee. This is the limit! In spite of my special letter to you and *your deputy,* they acted *to the contrary*!!

Lenin ordered Zinoviev to "influence Begge and *clear up the matter.*" One wonders whether the unfortunate Begge was "influenced" in the same manner as was the railroad official.

By now Lenin's health had deteriorated seriously. In 1918 a member of the Social Revolutionary Party had made an attempt on his life and lodged a bullet in him. In April 1922 he decided to undergo surgery for removal of the bullet, which his doctors thought was poisoning his bloodstream. Perhaps as a result of the operation, Lenin suffered a massive stroke on May 26 that left his right side partially paralyzed and temporarily robbed him of the ability to speak. Despite his frail condition, Lenin was especially concerned with seeing that Hammer was given special treatment. Two days before his stroke he began a letter—which he finished one day after the stroke—addressed to Joseph Stalin, the General Secretary of the Party. This last letter he was to write concerning the Hammers was marked "urgent" and "secret." Perhaps sensing he would soon die, Lenin wished to ensure that his successors maintained the personal camaraderie he had established with the Hammer family.

The cause of the letter was an apparently reassuring secret report he had received on the Hammers from Boris Reinstein. A footnote to Lenin's letter in a 1965 Soviet edition of his works describes "a report of B. I. Reinstein which contained detailed intelligence on Dr. J. Hammer and his son Doctor Armand Hammer and about the firm held by the family—the Allied American Drug and Chemical Company." The contents of this report will of course never be known. Whatever it said, it heartened Lenin. On May 24, he wrote:

> To *Comrade Stalin*
>
> with a request to circulate among all Politburo members
> (being sure to include Comrade Zinoviev)
>
> On the strength of this information from Comrade Reinstein, I am giving both Armand *Hammer* and B. *Mishell* a special recommendation on my own behalf and request all C. C. members to give these persons and their enterprise *particular* support. This is a small path leading to the American "business" world, and this path should be made use of *in every way.* If there are any objec-

tions, please *telephone* them to my secretary (Fotieva or Lepeshinskaya), to enable me to clear up the matter (and take a final decision through the Politburo) before I leave, that is, within the next few days.

Lenin

There were no objections, and on June 2, the Politburo—Stalin, Trotsky, Zinoviev, Kamenev, and the newly elected Rykov and Tomsky—unanimously approved Lenin's recommendation. Whatever "particular" support meant, they accepted it. The Hammer family niche was secure.

The S. S. *Majestic* sailed into the New York harbor on June 13, 1922. During the voyage, Hammer happened to strike up a conversation with a prominent American businessman during which he excitedly explained his asbestos concession in the Soviet Union. This businessman alerted reporters, who gathered to hear Hammer's tale when the ship docked.

Naturally Hammer made no mention of the special relationship his family had with the Soviet leadership. "When I conferred with officials of the Government," he told *The New York Times,* "I told them that I was a capitalist, that I was out to make money, but entertained no idea of grabbing their land or their empire." Of course, by denying being an anti-Bolshevik, land-grabbing capitalist, Hammer hoped to divert attention from the true, more suspicious circumstances. Lenin, after all, understood that the Hammers were anything but plundering industrialists. "The Allied American Company," he once wrote, "is to be distinguished from the usual capitalist companies in that it is well disposed toward the Soviet Union."

Hammer continued, "They said, in effect, 'We understand you didn't come here for love. As long as you do not mix in our politics, we will give you our help.'"

Later in June, Hammer gave a private dinner at the Hotel Commodore to interest other businessmen in the type of success he was enjoying. The *New York World* reported on the enthusiasm Hammer had generated: "A rich slice of the prospective trade with Russia which the financial centres of the world have been looking forward to for the last two years is within the grasp of American interests."

But the State Department was less pleased with the Hammer family's operations. It regarded the burgeoning activities of Allied American with increasing suspicion. One official in the American "listening post" of Riga, Latvia, reported to Washington on the odd staff of Allied American: "One personality involved is a Mr. Michell [*sic*], described as a naturalized American of Russian-Jewish origin; another is Dr. Hammer of New York, whose father is a well-known radical and a former friend of Trotsky."

The Department of Justice's Bureau of Investigation (the forerunner of the FBI) began an extensive, although ultimately fruitless, investigation of Julius Hammer. A number of disconcerting facts were compiled: Julius "was alleged to have received negotiable securities from Trotzky, which he delivered to Jules Magnus, who in turn delivered them to Ludwig C. A. K. Martens." Furthermore, in 1914 he had been involved in supplying dynamite to terrorist groups.

By this time, Allied American had an office in London and one in Berlin. During the summer of 1922, Armand traveled around Europe, buying machinery for the concession and signing contracts for the import of goods to the Soviet Union.

Armand's twenty-two-year-old brother, Victor, had spent a year at Colgate University and then a year at Princeton. He most of all wanted to be an actor. He had not been happy at either college, though, in part because he was Jewish; it was for this reason, for example, that he was excluded from Princeton's dramatic societies. His family wanted him to go to Moscow and lend a hand in the family enterprise instead. "The greatest actors are in Moscow," Armand told him. Victor agreed to go to Russia, enrolled in the Miller School of Shorthand and Typing in New York, and took a one-month course to train as his brother's secretary. In the fall of 1922 Victor sailed to Russia with Armand. On November 7, 1922—the fifth anniversary of the Bolshevik Revolution—Victor and Armand joined their father's friend Charles Recht and other American Communists at a celebration of the event. Later Victor went to work as a miner at Alapayevsk.

For much of 1922, Armand had orchestrated a campaign to get his father released from prison. He persuaded doctors, businessmen, and other influential friends to write letters to New York's Governor Alfred E. Smith. On January 23, 1923, Julius was paroled. He was not pardoned, however, and, since he was a naturalized citizen, Julius had no choice but to leave the country and reapply for American citizenship later, should he desire it. This fit in well with the family's plans.

After a reunion with Rose and their son Harry at the Hotel

Ansonia, Julius arranged through Alexander Gumberg to meet with Henry Ford at Dearborn. Julius's proposition was far bolder than another order of tractors. He attempted to persuade Ford to build an automotive plant in the Soviet Union, to be run by Russians and supervised by Ford engineers. Hammer explained that the Soviets preferred to construct factories rather than rely on imports.

The Soviet government had in fact placed a temporary ban on the import of American cars and tractors (perhaps to force Ford to agree to construct a factory on Soviet soil), but Ford was convinced that the ban was a slap at him personally for his anti-Bolshevik pronouncements. Julius assured him that it was not. Still, Ford was unwilling to undertake the project. Not wanting to give up hope, Julius promised to write to him from Russia after talking with Soviet trade officials in person.

Borrowing the passport of a socialist comrade, Julius Heiman, Julius set sail with his wife a few weeks later, leaving Harry in charge of the New York office. They spent a few weeks traveling in Europe. Julius, enjoying freedom at last, took the opportunity to check the operations of his company's London and Berlin offices. They arrived in Moscow on the first of May. The timing was perfect. Julius and Rose, returning to Russia for the first time since they were born, to the home of the first Communist Revolution, were just in time for the annual May Day workers' parade in Red Square. It seemed as if all of Moscow had turned out to celebrate their arrival.

3

AMERICAN ROYALTY

THE ACCOMMODATIONS the Soviet government gave the Hammer family were grand beyond the imagination of any other foreigners in Moscow, probably more luxurious than the dwellings of any of the Soviet leaders. The house was a stately, late-nineteenth-century mansion of beige stone with an ornate façade in one of the poshest sections of Moscow—an island of wealth, culture, and frivolity in a city racked by poverty.

The Brown House, as it was called, was located at Sadovo-Samotechnaya 14, near the Moscow Art Theatre and the circus. As the largest American home in the city, it became, in the absence of an official American embassy, "a sort of center of social life in the colony," as Eugene Lyons, then the Moscow correspondent for the Associated Press, writes in *Assignment in Utopia.* Lyons, who lived for a time in the Brown House, recalls, "Visiting Americans carried back tall tales of the splendors and comforts in which we luxuriated."

The Hammers, Lyons writes, "dispensed hospitality with a baronial hand." Actors and actresses, ballerinas from the Bolshoi, powerful commissars from the Kremlin, and visitors from abroad all mingled at the Brown House. "The vodka flowed generously," Lyons remembers, and the tables groaned with lavish buffets. This place of such peculiar mingling of Soviet and Western society became the center of Moscow's social life, the setting for social and political intrigue—and therefore the object of malicious and envious gossip.

Surrounded by gardens, with a terrace, tennis court, and carriage house for servants in the giant courtyard in back, the Brown House was set far back from the road. Inside, a wide staircase of marble spiraled to the two upper stories. Visitors were amazed by the icons and paintings, both priceless and gaudy, that covered practically every inch of the walls. "Reindeer heads looked down in astonishment from the vestibule walls," Lyons says.

On the first floor were three kitchens and pantries, several sitting rooms and bedrooms, and a spacious, elegant, wood-paneled dining room with cabinets full of crystal and fine china. On the ceiling above the dining table was a mural of fruits and flowers. Upstairs was a servants' sitting room, three connecting salons also lined with works of art, a great ballroom with a grand piano, and a kitchen with, in Lyons's words, "an oven as broad as a field." A private dining room, set off by sliding oak doors with frosted crystal windows, allowed the Hammer family a respite from the unending parade of guests.

Some of these guests preferred for one reason or another to enter or depart the house undetected. Among them, reportedly, were highly placed officials in the Party leadership, who entered the house through a secret passage to avoid identifying the Hammers as a family with close social and political ties to the Kremlin. The officials entered through a concealed door at the side of the house that opened into a narrow, labyrinthine passage ending in a panel, hidden beneath a large painting, beside the marble staircase.

Among the several servants was the cook, a wizened, bad-tempered old woman named Shura, who made bountiful if inelegant dishes such as barley-and-mushroom soup for the many houseguests. "Shura and her glowering ways were attaining international fame of a sort," Lyons recalls. "Her clumsy peasant figure, the flashes of earthly shrewdness and peasant greed out of the depths of her tight-lipped reticence, impressed foreigners as enigmatic."

The Hammers' palace of luxury did not escape the difficulties of the city in which it was located. To guard against intruders, Julius Hammer's untamed wolfhound, which was chained in a downstairs corridor during the day, was let loose at night at the servants' entrance. Somewhere deep within the bowels of the house dwelled the widow of the original owner. The Hammers and their guests never saw the woman, but occasionally, when a party in the ballroom grew too loud, she would angrily bang on her wall.

The courtyard of the house was ringed with apartments, once

stables, that now housed more than a dozen Russian families. "The sight of the foreigners' spacious life," Lyons observes, "the sound of their American gramophones, the odors of their daily meat must have been a constant taunt. The children stood on tiptoe and looked into the wonder-windows."

The Brown House served an indispensable function in Moscow. Important visitors to the Soviet Union, newspaper correspondents, businessmen, and Congressional delegations all were able to enjoy an oasis of Western-style comfort, which lent an aspect of good cheer to the drab capital. Walter Duranty, the famous Moscow correspondent for *The New York Times,* passed many an inebriated evening with the Hammers, which certainly did not detract from the rosy image of the Soviet Union his dispatches conveyed.

Visitors to the Brown House generally acknowledged that the Hammers were Soviet sympathizers. "Drawn to Russia from New York by their genuine interest in the revolution," Lyons explains, ". . . the Hammers . . . mixed the business of helping themselves with the pleasure of helping Russia." Julius was known as a passionate defender of Soviet Communism. When dinner guests ventured criticism of the regime, he urged patience: "Time, time, it takes time," he said.

The Hammers' visitors included H. G. Wells, Gene Tunney, Douglas Fairbanks and Mary Pickford, and Averell Harriman. Will Rogers came to Moscow in 1926, and one of the Hammers met him at the railroad station. As they crossed the Moskva River, Rogers was amazed to see Russians of both sexes swimming naked. Later he wrote a book entitled *There's Not a Bathing Suit in Russia.*

John Dewey came over in 1927 with a delegation of thirteen other educators that included Julius's friend Lucy Branham. They were all put up in the Brown House. One morning, Armand Hammer recounts, Dewey came down for breakfast and found Rose Hammer eating caviar and drinking glass thimbles of a clear liquid.

"May I ask what you are drinking?" Dewey said.

"Vodka," Rose replied.

"Vodka? For breakfast?"

"It's nothing but a cereal drink," she said.

Legends of the opulence in which the Hammers dwelled were so widespread that a Soviet motion-picture company once asked the Hammers for permission to film the interior of the Brown House, and the Hammers gladly acquiesced. Later they were dismayed to learn that the footage was used in a Soviet film depicting the evils of capitalism.

Seeking to downplay the importance of his father's political ties, Armand Hammer has always claimed that the Brown House belonged to him and Victor and that his parents came only for occasional visits. This is clearly not true.

The poet E. E. Cummings came to Moscow in May 1931 to see for himself what so many of his intellectual friends were hailing so enthusiastically. There was a room available at the Brown House, and Julius allowed him to stay for a few weeks. Cummings recorded his impressions of his month in Soviet Russia in a novel, *Eimi,* which is a masterful portrait of the cruelties and absurdities of Soviet Communism and the growing disillusionment of Americans in Moscow.

His description of Julius is perceptive, though unkind. Julius appears as a character named "Chinesy" because of his somewhat Asian-looking Jewish countenance, a regal, even imperious, strangely silent man of uncertain motives. Cummings dismisses Rose (Mrs. M.D.) as witless. (By the time Cummings visited Moscow, Armand and Victor had already departed the country.)

Cummings's first impression of Chinesy is one of a "huge . . . dangerous" man who "deferentially mentor murmurs," in Cummings's Joycean syntax. Cummings is astounded by the Brown House: it is not an apartment, like the residences of every other American in the city—"Why it's a house!" Chinesy "himself owns this house . . . O my yes, very rich indeed. Remind me to tell—but public spirited, very." Everything about Chinesy—especially, as Cummings intimates, the provenance of his wealth—is mysterious. When Cummings enters "the palatial residence of the Chinesy doctor" he sees Chinesy sitting "in a little plushy room" between two "typical American business gents of the Quiet, and how, variety." On second glance, Chinesy seems less imposing—"feeble? or merely not as I'd remembered."

One evening, the novel continues, Cummings, Chinesy and Mrs. M.D. and Turk (Charles Malamuth, a correspondent) go to a restaurant for dinner. Everyone has beer. Cummings overhears an argument between Mrs. M.D. and Turk.

"The state is queen," Turk tells Mrs. M.D., "and you'd be the first to hate that, despite your pretended procommunism." Chinesy/M.D. watches but says nothing: "Carefully meanwhile M.D. sips, alert, silent."

"Why?" Mrs. M.D. asks Turk.

"Suppose you were here and your husband had a private practice," Turk explains. "He'd be unable to make large amounts of money—"

"I wouldn't let him practice privately," Mrs. M.D. interrupts.

Later in the argument, Turk tells Mrs. M.D., "Not all these knowing millions can tell you a single god damned thing, because they're Russians. Do you understand? Russians. All of them are actually living (or rather dying) an unprecedented experiment, not merely observing it with an analytic eye, far less dreaming about it with a sentimental brain. What I tell you, I tell you because I can do what all those millions of human beings can't—speak."

Chinesy straightens. "Bravo," he whispers.

This passage is the only account of the disillusionment Julius might have felt, at least after eight years in Moscow, toward the regime. Nevertheless, whatever qualms he felt did not keep him from living magnificently in his palace filled with works of art acquired cheaply from the state.

Cummings describes another occasion, when several Americans exchange snide, anti-Semitic remarks about the doctor. "Well, if you will live with millionaire Jews," one begins to say.

"What's that?" Cummings asks.

The other American snickers. "I didn't mean anything derog- . . . as a matter of fact, I myself sponged off the doctor more than you; I didn't even pay for my room, and I assume you are." Cummings was not.

Shortly after Julius arrived in Moscow in 1923, he visited Rostov, where he looked into the possibilities of establishing a Ford plant, and spoke with regional trade officials. On June 1, he sent a long, cheery letter to Henry Ford. Still trying to persuade Ford to construct a tractor plant, Julius wrote that such an undertaking would "hasten greatly the reconstruction, not of Russia alone, but of the whole of Europe and would help to replace the atmosphere and danger of strife and warfare by the peaceful pursuits of agriculture and industry."

The three-page letter was typed on the new Allied American letterhead, with the company's name, Moscow address, and telephone number printed in Russian. A large engraving of a Fordson tractor floated above a legend that boasted, also in Russian: "Russian agent for the American automotive and tractor company 'Ford.'" Julius sent a copy of this letter to his other contact at Ford, Charles Sorensen, with the note: "I may add that since I saw you last, I have allowed no grass to grow under my feet. I found Russia to exceed all my expectations. . . . Living is most interesting here with Arts maintaining their excellent standards."

The Hammers also tried to persuade Sorensen and Ford to ship a display of Ford products to the agricultural exposition in Moscow during the summer of 1923, where Allied American had a pavilion. Julius's cable to Dearborn explained defensively: "WE ARE ONLY EXHIBITORS KEEPING AMERICAN FLAG FLYING." But Ford, still angered at the Russian embargo on his cars, refused to participate. Julius intervened personally with Trotsky, and the ban was lifted. Armand recalls that Trotsky had explained, in a singularly un-Trotskylike formulation, "No true Marxist would allow sentiment to interfere with business."

Not until 1929 would Ford agree to build a factory in Russia—and it would be at the urging of a delegation of Soviet trade officials. He paid little attention to the Hammers, however, and by the end of 1923, they lost interest in cultivating their contact in Dearborn. "I haven't heard from you for about six months and presume that you have probably dropped off the face of the earth," a concerned Charles Sorensen wrote to Armand in April 1924. "Why don't you write us once in a while? Have your folks returned from Russia? . . . When do you expect to come to Detroit again? Try and write when you have time." But the Hammers no longer had reason to visit Dearborn or, in fact, to return to the United States, at least for a long while.

The Allied American Corporation had become by now the Soviets' sole import-export agent for the United States. On July 14, the Hammers made the arrangement official by signing a contract to import as much as two hundred thousand gold rubles' worth of agricultural and mining equipment, and to export at least as much in any Russian commodity. The Soviets would determine all prices and receive 50 percent of the profits with an additional 10 percent as commission. The main export was to be asbestos, but a subsidiary firm was also formed that year to put Russian minks, sables, and hides on the American market. This company was Allied Fur Sales; Armand was its president.

As the Hammers' operations expanded, the reaction of the United States government grew divided. The Commerce Department began routinely to recommend them to American firms wishing to trade with the Soviet Union, yet the State Department concluded that they were "a pretty rotten bunch" who served as a "propaganda organ of the Soviet government." Most of the State Department's conclusions were based on grumblings from Foreign Service officials in Riga who were suspicious of Julius's known sympathy with Communism. Some suspicions, though, had a firmer foundation. In the spring of 1923, the State Department and the Department of War reported that the Allied American representative in New York, Alexander Gumberg, was regularly using company shipments to transmit mail and packages to Boris Reinstein in Moscow. Since Reinstein was the Soviet official most directly concerned with propaganda efforts in the United States, and Gumberg was known to be the Russians' chief political agent in New York, the Americans assumed that these exchanges related to pro-Soviet and Communist activities and that the packages contained Soviet funds for that purpose. None of these reports, however, was ever documented. In fact, despite such official concern about the Hammers, Governor Alfred E. Smith pardoned Julius on November 12, 1924, thereby restoring his American citizenship and allowing him to travel outside of Russia at will.

With the assistance of Gumberg, a congressional committee came on a junket to the Soviet Union in the fall of 1923 to see "whether Russia was heaven or hell." Congressman James Frear of Wisconsin and Senators Edwin Ladd of North Dakota and William King of Utah spent close to three months there, meeting with several top Soviet leaders and dining often at the Brown House. Their official sessions in the Kremlin were augmented by convivial banquets in the Hammers' stately dining room with Russian ballerinas and actors and actresses. The committee returned to the United States unanimously calling for the resumption of trade relations between the two countries. Russia, it turned out, was heaven.

After more than a year of incapacity, Lenin suffered a final, massive stroke, and died on January 21, 1924. Much of Moscow mourned (for even the most bitter opponents of the regime realized that things could only get worse), and the Hammer family of course attended the funeral. In his 1932 autobiography, Armand extolled Lenin with an explicit comparison to Jesus Christ: "Like One before him he forbade not little children to come to him, and rejoiced that they should be happy." Laboring for two and a half days, Soviet workers constructed a wooden mausoleum to enshrine Lenin's body. Armand recalled watching the Soviet leaders atop the tomb on the day of the funeral. Among them was an "unassuming" man with "keen and watchful" eyes—Stalin.

With Lenin's death went the liberal New Economic Policy that had permitted the Hammers to dwell in Moscow as nobility. The change, however, was by no means swift. The Hammers, who continued to serve an important function for the Soviet government, were allowed to remain, although their business was to undergo several changes. This was the result of Stalin's fierce struggle to succeed Lenin. Stalin was not Lenin's heir apparent; in the very last letter he dictated, a day before his death, Lenin had warned the Politburo that Stalin must not be permitted to succeed him. Within five years, though, Stalin had managed to outmaneuver and liquidate all of his potential rivals—Trotsky, Rykov, Tomsky, Zinoviev, and Kamenev.

Even when Stalin's dictatorial power was consolidated, the Hammer family was tolerated; this was probably because Julius, the head of the Allied American Corporation, maintained his ties with the leadership, perhaps even with Stalin himself.

As the Soviets methodically began amassing control of foreign trade, the Hammers' one-year term as import-export agents was terminated. By the middle of 1924, all American business was transferred from Allied American to the new, wholly Soviet-owned enterprise called Amtorg.

With this part of the business dissolved, the Hammers began to concentrate—or, more exactly, were told to concentrate—on operations within the Soviet Union. Alexander Gumberg resigned from the company to become vice-president of the All-Russian Textile Syndicate, which sold Soviet cotton in New York. One day Armand was summoned to the office of the Minister of Foreign Trade, Leonid Krassin, for new instructions.

The Soviets, Krassin announced, had decided to place the Hammers in charge of a state export bank, the Harju Bank in Reval. The arrangement was curious. As head of Allied American, Julius was to pay more than two hundred thousand dollars and thereby become the major shareholder in the bank, whose ostensible purpose was the export of butter. But butter may not have been the real reason. The Harju Bank may have been a surreptitious device for transferring Soviet money abroad, formally in the name of Allied American, to fund Comintern activities. As with so many of the Hammers' business transactions with the Soviet government, the methods of the Harju Bank were cloaked in mystery. One puzzle was how the Hammers had that much money to invest. Reports in the Soviet press made clear that the asbestos concession, far from making the Hammers rich, was faltering as world asbestos prices declined. Much of their money was tied up in the mine, which was producing little income.

The ever-suspicious State Department regarded this bank deal "with considerable apprehension, because of the close connection between this corporation and the Soviet government." Since "the Allied American Corporation could not have financed the undertaking itself in view of its failure to have made any considerable money up to that time from its Russian concessions," State Department officials in Riga concluded in a dispatch to Washington, it seemed clear that the Hammers were somehow using the bank's funds to make "profitable financial transactions for the authorities." A few months later, in May 1925, the bank was closed, a victim, the Hammers claimed, of major embezzlement by one of its employees.

Their stint as bankers having ended in failure, the Hammers then began a venture that would make them a lot of money—the manufacture of pens and pencils. With his father's approval, and Krassin's encouragement, Armand established yet another subsidiary firm, called A. Hammer and Company, incorporated in New York at 3 East 52nd Street, but based in Moscow. The agreement with the Soviet government was signed in 1925 and was to run until 1935, and then revert to the Soviets.

This was the first significant transfer of technology from the West to the East, though it was decidedly a nonmilitary one. Armand knew nothing about making pens or pencils but knew where to find the experts and equipment. He went to Birmingham, England, where pens were produced, and to Nuremberg, Germany, the bastion of the Faber pencil dynasty. In a series of shrewd maneuvers, Armand lured a number of disgruntled engineers away from their employers; his real coup, though, was obtaining the long-secret Faber process of turning out high-quality pencils.

The Soviet government provided Hammer with an abandoned soap factory on the outskirts of Moscow, cottages for the German and English employees, a school, and a restaurant. "It was a regular little city," Armand recalled.

Within half a year, the Hammers were manufacturing steel fountain pens and graphite pencils embossed with the name HAMMER in Russian. Armand selected as the company's coat of arms an overwhelmingly patriotic image of the upper half of the Statue of Liberty against a background of the American flag. Their trademark was a hammer and an anchor crossed, strongly resembling the two crossed hammers of the Johann Faber symbol (and bearing a slight, coincidental similarity to the hammer and sickle). Their motto was "The pens and pencils of the Hammer factory are always good."

The enterprise—especially the Hammer pencils—was a huge

success. Pencils had been scarce, and now Soviet stationery stores found it hard to keep Hammer pencils in stock. Older Russians remember going into stores and requesting "Two Hammers, please." The present members of the Politburo, including Leonid Brezhnev, learned to write with Hammer pencils.

Russians eagerly sought jobs at the Hammer pen and pencil factory; the pay was good and the work offered many Russians a means to conceal their non-Bolshevik backgrounds. A British observer noted:

> Professors, authors, generals, former captains of industry, ex-government officials, and ladies of noble birth, sit side by side at the cutting machines and lead filling machines, at the trimming and painting plants, and in the packing-rooms, with humble industrial workers. Their only ambition is to sink their individuality, and to destroy all records of their past, in order that they may keep their jobs. Nevertheless, the government agents and spies are constantly tracing their lineage and former careers, and insisting on their being turned into the streets to make room for the genuine proletariat.

By the end of 1924, the Hammers were turning out 51 million pencils and 10 million pens, and a year later were producing 72 million pencils and 95 million pens. Armand Hammer's first personal accomplishment was a hit. He began to export to England, Turkey, Persia, and China.

"We suddenly found ourselves eulogized in the Soviet press," he later wrote. "In two years we had turned Russia into an exporter of a manufactured product, which even before the war had been imported for millions of gold rubles. We received daily visits from Workers' delegations, student classes in engineering schools, and government commissions." The Hammers even published a booklet that proudly boasts of the virtues of the Hammer pencil. The back cover of the brochure, a copy of which is today in the Lenin Library in Moscow, features a dramatic depiction of an Allied American Corporation ship entering a New York harbor illuminated with spotlights.

From time to time, though, the Hammers were attacked in the Soviet press, which seems strange treatment for government-approved entrepreneurs. Once, at dinner at the Brown House, the Soviet Minister of Education, A. V. Lunacharsky, leaned over to Armand Hammer and confided, "I have been following the attacks on you in the newspapers; don't pay any attention to them.

You know, some of the comrades have to let off steam periodically, and since they haven't local capitalists to train their guns on, you have to be the goat." Not all of the attacks were to be ignored, though. Armand had initiated a program of profit sharing and piecework for his employees, a form of capitalism the Soviet authorities probably found repulsive and dangerous. Critical articles in the press may have been one way to warn the Hammers.

The Hammers did profit from the factory, but far less than they advertised. Walter Duranty regularly reported in *The New York Times* that the Hammers were clearing a million dollars a year. It did not come from the asbestos concession (which Victor later remembered as "a flop") or, in fact, from the pen and pencil business. In 1928, Armand submitted a confidential report to the American Embassy in Berlin, in response to a U.S. request, revealing his profits to be about half of what Duranty claimed. In 1926, for example, Allied American had made $600,000, and in 1927, $500,000.

The Hammers had been able to export their profits in 1924 through the Harju Bank, but since that institution's demise, all of their money remained in rubles in the State Bank. Some of it subsidized the vodka, caviar, and household expenses of their royal existence. But while Julius was a dedicated Communist, at least in sympathy, he and Armand were also dedicated moneymakers. And by the late twenties, when Stalin decided that all foreign businessmen—even the Hammers—should leave Russia, a way had to be devised to enable the Allied American Corporation to take its profits out. This launched the Hammer family on another profitable partnership with the Soviet government: the export of Russian art.

4

TROTSKY AND THE YALIE

FOR ALL THEIR revolutionary fervor and Kremlin friends, the Hammers lacked clout where it counted most—in the United States. The Soviets needed to interest influential Americans in the economic potential of, and, perhaps more important, the diplomatic recognition of Russia. But most Americans were uninterested.

One exception was the financier Bernard Baruch, who entertained a tolerant attitude toward the Bolsheviks. "The Russian people have a right, it seems to me, to set up any form of government they wish," he wrote in 1920. He thought capitalism would be restored to Russia only by means of trade with the West, and for this reason he advocated doing business with Russia, although he did none himself. In 1925 an American journalist introduced Baruch to Leonid Krassin, the Soviet Minister of Foreign Trade, at Versailles. Krassin described at length the Soviet plan for building heavy industry, and offered Baruch whatever concession he chose if he would be willing to give the Soviets advice. Baruch replied that he would be only too glad to help them, even without any reimbursement, if they would simply give up Communism. Krassin lost interest in Baruch.

Henry Ford's relationship with the Soviets was happier. By the end of the twenties, he had sold them a total of twenty-four thousand tractors and a few thousand touring cars. On May 31, 1929, the Ford Motor Company signed a contract with Amtorg to provide plans for an immense factory to produce Model A cars and

Model AA trucks. "Abandon any theory," Ford began to assert at the time, "if the success of the job requires it." The Soviet Union deified him in return. "If Lenin is Russia's God today," an American journalist wrote in the *Nation's Business* at the time, "Ford is its St. Peter." For a time, the word *Fordizatsiya* entered the Russian vocabulary as a synonym for American-style automation. In the late twenties, a Russian couple in the Volga area was married in a cart pulled by a Fordson tractor; their ceremony exalted Henry Ford and his tractor. But Stalin decanonized Ford in 1934, as soon as Soviet engineers figured out—thanks to Ford's technology—how to build their own cars, trucks, and tractors.

Throughout the twenties, Russia searched for prominent American businessmen to take a Soviet concession and thus act as bellwethers for large-scale Western investment. Only with capitalist help, the Bolsheviks reasoned, would they rebuild Russian industry. Lenin had decreed that the capitalists would build Communism, and Stalin concurred. Yet in the middle twenties, when it seemed as if no major Western investor was interested in the Russian market, the Soviets grew desperate. And then, out of the blue, there came an American with a famous name, a fortune, and an industrial empire, who wanted to do business. The Russians were, initially, thrilled.

William Averell Harriman was born in 1891, the eldest son of the "robber baron" Edward Henry Harriman, who created the Union Pacific Railroad and was known, not always with affection, as the Napoleon of American railroads. Theodore Roosevelt more simply called him one of the "malefactors of great wealth." E. H. Harriman's fortune was once estimated at one hundred million dollars. The five Harriman children were raised as true American aristocrats, playing croquet and polo with the Morgans, Vanderbilts, Whitneys, and Rockefellers—all of whom were, like the Harrimans, only first- or second-generation rich.

E. H. Harriman had grandiose schemes for a global transportation network, railroads linking vast shipping empires. Frequently he would take the family on trips around the country in a private Pullman car. One famous Harriman family expedition in 1898 took them to Alaska in typical Harriman style: they set sail from Seattle on a private steamer, accompanied by a staff of sixty-five that included two doctors, two photographers, three artists, and twenty-five scientists (among whom was the naturalist John Burroughs). When the party reached the Bering Sea, they briefly entered Russian territory. Years later, during the Second World War, Averell Harriman recounted to Stalin the story of his first visit to Russia when he was seven; Harriman remembered little of it except that no one in his family had a passport.

Averell attended private school in New York, and then was sent to Groton. By the time he finished school in 1909, his family had moved into their great estate, Arden House, located on thirty-five thousand acres in the Orange County town of Turners (later renamed Harriman), New York. Six hundred workers had spent three years building Arden House. A few months after moving in, E. H. Harriman died, leaving his entire fortune to his wife in a one-sentence will. In time, the assets and responsibilities of the Harriman empire passed to Averell.

That fall, Averell entered Yale College. He was too light for the crew, and so, after two months of studying rowing technique at Oxford, became one of the few undergraduates ever to be appointed chief coach. The freshman crew he coached included Dean Acheson. Later Harriman bragged, "Most of the rest of Washington thinks of Dean Acheson as the Secretary of State under Harry Truman and a great figure of another time. I still think of him as someone I taught rowing to on the freshman crew at Yale." The tall, attractive, dark-haired Harriman was not terribly popular—too rich for the poor men's sons and too driven for the rich. Yet he was elected to Skull and Bones, the undergraduate secret society whose members deemed themselves the fifteen men in their class most likely to succeed in life.

His class-book entry concerning his future was concise: "Harriman will go into railroading." He had no choice. In his senior year he was elected to the Union Pacific board of directors; upon graduation, though a vice-president, he went to work on the railroad's surveying gang to learn the business. The fact that the son of the railroad's founder was working as a laborer was kept secret until a newspaper reporter, noting that "young Harriman is as averse to publicity as a mouse is to a cat," discovered that the twenty-two-year-old heir was working

> on a handcar along the line of the Union Pacific in Wyoming and Colorado, serving as a section hand in one of the railroads of which he is vice president. Attired in blue overalls, he is mixing with the section men and the ordinary day laborers along the line. . . . At noon Harriman's dinner is taken from a tin bucket, and he eats it in company with his fellow laborers. To them he is simply "Bill" and a cub engineer, who doesn't know much about the business but is learning.

In 1915 his father's successor as chairman of the railroad, Robert S. Lovett, promoted Averell to vice-president for purchasing. That same year, he married Kitty Lanier Lawrence (with whom he was to have two daughters before they were divorced fourteen years later), and his mother deeded Arden House to him.

When the Great War came, Harriman was twenty-three; though many men of his age enlisted, he did not. Instead, he built a shipyard near Chester, Pennsylvania, and announced that America's defense effort would be better served by his running the shipyard and producing steel cargo ships than by his serving in the army in Europe. It is said that his eagerness to take on dangerous missions later in life, such as serving as ambassador to the Court of St. James's while London was being bombed, was psychological compensation for his decision, which he later regretted, to stay out of the First World War.

From shipbuilding he progressed to shipowning, and set up the American Ship & Commerce Corporation, which owned a fleet of a hundred ships. In 1920, at the age of twenty-nine, Harriman told B. C. Forbes in an interview in *Forbes* magazine, that "it is as indefensible for a man who has capital not to apply himself diligently to using it in a way that will be of most benefit for the country as it is for a laborer to refuse to work or for a revolutionary to resort to bombs in this country." With this high-minded purpose, he plunged into expanding his financial interests. That year he organized W. A. Harriman & Co., an international investment house. A few years later he and his brother Roland would organize Harriman Brothers & Co., an international banking firm. Both would merge, in 1931, with the century-old Brown Brothers & Co. to form the great private bank, Brown Brothers Harriman & Co.

Averell knew that he could not hope to outdo his father in commerce. Perhaps it was for this reason that he entered the world of international business, which would bring him into contact with the statesmen of the day and would eventually propel him into government service when Franklin Roosevelt became President. With his financial empire established in the early twenties, he began visiting Europe twice a year in search of business opportunities. Soon W. A. Harriman & Co. was marketing a twenty-million-dollar investment in a zinc and coal property in Upper Silesia, Poland, which earned Averell a directorship in a Polish bank. At about the same time, he joined with a Hamburg banking firm, M. M. Warburg and Company, to purchase Soviet bills from German firms. The Soviets, he found, were financially trustworthy.

"I was very anxious to know what the Soviet Union was all

about," Harriman recalled. "I thought the Russian Revolution would have an influence on world affairs for as long as I lived, and, being a businessman, the only way to get in touch with them was to do business with them." In 1922 he, a German firm, and the Soviet government formed a short-lived joint trading corporation. Although little trade resulted from the venture, Lenin himself followed it with great interest. He referred to it as "the project for Harriman's entry."

Lenin was well informed about the Harrimans. In Zurich, before the Revolution, he had done vast research into the giants of American capitalism and knew well the name of E. H. Harriman. The entry of young Harriman—whose very name symbolized the class Lenin sought to eradicate—into the Soviet market was a tantalizing prospect.

When the Russian Revolution came, Harriman belonged to what he calls the Five Year Club—the school of thought that contended that the Bolshevik regime would collapse within five years. Each year the five-year estimate was revised. By the twenties, though, Harriman says that he recognized "it was a permanent affair." When the opportunity arose for a major concession in the Soviet Union, he seized it. While most businessmen at the time thought such a venture risky or repugnant, or both, Averell Harriman was more adventurous—more enlightened, he likes to recall.

In 1924 Harriman heard that the world's largest deposit of manganese ore was being offered for rent by the Soviet government. The field, in Chiatura, near Tiflis, Georgia, had before the Revolution supplied half of the world's output of manganese, a vital ingredient in the manufacture of steel. The Chiatura field was estimated to contain at least a billion dollars' worth of ore, enough to supply the world for the next half-century.

Harriman immediately dispatched an associate, J. Speed Elliott, to work out a deal with the Russians. Because of the Harriman name, negotiations went quickly. On January 19, 1925, Speed reported triumphantly from Moscow, "Everything looks good here so far." At a cost of $3,450,000, Harriman bought the rights to mine the Chiatura field for twenty years and to export its manganese ore. This would be the biggest American venture yet granted in Soviet Russia.

The contract specified that Harriman was to produce 300,000 tons of ore per year during the first three years, and 500,000 a year during the remainder of the twenty-year period, a total of 16 million tons. Harriman was also to transform the existing narrow-gauge railway at the field into a full-fledged line extending to the port at Poti. He was required to loan the Soviet State Bank one million dollars as a "security deposit," and put down another million dollars as advance royalties. In addition, the Soviets requested a fixed royalty of eight dollars a ton, which, with the world price of manganese high, seemed reasonable—a condition that was later to cause great difficulties. In return, the Soviet government agreed not to grant any other manganese concessions "in the area." Speed Elliott, as vice-president of W. A. Harriman & Co., and Felix Dzerzhinsky, chairman of the People's Supreme Economic Council (and head of the Cheka, the secret police), signed the fifty-two-page contract in a ceremony in the Kremlin on June 12, 1924.

The Chiatura field had once belonged to a group of Russian businessmen, all of whom were forced to leave the country after the Revolution. As one of the conditions of the concession contract, Harriman agreed to give a percentage of the profits to the former owners, most of whom had moved to the United States. This money came out of Harriman's account. For years afterward, Harriman received letters of thanks from these émigrés, one of the last coming from a Palo Alto nursing home in 1981.

Three other investors went in on the deal with Harriman, and on July 27, 1925, they and three officers of W. A. Harriman & Co. met at the office of the United States Corporation in Dover, Delaware. The Georgian Manganese Company, Ltd., was formally incorporated. Harriman was named chairman of the board, and the company set up an office at 39 Broadway in New York. Harriman was pleased. He expected to make something like $120,000,000 from the project.

But almost at once there were serious problems. The vice-chairman of the Soviet Concessions Committee, Adolph Joffe, accused Harriman of being tightfisted and demanded a 15 percent raise for the Soviet mine employees. The double-track railroad Harriman was to build for two million dollars soon doubled in cost. More seriously, the Russians, who had agreed not to allow any competing manganese mines "in the area," granted one in Nikopol, the Ukraine—officially not then a part of the Soviet Union—to a German consortium, and on more favorable terms. The Germans undersold the Harriman group. At the same time, Brazil and Africa began to unload manganese on the world market. A worldwide glut resulted. Instead of becoming the baron of manganese as he had anticipated, Harriman had to dispose of the ore at vastly depressed prices. With the royalty rate fixed at eight dollars, the Georgian Manganese Company began to lose money at an alarming rate.

"The greatest American concession in the U.S.S.R.," as the Russians called it, came to be known as Harriman's Folly. Americans laughed at this vision of a capitalist dream of empire dashed upon the shoals of Bolshevik perfidy. A Soviet historian later charged that Averell Harriman "wanted to establish a monopoly in the world market," which went against Soviet principles.

Harriman felt that the Soviets had violated the spirit if not exactly the letter of the contract, and, in an effort to halt the price decline of the ore, he began to produce less manganese than agreed upon. The Soviets were incensed. Leonid Krassin, one of the gurus of Soviet economic policy, who was then ambassador to Great Britain, railed against this American "smart-dealer." "To allow a monopoly, all the more to someone so hostile to the Soviet Union, may turn out to be the gravest political error," he raged.

But playing the Germans off against the Americans was not so easy, the Soviets realized. Evidently the capitalists could be every bit as devious as the Communists. Still, Averell Harriman was hardly hostile to the Soviet government; he was one of the few Americans who was not. Even while his manganese concession was failing, he announced to the American press a "tentative" agreement he had made to exploit a 120-acre oil tract in the Bibi Eibat region of Russia, at a cost of seven million dollars plus royalties. But that was not to be. By the fall of 1926 Harriman realized he would have to go to Moscow himself to straighten out the manganese difficulties. He called on Secretary of Commerce Herbert Hoover for advice. Hoover was entirely uninterested in international developments, Harriman remembers, and warned that the United States would not be responsible if anything happened to him in the Soviet Union. Harriman was annoyed by Hoover's brusqueness and was glad, when Hoover ran for President in 1928, to vote for his opponent, Al Smith, a friend and a Democrat. Until then a good Republican, Harriman credited Hoover with his conversion to the Democratic Party.

He spent a few weeks in Europe, partly on other business and partly to find out what he could about the strange land he was about to visit. Many of the officials with whom he spoke knew little about the Soviet Union and cared less; others assured him that the Bolshevik regime was about to collapse. The only people who seemed to know anything were newspapermen who had been in Moscow.

Harriman reached Moscow by December, accompanied by a coterie of aides. Russia was not at all as he had expected. Life seemed reasonably free. He went to the theater and to concerts and was impressed; he had drinks with prominent Russian intellectuals, writers, painters, and musicians. The Moscow correspondents, including H. R. Knickerbocker and Walter Duranty, had much to tell him, although Duranty was by far the most enthusiastic. Yet "conditions of life of the people were pretty bad," Harriman recalls. "I remember the wild children living in the streets and in manure traps. It was a tragic spectacle."

His party hired women of the old Russian aristocracy as translators. (After Harriman left, the women were rounded up and interrogated.) "I had a feeling that I was being watched," he says, but he was not much concerned since there was nothing he could do about it.

Also, he observes, "I was one of the few businessmen of any prominence to go to Moscow." Doors in the ministries seemed to fly open faster even than they did in the United States. Virtually everyone he wished to see was available, with the single, important exception of Stalin, who was said to be out of town. Stalin was not; although during the war he assured Harriman that he would have seen him had he known he was in town, but he had not been told.

All of the commissars Harriman saw asked him about the chances of American recognition of Russia. Many of them, ignorant of anything but a good Marxist view of America, believed that a persuasive talk with this American millionaire might make the difference. Harriman delivered the same reply to all: one of the main obstacles was Communist financing of the American Communist Party and the Third International. Harriman was regularly informed that the Soviet Communist Party was entirely separate from the Soviet government, and that the government officials had no control over the doings of the Party. "I pointed out," Harriman says, "that no one believed that."

But the main purpose of his journey was the concession, and the official with whom he met for that purpose was none other than the once mighty Leon Trotsky. Even before Lenin's death, Trotsky had been steadily outmaneuvered by Stalin, until by 1926 he had been reduced to the menial position of head of concessions. A month before he saw Harriman, Trotsky had been removed from the Politburo; a year later, he was to be thrown out of the Party and then out of the country, eventually to be axed to death in Mexico in 1940 by Stalin's agents.

It is significant that, although Armand Hammer got to see

Lenin, Harriman was assigned to negotiate with the demoted and disgraced Trotsky. The four years since Hammer had come to Russia had seen a major change in the official attitude toward capitalists. They were to be courted, but not by the top Communists, for it was now considered grubby work. Lenin's New Economic Policy was in the process of being overturned—a casualty of Stalin's rise. The Soviet leadership was in turmoil, and Trotsky and other members of the opposition to Stalin lay in wait, planning, in vain, their comeback. When Averell Harriman came to see him, Trotsky had far more pressing matters on his mind than an American's complaints about a manganese mine down south in Georgia.

Two years earlier, the Soviets had made a fuss over the idea of an American of Harriman's prominence taking a concession. But now, while lower-level commissars treated him as a celebrity, participants in the power struggle at the top found him dangerous company. A shift in policy was under way, although Harriman did not find that out until too late: American factories would always be welcome, but all private ownership—which included concessions—was being phased out. This may explain why Stalin refused to see him. It may also explain why Trotsky was relegated to meet him, and why Trotsky was extremely stiff and formal. Harriman believes that Trotsky suspected they were being observed or listened to.

Trotsky greeted Harriman courteously and, without small talk, guided him to a conference table, where they reviewed the terms of the contract item by item. They spoke through an interpreter, George Andreychin, who was later sent to a labor camp for his association with Trotsky. For four hours, Trotsky listened to Harriman's proposed emendations without saying a word. "We dealt entirely with the business before us," Harriman recalls. "There was not a word of 'How are you enjoying Moscow?' or 'How is your health?' or the normal chitter-chatter." At the end, Trotsky said abruptly, "Now, Mr. Harriman, have you got anything else to say?"

"No," Harriman replied, "I think we've had a complete conversation." And Trotsky got up, shook hands briskly, and left the large room through a different door from the one through which Harriman had entered. "He struck me as cold, entirely the intellectual, with a very penetrating mind," Harriman says.

The official verdict on Harriman's suggestions had to go through the sludge of Soviet bureaucracy. An answer would not come for several months. Harriman remained in Moscow for a few more days. While he was there, Leonid Krassin—who had publicly reviled him a few weeks earlier—died in London. His body was brought to Moscow for a state funeral, since he was one of the early heroes of the Revolution. His widow Lubov, a White Russian émigré and an outspoken opponent of the Bolsheviks, and her three daughters, who had been raised in Britain, came to Moscow for the funeral.

One day, two of the girls came in tears to see Harriman. They had been forbidden to leave the country, they explained, because the Soviet authorities were convinced that Krassin's widow would write a damaging anti-Bolshevik book. Harriman went to see Foreign Minister Maxim Litvinov to protest. The United States would get a terrible impression of the Soviet Union, he insisted, if the family of such a prominent man was so cruelly treated. Litvinov agreed, and issued the exit visas. A few years later, just as the Bolsheviks feared, Madame Krassin published a biography of her husband that contained a damning exposé of the Soviet regime.

On his way home, instead of returning via Europe, Harriman went south to visit his mine. He would thus be able to prospect for other business opportunities in the Russian countryside. Accustomed to the very best in railroad transportation, he requested a private car. The Soviets gave him one of the most resplendent relics of czarist days, all ornate scrollwork with wood inlay and gilt.

He stopped at Baku to observe oil fields. At his hotel, he vividly remembers, there was no butter on the tables—instead there was caviar, and "you could take as much as you wanted." In Tblisi he spent a day with the American Relief team and was taken by the local dignitaries to visit what they called the State Wine Library, once the cellar of Grand Duke Nicholas. It was stocked with fine old wines of choice French and German vintage, and Napoleon brandy. The tasting session (conducted, as the Soviets like to say, "in a warm and friendly atmosphere") lasted for several inebriated hours.

When he reached Chiatura, he inspected his mine and spoke with the American engineers there. He tried to meet with the regional commissar to discuss the mine's difficulties, but the man was nowhere to be found. Harriman went to the official's office to track him down but, as he remembers, the commissar "was probably terrified to see me and stayed away." Here, again, was that peculiar reception he met throughout Russia: friendly meetings with anyone not directly involved with the concession business.

He left Russia in January 1927, from Poti on the Black Sea, aboard a Danish ore freighter. In Milan he discussed with Italian bankers the financing of a hydroelectric power project. One obstacle to the financing was Mussolini's plan to revalue the lira, so the bankers suggested that Harriman explain this to Mussolini in person. Harriman, who would never miss the chance to meet a world leader, thought this a grand idea, and arranged an appointment.

He was ushered into Mussolini's enormous office, where the dictator was standing at his desk. Mussolini had recently begun to learn English, and so insisted upon speaking it without the aid of a translator. The conversation was not easy. Mussolini listened to Harriman's advice on the revaluation, and disagreed. When they came around to the subject of the Soviet Union, he explained that while he deplored Communism, "he was prepared to deal with Russia on a commercial basis, since Italy needed trade with Russia." Mussolini spoke as if to think otherwise were insane.

After Milan, Harriman went on to Cannes, where he arranged to meet Winston Churchill for the first time. "I wanted an excuse to meet him," Harriman admits, "and so talked to him about Russia." Although Harriman attempted to give his impressions of Russia, Churchill did most of the talking. He explained that he was a staunch opponent of the Soviet Union and described his attempts to persuade the British cabinet to lend support to the American intervention in the Soviet civil war after the Revolution. Had his efforts succeeded, Churchill was sure, "the Bolshevik government would have fallen." Churchill told Harriman to get out of the Russian business as soon as possible, abandon the mess altogether, and forget about renegotiating the contract. Eventually Harriman would take his advice—although it was not to be for a year—and when the two met again during the war, Churchill boasted that his advice had saved the American millions of dollars.

Harriman returned to the United States in early 1927, and announced that the Soviets had agreed "in principle" to several important changes in his manganese contract, such as sliding rather than fixed royalties, and a release from the obligation to build the railroad. When the Russians made it official in July, Harriman told reporters that "the Soviet government has met us in a fair spirit." Outwardly he was optimistic, but he had decided after his trip to Moscow to ask his president, Richard Robinson, to negotiate a termination to the concession. The word got around, by June 1928, that the celebrated Harriman concession was moribund. *The New York Times* reported sarcastically that "It would seem certain that Harriman Manganese has passed away after several months' illness, aged 3½ years. Though its birth was accompanied by prodigious hopes, it never was a healthy child. . . ."

The rumors were accurate, for two weeks later the Soviet government announced that Averell Harriman had given up on his manganese mine and that Harriman's four-million-dollar investment was to be repaid over fifteen years at 7 percent interest. Harriman has denied, throughout his life, that he lost money on his Soviet venture; he claims that he even made a small profit. But years later he remembers that his real motivation for opening the concession was not money; it was, instead, the adventure of the thing: "I was in it more for the interest of doing business with the Russians than for the operation itself. I don't want to say that we didn't want to make money, but we were very glad to get out of it. And I profited very much from the experience."

Far from discouraging him, the 1926 visit to Moscow fascinated Harriman, and brushed the scales from this internationalist businessman's eyes. In 1928 Wall Street lawyer Paul Cravath published a "confidential" brochure for fellow traders with Russia, assessing the future of Soviet Communism. Harriman pored over the pamphlet, penciling in extensive annotations. Cravath had written that the Soviet Union needed a liberal infusion of Western capital to make it abandon its most radical tendencies—one of the great rationalizations of East-West trade—and Harriman wrote "Essential!" in the margin. But at the end of the pamphlet, Harriman added several thoughts of his own in hastily scrawled script. Cravath "does not emphasize enough the fanaticism of the communistic believers," he wrote. A business failure had made Averell Harriman into an expert of a sort, an education that he could, and would, parlay into a career in diplomacy with Russia.

"Harriman came out of the period much better off, all things considered, than Trotsky did," E. J. Kahn, Jr., wrote in a *New Yorker* profile of Harriman in 1952. Stalin's ascent to power had brought Harriman's dreams of a manganese empire to a swift end, and, like Trotsky, Averell Harriman came to reassess the regime with which he had once cooperated.

5

HOUSEHOLD EFFECTS

A DELEGATION OF American Communists—Jay Lovestone, Bertram Wolfe, and Ben Gitlow—came to Moscow in 1928 to attend the Sixth Congress of the Communist International. Their old comrade, Julius Hammer, who continued to pay his party dues every year, invited them to dinner at the Brown House. In many ways Julius was an adviser to these men: he knew the ways of Moscow and, after a lifetime in illegal politics, was versed in the methods of circumventing the authorities. Drawing upon his experience, he explained how to smuggle Party documents past U.S. customs. He also asked them a favor. Because he was not a Comintern delegate he did not have tickets to the Congress, which was being held in the Kremlin. Could they get him two tickets, one for himself and one for Rose? Lovestone said he would be delighted to, and arranged it the next day.

On the opening day of the Congress, Lovestone, seated in the Throne Room of the Czar's Palace in the Kremlin, was startled to see two grim-looking Russians—obviously agents of the Soviet secret police, the OGPU*—slip into the seats on either side of him. One of them asked, "Are you aware that you gave two tickets

*The names of the KGB's forerunners are often a point of confusion. The Soviet secret police was founded in 1918; its head was Felix Dzerzhinsky. In 1922 the Cheka became the GPU, part of the NKVD; in 1923, detached from the NKVD, the GPU became OGPU, directed by Dzerzhinsky until his death in 1926. After a series of further changes, it became, in 1954, the KGB.

to bourgeois capitalists?" Lovestone was puzzled. When he realized that the agents were referring to the tickets he had given Julius, he grew angry. "Yes, I am aware," he said. "And I would do it again if they asked me." After a few silent minutes of threatening looks, the agents left.

That evening, Lovestone related this bizarre incident to the other Americans at their hotel. What was all that about "bourgeois capitalists"? the Americans wondered. Everyone knew Julius was a card-carrying Communist. It was commonly accepted that Julius Hammer worked in some capacity for the OGPU, although it was not known for certain; such things never were. Still, these men never doubted it. A comrade did not spend five years in Moscow socializing with every visiting American of any importance and *not* keep the OGPU apprised.

They concluded that Lovestone's strange encounter was some kind of a charade. Maybe it was the Soviets' way of creating a false image that the Hammer family were good, clean capitalists. If that had really been the OGPU's intention, it hadn't worked. Lovestone, Wolfe, and Gitlow remained unconvinced. Yet neither Gitlow's *I Confess* nor Wolfe's *A Life in Two Centuries,* both of which discuss the Hammers, mention Julius's suspected connection with Soviet intelligence. In fact, when Gitlow published a second edition of his book in the forties, he deleted all references to Julius, perhaps hoping to spare him and his family embarrassment in a hostile, anti-Communist America.

In 1929 an equally strange incident took place, described by both Gitlow and Wolfe in their memoirs. The same group of American Communists came to Moscow in April 1929, in circumstances much less happy than those of the previous year.

Stalin had at last attained unrivaled dictatorship of the Soviet Union, and was now calling himself the "Leader" of the nation and of world Communism. He had begun systematically to remove from power anyone he suspected of being less than completely loyal to him. The American Communist Party, once a relatively autonomous organization, now faced Stalin's fire. It had been sundered into a pro-Stalin faction and a larger anti-Stalin one, led by Jay Lovestone.

Lovestone, Gitlow, and Wolfe had therefore been summoned to attend a special tribunal of the Communist International—a trial to consider Lovestone's opposition. The commission's charges were wrathful, but Lovestone, Gitlow, and Wolfe, who resented control of their Party by Stalin, fought back.

Stalin decided to undercut them entirely by sending an "Open

Letter" to the members of the American Communist Party on May 11, 1929, appealing to members over the heads of their leaders to select a new leadership that Stalin preferred. Stalin told Lovestone that the contents of the letter would be kept secret until the American party had a chance to decide its course of action but that Lovestone was to remain in Moscow as an "exile"—a captive, really—to ensure that he did not return to the United States and act against Stalin's wishes. The Americans had never heard of a Party member kept hostage in Moscow in order to keep him from doing battle with Stalin, and they were understandably terrified.

On May 15 Gitlow and Lovestone paid a visit to the Brown House to see Julius Hammer and ask how they could get back to America. Gitlow, at the same time, wanted to collect Julius's Party dues.

"He was very glad to see us," Gitlow remembered, "for he had some very startling news to give us concerning the American Party." He told them about Stalin's "Open Letter." "We wondered how the news reached Hammer so quickly," Gitlow writes. "It was supposed to be kept a secret until the Central Executive Committee in the United States had an opportunity to act upon it."

Julius supplied the answer without their asking for it. "His son Armand had seen Walter Duranty of *The New York Times* that morning," Gitlow continues. "Duranty informed him that he had been given news of the decision on the American Party with the request to cable it to the United States immediately. He had shown Armand a copy of the cable which he had sent that morning upon Stalin's request."

The Americans were amazed that both Duranty and the Hammers had been given the details of Stalin's secret letter. It was clear that Stalin was using *The New York Times* to effect the ouster of the men from the Party's leadership before the members of the Party could make their own decision. But how had Duranty gotten his information? Was it true that the Hammers had learned it from him, and not the other way around?

When Duranty did not immediately submit his report on the "Open Letter," but waited a few days until *Pravda* published an account of Stalin's decision, the Americans came to suspect that Duranty had gotten the news not from Stalin or Stalin's deputies, but rather from Julius Hammer. It was all very puzzling and, though the three Americans as usual could not be sure about Julius, they were dismayed at the possibility that he had in effect sided with Stalin against the American Communist Party.

It was all the more surprising because Julius Hammer had been involved in transferring funds from Moscow to the American Communist Party, using the Allied American Corporation as a conduit. Benjamin Gitlow has recorded that Soviet funding for the American Communists continued throughout the twenties. Sailors with diamonds in their shoes were relied upon less often; "as the Comintern organization was improved, better ways were developed for shipping money," Gitlow writes. As noted earlier, packages suspected of containing money were intercepted on their way between Boris Reinstein in Moscow and Alexander Gumberg in New York in 1923, but when Allied American was phased out of the export-import business in 1924, it was apparently no longer used for this purpose. A different operation may have been devised.

In 1924 a Soviet trade organization was established in England, known as Arcos, an acronym for All-Russian Cooperative Society. From then on, Gitlow notes, "the money destined for the United States and Canada was shipped through the Arcos." Scotland Yard raided Arcos in 1927, suspecting that it was engaged in subversive activities. Tons of files were removed from the Arcos headquarters. No details were made public, but shortly after the raid, according to a confidential document in the intelligence files of the U.S. State Department, Julius Hammer was denied permission to enter the United Kingdom because he was "a political agent" and "the controlling personage of the Allied American Corporation which was used as a cover for the transmission of funds to American revolutionary organizations." Several former agents of the Central Intelligence Agency insist that they have seen documents, removed from the Arcos office in London, that prove that the Hammers' company was used as a channel for financing Communist activities in England and the United States.

The shipment of monies through Arcos ended with the raid in 1927, Gitlow writes, because the names of persons in the United States who received money were now known by the British authorities. New methods had to be devised. "In later years most of the money was cabled to us through an office maintained for that purpose in Berlin," Gitlow notes. "The money was cabled to relatives of party leaders, business men who were party members or sympathetic to the party, through firms of these in Canada and in New York. Our Party members, usually when they returned from trips to Moscow, brought back with them money for the Party's activities." It is likely that Julius Hammer continued to help, at least until 1929.

Jay Lovestone maintains that Walter Duranty was involved, as was Julius Hammer, in working for the OGPU. While there is no proof of this charge apart from Lovestone's testimony, there is clear evidence that Duranty assisted the Hammers in publicizing the extreme profitability of their Soviet business—which, as it turned out, was largely invented.

Throughout the twenties, Duranty reported in glowing terms the Hammers' huge financial success. He repeatedly denied their serious difficulties with Soviet labor at the asbestos mine, and, as the worldwide demand for asbestos declined and the concession began to lose money, Duranty continued to report in the *Times* that Allied American was making multimillion-dollar profits.

In late 1926 the Hammers gave up on the asbestos concession once and for all. They were now left with the pen and pencil factory, which continued to make money. Julius went to New York in 1927 to obtain a loan of $500,000 to expand the factory's operations, but the U.S. government denied his request.

Soon there were other problems with the factory. Stalin, ever reluctant to be dependent on foreigners, established a rival, state-controlled pencil concern, which began to prosper. The first Five-Year Plan, initiated in 1928, sought to build strong, independent Soviet industries not reliant on foreign assistance. That meant that the Hammers, as useful as they had been, had to go.

The Hammer pen and pencil factory was sold to the Soviet government on February 18, 1930, and renamed the Sacco and Vanzetti Pencil Manufacturing Company. When the news of the liquidation first broke in late 1929, Walter Duranty filed one of his most defensive dispatches: "It is admitted that the Hammer interests made big profits, but they built up the big and profitable business at their own risk. The Hammer interests were the first Americans to do business in Russia and—profits or no profits—they have not been treated over-generously."

A few months earlier, Armand Hammer had visited the American ambassador to Germany, Jacob Schurman, in Berlin, and told him excitedly of the enormous profits his family was making in Moscow. Ambassador Schurman, who was skeptical of Hammer's enthusiasm, noted in a report to Washington, "It would be interesting to watch his export of profits from his present concession."

It was indeed interesting. By the terms of the liquidation agreement of February 18, 1930, the Hammers turned the factory over to the Soviets "in return for several million dollars paid in rubles cash, Soviet bonds, and permission to remove all of the Hammers' 'household effects,'" according to an account in the Soviet press at the time. But since rubles were not allowed out of the country, how were the Hammers really paid? And what were these unspecified "household effects"?

The answer in both cases, of course, was art—the treasures of the czarist aristocracy that the Bolsheviks had plundered after the Revolution. This included knickknacks of the royal family whose only worth was sentimental or historical; the jeweled objects of the workrooms of Peter Karl Fabergé, such as Imperial Easter Eggs commissioned for the czar's family, and the vast collection of valuable Russian and European paintings that now sat gathering dust in state warehouses. To a regime with little appreciation for the valuables of pre-Revolutionary Russia and a great need for convertible currency to finance imports of heavy machinery—as well as Comintern activities aimed at destabilizing Western democracies—these objects were suddenly a precious commodity.

And the Hammers, who had to be paid somehow as a price for their departure, now could help the Soviets dispose of this art—and thereby embark upon their second Soviet enterprise. Even before they ended operations in Moscow in 1928, the Hammers opened a gallery in New York, called L'Ermitage Galleries, to sell Russian art on commission for the Soviet government. Anastas Mikoyan, then a candidate member of the Politburo and the People's Commissar for Domestic and Foreign Trade, offered the Hammers a commission of 10 percent on any works from the Hermitage they could sell in America. L'Ermitage Galleries, a magnificent establishment at 3 East 52nd Street in New York became the Soviet Union's first significant outlet for the treasures of the Hermitage. Russian émigrés, realizing that the Bolsheviks had begun to sell invaluable canvases from the Hermitage, were outraged.

Late in 1928, the Hammers received a telegram from a syndicate of New York art dealers, among them Joseph Duveen and Bernard Berenson, that was interested in purchasing works from the Hermitage. The dealers sent a list of forty masterpieces for which they were willing to pay five million dollars. The Hammers brought this offer to the head of the Soviet agency for art export, a man named Shapiro, who was insulted by the low figure.

"What do they think we are? Children?" Shapiro asked angrily. "Don't they realize we know what is being sold in Paris, London, and New York? If they want to deal with us seriously, let them make serious offers." But the American dealers would not raise their offer. Armand then went to see Mikoyan, who admitted that "We do need money" but would not settle at such a price.

With the liquidation of the asbestos concession and the pen and pencil factory, Hammer explains, his family left Moscow in the early thirties with their personal art collection, which filled the Brown House and also "overflowed into several warehouses." The Soviets generously allowed them to take everything with them, asking only a 15 percent export tax, he says.

Hammer further explains that the family was prodded into this enterprise by an American antique dealer named E. Sakho who, frustrated by his inability to export Russian art, offered to make the Hammers partners in his export business. Robert Williams, author of the book *Russian Art and American Money,* has been unable to find any record of this antique dealer: "Regrettably, Sakho himself left no trace except in the memory of the Hammers."

Perhaps this Sakho is but an invention to portray the Hammers' decision to go into the art business as an entirely serendipitous one. For it certainly was not . Undoubtedly the Hammers did apply their shrewd business talents to art collecting, but it is unlikely that a "hobby" that filled "several warehouses" would have gone unnoticed or even benignly overlooked by the Soviets. Apart from whatever filled the Brown House, most of the "Hammer Collection," as it was later to be called, consisted of objects sold *on commission* for the Soviet government. In other words, the Hammers acted as brokers for the Soviets.

Many of the pieces bore yellowed tags embossed with the double-headed eagle crest of the Russian czars and typewritten descriptions in Russian. The tags, Hammer recalls, "looked as authentic as if they had come directly from the Winter Palace." In fact, many of them had. Other objects still had labels and numbers from Soviet museums on them. The Hammers were partners of the Soviet government once again.

As the family prepared to leave Moscow, they had to dispose of their mansion. Victor and Armand left the city in 1930, and Julius and Rose remained a year and a half longer, settling the final details of their Moscow operations and picking out objects to sell in America.

With the family and much of their possessions gone, Julius negotiated the transfer of the premises to the Soviet government "in great secrecy," Eugene Lyons recalls. Lyons was suddenly asked to leave the Brown House and move elsewhere. Julius and Rose received, in exchange for the house, "a large apartment elsewhere and divers other considerations," Lyons says.

Suddenly, the Hammer mansion was the headquarters for the *Moscow Daily News,* a Soviet English-language paper. "It took nearly as large a staff and ten times as much noise to produce this amateur four-page newspaper as it does to get out *The New York*

Times," recalls Lyons, who was forced to share the house with the newspaper staff before he found an apartment. "Both the noise and the staff flowed in turgid streams past our doors and overflowed our thresholds. The *Moscow Daily News* was a haven of economic refuge for the more literate Americans and Britishers wishing to remain in the Soviet capital." Now the Brown House was lorded over by Michael Borodin, the Soviet "Colonel Lawrence" of the Chinese Revolution.

The spacious comfort had disappeared:

> No more bourgeois amplitude and quiet and cleanliness; now the broad corridors and marble staircase were slimy with Moscow's mud, now a hundred voices outshouted each other and doors banged and strangers dashed into our living room and sleeping room, now the field-like ballroom upstairs was crowded with desks, and Shura's lordly domain turned into a factory kitchen.

And—the final indignity—the giant bathtub was removed, and the bathroom converted to a lunch counter.

The Brown House was not the only reminder of the Hammer family's regal existence in Moscow. There was also a child.

Both Armand and Victor married Russian women. During the summer of 1925 Armand met an actress and singer, Olga Vadina, who, Armand says, was really the Baroness Olga von Root, daughter of a czarist general and a descendant of the Polish general Kosciusko. After the Revolution, Olga and her family, opponents of the Bolsheviks who switched to the Bolshevik side only to save their lives, moved from Petrograd to Kiev, where Olga found work singing gypsy songs in cabarets. When she met Armand at Yalta, she was already married to her manager. "We took a train to Moscow and Olga obtained a divorce," Hammer recounts. "It was easy in those days. We were married in a civil ceremony and had a wonderful reception at the Brown House for our families and friends." Years later, Armand reminisced to an acquaintance that "Olga was the love of my life." In 1929 they had a son, whom they named Julian (for Julius).

Apparently, when it came time for the Hammers to leave Moscow, Olga and Armand had decided to divorce. But since Armand was a U.S. citizen and Olga a Soviet citizen, the process was complicated. If the marriage was dissolved in Moscow, Olga would be forced to remain in Russia and, according to Soviet law, so would their young son. They left the country together in 1930 and spent a year in Paris, where Armand began dealing in the purchase of Soviet promissory notes from American and European concessionaries who did not trust the Soviet government to make good on them. At least this is the version Hammer relates. Hammer paid half of the face value of such notes, which the businessmen gladly accepted, and was then paid by the Russians. He thereby earned "millions of dollars," he claims.

Actually, he was probably paid not in hard currency, with which the Soviets were stingy, but in art, which his family would later sell in the United States. This benefited the Soviet government as well, enabling it to pay Westerners much less than they had agreed. British and American intelligence, ever suspicious of the Hammers, were convinced that Armand's Russian wife was an OGPU agent, although it is doubtful that she ever moved in circles important enough to gather any intelligence worth conveying to Moscow.

The story of Victor's Russian marriage is far sadder. Neither he nor Armand has ever discussed it with even their American friends, although several of their Moscow acquaintances from the 1920s remember the tale. Sometime in the mid-twenties, Victor married a beautiful Russian singer named Varvara, known as Vava. They moved into the Brown House, where the couple was quickly absorbed into the fast-paced life of inebriated, song-filled parties with actors and actresses from the Moscow Art Theatre. In 1927 Vava gave birth to a son. They named him Armand Victorovich. He lived in his own room, with his own servants, like a modern-day boyar. This idyll was shattered one day in the late twenties, when Victor left Moscow to take care of business in Berlin. When he reached the Soviet-Polish border, he realized that he had forgotten his passport, and returned to the Brown House to retrieve it. There he was shocked to discover Vava in bed with an actor.

Furious, Victor would have nothing more to do with his wife. But he was concerned about the fate of his son and realized that if they divorced, Armand Victorovich would be compelled to remain in Moscow when the Hammer family left. So Vava and their son stayed in the Brown House although Vava and Victor were estranged.

As Victor prepared to leave Russia for good, he discovered that Vava refused to leave the country with him as a legal couple so that they could divorce in the United States. Perhaps because

Vava was in love with another man, she insisted on remaining in Moscow, with Armand Victorovich. Victor pleaded desperately. Their son, he argued, who because of his American father and Russian mother had dual citizenship, would be subjected to the suspicion with which Stalin's regime regarded all half-foreign children. But Vava was unyielding.

Throughout the early thirties, Victor continued to make regular visits to Moscow, on buying missions for L'Ermitage Galleries and to visit his son. In 1934 Victor was denied a visa to enter the Soviet Union. He stayed in touch with his son through letters delivered by American visitors to Moscow and through American ambassadors to the Soviet Union.

The Soviet authorities, who kept Victor's son under surveillance, regarded him with gradually increasing suspicion. Armand Victorovich, who had become a sort of hostage to ensure that the Hammers continued to deal fairly in their transactions with the Soviets, grew up with a famous American name in a land that now distrusted all Americans. Only when the Hammers returned to the good graces of the Soviet government would Armand Victorovich Hammer be restored to the life of aristocracy in which he had spent his early years.

Julius and Rose left Moscow on September 27, 1931, and began a long trip home by way of several European countries. Julius renewed his American passport on October 21, stating that he was still engaged in "settling the affairs of the family pencil concession" and in "purchasing antiques and art objects for the L'Ermitage Galleries," of which he was president and his son Armand vice-president and treasurer. In December he tried to enter Britain but was rebuffed because of the findings of the Arcos raid of a few years earlier. He then proceeded to Switzerland.

En route, during a stop in Erfurt, Germany, Julius was arrested for the second time in his life. Several German firms, creditors of the Hammers' pencil factory, claimed that the Hammers still owed them $106,000 for equipment. Julius refused to pay the debt—for the now defunct Allied American Corporation did not have the cash—and was thrown in jail. Bail was set at three hundred thousand marks.

The U.S. consul in Berlin attended Hammer's trial and reported in January 1932, "A swindle is involved, and if Hammer got away from Germany, I am afraid the German creditors would have had a hard time getting any money." Julius was helped out of the legal tangle by the intercession of a powerful American friend, his attorney, Henry French Hollis, formerly a Senator from New Hampshire. An out-of-court settlement was reached, and Julius was released.

In early 1932, the Hammers decided they wanted to become involved in the presidential campaign of Franklin D. Roosevelt, who seemed of all the candidates the most sympathetic toward the Soviet Union. They also may have surmised—accurately, it turned out—that this support might give them a measure of power if Roosevelt were elected.

Armand wrote to Henry Hollis, who was a major Roosevelt supporter, and announced that he had decided to "take an active interest in American politics in general and the coming elections in particular." He now wanted to become involved in a "worthy political movement"—the Roosevelt campaign.

Hammer explained that he was helping to raise money from American representatives of French wine and spirits producers, who were most interested in Roosevelt because they believed he would repeal Prohibition, as he did. Hollis wrote to Louis Howe, a Roosevelt adviser, that "the advice of Dr. Hammer regarding affairs in Russia and the best way to deal with the present government would be extremely valuable." With this introduction, Hammer cabled Roosevelt:

> PRESS DESPATCHES HERE FEATURE YOUR INCLINATION TOWARDS RECOGNITION OF RUSSIAN GOVERNMENT. AFTER BUSINESS IN RUSSIA AS AMERICAN CITIZEN LAST THREE YEARS I HEARTILY FAVOR SUCH RECOGNITION.

As Robert Williams notes dryly in *Russian Art and American Money,* "Hammer's modesty in compressing more than a decade of trading with the Soviet government into three years was a curious oversight." Doubtless it was not an oversight; more likely, three years seemed less suspicious than eleven.

Now that the Hammers were in the West, the State Department was more suspicious of them than ever and compiled unsubstantiated secret reports that hinted at evil doings. "Armand Julievich HAMMER and Victor Julievich HAMMER, who also calls himself VYER, both continue to carry out secret missions for the Soviet government and travel between the United States and Europe for that purpose," one document insisted. "It is further stated that they are frequently accompanied by a woman, Olga VADINA, said to be an O.G.P.U. agent, and who was allowed to leave Russia for the purpose of helping them."

By the middle of 1932 the family had returned to New York, and at least one Russian émigré, Boris Lyubyashchi, was vigilant enough to warn the Secretary of State in a letter in Russian dated December 30, 1932:

> Is it known to you that Dr. Julius Hammer returned from Soviet Russia? He was serving a sentence in 1919 at Sing Sing. In 1922 he went to the Bolsheviks' country and lived there 10 years. He was engaged in propaganda. Now he has returned and nobody knows about it at the State Department, but many are interested in his career. Now he announced in the Russian paper that he is going to sell jewels of the Russian Czar at Lord and Taylor 5th Avenue, and it is a question as to how he managed to bring them here. Excuse me for bothering you, but I would like to call your attention to the fact that he will lead propaganda here. His wife quite frequently makes trips to Moscow.

But the State Department had taken notice of the Hammers' arrival, and, just as Mr. Lyubyashchi had feared, nobody really did know about it there. "It appears that the Hammers are no longer interested in any concessions in Russia," one State Department report concluded at the time, "and that they are now buying for their own account on a moderate scale merchandise intended for sale in the United States." When it came to precisely what the Hammers were doing, and what the Soviet government had to do with it all, the United States government had not a clue.

Armand and Olga were divorced as soon as they reached the United States, and Olga, with their four-year-old son, Julian, went off to Hollywood to try to rebuild—ultimately unsuccessfully—her singing career. L'Ermitage Galleries became the Hammer Galleries run by Julius, Rose, Armand, and Victor. While the rest of the United States suffered the bleakest period of the Depression, the Hammers were able, thanks to their Russian business, to live in high style—not as luxuriously, perhaps, as they did in Moscow, but quite well nevertheless. Armand and Victor bought huge apartments on Fifth Avenue, and began to spread the word about their new enterprise.

Armand was the marketing genius behind it. He aroused the scorn of the art world—and, at the same time, made gigantic profits—with what can only be described as lowbrow huckstering. Who had ever heard before of selling a collection of "Russian

Imperial Treasures from the Winter Palace, Tsarskoye Selo, and other Royal Palaces" in a department store? But they were not exactly crown jewels as Armand's brochure advertised; they were, as Robert Williams explains, "the debris of Russian hotels, monasteries, shops, and palaces which the Hammers were getting from the Soviet government, brocades, fabrics, priests' vestments, silver, porcelain, glassware, icons, and Fabergé jewelry."

Yet they were indeed sold in department stores. Armand informed the heads of department stores throughout the nation that he had just returned from Russia, where he had acquired a great and valuable collection. Now, because of "the failing ruble and my desire to convert my rubles into something tangible," he was interested in "disposing of this art." He did not mention that a good portion of what he had to sell came from Soviet warehouses and museums and belonged to the Soviet government, but the merchants would hardly have cared. It was a special bargain, Hammer told the department-store chiefs—40 percent off the "listed retail selling price," whatever that was.

For a long time, there was no response. Then Scruggs-Vandervoort and Barney in St. Louis ordered a shipment. The Hammers bought a load of secondhand theatrical trunks and shipped off a few trunkfuls.

It was a great success, and Scruggs-Vandervoort wanted more. It appeared that, Depression or no Depression, people could not overlook such a bargain. Valuables and schlock alike were tagged with bargain-basement-sounding prices such as \$19.95, \$49.50, or \$499. It was a hit. Marshall Field in Chicago allowed the Hammers to set up a display at its "Century of Progress" exhibition in 1933–34. In time requests came from department stores in Los Angeles, Cleveland, Detroit, San Francisco, Pittsburgh, Baltimore, Washington, and finally Lord and Taylor in New York.

The New Yorker published a profile of Armand Hammer by Geoffrey Hellmann, entitled—without irony—"The Innocents Abroad." It described a "short, forceful, dark-haired man by the name of Armand Hammer" who drives around every day "in an old Rolls-Royce, and works so hard that he sometimes falls asleep in his clothes, too exhausted to go to bed."

The story related is essentially the one Hammer had just begun to invent and would retell throughout his life. The central role his father played in it all had become but a cameo appearance in the epic of Armand: "Armand was responsible for much of this prosperity, for in 1920 his father's far-flung activities were interrupted by a protracted absence." There was no mention of Julius's jail term, involvement in Communism, close friends in the Soviet leadership, or leadership in the family businesses, for Hellmann reported the tale that all of the Hammer family had agreed to furnish. It was bad business, they probably thought, to call public attention to a political connection that looked unseemly.

"The late Czar would undoubtedly be dismayed," Hellmann writes, "if he could know many of his most intimate possessions, as well as the toys of his children, are now being disposed of by the son of a Russian Jew." The collection was appraised at over a million dollars, and received rave reviews in art journals. Moreover, Hellman writes, it was

> recognized as authentic by such indisputable local Romanoffs as Grand Duchess Marie and Princess Paul Chavchavadze, who must find it difficult to reconcile themselves to the idea of dinner sets and salt cellars formerly belonging to their brothers and their sisters and their cousins and their aunts now being in the hands of a person who was born and brought up in the Bronx. Many White Russians, moreover, disapprove of Hammer's habit of cutting up church brocades to make handbags, but others, who have met him, regard him as a likable fellow and are not above attending occasional vodka parties that he gives. Only the other night, Prince George of Russia went to Hammer's house for dinner bringing with him a high dignitary of the Greek Orthodox Church. Hammer won the Prince's respect two or three years ago when he presented him with a silver box formerly belonging to the latter's brother, Grand Duke Constantine.

Twice in the profile, Hellmann makes gentle digs at Hammer's social background—as "the son of a Russian Jew" and "a person who was born and brought up in the Bronx"—to explain the irony of the Hammers selling the spoils of the Russian aristocracy. The ultimate irony, never specified here, is that the goods, which had been confiscated by the Bolsheviks, were being dispensed, in effect, by agents of the Bolsheviks. The dollar commission paid to the Soviets was used to fund Comintern activities and possibly American Communist activities as well.

Old Russian aristocrats in emigration, won over with gifts and flattered with dinners, began to flock to the Hammers and to the Hammer Galleries. The Palm Beach branch of the gallery was ostensibly managed by Harry, but Harry was such an inept businessman that it was really run by a new acquaintance of the Hammers named Prince Michael. Anytime a Russian émigré needed cash, all he had to do was pay a visit to the Hammers and part with a family heirloom.

Not all émigrés liked what the Hammers were doing, particularly when word got around that some of the goods were imported directly from Soviet state warehouses. The gallery became a target of occasional attacks. In March 1934 a sword that had belonged to Grand Duke Vladimir was stolen. The thieves turned out to be disgruntled émigrés.

In keeping with this new grand company the Hammers were now keeping in the United States, Armand began to tell people that his family came from the Alsace region of France, not from Odessa. Although Julius remained a Party member, he rarely associated with his old comrades. Old friends of the family, who had known them in simpler days, were no longer invited to dinner.

Armand's *Quest of the Romanoff Treasure* was intended more as promotion for the Hammer Collection than as autobiography. A slick book of slightly more than two hundred pages, it appears to be the work of a ghostwriter—names of close friends are misspelled and there are serious errors of chronology—although Hammer claims in his introduction that he wrote it himself "in only a few weeks."

Walter Duranty wrote a brief but glowing introduction, lending the account credibility; he guaranteed that Hammer "has set down on paper a true and faithful record." *Quest* received favorable reviews. *The New York Times Book Review* praised it, noting that it must be reliable because it comes recommended by Walter Duranty, who "knows his Russia as thoroughly as any foreigner can."

Quest featured several stunning black-and-white photographs of the finest of the Hammers' wares and several crown jewels they were not selling. The book is a clever bit of propaganda, disseminated at a time when American information about actual conditions in the Soviet Union was seriously deficient. Hammer describes a Russia so far removed from reality that one must conclude that he intended either to advertise the Hammer Collection or to aid the cause of diplomatic recognition by convincing Americans that the Soviet Union really was Utopia—or both.

For the Hammers could not have believed in the Russia that *Quest* presents. By the time they left Moscow, Stalin had begun the bloody drive to force millions of peasants into collective farms. Since the early twenties, the Hammers must have witnessed the evolution of a society ruled by fear. Many of the so-called political pilgrims of the thirties touted Stalinism out of various degrees of ignorance. After more than ten years in Moscow, Hammer had obviously seen the horrors of Stalin's Russia. But he was not letting on.

Hammer compares Lenin to Christ; he portrays Felix Dzerzhinsky, the ruthless founder of the Soviet secret police, as a "remarkable man"; and Yosif Vissarionovich Stalin, whom the great Russian poet Joseph Mandelstam had called in a famous verse for which he was executed, "the Kremlin mountaineer,/The murderer and peasant-slayer," Hammer depicts as "unassuming." Most remarkable is Hammer's description of the Bolshevik regime as not a gang of oppressors but rather humane servants of the people's desires: "The new regime is, of course, not universally popular—what government is?—but it rests upon a much wider and more solid foundation than is generally believed abroad."

The Bolsheviks were not "a relatively small group who have seized power and hold it through the army and the secret police," Hammer explains. The Soviets have the full and enthusiastic support of "over ten million organized workers who are the most vigorous and energetic element in Russian national life." Hammer's reassuring defense of Soviet Russia seems at times an export version of the *Pravda* line:

> There is, too, a psychological element of stability which seems to have been somewhat overlooked by the outer world in its estimate of conditions in Russia. This country has had its Revolution, has realized the wildest dreams of the wildest strike leader or labor agitator. The working class has seized power and attempted to put into being the theory of integral Communism as a practical system of politics and economics. . . . During all these years the workers have been flattered to think that the power is in their hands. They have no incentive to strike for that would injure their interests. In short, by a curious paradox, Soviet Russia, the country of Revolution, is today the least revolutionary of countries.

The disillusionment with the Soviet regime, which E. E. Cummings details in *Eimi* and ascribes to Julius, is here supplanted by idealistic fervor. Most important, perhaps, is Armand's unmistakable placation of the American worry that Soviet Russia might be expansionist. The Soviet Union, he insists, is happy, contented, and above all docile.

President Roosevelt signed the repeal of Prohibition in 1933, and Hammer was prepared. He had foreseen that American brewers would face a dearth of beer barrels, and had arranged with the Soviet government through Amtorg in New York to import Russian lumber—white-oak staves and barrel heads—which one of his new companies, the A. Hammer Cooperage Corporation of Milltown, New Jersey, would use to become the leading manufacturer of beer barrels. Little is actually known about Hammer's beer-barrel enterprise—such as why it was necessary to *import* lumber. But in any case, the undertaking provided an ongoing financial link between the Hammers in New York and the Soviet government.

At the same time, the Hammer family continued to expand Hammer Galleries. They employed as a buyer a Russian, Alexander Schaffer, whom they had brought with them out of the Soviet Union in 1932. Schaffer bought gold snuffboxes, paintings, silver, and glassware for his own store in Rockefeller Center and for the Hammers as well. It is likely that the Hammers continued to visit Europe throughout the thirties. As late as 1936, Victor made several return trips to the Soviet Union. When he visited Italy, Egypt, and London in 1940, American intelligence officers in London compiled a confidential dossier on him. "Victor Julius Hammer described himself as an antique dealer," the report stated skeptically, "but the records of our friends"—"friends" being a code word for British intelligence—"show that he was formerly actively associated with the Allied American Association [*sic*]."

It appeared to many in British and American intelligence that the Hammers' new art venture differed little from their Moscow-based activities. Although *Time* wrote of Armand Hammer in 1935, "In his Manhattan galleries, he makes his final conversion of profits to cash," a brief glance at the Hammers' account books told a different story. The collection the Hammers took out of the Soviet Union in the early thirties was appraised at one million dollars, yet by 1940, Hammer says, the Hammer Galleries made more than eleven million dollars. Evidently, by far the greatest part of their merchandise was steadily imported from Moscow. The Hammers' connection with the Soviet government continued to prove lucrative.

6

"A VERY UNUSUAL KNOWLEDGE"

When the publisher William Randolph Hearst ran into hard times and decided to auction off the bulk of his estate in 1940, Armand and Victor Hammer managed to become his agents, offering to apply the sales techniques that had worked so well with their Russian art. They arranged to sell Hearst's possessions at two stores owned by their friends the Gimbels—Gimbels and Saks Fifth Avenue—though the idea of the hoi polloi rummaging through his treasures "in Gimbels' basement," as he put it, made Hearst uneasy.

Hammer promised to "give tone to the sale," though. He published a flossy art magazine, *The Compleat Collector,* that featured articles on the Hearst collection. Hammer wrote the articles himself and even appeared, pseudonymously, as the editor: "Braset Marteau," French for "arm and hammer."

The opening was set for January 27, 1941. Hammer, who regularly contributed to Franklin Roosevelt's campaigns, even attempted to snare Eleanor Roosevelt to cut the ribbon. "This exhibition and sale is under my direction and I am intensely interested in it," he wrote to Mrs. Roosevelt, "not only from a selfish commercial point of view but also because it is an interesting experiment with great social implications—namely—a dispersal of what is probably the largest private art collection in the world, to the general public at prices within the reach of all." He promised to donate the proceeds from the sale of *The Compleat Collector,* at one dollar each, to the Infantile Paralysis Fund ("in which the President is interested," he reminded her). But Mrs. Roosevelt was uninterested in Hammer's particular brand of socialism and sent her regrets.

Undoubtedly this slight wounded Hammer, who was fond of courting the high and mighty. Later he was to brag that he was a confidant and influential adviser to President Roosevelt: the chairman of Macy's, Beardsley Ruml, and Nelson Rockefeller would often fly to Washington on Hammer's private Executive Beechcraft, Hammer claimed, where all three would give counsel to the President. But this was not true. The attention of the powerful remained out of Hammer's reach until he was in his sixties.

When Roosevelt gave his Jackson Day address in January 1936, attacking businessmen and financiers who opposed his New Deal, Armand fired off a long, proud telegram:

> IN YOUR HEROIC STRUGGLE FOR SOCIAL JUSTICE YOU HAVE THE SUPPORT AND THANKFULNESS OF ALL FAIRMINDED INTELLIGENT CITIZENS WHO ARE NOT BLINDED BY PREJUDICE OR MISLED BY FALSE INFORMATION STOP MORE POWER TO YOU.

In the summer of 1940, Hammer sent several "Icesaver" ice chests, made of white oak imported from the Soviet Union, to Mrs. Roosevelt. Before the 1940 election, he paid for a radio dramatization of "the achievements of the New Deal in social legislation" to be broadcast in New York as campaign advertisements for Roosevelt. He sent a recording of the broadcast to Mrs. Roosevelt, adding, "we all hope that it will help to decide the election in favor of the President." In a letter that Hammer treasured ever afterward, Eleanor thanked him, exclaiming, "What a grand thing you did to help the President!"

Until World War II cut off all Soviet exports, the Hammers continued to make much of their money from such Soviet items as art and barrel staves. It seems strange, therefore, that Hammer assumed a public posture during the summer of 1940 in favor of extending Lend-Lease aid to Britain—for the Soviet Union was at the time allied with Nazi Germany against Britain. Technically, to strengthen England was to oppose the Soviet Union.

Hammer often refers to his stand on Lend-Lease as evidence that he has not consistently been a defender of the Soviets. "When the war with Hitler broke out, of course, at first Russia was on the side of Hitler and I came out very strongly against Russia," he says. "People don't realize that. Some people accuse me of being so pro-Soviet that, right or wrong, I'm always defending the Soviets. Well, that wasn't true. I was a strong supporter of the free world."

When it came to Lend-Lease, Hammer was not exactly a Harry Hopkins or an Averell Harriman. Much of what he did during 1940 seems aimed at bolstering his image as a fervent American patriot.

An old friend of the family's, Senator William H. King, who was a guest at the Brown House during his congressional junket to Russia in 1923, was one of the sponsors of a Lend-Lease bill. He asked Hammer to give his support by publishing a pamphlet in favor of a plan to exchange financial aid to Britain for leases on British bases in the western hemisphere. Hammer did so at his own expense.

Not content with the brochure, Hammer wrote Roosevelt on September 21. He described the King plan and advised the President to form a committee "to study the question" made up of "An economist (such as Dr. Moulton of Brookings Institution); a practical businessman; a banker with an international outlook (such as Mr. Winthrop Aldrich); a representative of the labor unions; a representative of the farming interests." Presumably, the "practicil businessman" was meant to be Armand Hammer. At the end of the letter he summoned "the courage to ask for a few minutes of your time so that I may amplify this proposal." Roosevelt's personal secretary, General Edwin Watson, thanked Hammer but refused to grant an interview.

After the election, Hammer tried once again to see Roosevelt. He asked Senator King to make the request through General Watson, and also wrote Watson himself, explaining that

> the purpose of my desire for an interview is to enable me to inform the President of the result of a survey of public opinion I have made on the question of financial aid to Great Britain. I would like to present to him, with my compliments, a volume of newspaper clippings gathered during the month of October 1940, showing to what extent public opinion, as represented by editorial comment, is in favor of financial aid to Great Britain.

King came through. He told Watson that "Dr. Hammer did great work for the President during the campaign." Roosevelt agreed to a token five-minute appointment, and Hammer, who was staying at the Mayflower Hotel in Washington, came in on November 28, 1940, around 12:30 P.M.

When he arrived at the White House, he learned that the appointment had been rescheduled to 4:30 in the afternoon. Hammer returned later in the day. General Watson ushered him into the Oval Office, where Hammer made his brief presentation and was escorted out.

The next day, Roosevelt gave his 698th press conference.

The New York Times that day had reported that an "Arnold Hammer" had met with the President the day before to discuss a proposal for Lend-Lease. One reporter asked, "Can you tell us about your conference with Dr. Armand Hammer on the naval defense bases?"

"Never talked about it," Roosevelt replied.

"He rather gave the impression you had talked about it," the reporter persisted.

"No, he gave me a long book here which I have not had a chance to look at yet. If you are really interested, you may look at it. It has"—and here Roosevelt picked up Hammer's gift scrapbook—"twenty-eight million, six hundred and thirty-six thousand, nine hundred and forty news clippings."

"All for Willkie?" someone asked. There was hearty laughter.

"No, no," the President answered, "but these news clippings are on a bill proposing settlement of World War debts. I thought it was political, but it isn't, for it says, 'Leasing of Pacific Bases and Granting Credits to Great Britain,' and then each paper that has favored it, editorially, with the circulation of the paper after it; and there are twenty-eight million of those; and—oh, yes, editorials favorable for buying the earth, 5,577,580; unfavorable, 456,832." Then Roosevelt looked up and said archly, "It is a very interesting compilation—which I haven't had time to scan." Everyone laughed again.

Joseph Alsop has written, in his book *FDR,* that Roosevelt favored the plan to transfer fifty mothballed American destroyers to the British navy, but waited until he saw that American public opinion was solidly behind him—in fact, until he was criticized for being dilatory about it. Perhaps Hammer saw a wave about to crest and jumped on top of it for the opportunity to meet the President.

Hammer's public posture as an advocate of Lend-Lease was not necessarily an anti-Soviet act. Stalin's nervous alliance with Hitler was based on his fear of being overpowered by the Nazis. A strong Britain would mean a Nazi defeat, and it is likely that Stalin more than anything desired to crush the German menace.

There is little reason to believe that the Hammers broke with their longtime business partner, the Soviet government. A better explanation is that Hammer sought both access to the President and a public identification with a popular cause.

This hypothesis is strengthened when one examines Hammer's rapid return to the Russian fold as soon as that became publicly acceptable. On May 18, 1943, for instance—when the United States was allied with the Soviet Union—he organized an exhibition of paintings entitled "Five Hundred Years of Russian Art." The show, which was held at the Jay Gould Mansion on Fifth Avenue in New York, was designed to raise money for the Russian War Relief Fund.

Many of the works belonged to Joseph E. Davies, who had acquired a magnificent collection of Russian art during his stay in Moscow as American ambassador to the Soviet Union in 1937 and 1938. Davies approved of the idea of the benefit and was pleased to loan his collection.

Hammer had given a Russian seascape to President Roosevelt a few years earlier, and used the occasion of asking to borrow it to ask him whether he would agree to serve as an honorary patron. He explained that the guests of honor included Davies and the Soviet Ambassador, Maxim Litvinov. The show, he said, "will have an important influence in bringing closer together the peoples of the United States and Russia not only during the present war, but also during the post-war period."

Hammer also wrote to Eleanor Roosevelt: "In view of the prejudice which still exists against Russia in certain quarters, won't you help us by setting an example to the rest of the country and honoring our opening with your presence?" He included a copy of her "What a grand thing you did to help the President!" letter of three years before. But both Roosevelts sent their regrets.

Apart from making a number of trips to the Soviet Union during the thirties, it is not clear what Julius and Rose Hammer did after their return to America in 1932. They settled down in a large, comfortable house in Scarsdale, New York, perhaps acting as advisers to the family business in which Armand was playing a greater and greater role. In 1943 Julius's medical license, which had been rescinded when he was imprisoned, was restored, in part because of the wartime shortage of doctors. They moved back to New York City, where Julius resumed practicing medicine.

Julius also remained active in Communist causes. In December 1944 he served as a member of the Committee for the Celebration of the Twentieth Anniversary of the Icor Association. A report in the *Congressional Record* almost thirty years later asserts that "This group, which has been officially cited as a Communist front by California and Massachusetts state committees, had the responsibility of raising funds for the Soviet Jewish Autonomous Republic of Biro Bidjan." The same report states that in 1945 Julius Hammer

> appeared as a stockholder for the Peoples Radio Foundation, Inc., which was cited as a Communist front by Attorney General Tom Clark. This group, which was controlled by the International Workers Order, had as its purpose the establishment of a pro-Communist FM radio station in New York City.
>
> In February 1946, Julius Hammer was listed as a member of the National Board of the American Committee of Jewish Artists, Writers, and Scientists, a Communist front which has been officially cited by the California committee. On February 25, 1946, he also served as a sponsor of a testimonial dinner given by this organization for Communist Party member Albert Kahn.

It is hard to say whether these organizations were Communist or merely activist, a distinction that Red-baiting congressmen have been loath to make. Was the Julius Hammer who in 1919 planned, from the safety of the Ansonia Hotel, a Communist Revolution in the United States a leftist or a Soviet Communist? After years in Moscow during which he observed the horrors of Stalinism, could he really still have been a Communist? His former comrades Bertram Wolfe and Jay Lovestone, who emerged from their radicalism of the twenties disillusioned and embittered, were amazed that Julius had not undergone a similar change of heart and mind.

On October 17, 1948, Julius died of a heart attack at the Barbizon-Plaza Hotel in New York. He was seventy-four, and from all indications still loved the nation he had done so much to help, Soviet Russia. But because he was known as a gentle, generous, and humanitarian man, his friends remembered him fondly.

His *New York Times* obituary omitted any mention of his involvement in Communism. He was described simply as a "retired general practitioner" and a graduate of the Columbia College of Physicians and Surgeons. His funeral service was conducted by Rabbi Samuel Goldenson of Temple Emanu-El. The pallbearers included several prominent New York judges and professors, as well as the chairmen of Macy's and Gimbels.

Armand, in the meantime, had gone into the whiskey business, at the urging of Fred Gimbel. In 1943, the A. Hammer Cooperage Corporation became United Distillers, Ltd.; its board of directors consisted of Armand, Harry, and Victor—again, a family operation with Armand in charge.

Armand's fortunes improved dramatically with his marriage to a rich divorcée, Angela Carey Zevely. A singer, as was Armand's first wife, Angela had attended the Boston Conservatory of Music and later attained some recognition in amateur operatic roles; in the early thirties she sang on national radio for the Columbia Broadcasting System. But at the height of her career she was seriously injured in an automobile accident in Florida. Her hearing was impaired, and her singing career ended.

After she was divorced from her first husband, she bought an estate in Red Bank, New Jersey, and raised thoroughbred horses, prize pigs, and cattle. In 1936 she met Hammer. He told her that it was unusual for a woman of her "background" to become a serious farmer. They soon became good friends, and Hammer helped her expand her farm and cattle-raising business, which he incorporated as Shadow Isle Farms, Inc. This was really her undertaking, although they were now co-owners, because Hammer devoted most of his time to his new distilling company. On December 19, 1943, Armand and Angela were married.

As Angela was by now well established in New Jersey society, the couple used Shadow Isle as a showplace for entertaining businessmen and politicians. In the winter they lived in a carriage house that Hammer had bought sometime in the twenties, at 183 West Fourth Street in Greenwich Village. As United Distillers grew, Hammer bought the Executive Beechcraft for jaunts to Washington, and a seventy-eight-foot yacht, the *Lansdowne,* on which he commuted, via the East River, between Red Bank and his office in the Empire State Building.

United Distillers, which evidently had no connection with the Soviet Union (the Second World War brought a temporary halt to Hammer's trade with Moscow), began with a distillery in New Hampshire and a molasses importing firm. Because of grain shortages caused by the war, the production of alcohol from grain was prohibited, and so United Distillers produced whiskey from alcohol made from rotten potatoes. They began to bottle bourbon called "Old Cooperage."

When grain controls ended, the Hammers acquired grain-alcohol distilleries in Kentucky and the J. W. Dant Company, producers of higher quality, bonded bourbon. Hammer applied his promotional skills to the sale of Dant bourbon. He sent displays of the bottles, draped in what looked like Romanov jewels, around the country, calling it "the crown jewel of Kentucky Bourbons." He also reduced its price by a third. Before long, it was one of the biggest selling whiskeys in the country, and Hammer was making a lot of money once again.

Armand Hammer was never dragged before the House Un-American Activities Committee, though so many others who had nothing at all to do with Soviet Communism were. Perhaps this was because he learned from his father's bitter experience with Tammany Hall the importance of having powerful friends. Already he had begun to translate his wealth into political influence by contributing generously and shrewdly to the campaigns of state and national politicians.

His brother Victor was less fortunate. In 1940 Victor had married a young, pretty singer named Ireene Wicker, who was famous as "The Singing Lady" of the airwaves. The Un-American Activities Committee decided in the early fifties that she had been involved in Communist causes, and she was blacklisted. The charges were investigated by the Committee several years later. Vincent Hartnett, author of the book *Red Channels: The Report of Communist Influence in Radio and Television,* defended the blacklisting of Miss Wicker:

> I knew . . . that Ireene Wicker was married, her second marriage, to Victor Hammer, his second marriage. Victor Hammer was a son of one of the founding members of the Communist Party. Old Doctor Hammer was such a big wheel in the party that he used to pay the rent on the party headquarters in the old days. I have a memory on these things—I am older than I look—whether by direct or indirect knowledge.
>
> Miss Wicker had married into what had been the aristocracy of the Communist movement. I knew that.

Hartnett described two charges against Ireene. In June 1946, he said, she had lent her apartment (which was also Victor's) for "a fund-raising gambling party" for the Joint Anti-Fascist Refugee Committee—which was, he said, "one of the top fund-raising arms of the Communist Party." The party had raised half a million dollars for the Communist Party, he said. The second charge was that Ireene and Victor "had taken a whole table at $100 a plate at the Waldorf for a fund-raising luncheon for the Joint Anti-Fascist Refugee Committee. I knew this from witnesses and I had photostatic copies of checks from the gambling party."

In 1949, when *Sign* magazine published information that Ireene had been a sponsor of the political campaign of a Communist Party candidate for the New York City Council, Armand Hammer had protested to the magazine that the accusation was false. Victor also complained that Ireene was "unjustly accused." At length Ireene admitted to having attended the Waldorf luncheon. After the witness related this final incident, the Un-American Activities Committee decided that Ireene's blacklisting had been fair. Armand's political pull was insufficient.

"PLEASE BE ASSURED OF MY GOOD WISHES AND COOPERATION," Hammer cabled Harry Truman on April 13, 1945, the day after the death of Franklin Roosevelt, "IN THIS HOUR WHEN YOU ARE ASSUMING THE SUPERHUMAN BURDEN OF LEADERSHIP OF A GREAT COUNTRY AND A GREAT CAUSE." A year later, Hammer found reason to write again. He had a plan to help the United Nations Relief and Rehabilitation Administration (UNRRA) in its efforts to combat the European famine caused by the war.

He was donating one million pounds of wheat flour, he told President Truman, which he would otherwise use in distilling, to the UNRRA, in order "to augment the supply of food so urgently needed by the starving peoples of the world." Perhaps this would inspire other distillers to do likewise. Hammer was, as usual, not reticent about the gesture. He saw that it made *The New York Times* and that Drew Pearson discussed it on his radio show.

Truman would not see Hammer but suggested he talk with the head of UNRRA, former President Herbert Hoover. Hammer had a friend, Senator R. Owen Brewster, send Hoover a letter of introduction on Hammer's behalf. Hammer "is one in whom you can place complete confidence," Brewster assured Hoover, "and one who has a very unusual knowledge of Russian conditions as a result of his residence there from 1920 [*sic*] to 1930."

Hammer met with Hoover on July 11, 1946, at five o'clock in the afternoon, at Hoover's suite at the Waldorf-Astoria in New York. He described his plan to donate wheat flour to the UNRRA. Eight days later, Hammer managed to arrange an interview with President Truman, insisting that he had "no favors to ask." There is no record of what transpired, and there is no reason to believe the meeting was any more substantive than was Hammer's talk with Franklin Roosevelt. Immediately afterward, he announced publicly that he was embarking on a tour of Europe to "get a first-hand view of the need for famine relief."

Where in Europe did Hammer go? Russia is as good a guess as any. Not only was his "very unusual knowledge of Russian conditions" what recommended him to Hoover and Truman, but the Soviet Union was, as it turned out, the major beneficiary of UNRRA largesse.

The uneasy postwar relationship between the United States and the Soviet Union, which became the Cold War, began even before the last shots of the Second World War were fired. When the formation of UNRRA was being discussed in 1945, Ambassador Averell Harriman sent a secret telegram from Moscow warning that giving aid to Russia would be a mistake:

> HAVING OBSERVED CAREFULLY THE EFFECT ON THE SOVIET GOVERNMENT OF OUR GENEROUS LEND LEASE POLICY OVER THE PAST FOUR YEARS I HAVE NOT (REPEAT: NOT) FOUND THAT WE HAVE OBTAINED ANY BENEFIT IN GOODWILL ON THE PART OF THE SOVIET GOVERNMENT, IN CONNECTION WITH THEIR ACTIONS WHICH EFFECT OUR INTERESTS. DURING THE WAR WE HAVE OBTAINED IN MY OPINION FULL VALUE FOR OUR LEND LEASE SHIPMENTS THROUGH THE STRENGTHENING OF THE SOVIET WAR EFFORT. HOWEVER, NOW THAT THE WAR IS OVER I SEE NO GAIN TO THE UNITED STATES IN DEALING WITH THE SOVIETS ON ANY OTHER THAN A REALISTIC RECIPROCAL BASIS.

But Harriman's warning went unheeded. UNRRA aid was extended to all of Europe, and Russia took the lion's share. The United States contributed about 95 percent of the funds and food provided by the relief plan, and the Soviets gave less than one-tenth of one percent. Of the $1.7 billion worth of foodstuffs distributed in Europe, the Soviet Union and Soviet-occupied countries took 60 percent. Moreover, the Red Army had completely looted the three million tons of food stores that Japan had left in Manchuria, which was to have gone to China, Korea, and Japan. With this added in, the final result was that 80 percent of all UNRRA food went to Russia or the Eastern bloc. Herbert Hoover seems to have been unhappy with the results of his mission. He had a bitter memorandum compiled for his personal records, concluding that "the idea of an international relief organization is nothing more than a false front."

As for Armand Hammer, it is doubtful that he was similarly depressed. This is another hazy period of his life, about which there seem to be no available records. If he did go to Russia, as seems likely, what did he seek to accomplish there? As the UNRRA never heard from him again, it seems unlikely that he inspected Russian sites of famine and devastation.

Almost exactly twenty-five years earlier, Hammer went to Russia on the pretext of combating famine. The parallel is unmistakable. Although no business was to result from the 1946 journey to Russia—if it did take place—the Hammers at least reestablished their old contacts. Several diplomats who have spent time in Moscow, as well as a number of Muscovites, report that since 1946 Armand and Victor Hammer have kept apartments in Moscow. Some insist that only Armand has.

So, once again, Armand Hammer had a *pied-à-terre* in the Soviet Union. And the money and power to accompany it—well, that would come later, when the time was right.

PART TWO

The rotten capitalist world is collapsing.
Friends, let's drink, let's laugh,
let's rejoice.
—NIKITA S. KHRUSHCHEV, *June 26, 1956*

THE THAW

7

"JOHN FOSTER DULLES FIRING AT US FROM UNDER THE TABLE"

It was 1954, one of the most glacial years of the Cold War. Armand Hammer, having given up selling beer barrels and Russian art, was selling bonded bourbon and prize cattle. Averell Harriman, having long since departed the American Embassy in Moscow, had just been elected governor of New York.

The wartime alliance between Russia and America, which had transformed "the peasant-slayer" into Uncle Joe Stalin, was now replaced by a fierce political struggle. Even Stalin's death in 1953 had not immediately changed things. But now, virtually no American cared to be associated with the Soviet Union. Even the most aggressive merchant refused to risk the hostility he would face after a sales trip to Moscow.

Then, suddenly, seventy-one-year-old Cyrus Eaton, a titan of American industry whom the *National Review* once described as "the most fearsome living incarnation of the old-time competitive capitalist spirit," contacted the Russians. He was interested in a private détente of sorts.

Eaton was the founder of the Republic Steel Corporation, one of the country's largest manufacturers of flat steel, with a long history of ill treatment of its workers. He was also the head of a gigantic empire that included the Chesapeake & Ohio Railroad. It is unclear exactly why he decided that Russia might be a good client. Trade with the Soviet Union, after all, was so restricted after the war as to be virtually nonexistent. Nothing that might possibly have a military use could be exported to Communist nations; the list of restricted items covered everything from steel to brassieres. But there were ways around the restrictions and Eaton was determined to sell steel to the Soviets—secretly, of course. He dispatched his son, Cyrus, Jr., to Moscow that year to make an offer.

His son came back with the good news that the Russians were indeed interested in doing business. Unfortunately, there were problems. Not only would such a transaction violate American law, but the Soviet government had a long-standing policy of not parting with hard currency whenever it was avoidable. So Eaton, drawing on the extensive resources of his financial network, set up an ingenious circumvention. In exchange for his flat steel, the Russians would supply chrome ore, which they had in great supply; the exchange was made through a Canadian middleman firm, since Canada was considerably more lax on trade with the Communists. Republic Steel furnished the flat steel—Eaton had sold the company but still maintained large holdings—and Union Carbide (one of Eaton's major clients) received the chrome. Everything was shipped on the Chesapeake & Ohio.

Of course, it was all conducted in the strictest secrecy. None of the American companies involved cared to imagine the uproar that might result if the deal came to light. The situation led to some comical moments at which Cyrus and his son could laugh only in private. The chairman of Republic Steel, for instance, while profiting handsomely from his clandestine partnership with the Soviet government, delivered good Republican speeches to the Cleveland Chamber of Commerce and other organizations, warning darkly, as was then the fashion, of the horrible Soviet military threat facing America. His Chamber of Commerce audiences, as well as his stockholders, remained blissfully unaware that Republic Steel was supplying the steel for the Russians' military industry. From 1954 on, the Eatons continued to do quiet business with the Soviet Union, on a modest scale.

In that year, 1954, a group of Russian farmers came to visit Eaton at his estate outside Cleveland. He entertained them generously, put them all up for several days, and proudly showed them his livestock. A year later, in 1955, Premier Nikita Khrushchev's son-in-law, Alexei Adzhubei, the editor of *Izvestiya,* led a group of Soviet journalists on a visit around the United States. The State Department escorted Adzhubei's group everywhere and arranged for them to see a football game in Cleveland.

But the Russians were uninterested in football. Instead, they wanted to meet with a real, live capitalist—Cyrus Eaton. When the State Department escort called him, Eaton protested that he was not a typical American capitalist. Finding that no other businessman in Cleveland was willing to receive the Soviet delegation, however, he relented.

He set off in his limousine to pick up the journalists at their hotel in Cleveland and was dismayed to find a crowd of Americans surrounding the hotel shouting threats and obscenities at the Russians. Many of the hecklers, Eaton later claimed to have determined for certain, were on the payroll of the FBI. This was Eaton's first taste of the violent antagonism he would encounter throughout the next twenty years because of his friendship with the leaders of the Soviet Union. It was a rancor he came to find delicious.

Cyrus Eaton was fabulously wealthy, courtly, and aristocratic in demeanor. E. J. Kahn, Jr., described his appearance in a *New Yorker* profile many years later:

> Physically, Eaton is the epitome of a capitalist—almost a caricature of one. He is tall, robust, silver-haired, blue-eyed, ruddy-cheeked, and always impeccably dressed. His day-in-and-day-out costume, even when down on the farm, consists of a well-cut (Wetzel) double-breasted dark-blue serge suit, with a white shirt, a gray silk four-in-hand, and highly polished black shoes.

Eaton was also an athlete; he played ice hockey until he was seventy, skied until eighty-seven, and did not give up horseback riding until he was ninety-two.

The fifth of nine children of Mary Adelle McPherson and Joseph Howe Eaton, Cyrus was born in the town of Pugwash, Nova Scotia, on December 27, 1883. His father, a farmer and a lumberman, was also the town postmaster and manager of the general store. Cyrus attended the town elementary school (which is now named for him) and the Amherst Academy a few miles away.

In 1901, having just finished high school, seventeen-year-old Cyrus was invited to spend the summer in Cleveland with his uncle, Charles Eaton. Cleveland's leading Baptist minister, Uncle Charles was a good friend of the town's most famous Baptist, John D. Rockefeller. Rockefeller spent five months a year at Forest Hill, his estate in Cleveland, and was the superintendent of Reverend Eaton's Sunday school.

The reverend frequently went to dinner at Forest Hill, and one night during the summer of 1901 he brought along his visiting nephew. Mrs. Rockefeller was distressed to learn that young

Cyrus was planning to take a job as night clerk at the Euclid Hotel for the summer. "Isn't there something he can do around here, John?" she asked her husband. There was, Mr. Rockefeller replied; and he hired Cyrus as an errand boy, golf caddy, and bodyguard, at a salary of two dollars a day.

During the next four summers, while attending McMaster University in Toronto, Eaton continued to work for Rockefeller, and developed an immense respect for him. "There's never been any man in finance or industry who came close to matching John D. Rockefeller in imagination or in application," he once remarked.

Rockefeller repeatedly pressed Eaton to quit McMaster and work for him full time. But Cyrus held out until he graduated in 1905, and then moved to Cleveland. After two years as one of Rockefeller's factotums, Eaton came upon an opportunity to purchase an electric-power-plant franchise in Manitoba, Canada. He borrowed the money, and within a few years had formed the Canada Gas & Electric Corporation. By 1912 he had combined hundreds of American Midwestern companies into a broad syndicate, the Continental Gas & Electric Company, and so was, by the age of thirty, a millionaire. He married Margaret House, the daughter of a Cleveland physician, and became an American citizen.

By the mid-twenties he controlled the United Light & Power Company and one of America's largest brokerage houses, Otis & Company. This made his utilities empire second only to that of Chicago's utilities baron, Samuel Insull—and when Eaton began methodically buying into Insull's companies, Insull was forced to battle until Eaton had bankrupted him.

Eaton's dynasty grew to include Goodyear Tire & Rubber and large chunks of Firestone and Goodrich; by the late twenties he had formed the Republic Steel Corporation from five steel and iron concerns. As he struggled against established firms such as Bethlehem Steel, he began to identify as his enemy the Eastern financial elite. "How are we going to have leadership in this vast country if everything must be directed from Wall Street?" he demanded. "It would make clerks of us all here in the Middle West."

By 1929 he had acquired a reputation as one of the nation's most bloodthirsty industrialists. For example, in the course of a lengthy and acrid litigation, Bethlehem Steel's attorney depicted Eaton as a Napoleon riding to victory through rows of corpses. The Crash of 1929 wiped out the Eaton dynasty, although Cyrus hardly went broke: his fortune dwindled from one hundred million dollars to five million. The disaster took a toll on his twenty-six-year marriage to Margaret House, with whom he had seven children; they were divorced in 1934.

In the early thirties, Eaton fought his way back by laying siege to Wall Street once again. Traditionally, Morgan Stanley, Kuhn Loeb, and the other New York—based investment banks underwrote all railroad bonds without competitive bidding, but Eaton was now determined to share the action. His Otis & Company joined Halsey, Stuart of Chicago to compete for a thirty-million-dollar bond issue that the Chesapeake & Ohio Railroad was planning to take from its customary Wall Street underwriters. By offering the bond issue at two million dollars less than Morgan Stanley and Kuhn Loeb, Eaton's group won the C & O's business. When the head of the C & O, Robert Young, departed to bid for control of the New York Central Railroad, he sold his C & O stock to Eaton, who then succeeded him as chairman.

He had won the battle, and when seventeen Eastern investment banking houses were indicted by the government for allegedly cooperating to control two-thirds of the nation's underwriting business, Eaton happily twisted the knife by submitting a statement into testimony that assailed the New York houses as "a colorless fraternity" that "militates against the creative and constructive finance that is the keystone of our free-enterprise system."

His crusade against Wall Street may have turned him into a Democrat. He supported Roosevelt in 1932, some believe, because he wanted to stop Newton D. Baker, Woodrow Wilson's Secretary of War, who had connections to New York financiers. In the twenties, as the public utilities lord of Kansas City, Eaton had met Harry Truman. When Senator Truman was chairman of a Senate committee on the national defense, he persuaded the War Production Board to approve an Eaton project to mine the rich iron ore reserves beneath Steep Rock Lake in northwestern Ontario. In 1948, when Truman's presidential campaign ran short of money just before an important whistle-stop rally, Eaton came through with the five thousand dollars to pay for the cost of the train.

Eaton's most notorious court battle began in the early fifties and lasted five years. In 1948 he had promised Henry J. Kaiser, the California industrialist, and Joseph W. Frazer, another manufacturer and a friend, to help them enter the postwar automobile market by underwriting a sale of steel. When the securities market went bad, Eaton pulled out, and Kaiser-Frazer sued him for breach of contract. Although Eaton eventually won the trial, the Kaiser-Frazer controversy only added to his reputation as a ruthless tycoon.

Ruthless, perhaps, and usually victorious—yet he had acquired the image of a spoiler. A longtime Eaton nemesis was Robert A. Taft, "Mr. Republican," who had fought Eaton's attempts to enter the railroad financing business in the late thirties. When Taft ran for reelection to the Senate in 1950, Eaton contributed thirty thousand dollars to Taft's opponent, Joe Ferguson. Since no individual was allowed to give more than five thousand dollars to a political campaign, Eaton had his Otis & Company employees contribute some of the money—for which he later reimbursed them. The rest was in the name of John L. Lewis's Non-Partisan League. A Senate investigating committee became concerned but finally dropped the matter. Then, when the Taft family attempted to buy the *Cincinnati Enquirer,* Eaton rushed in to loan the newspaper's employees almost eight million dollars to keep it from falling into the hands of the Tafts. The Tafts symbolized to him Eastern financial interests, and fighting them, as well as the rest of Wall Street, had become a game for Eaton.

By the time he reached his seventies, Eaton could rest on his accomplishments. He lived baronially in his large late-eighteenth-century farmhouse on eight hundred acres near Cleveland that he had purchased in 1912 and named Acadia Farms, after the French name for Nova Scotia. Unlike most gentleman-farmers, Eaton was actively interested in the breeding of his cattle. The star of his stable was P. S. Troubadour, an International Grand Champion bull that once appeared, along with Eaton, on Ed Murrow's "Person to Person" television show. Eaton knew every tree on his estate by name, and was said to have been able to name all the trees and birds native to North America.

He maintained another residence in Upper Blandford, Nova Scotia—a three-thousand-acre estate called Deep Cove Farms, where he spent summer and winter vacations. A hundred fifty miles south was the ancestral home of Eaton's forebears. It was Pineo Lodge, a white, fifteen-room, one-hundred-fifty-year-old house on the Northumberland Strait that had belonged to the Eaton family until the mid-nineteenth century, when Cyrus's grandfather gave it up to look for gold—unsuccessfully—in California. Eaton had always admired the lodge, and when he became rich he bought it.

There, he partook of his greatest loves: reading and philosophical discussion. Throughout his life he read works of philosophy voraciously, favoring Darwin, T. H. Huxley, and the other rationalists. As a wealthy and prominent man, he invited university presidents and scholars to spend vacations with him at Pugwash. "I found pleasure in talking to thinkers, for a change," he once recalled. "I would sometimes take them on salmon-fishing expeditions, maybe half a dozen college presidents at a clip, casting in the daytime and in the evening discussing the best way of getting people interested in great books."

Early in the 1950s he formalized this ritual. Cooperating with the Association of American Colleges, he founded what he called Intellectual Life Conferences, in which academics from around the country were invited to Nova Scotia to play tennis and discuss Plato. The first was held in 1955.

About a dozen university professors attended, including British biologist Sir Julian Huxley; Julian Boyd, editor of the Jefferson Papers at Princeton; and Henry Steele Commager, the historian, then at Columbia. "They wandered," reported *MacLean's* magazine, "with their heads in the clouds, through a variety of academic pastures."

It might have been Eaton's secret commerce with Russia that sparked his interest in Soviet-American relations, but more likely it was the other way around. He later claimed that his interest in the Soviet Union had been indirectly spawned by John D. Rockefeller. He was greatly influenced by Samuel Harper, the head of the Russian department at the University of Chicago (which John D. Rockefeller founded), and the son of William Rainey Harper, the university's first president. Sam Harper spent half of almost every year of his life in Russia. He was a staunch defender of the Hitler-Stalin pact of 1939, and wrote a book, *The Russia I Believe In,* that was published posthumously in 1945. "Sam's enthusiasm for Russian culture and Russian children had a great impact on my life," Eaton once said.

By the time of the second Intellectual Life Conference in 1956, Eaton had decided to take an active public interest in Soviet-American relations, though his business dealings remained a secret to his death. This conference, which focused on the Suez crisis then brewing, was considerably larger and more international in scope. Eleven men from nine countries gathered at the lodge from August 3 to 11 to play croquet, eat lobster, drink vintage wines, picnic by the sea, swim, sail, and meet for two hours each morning and two hours each evening in the book-lined study of the house, which had recently been renamed "Thinkers Lodge." Two weeks earlier, Nasser had seized the Suez Canal; now, in the relaxed, even epicurean atmosphere of Pugwash, intellectuals from

Israel and Arab countries—and from both Communist and non-Communist ones—discussed the situation without rancor (and, it is also true, without reaching any consensus).

Eaton was "a multimillionaire who collects thinkers the way other multimillionaires collect yachts, race horses, or rare postage stamps," a journalist observed at the time. The guests were even more colorful than those of the previous year. Apart from the usual collection of dignitaries, there was a representative of Communist China: Dr. Chien Tuan-Sheng, president of the Peking Institute of Politics and Law, who arrived with a Chinese watercolor as a gift for Eaton. And there was a delegate from Russia—Alexander Samarin, a leading Soviet metallurgist who was instrumental in constructing the Russian steel mills in the Urals during the thirties. He came with a large silver samovar, a bottle of vodka, and a tub of the best Russian caviar as house gifts. No explanation was furnished as to why the Soviet representative was a steel expert. One reporter did ask Eaton whether it was not slightly unorthodox for "a man of his standing in conservative financial circles to be entertaining a Russian." "I make steel," Eaton replied. "The people of Russia have an idea that many industrialists in the United States are interested in war to create an outlet for steel and munitions. Now I have had an outstanding Russian here with me and he has seen a United States industrialist who hates war and doesn't believe that war ever settles anything." But Samarin hardly had to be convinced of Eaton's good feelings toward Russia, and toward its steel industry.

Throughout the United States and Canada, people were intrigued that such a fierce industrial warrior could take an interest in something so high-minded. Padding about the grounds of his estate in baggy gray flannel pants, a blue sport shirt, a blue sweater, and scuffed moccasins, he seemed, as *MacLean's* marveled,

> utterly unlike the Cyrus Eaton pictured by newspaper readers—the wily nerveless financier who amassed a great fortune by cold-bloodedly outwitting his opponents in several of the most famous financial struggles of this century. Here, he was a simple, gracious, extremely courteous Nova Scotian, who insisted on shoving garden chairs around for his younger guests so they would be in the cool shade instead of the hot sun.

Although two Communists were in attendance, the Intellectual Life Conference of 1956 did wonders for Eaton's image. Even Cleveland, full of businessmen outmaneuvered by him or envious that he had survived the Crash and they had not, came around to thinking well of him. The *Cleveland Plain Dealer* described him as "the tycoon who looks like a cardinal." In an interview with the newspaper, Eaton prattled on happily about his favorite authors: "the Greek historians Herodotus and Thucydides; the British historians Macaulay, Hume and Green . . . the poets Homer, Shakespeare, Milton, Burns, Shelley, Keats, and Byron . . . John Dewey . . . George Santayana . . . Bertrand Russell . . . ." He went on to say that he was beginning to read the works of Karl Marx, to learn "of the forces that made it possible for the vast populations of Russia and China to throw away, for the most part, their age-old political and religious beliefs and accept the doctrines of Karl Marx and his disciples."

His *Plain Dealer* interviewer could not understand the significance of Eaton's new reading list. Even when Radio Moscow broadcast a brief interview with him, in which he urged commerce between the United States and Russia, no one took it to be the least bit anomalous. *The New York Times* even printed a scant notice of the transmission under the headline, "SOVIET BROADCASTS U.S. ANTI-REDS' VOICE."

Now almost seventy-three, the man who had almost everything had begun, though tenuously, to embark upon a second career: the alluring and murky world of international affairs, with an emphasis on the tangled realm of Soviet-American relations. After a two-year dalliance of the mildest sort, he came upon an opportunity he would not pass up.

In 1955, Bertrand Russell and Albert Einstein issued a manifesto to "the scientists of the world and the general public" that called for a conference of "men of science of the most divergent political opinions—Communist, anti-Communist, and neutral" to agree upon the means of limiting the threat of nuclear war. Captivated by the idea, Eaton sent Russell a glowing letter, offering to help finance such a parley.

He was not the first to make an offer, though. Aristotle Onassis had written Russell to say that he would help sponsor a scientists' conference if it were held in Monte Carlo. Russell explained this to Eaton, who then made a counteroffer: if it were to take place in Pugwash, he would foot the bill entirely. He added that he was already in the intellectual-conference business anyway.

Russell accepted Eaton's generous proposal. The Pugwash Conference of Nuclear Scientists was born; the first was scheduled for July 1957. Two of Russell's friends, C. F. Powell of the Wills Physical Laboratory at Bristol, England, and Joseph Rothblat of the University of London, invited forty eminent scientists from around the world. Twenty-four accepted. Eaton paid the travel costs of all participants, which totaled $100,000. Only a few could be put up in Thinkers Lodge, so some had to stay in private cars of a Chesapeake & Ohio train that Eaton had had brought in. Others were put up in the local inn. The twenty-four scientists could not comfortably meet in the library of the lodge, so Eaton converted a schoolroom in Pugwash's Masonic Lodge into a conference room by having the desks removed and a triangular trestle table installed.

The guests arrived over on the weekend of July Fourth and began meeting by the sixth, morning and afternoon, with the evenings free for drinks and dinner. Albert Einstein had died the year before; and Bertrand Russell was too ill to attend, but sent a tape-recorded message. Russell's deputy, C. F. Powell, stood at the head of the conference table at the Masonic Lodge, pencil perched behind his ear, and presided. Eaton stayed away from the sessions.

The Russian delegates, all members of the Soviet Academy of Sciences, sat together at all meetings. One was A. M. Kuzin, a biochemist who took to wearing a blue beret and spending much of his time talking with his American opposite, H. J. Muller, a Nobel-prize-winning biologist at Indiana University. Another was the chemist A. V. Topchiev, secretary-general of the Academy and the Soviet Union's number-two scientist, who spoke no English. A tall, dark-haired, round-shouldered man in boxy suits, Topchiev was able to speak with only one American, the Russian-speaking editor of the *Bulletin of the Atomic Scientists,* Eugene Rabinowitch of the University of Illinois, who conveniently happened to be his opposite. The third member of the Soviet delegation was a distinguished-looking physicist named D. F. Skobeltsyn, who came to be known as the "aristocrat" of the conference—he spoke eloquent English and French, and several times accidentally referred to Leningrad by its old name of St. Petersburg.

Not only did the Soviet scientists make friends among some of the most eminent scientists in the Western world at Pugwash, they also impressed everyone present with their formidable knowledge of nuclear science. One evening Rabinowitch came up to Eaton, slightly awed, and observed, "There is nothing we can tell the Russians about the nuclear art. They know as much as we do, and probably more." The Soviet government could not have done more to disturb the smugness of the Western scientific elite. And there was no question that the Russians were official emissaries of the Soviet Union; although they had been invited as private citizens they admitted "our views represent those of the Academy."

The scientists met in private, on the assumption that public sessions would lead to grandstanding and would hinder candid discussion. Most of the participants were pleased with the conference. "Everyone talked sense," Rabinowitch remarked, "and if anyone brought a soapbox he left it outside."

They issued a statement that all but two—Leo Szilard of the University of Chicago and John Stuart Foster of McGill—signed. Much of it was vague yet ardent. "We are all convinced that mankind must abolish war or suffer catastrophe," it said, " . . . and the establishment of lasting peace will mark the opening of a new and triumphant epoch for the whole of mankind." One section of the report concluded that the strontium-90 in fallout from nuclear *tests* would dramatically increase the worldwide incidence of leukemia, bone cancer, widespread genetic mutations, and that

> it cannot be disputed that a full-scale nuclear war would be an utter catastrophe. . . . In the combatant countries, hundreds of millions of people would be killed outright, by the flash and heat, and by the ionizing radiation produced at the instant of explosion. . . .

The report ended with an appeal to all scientists to "do all in our power to prevent war." This, it said, "we can do by contributing to the task of public enlightenment concerning the great dilemma of our times."

On the last evening of the conference, everyone gathered for dinner at Thinkers Lodge. Pledging to work for peace, they raised their glasses at the end of dinner and toasted their sponsor, Cyrus Eaton.

Public reaction to the Pugwash Conference was almost universally admiring. The *Washington Evening Star* announced on its editorial page that the Pugwash scientists had demonstrated that "war is obsolete." *Life* featured a photo spread of the now famous meeting, entitled "Atomic Age Powwow in Pugwash." The British journal *Nature* reprinted the scientists' report in its entirety and observed that "never before had a group of scientists, so widely representative, met to discuss topics of such general importance." Even Leo Szilard, who had dissented from the Pugwash report, admitted that "this meeting was, I believe, a very important experiment."

The real star of the show, however, was Eaton. His picture was splashed over the pages of newspapers around the country. *The New York Times* called him "The Millionaire Philosopher"—"a benign Uncle Sam without the beard." His credo that "A man's first moral obligation is to earn his living and his second is to be intelligent" was widely published—confirming his new image as that rare creature, the intellectual industrialist.

Determined to make Pugwash his debut as a statesman, Eaton wrote to President Eisenhower. The year before, Eaton had offered him use of the Chesapeake & Ohio's resort hotel, the Greenbrier, in White Sulphur Springs, West Virginia, for Eisenhower's meeting with the President of Mexico and Prime Minister of Canada. Eisenhower accepted, and found the setting luxurious, the staff gracious—and Cyrus Eaton present. He and Eaton had several cordial talks about politics and baseball; Eisenhower found that Eaton had an opinion on just about everything. Though a Democrat, Eaton understood the importance of cultivating the President.

On October 9, 1957, Eaton wrote to the President to tell him about the Soviet nuclear scientists he had met at Pugwash, who "gave every evidence of equalling the best of the brains of the dozen nations represented there." He explained that Soviet advances in the field of metallurgy were as impressive. "Your genius for frank and friendly diplomacy," he wrote, "coupled with your universally recognized integrity and honesty, designate you as the one man in the world who can work out the accommodation with Soviet Russia and Red China needed to guarantee honorable peace."

Eisenhower's reply was polite and noncommittal. He prayed that the Soviets' "impressive advancements" would "be utilized for the betterment of all mankind" and added, "to that effort I continue to devote every energy I personally possess."

On November 6, Eaton joined forty-nine other American businessmen, from David Sarnoff to Henry Luce, on a three-tiered, wedding-cake-like dais at a dinner in the Waldorf-Astoria. They were being honored as the *Forbes* magazine's "Fifty Foremost Business Leaders of America." Eaton's newfound prominence as a politically concerned businessman had evidently put a patina of philanthropy on his old cutthroat image.

This prominence was swiftly tested. Soon after the Soviet delegation left Pugwash, a decision was made somewhere at the top of the Kremlin hierarchy. Pugwash was quite useful, the Soviets decided; it coincided perfectly with the Politburo-directed Soviet peace movement then under way. What if Pugwash were expanded enormously—say, into a worldwide conference, initiated by Russia? The propaganda value would be incalculable.

One hundred fifty-five members of the Academy of Sciences then issued a declaration, sent to Eugene Rabinowitch for publication in the *Bulletin of the Atomic Scientists,* which called for "a broad international conference of scientists to discuss the perils of a thermonuclear war." The West responded favorably.

The *Financial Post* of Toronto enthusiastically endorsed the appeal, adding that this view was shared by Cyrus Eaton, "a supercapitalist and stout defender of democracy and free enterprise." Other Canadian reactions were as positive, yet characterized by an amazing naïveté. Prime Minister John Diefenbaker announced in the House of Commons, "I conclude that the proposal made by the scientists of the U.S.S.R. was one outside of governmental consideration in any way." For the Prime Minister of Canada not to realize that all such declarations by Soviet groups are not only government-sanctioned but usually government-inspired was disconcerting. Even the *New York Herald Tribune,* a staunchly conservative paper, called the appeal "A Soviet Hand of Friendship." "Interestingly enough," an editorial pointed out, "this Soviet offer has grown out of a meeting arranged by one of this country's leading capitalists, Cyrus S. Eaton." The *Herald Tribune* published, below the editorial, an article by Eaton entitled, "Let's Meet the Soviets Half-Way." He wrote:

> I take the declaration of these 155 top scientists seriously. I think that any man who refuses to respond to that appeal is lacking in wisdom and not serving the best interest of the United States. I think the more contact we have between people of the two nations the quicker we'll realize that we are all human, with weaknesses, with limitations, and that for better or for worse we had better agree not to annihilate each other. Either we'll live together or we'll perish together.

This elicited a few angry letters, but most responses were positive. "If given a chance," one reader said, "millions of Americans would support Eaton's statesmanship as opposed to Dulles' puerile 'brinkmanship.'" Another wrote, "Let's have more articles by Cyrus Eaton and other *sane* men!" Eaton's career as a sort of dollar-a-year ambassador-at-large was under way.

But Eaton had now become a renegade, capitalism's prodigal son. A reporter asked him in early December why he defended Communists. He retorted, "No one can accuse me of being a Communist, but the time is short, and our politicians need some good advice and need it quickly." He was not slow with the advice. At a banquet at Philadelphia's Union League, he announced that the Cold War was largely America's doing, because after the Second World War, the United States kept the details of the atomic bomb a secret.

In Montreal in February 1958, Eaton told eight hundred members of the Canadian Club that John Foster Dulles—who just six months earlier he had gently mocked as "an able lawyer"—was "a self-appointed Soviet-hate-monger, still making a career of stirring up enmity between the Western and Eastern worlds." He called for Dulles's removal. Not long afterward, Eaton had Soviet Ambassador Mikhail Menshikov and his wife for a weekend at Acadia Farms. Clevelanders grumbled. One did not keep such company and avoid criticism.

Then, literally overnight, Eaton plunged himself into national controversy. In an ABC television interview with Mike Wallace on Sunday evening, May 4, 1958, he declared, "I always worry when I see a nation feel that it is coming to greatness through the activities of its policemen." He proceeded to launch into a devastating attack on American policies:

> The F.B.I. is just one of the scores of agencies in the United States engaged in investigating, in snooping, in informing, in creeping up on people. . . . I am just as sure as I am alive that one of these days there will be an enormous reaction against this in the United States. . . . We can't destroy Communism. It's there to stay. . . . And to imagine that they could convert us to Communism is just silly. . . . No one in the world would be more unhappy under Communism than I, because I am dedicated to the other principle.

There were no Communists in the United States to speak of, he went on,

> except in the mind of those on the payroll of the F.B.I. . . . If you were to take the police forces of the cities and of the counties and of the state and governmental agencies and add them up, Hitler in his prime, through the Gestapo, never had any such spy organization as we have in this country today. We're certainly worse in that respect than the Russians.

The House Un-American Activities Committee was furious. Never before had it been attacked with such virulence on national television—and especially by one of the most famous businessmen in the country. Three days later, at an anti-Communist rally at Hunter College in New York, one of the committee's members lashed out. Eaton, he charged, had "made a tremendous contribution to the Soviet cause."

The committee demanded that ABC television grant equal time, and a few days later its staff director, Richard Arens, delivered a vehement rebuttal. He said that Eaton's remarks were "typical of a campaign of vilification which the Communist conspiracy is promoting in the United States against our security agencies and will accelerate in the future by its devious devices to weaken our internal defenses." Although a year before no one, including Mr. Arens, would ever have publicly criticized Eaton, now Arens said that Eaton's charges were the climax of a "series of his public utterances which have appeared over the course of the last several years in the world Communist press. The international Communist machine, which we estimate expends an average of three million dollars a year on propaganda, is now using Mr. Eaton's statements all over the world against the United States and our internal security systems." Finally, Arens casually mentioned that the committee planned to subpoena Eaton for an appearance.

The battle was on. Eaton instantly issued a response. He had not yet heard from "the so-called Un-American Activities Committee," he said, but, "needless to add, I shall be delighted to appear before any Congressional committee for a serious discussion of the Federal secret police and intelligence agencies and the effects, as I see them, of their *sub rosa* activities on the freedoms guaranteed to the citizens by the Constitution and the Bill of Rights." With a flourish that only one with such a legendary business career could make, he proclaimed: "For nearly three-quarters of a century I have been dedicated to the development of the capitalistic system and the democratic form of government under which it flourishes. I shall be proud to match records with any member of the Un-American Activities Committee, as well as any secret police or intelligence agent."

The Un-American Activities Committee was by 1958 only a shadow of its once-dread self, but Eaton had stirred up the old antagonisms. Democratic Senators Hubert Humphrey and Paul Douglas mildly reprimanded the committee for its "perhaps impetuous" and "ill-considered" action, while conceding that Eaton was too "trusting" of the Russians. The American Civil Liberties Union called the subpoena "harassment" that could "only intimidate other Americans who wish to express their opinions on controversial issues."

The *New York Daily News,* on the other hand, thought it a great idea. Which side would Eaton be on if war broke out between Russia and America? the paper asked. Herbert Brownell, the former U.S. Attorney General, told the Cleveland Bar Association that Eaton's comments were "wild and reckless." The Cleveland chapter of the Lithuanian-American Council sent Eaton a copy of J. Edgar Hoover's *Masters of Deceit.*

Not long afterward, Eaton happened to be in Washington for a dinner at the Soviet Embassy. He let the House Un-American Activities Committee know he was available—would they like to get together with him for a chat? The committee's chairman, Francis E. Walter, said he would, and arranged an informal meeting with Eaton.

It was a stormy confrontation. Eaton charged that he was being bullied, and Walter walked out, saying that his stomach could not take it. Later, he decided not to serve the subpoena. "No useful purpose can be served by permitting Mr. Eaton to repeat the groundless accusations that Iron Curtain countries have used for propaganda purposes," Walter said. Neither he nor anyone else on the committee relished the thought of taking on, before the public, the eloquent, literate, and outraged Cyrus Eaton.

At the end of August 1958, Eaton went to Moscow for the first time in his life. He was accompanied by his new wife, a thirty-six-year-old divorcée from Cleveland, Anne Kinder Jones. A judge's daughter from good Cleveland society who had been confined to a wheelchair for years because of polio, Anne had been a classmate of Cyrus's daughters at the leading Cleveland school for young ladies, Hathaway Brown. She was attracted to Eaton and to his outspoken views, and he admired her sparkling wit and keen intellect. She served as a hostess at the various conferences at Pugwash before they were married in December 1957. Eaton was almost seventy-four.

"Cyrus and I had decided after meeting the Russians at Pugwash in 1957 that we would like to see the Soviet Union for ourselves," Anne later recalled. "This was in part because what we were hearing from them was quite different from what we were reading in the American newspapers—or anybody else's newspapers, for that matter. And so we decided to go as tourists."

But it would not be a simple tourist visit. When they boarded the plane at Idlewild Airport, they found in the seat immediately behind them the Soviet Foreign Minister, Andrei Gromyko, returning home from a U.N. meeting. The Eatons struck up a conversation with him. The Russian knew all about Eaton. He asked him to point out Pugwash as they flew over Nova Scotia. Eaton and Gromyko talked in English long into the night.

By the time the Eatons arrived in Moscow, the Soviet government, having been apprised by Gromyko, was expecting them. To their surprise, they were met at the airport by the Soviet Minister of Agriculture, V. V. Matskevich, who escorted them to their hotel, the Sovietskaya, and was their host during their entire stay.

Matskevich took Eaton to an agricultural exhibition on the outskirts of Moscow, to a race of troikas (carriages pulled by three horses), and to steel mills. One day he asked whether Eaton would be interested in meeting Khrushchev.

"But of course," Eaton replied.

Matskevich explained that the Premier was then vacationing at the Black Sea. Eaton said he would gladly fly down to see him. No, Matskevich said, Khrushchev was so eager to meet Cyrus Eaton that he would cut short his vacation and fly to Moscow just for the occasion.

On Monday, September 1, 1958, Eaton joined Matskevich and A. I. Tulipnikov, the leading Soviet agriculture expert, for a meeting with Khrushchev in the Kremlin. They sat at a long, green-baize-covered table and spoke for about ninety minutes.

"We had an absolutely hilarious time," Eaton recalled. "I was feeling relaxed and full of fun and jokes." At the middle of the table there were bottles of mineral water, old-fashioned cut-glass goblets, chocolates, and fruit. Suddenly, in the middle of the conversation, there was a loud noise like a pistol shot. It was a bottle of mineral water exploding, its cork hitting the ceiling.

"What was that?" Khrushchev gasped.

"That was John Foster Dulles firing at us from under the table," Eaton replied, and Khrushchev roared with laughter. Eaton had good fun poking fun at his own government. He compared the State Department to "the little guy in the Artemus Ward story who said that he had outmaneuvered a big guy he was fighting until he got his eye right on the other guy's fist."

After they had finished talking, Khrushchev took Cyrus and Anne on a tour of the Kremlin, the Czar Bell, and Czar Cannon, and the several ancient cathedrals that tourists are allowed to visit. When the other sightseers (predominantly Soviet) realized that the leader of the Soviet Union was in their midst, they broke into applause. "It was sort of like having the President of the United States showing someone around Mount Vernon in the middle of a tourist group," Anne remembered.

Naturally, the meeting between Eaton and Khrushchev made sensational, front-page news around the world. *Pravda* ran a photograph of both men on its front page and an article on the meeting of the Soviet leader with "the eminent American public figure." Radio Moscow praised Eaton for his interest in "the preservation and strengthening of peace throughout the world."

The New York Times printed the same photograph on its front page. The American and the Russian seemed to be dressed in identical suits; it must have appeared to American readers that Khrushchev had put on his very best American-capitalist-aristocrat outfit. The *Times* headline read, "KHRUSHCHEV TELLS EATON THAT SOVIET WANTS PEACE." Eaton expressed his now customary assertions that the Soviet Union was interested in peace and prosperity, not expansion. He also announced that Khrushchev wanted to be invited to visit the United States to see America's farms, industries, and transportation systems. (A few years later, the conservative journal *American Mercury* angrily accused Eaton of having been "immensely" influential in securing an invitation for Khrushchev by means of the *Times* article.)

Eaton later charged the American correspondents in Moscow with attempting to distort the news of his meeting with Khrushchev. Two correspondents interviewed him, Eaton said, and returned shortly to show him how the Soviet censors had altered their stories. Eaton was astonished to read the uncensored versions—they reported that Eaton had attacked Khrushchev. Why, Eaton asked, had they written something so patently false?

"But you're an American capitalist," Eaton said one of them told him, "and we assumed you'd denounce Communism."

Eaton recalled that he then replied, "I'd never have the bad taste to say anything like that about the head of a country while in his country."

On his way back from Moscow, Eaton stopped in Austria for the third Pugwash Conference. (The second, held in Lac Beauport, Quebec, in March 1958, was mainly devoted to planning for this ambitious, larger one in Austria.) This conference was jointly sponsored by Eaton and the Austrian government. Seventy-three scientists from twenty-one countries attended. Meetings were conducted in English and Russian.

The high point of the conference was a public session in Vienna, at which fifteen thousand people packed an auditorium to hear the scientists discuss the dangers of nuclear war. Since it was in Europe, Bertrand Russell was able to drive down and participate.

Russell was scheduled to speak for ten minutes after one eminent German scientist gave his ten-minute delivery. But the German went on for forty minutes, and threatened to continue interminably. Russell turned to Eaton and stage-whispered, loudly enough for the microphones to pick up, "It's time to drop the bomb."

Eaton and his wife returned to the United States at the end of September 1958, and immediately went on the lecture circuit. He gave a series of fiery speeches titled "A Capitalist Speaks: Let's Meet the Soviets Half-Way." John Foster Dulles was "an insane fanatic," he bluntly told the National Press Club in Washington and the Cleveland City Club. "There is no use having a land of liberty," he said before the Kansas City Chamber of Commerce, "if there is no one left to enjoy it." He attacked Dulles's tirades against the Soviet Union, explaining that "the Russians do not forget criticism and are deeply hurt by insinuations made against them . . . they continue to brood over them."

He explained the Eaton theory of rapprochement to the Cleveland Advertising Club. Having sized up the Russians as one would a business competitor, he said, he had decided that the United States could make a deal with them. Many club members shunned the event, and some who went said afterward that Eaton should not have been allowed the platform. Still, as the *Plain Dealer* reported, "the audience was full of prominent, thoughtful citizens who listened so attentively you could hear a pin drop. They were there to hear him out, whether they agreed or not."

America did not know quite what to make of Cyrus Eaton. Early in 1959, two journals with entirely opposing political viewpoints ran profiles of Eaton so different that they seemed to be describing different people. On the left, the *Nation* waxed exuberant. It called Eaton a "merchant of peace" and praised his "enlightened capitalism." In the *National Review,* John Chamberlain was at once perplexed and despondent. How could this "towering figure in American industrial history" in "the great mold of the Rockefellers, the Guggenheims, the Vanderbilts, and all the other builders who were traduced by the pigmies of the Rooseveltian decade as 'robber barons,' suddenly emerge in his old age as America's Number One Fellow Traveler and Communophile?" How could Eaton swallow the entire Communist line? Chamberlain asked. After all, he argued, "If Khrushchev is really afraid of atomic war, there is no reason why the West should hurry to deal with him. If we hold the cards, why not wait?" He could only conclude that Eaton's pronouncements arose out of profound ignorance or tremendous vanity. "Father, forgive them," Chamberlain wrote of Eaton and his ilk, "for they know not what they do."

At the end of December 1958, on his seventy-fifth birthday, Eaton received from his new friend Nikita Khrushchev three matched white stallions, a two-wheeled carriage, and a sleigh—

the only authentic troika in the United States. It was accompanied by a Russian trainer and a veterinarian, who spent a week at Acadia Farms instructing the Eatons' employees in handling the horses.

No sooner had Eaton gotten the hang of driving the troika than a Soviet guest arrived at the farm for a ride and a visit—Soviet Deputy Premier Anastas Mikoyan. On January 7, he joined the Eatons for a troika ride. The Russian trainer drove, Cyrus and Anne got into the carriage seats, and Mikoyan clung to the side on a narrow running board as the horses galloped along at twenty miles an hour. "Mr. Mikoyan is the bravest man I ever heard of," Anne marveled.

This feat marked the beginning of Mikoyan's ten-day campaign across the country to pave the way for the as yet unannounced visit of Nikita Khrushchev in the fall. The Eaton estate was the natural place to launch the tour; Mikoyan knew he could count on an enthusiastic reception.

Always the good host, Eaton gave a lunch in Mikoyan's honor at the very proper, Republican, Union Club in Cleveland. The crowd that gathered outside the club was less than hospitable. They spat, hurled rocks and rotten eggs at Mikoyan's car, and chanted, *"Mik-o-yan—murderer!"*

Inside, Mikoyan told a polite audience of businessmen that he was interested in placing the biggest order for steel in the history of the world—which would not, he assured them, be used for military purposes, and for which he was prepared to pay in advance in hard cash. A number of steel industrialists made offers. Mikoyan told Eaton that it was the happiest day of his life.

But when Mikoyan reached Washington and tried to persuade the newly appointed Secretary of Commerce, Lewis Strauss, to grant export permits, he was rebuffed. Mikoyan tried to assuage Strauss with a gift of vodka and caviar, but Strauss gave him, in exchange, a copy of George Washington's Farewell Address, which warns that "national morality" cannot prevail "in exclusion of religious principle." "We won't do business with you," Strauss told him, "because you don't believe in God." It was an inflammatory remark and, as Eaton remarked when Mikoyan recounted it, "hardly tactful, to say the least."

Mikoyan appreciated Eaton's sympathy all the more after this rebuff—and probably also his steel, successfully conveyed through Canada. He proclaimed that Eaton had "become more popular in our country than any capitalist has ever been before. This is not a normal capitalist."

8

THE RULING CIRCLES

ON THE SAME TRIP, out of nostalgia more than anything else, Mikoyan paid a visit on another old friend, Averell Harriman. The two had known each other since the days of the Second World War, when Mikoyan was one of the Soviet officials in charge of receiving the trucks, tanks, and weapons Harriman was transferring. Now, in January 1959, Harriman was a political nonentity. Having been defeated just a few months earlier for reelection as Governor of New York by Nelson Rockefeller, he sat in his elegant East Side town house, the walls of which were covered with Cézannes, Rousseaus, Matisses, and Picassos, and did nothing. For the first time in his long career in government, he was out of a job. The partners at his bank, Brown Brothers Harriman, trembled that the old man might, for lack of anything else to do, come back and try to take charge.

"It was as if the earth had opened and swallowed him up," Harriman's friend Daniel Patrick Moynihan observes. "The Bronx County Democratic Party wouldn't give him a free seat at their annual dinner. A Shenango County leader wouldn't have had him to breakfast. He was finished."

Moynihan called another friend of Harriman's, Michael Forrestal, and suggested they have dinner to discuss what the ex-Governor could do now. Forrestal had been raised by Harriman after his father's suicide. He and Moynihan were worried about their old boss. They wondered what sort of job—"just a little job with a little office so he could fuss around," suggested Moynihan—they could find for him that had something to do with Russia. For if Averell Harriman was identified with anything, he was identified with the Soviet Union. He fancied himself the one American the Soviets trusted. He had after all invested in Soviet manganese mines when practically no one else of any standing was investing. More important, he had negotiated Lend-Lease aid to Russia during Stalin's desperate days after the German invasion in 1941. After that he had been Roosevelt's all-important ambassador to Moscow when it was of utmost importance that the two powers work together.

"I've seen Stalin more than any other foreigner has, you know," he once bragged with almost childlike pride. C. L. Sulzberger of *The New York Times* once asked him who he thought was the greatest of all great men of their time, and Harriman without hesitation answered Stalin. He insisted that Stalin was as powerful a leader as Churchill and Roosevelt, and more able.

After his defeat in 1958 Harriman preferred to be addressed as Governor (it was the only elected office he ever had or would hold), but without question the most exciting time of his life was his wartime service in Moscow. His fascination with Russia came partly from nostalgia for those days and partly from the curious fascination that only the richest men can feel for the regime that holds them at once in disrepute and admiration. A lot of people had thought he would make a poor ambassador to Moscow. Bernard Baruch thought he was nothing more than "a spoiled rich man's son," and Harold Ickes agreed.

But the Americans misunderstood the Soviets. Stalin once turned to Harriman in the middle of a tough negotiating session and made a reference to the Harriman manganese concession. "Well, we know you are our friend," Stalin said, "because you came to us at a time of need and were ready to cooperate with us." During the war, Russians regarded Harriman with a measure of awe. George Kennan, who served under him in the American Embassy in Moscow, writes, a touch enviously, in his memoirs that a Russian woman once remarked, "They look at him and they say to themselves: there goes a man!"

Russia's adoration for Harriman abruptly vanished in 1945, when Harriman decided that Stalin was seeking to plunder Europe, and that American journalists, who were still in the habit of praising America's wartime partner, should be warned. At the first session of the United Nations in San Francisco, Harriman held an off-the-record press conference. He told reporters that Russia was now striving for a world Communist dictatorship.

"Our objectives and the Kremlin's objectives," he said, "are irreconcilable." A few of the journalists were outraged by Harriman's warlike talk, which they considered inappropriate for someone who was at the time Ambassador to the Soviet Union. Two of them got up, announced that they would not listen to this "warmonger" anymore, and left the room. One was the newscaster Raymond Gram Swing, who came to Harriman a year later and apologized. The other was Walter Lippmann—"and he never apologized to anyone," Harriman recalls.

From then on, Stalin disliked Harriman. When Harriman was named to head the Marshall Plan in Europe, the Soviets were outraged. He was now one of their great enemies, an integral part of anti-American propaganda. Cartoons in the Soviet satire magazine, *Krokodil,* began to portray him as a symbol of evil, venal capitalism—drawings of his face resembled Al Capone's, with a large gray fedora, a menacing scowl, and a fist clenching dollar bills.

One Soviet journal of opinion published an acerbic profile of him in 1951 entitled "Averell Harriman—Warmonger." Now an influential assistant to President Truman, Harriman was cast as a singularly unsavory character:

> When this man, with a foppishness unsuited to his age and a haughty and dour visage, appears at the White House, the presidential flunkies hastily fling open all doors before him, while approaching officials quickly get out of his way, beaming the sweetest smiles.
>
> Apparently, however, he does not even notice them. He passes by indifferently without even a flicker of his eyelids, which are usually half closed.
>
> It cannot be said that he scorns people—that is not the right word. People simply do not exist for him. The whole world serves in his eyes merely as a God-given background for him, himself, William Averell Harriman, and for the narrow circles of his partners in big business, the magnates of Wall Street.

The article—only one of many similar ones that began appearing in the Soviet press especially after 1950—went on to discuss Harriman's "unshakable belief in his absolute superiority over those about him and in his mission to rule and to decide the fate of the world." It charged that Brown Brothers Harriman had helped fund Hitler, that the Second World War had made him huge profits. And when Eastern Germany and Poland came under Soviet influence after the war, the article continued, "lucrative Harriman undertakings came into the hands of the people"—so that, now, "Harriman chokes with frantic rage—the rage of a beast of prey from whose claws the desired prey has slipped."

Harriman's drastically altered status was similarly reflected in the different entries on him in the *Great Soviet Encyclopedia* over the years. The 1929 article describes "Harriman & Co." in an absolutely straightforward manner. By the 1952 edition, Harriman had become a "capital finance magnate, reactionary statesman of the U.S.A., enemy of the U.S.S.R. and countries of peoples' democracy, one of the main mongers of the third world war who strives for the establishment of supremacy of American imperialism." Words were not minced; the heady, almost fraternal days of the war had been long forgotten.

And then, in 1958, the Soviet encyclopedia was back to regarding Harriman more blandly as a "U.S. political figure, one of the leaders of the Democratic party, millionaire." A new era had begun. With the death of Stalin in 1953 and the accession of Nikita Khrushchev to the premiership in 1957, the Politburo seemed to assume a new, conciliatory tone.

From time to time, though, Khrushchev could not resist making a crack about Harriman. In 1958, for example, he ridiculed the New York State gubernatorial race between Harriman and Rockefeller. It had been a battle between "two prominent capitalist exploiters," he told the Central Committee, and "in keeping with the way things are in America, the man with the most money won." (Actually, he was not too far wrong; Rockefeller vastly outspent his tightfisted opponent.)

When, shortly after his humiliating defeat, Harriman heard that Anastas Mikoyan was planning a tour of the United States in January 1959, he wrote to Mikoyan and invited him to come to his town house and meet some prominent New Yorkers. Mikoyan, who was a close adviser to Khrushchev, probably mentioned the invitation to the Premier. With a Democratic victory in 1960 likely, it made good sense, they might have reasoned, to establish good rapport with Harriman, who was not only extremely wealthy but also probably had good contacts in the Democratic Party. How were the Soviets to know how unpopular Harriman was in the Democratic Party, even within his own state?

Moynihan and Forrestal were not alone in pondering Harriman's future; the Governor was mking plans himself. If a Democratic President was indeed elected in 1960, he would need a seasoned Soviet specialist. Perhaps Harriman would even be named Secretary of State. This would be sealed if he were able to display his expertise publicly. That could only be done if he could see Khrushchev. The first step was Mikoyan.

A small group of New Yorkers, including David Rockefeller, gathered in Harriman's town house at 16 East Eighty-first Street in New York. Mikoyan, having just met with Midwestern industrialists in Cleveland, was delighted to have the chance to meet a few Wall Street magnates. He made his standard pitch and then turned to Harriman. "Why is it that you spent so many years in the Soviet Union and have never been back there since the war to see what is going on in our country?" he asked. "I cannot understand this. Friendship should not be forgotten—it must be restored." Harriman replied that now that Nelson Rockefeller had given him some free time, he would be glad to make a trip. Mikoyan jokingly said to David Rockefeller, "Please convey my thanks to your brother for his defeat of Mr. Harriman, who can now come to Moscow and see his friends."

After the others had left, Harriman told Mikoyan that he wanted to meet with Khrushchev when he went to Russia. Mikoyan replied that it could be easily arranged. Khrushchev would be only too happy to see him.

Harriman came to Russia in the middle of May 1959, accompanied by a small retinue that included Charles W. Thayer, formerly a specialist on Soviet affairs in the State Department. Harriman had ensured that his journey would receive publicity by covering it himself, having signed contracts with the North American Newspaper Alliance for a series of syndicated newspaper articles and with Time, Inc., for a long article in *Life,* for which he was to be paid the customary fee of three thousand dollars.

For six weeks, the Harriman party traveled about the country, from Moscow, Leningrad, Stalingrad, and Yalta to Bratsk, Western Siberia, and the new agricultural regions of Kazakhstan. Everywhere he went he was interviewed by Soviet journalists. He reported proudly in his first article that within forty-eight hours of his arrival in Russia, "no less than three members of the Cabinet offered me everything from a bear hunt to a non-aggression pact. Premier Nikita S. Khrushchev, in a speech in Moldavia, publicly stated that I might go wherever I like in the Soviet Union."

He met with the mayor of Moscow to discuss the housing shortage, and visited Anastas Mikoyan in the Kremlin. Even the Kremlin, he noticed, had changed since the war. After the death of Stalin, the Kremlin had been opened to tourist groups; in the old days, only VIPs could enter. Harriman thought this symbolized a new era of openness in the Soviet Union. The people looked amazingly different as well, he reported: "On the sidewalks, instead of the formless bundles of shabby black coats that once plodded the streets, you now see neatly dressed women in bright clothing, their hair carefully brushed and their faces made up. With them hurry men in business suits that might have come from Seventh Avenue."

Khrushchev, as was his tendency, kept Harriman waiting until his last day in the country before he consented to a meeting. He summoned Harriman and Thayer to the Kremlin on June 23 for a free-wheeling conversation that was the longest Khrushchev had ever held with a foreign private citizen. It began in Khrushchev's office around noon; after an hour and a half Khrushchev invited them to drive with him to his dacha outside Moscow for dinner and more talk.

Radio Moscow broadcast news of the meeting as it proceeded. At the same time, Harrison Salisbury noted in a dispatch in *The New York Times* that "No American in recent times has received a more cordial and enthusiastic reception than Mr. Harriman" in Moscow.

The twenty-minute limousine ride was at top speed all the way. As they left the city, Khrushchev mentioned that he had read a speech by George Kennan that called for a gradual American withdrawal of troops from Europe. Kennan was an intelligent man, Khrushchev said. His ideas were good.

"Would you be willing to pull Soviet troops out of Eastern Europe?" Harriman asked.

"Under certain conditions, yes," Khrushchev said but did not elaborate. There was silence for the remainder of the ride.

At the dacha they were met by Mikoyan, Andrei Gromyko, Yuri Zhukov (the editor of *Pravda*), and Frol Kozlov (Khrushchev's deputy and heir apparent). Khrushchev announced that, in order to work up an appetite, everyone would go for a walk in the woods. After ambling along for a few minutes, Khrushchev spied a hedgehog on the path and, showing off to Harriman and Thayer, picked it up to display it to his guests.

Harriman had brought with him a yellow legal pad on which he had scribbled a few questions he wanted to ask Khrushchev. "Is K. the boss of the whole show," he had written, "or does he have to consult and be guided by military or political—? How far will K. go in risking nuclear war?" During dinner Harriman asked, as tactfully as he could, the first question. Who was really in charge? Surrounded by his aides, Khrushchev could not be as blustery as he might ordinarily have been. He assured Harriman that all decisions were made by consensus among the Politburo members. He left the distinct impression that what he really meant was that he made policy and everyone else agreed. He looked down the length of the table at Gromyko, who sat glumly at the foot, saying nothing. "Gromyko only says what we tell him to," Khrushchev announced loudly. "At the next Geneva meeting he will repeat what he has already told you. If he doesn't, we'll fire him and get someone who does."

This brought Khrushchev to the subject of the division of Berlin. He grew hostile. If America sent in tanks, he warned, "they will burn, and make no mistake about it. If you want war, you can have it, but remember it will be your war. Our rockets will fly *automatically.*"

"Automatically," the other Russians repeated solemnly.

Harriman argued that all of the United States supported the policies of President Eisenhower. Khrushchev laughed and said that the American working class had no voice in its government. This idea obsessed Khrushchev. As the night wore on, and Khrushchev proposed toast after toast with Armenian cognac ("which he drank liberally," Thayer noted), the Chairman became increasingly vociferous on the subject.

Patronizingly, as if giving a lecture, Khrushchev informed Harriman that the United States was completely controlled by tiny, powerful "ruling circles" of big businessmen. Harriman asked curiously who the members of these circles were. Khrushchev tapped his arm and smiled. "You're one of them," he said.

Harriman, that true-blue capitalist, always found the word "capitalism" odious. He several times proposed that Americans ignore the word entirely, since it was loaded with a Soviet-Marxist conception of the Western world. Once, Khrushchev ridiculed Harriman's idea in a speech before the Central Committee:

> What's true is true. Not even the most perfect chemical cleaning can wash the blood and dirt out of this black word. There is a pointed saying among the people: "You cannot wash a black dog white" [*Laughter in the hall, applause*]. One may welcome the efforts of Mr. Harriman, who has picked up a spade to dig a grave for the word "capitalism." The peoples of the capitalist countries will, however, make their own, and more correct, deductions, and will bury, not the word "capitalism," but the very capitalist system itself, rotten to the core, with all its vice. [*Stormy applause.*]

Harriman had asked Mikoyan in New York whether Khrushchev really believed a few rich men ran America, and Mikoyan said yes, because Khrushchev was "completely uneducated." "But didn't he go for a couple of years to a Communist night school?" Harriman persisted.

"Oh, that Communist school, there's nothing to that at all," Mikoyan had laughed. "That's just to teach them propaganda."

Now, at the dinner table in his dacha, Khrushchev went on for what seemed an eternity about how enormously powerful Averell Harriman was. He poked fun at the Harriman-Rockefeller contest. "We consider the choice of a Rockefeller impossible to understand," he said, "but we will let you decide for yourselves in the United States. You may have millions, but I have grandsons." Harriman started to protest that he had grandsons, too, but Khrushchev continued. "I am a miner by origin," he said, "now a Prime Minister, and that is a characteristic of this country."

"I was a plumber," Mikoyan put in. Kozlov added that he had been a "homeless waif," and Gromyko, breaking his long silence, said that he was the son of a beggar. Harriman lamely argued that he had "many contacts among working people," but Khrushchev found this notion ridiculous. He compared Harriman to Leo Tolstoy, who tried to atone for his wealth by living a simple life on his great estate. "Tolstoy wanted to till the soil like a peasant," he said, "but the peasants called him the stupid count, and said the count had worms in his backside."

Later, Khrushchev, by now fairly well inebriated, returned to world affairs. Within five to seven years, he warned, "we will be stronger than you." At the bargain price of only thirty billion dollars, he said, Russia could destroy all of Europe and the United States. "We have this possibility," he said. "I am frank because I like you as a frank capitalist. You charm us as a snake charms rabbits." He added that after he died, if a capitalist came near his grave, he would turn over—"but if you, Mr. Harriman, approach, I won't turn over."

Harriman was an exception, a *good* capitalist. This brought Khrushchev to reminiscing about the war. He confided that Stalin, when he seized Poland, realized that some of the Polish nickel mines were partly owned by Harriman interests, and felt the United States should be reimbursed. But Harriman did not know what Khrushchev was talking about. He no longer had interests in Polish mines. "Perhaps Stalin was misinformed," Khrushchev admitted.

"I know that you knew Stalin and had respect for him," he continued. "I must tell you that during the latter days of his life he became increasingly suspicious. At the end he trusted nobody. When we were called to his office, we never knew whether we would see our families again." With some understatement, he added, "You know, people can't work in that kind of an atmosphere."

Abruptly, Khrushchev turned to the subject most on his mind: a summit meeting with President Eisenhower at Camp David. What were the chances of that? Would Harriman be willing to come out publicly in favor of it?

Harriman replied that he would, that a summit meeting would be a wise idea. He then asked Khrushchev whether he would be interested in meeting the men whom he insisted were the secret rulers of America. If Khrushchev did come to the United States, perhaps he would like to come to the Harriman town house and meet the richest men in America. Khrushchev said he would most definitely be interested—provided Eisenhower invited him to visit.

It seemed as though this party would never break up. Already it was getting late, and the Russians around the table were seriously drunk. Whenever Harriman would stand up to leave, Khrushchev would order him to sit down, and then propose another toast. Once, Khrushchev looked hurt. "Why do you leave now?" he asked.

"Well, we can't keep you up too late," Harriman said in his best diplomatic manner.

"Oh, this is the early part of the evening," Khrushchev said airily, and gestured for him to sit. "The evening hasn't hardly started."

A while later, when Harriman again tried to escape, Khrushchev became stern. "Our working day is over, and we are ready to spend *all night* talking with you," he said.

Harriman began to feel desperate. There was no civil way he could escape these besotted heads of world Communism without insulting their hospitality.

Finally, as Harriman later recalled, "I'd had enough. I couldn't take it any more. Ten hours was enough." He would be firm. At 10:30, he announced he was exhausted, and he and Thayer got up and walked to the door.

Khrushchev would have none of it, and beat the Americans to the door, blocked their exit, and continued to talk, standing up, for another fifteen minutes. Harriman and Thayer were relieved when at last Khrushchev said good-night. He told them he would announce to the Soviet press only that "the conversation had taken place in a warm and friendly atmosphere." But he had one request: please, he asked, do not tell anyone about his having picked up the hedgehog in the woods earlier in the evening. Hedgehogs, he said, had a peculiar, embarrassing connotation in Russia. He did not explain, and the remark remained a mystery.

Harriman was unsure how to report to the American press on this bizarre encounter. How could he explain Khrushchev's alternately jovial and menacing remarks without mentioning the endless round of cognac toasts? How much should he make public?

He and Thayer decided to send a report of the real nature of the evening to the State Department, through the American Embassy in Moscow. Two days later, Harriman called a news conference for the Moscow correspondents of the American papers. He explained that Khrushchev, though unyielding on the question of Berlin, "had expressed his continued and firm desire for better Soviet–United States relations." He also urged that Khrushchev be invited to tour the United States. "Increased knowledge and information will help," he said. "Mystery normally encourages misunderstanding and suspicion."

But Harriman's conciliatory talk was too much for some hardliners in the State Department who had read the report of the Khrushchev meeting. Someone apparently leaked a distorted version of Thayer's notes, with an emphasis on Khrushchev's more bellicose pronouncements. Two top-notch journalists, Joseph Alsop, then a syndicated columnist, and Harry Schwartz of *The New York Times,* were given the account. On July 3, Alsop revealed Khrushchev's "crude threats" about Berlin, couched in a "brutal tone and unprintable language." "The inner circle of the American government," he wrote, "has been shaken and alarmed by the 'Hitler-like' interview." In the *Times,* Schwartz quoted an unnamed source who said, "Khrushchev was very rough in his talks with Harriman."

Time, Inc. was upset about the leak, and suspected Harriman of having supplied the information himself. They angrily demanded an additional thousand words for the *Life* article as recompense. Harriman protested that he was not the source, and they dropped their demand.

In his *Life* article, though, Harriman was now forced to be more blunt. In fact, he changed his version of the interview from the one he had told in Moscow to one of dismay. It was entitled, "My Alarming Interview with Khrushchev." The headnote called it "the full story of Khrushchev and his bullying demands." Nikita Khrushchev cannot have been pleased with the article. Alongside the article was a photograph of the Premier holding the hedgehog aloft.

Harriman told of Khrushchev's "blunt and brutal language" and "forceful and provocative talk." Khrushchev "spoke with angry emphasis," "asked contemptuously," "retorted contemptuously," "became heated," "asked hotly," "said sarcastically," and so on. Harriman even added ominously that Khrushchev "might well overplay his hand." The only solution, Harriman averred, was to invite Khrushchev to visit the United States and correct his terrifying misconceptions. Eisenhower did invite Khrushchev that summer, perhaps in part because of the calls from Harriman and Eaton and others, perhaps not. Khrushchev then told Harriman he would be pleased to meet the "ruling circles" at his house.

This was to be the best thing that happened that year to Harriman. A visit by Khrushchev would be, as David Halberstam observes in *The Best and the Brightest,* "a marvelous piece of wampum to barter with a new President."

A year later, Harriman was to employ the wampum energetically. On November 12, 1960, Harriman wrote to John F. Kennedy in Palm Beach to report on a talk he had had in New York with Alexander Korneichuk, a member of the Soviet Central Committee who was, he assured the President-elect, "quite close to Khrushchev." Korneichuk told him that Khrushchev was anxious to make a fresh start. "I would like to have an opportunity to talk with you about our relations with the Soviet Union," Harriman concluded. "I would be glad to come to Palm Beach for a brief chat, if that would suit your convenience."

Three days later Harriman sent another letter to Palm Beach. The Soviet Ambassador, Mikhail Menshikov, had asked him to the Soviet Embassy, he wrote, to relay a message Khrushchev wanted to give to Kennedy. Khrushchev sought disarmament and an improvement in relations. "This message is intriguing in that it was obviously written by Khrushchev himself," Harriman told Kennedy. "During the war I found out I couldn't get anywhere on matters of importance without getting to Stalin himself. Undoubtedly the same situation exists today with Khrushchev." The implication was unmistakable: only Harriman had the necessary access to the Soviet leader.

Within six days, Harriman sent along another message from Khrushchev. Now the Premier wanted Kennedy to permit Harriman to "talk over these matters unofficially" as a representative of the incoming Democratic administration. "It would be still better," Khrushchev had written, "if Mr. Harriman were authorized to state the views of President Kennedy himself on any particular issue." Harriman reported that he had told the Soviets

> that I felt sure that President-elect Kennedy would not authorize anyone to have talks until he had assumed office. I explained that it was not customary for our President-elect to take any substantive positions during the interval between the election and inauguration. The first step in international affairs would be the appointment of the Secretary of State.

Kennedy got the hint and responded brusquely. He thanked Harriman for the messages and added, "I hope to have the chance to see you sometime soon." Eventually Kennedy gave Harriman the embarrassingly minor post of roving ambassador. The new President and his aides did not hold great affection for the old man. They ridiculed his vanity—Harriman was so vain that he refused to wear a hearing aid although he was quite deaf. Once Kennedy asked Harriman his opinion about some aspect of Soviet policy and Harriman answered, "Yes." Kennedy finally had to ask Forrestal to persuade Harriman to get a hearing aid.

Harriman wanted to be Secretary of State, but he accepted Kennedy's offer with hardly a whimper. "Kennedy would give him dirty little jobs," one diplomat recalled, "which Harriman would snatch up—he'd pack his bags and go off to the Far East or wherever." Besides vanity, Harriman had a reputation as a meddler, which his correspondence on Khrushchev did not help. "Averell has to be the bride at every wedding and the corpse at every funeral," an acquaintance once said.

On Thursday, September 17, 1959, Nikita Khrushchev, who was staying at Blair House in Washington, awoke early and boarded a special Pennsylvania Railroad train at Washington's Union Station at 8:20 A.M. He reached New York at 12:05. A half hour later, New York's Mayor Robert F. Wagner gave a luncheon in his honor at the Waldorf-Astoria.

At 5:30 in the afternoon, Khrushchev and his party, which included his son-in-law Alexei Adzhubei, his interpreter Oleg Troyanovsky, and a few others, arrived at Harriman's residence. Twenty-seven extremely well-to-do men were assembled in the large, handsome library on the second floor. Its walls were covered with splendid paintings; a large Picasso hung over the fireplace.

Positioned about the room were busts of Franklin Roosevelt, Dwight Eisenhower, and Benjamin Franklin.

How these men had come to be invited is a story in itself. A few weeks earlier, Harriman had called his friend John J. McCloy, chairman of Chase Manhattan, of the Council on Foreign Relations, and, some said, of the establishment itself, and asked him to send a list of twelve of his "business friends." McCloy furnished a list that included two Rockefellers, David and John III; Harriman apparently decided that David had seen enough of Khrushchev and scratched his name off. Harriman settled on a list of thirty-odd people, all of whom possessed or controlled assets of over one hundred million dollars, and grouped them into categories: General Business, Finance, Fabrics, Metals, and Foundations. He asked a secretary to determine the total wealth these men represented. The sum was $38.9 billion.

Among the guests invited were General David Sarnoff of R.C.A.; Philip Mosely of the Council on Foreign Relations; Herbert H. Lehman, the former Senator; Henry Heald of the Ford Foundation; Dean Rusk of the Rockefeller Foundation; and George A. Woods of the First Boston Corporation. Only one "ringer" was invited—the former Secretary of the Air Force and a senior partner of Coudert Brothers, Thomas K. Finletter, who was merely a high-powered lawyer. The day before the reception, Harriman happened to be talking with John Kenneth Galbraith, who had heard about the occasion and wanted to be invited (as a "representative of the proletariat," he said). After some arm-twisting, Harriman agreed.

Word of the Harriman Millionaire Party had gotten around. That day, Harriman received a number of telegrams. Several came from Russian émigrés who asked Harriman to persuade Khrushchev to issue exit visas for their relatives. The chairman of the Hungarian Committee of America asked him to raise the topic of the subjugation of Hungary. The Secretary of the Donut Institute in New York cabled:

> SIR NO GREATER COMMON AMERICAN TOUCH COULD BE AFFORDED PREMIER KHRUSHCHEV THAN HIS OPPORTUNITY TO MUNCH AN AMERICAN DOUGHNUT. SUCH A PHOTOGRAPH WOULD MERIT MOST UNUSUAL INTERNATIONAL HUMAN INTEREST FRONT PAGE SPACE.

Harriman ignored the messages.

He, his wife, and his daughter greeted the Russians at the door and led them upstairs. The Americans were seated in a large, elongated circle, and Harriman took the guest of honor around to be introduced to each one. Halfway through he spotted Herbert Lehman, who had been the chief of UNRRA operations in Europe after the war—Khrushchev was at the time in charge of receiving the shipments in the Ukraine—and embraced him, calling him "my boss." He shook Henry Heald's hand without interest until he realized that this was the president of the Ford Foundation—and then he shook hands again, saying, "Oh, Mr. Heald of the *Ford* Foundation."

Khrushchev took his seat in front of the fireplace, next to Harriman, and refused an offer of vodka because it was not Russian.

Harriman then offered New York State brandy, which was, he said, "mild, like the Armenian type Mikoyan enjoys." Khrushchev took a small glass, but refused an offer of Russian caviar. Especially sensitive to the image he projected before these men, Khrushchev probably preferred not to propagate the notion that Communist leaders regularly dine on caviar.

Harriman gave a little introductory speech, explaining that the guests represented both political parties, many industries and professions, and all were united in support of Eisenhower's foreign policy. All would support any moves Eisenhower might make to relax tensions between Russia and America, he said, and such moves would certainly be honored by any Democratic administration that might follow.

Khrushchev interjected that he could not really tell the difference between Republicans and Democrats and then, musing aloud that the remark might constitute "interference in your internal affairs," apologized. He looked around the room and declared, "You rule America. You are the ruling circle. I don't believe in any other view. You are clever. You stay in the shadows and have your representatives, men without capital, who figure on the stage." The Americans appeared stunned. Khrushchev went on, softening his words. "You have your system and we have ours," he said. "Much depends on your policy, and we want an understanding with you so that relations will improve."

The leader of the Bolshevik clique, addressing the presumably all-powerful capitalist clique, suddenly appeared confused. "The ruling group *is* a secret one, isn't it?" he asked.

After laughing off Khrushchev's question, Harriman suggested that, since the Premier would have to answer so many questions on his visit, perhaps he would prefer to ask them instead. Wary that he would only receive thirty miniature lectures on capitalism, Khrushchev declined. The lectures came anyway, in question form—great, windy speeches disavowing Communist sympathies, expressing faith in American free enterprise, and making heavy-handed points. McCloy spoke first, with a discourse on the powerlessness of Wall Street. Any piece of legislation Wall Street supported, he said, was automatically rejected in Congress.

Khrushchev was unsympathetic. "It appears that I have before me America's poor relations," he said, and everyone in the room broke into laughter. He had made his point.

The next broadside came from the chairman of General Dynamics, Frank Pace, who described his rise from rags (a farm in Arkansas) to riches (chief executive of a giant corporation). He assured Khrushchev that he would gladly disband General Dynamics' military business if it would bring peace to the world. (Later, in fact, General Dynamics saved itself from bankruptcy by expanding its weapons operations.)

David Sarnoff, the Russian-born head of R.C.A., followed with a twenty-minute sermon, the main point of which seemed to have been that the Soviet Union should adopt American-style television programming. "You want to propagandize us," Khrushchev said. Sarnoff argued that he wanted simply a "free interchange of information such as we are having in this room." Khrushchev retorted only that Russian tastes were different from American ones, and that "Things have changed in Minsk since you were a boy."

Khrushchev then had the tactlessness to make a crack against *both* the United States and American business. "You must concede that the Soviet Union and other socialist countries are lost forever to the capitalist world," he said. "You had better write off the socialist countries from your balance sheet."

The businessmen were enraged. "Are you ready to write off the rest of the world from *your* balance sheet?" McCloy burst out.

"We have never put it on our balance sheet," Khrushchev said.

Harriman interrupted, "But it is on your *future* balance sheet."

"My balance sheet," Khrushchev replied sourly, "is restricted to the Soviet Union."

After about ninety minutes of such vapid interchange, the meeting between the leaders of the capitalist and Communist worlds broke up. Harriman later recalled in *Life* magazine that he thought Khrushchev's concept of American businessmen "was a bit dented" by this encounter. It probably was. Alexei Adzhubei described the meeting a few days later in *Izvestiya,* remarking with disappointment that the great capitalists had been "deliberately attired in everyday suits"—presumably instead of top hat, white tie, and tails.

Many of the Americans came away disenchanted as well. Herbert Lehman told Harriman afterward that he was "not much encouraged by either the answers or the attitude of Mr. Khrushchev." Another businessman present anonymously supplied the Central Intelligence Agency with a "personality sketch" of Khrushchev that was garnered from the Harriman cocktail party; he found the Premier "very tired," "less alert than usual," and "repeatedly fumbling for words."

But the two ringers, Galbraith and Finletter, were more impressed. As they walked out of the meeting, avoiding the crowd of newsmen and photographers, Finletter asked, "Do you have any doubt as to who was the smartest man in there tonight?"

Nikita Khrushchev returned to the Waldorf-Astoria that evening for a dinner sponsored by the Economic Club of New York. The atmosphere was even more hostile than at the Harriman reception. Henry Cabot Lodge, Khrushchev's official escort, read him a stern lesson on capitalism. Hecklers from time to time shouted Khrushchev down. When the outcries grew too loud, Khrushchev threatened to leave. At one point, the two thousand dinner guests in the Grand Ballroom rose spontaneously, placed hands across their chests, and sang, with defiant patriotic fervor, "The Star-Spangled Banner."

Sitting on the dais, Harriman doodled on his blue rag-paper program throughout Khrushchev's speech. On the back he sketched "COMMUNISM" in large block letters, on the front a passable rendering of a horse, and inside the front cover a phrase Khrushchev seemed to utter almost all the time: "Ruling Circles."

In the course of his largely genial talk, Khrushchev revealed that he had offered Averell Harriman, when he came to visit in June, the post of economic adviser to the Soviet government. He explained that Harriman, now unemployed, might find the perquisites tempting—a good salary and a nice dacha not far from Moscow.

Khrushchev then looked around at the Economic Club members and their guests and announced that the offer stood for anyone in the audience who wanted to "lend his hand at building socialism." The pay would be just as good as in the United States. Interested parties should, he said, just give him a call at his suite at the Waldorf. The capitalists roared with laughter.

9

THE RETURN OF THE "PRODIGAL SON"

When Khrushchev returned to the United States in September 1960 to attend a session of the United Nations, he found the time to drive out to Hyde Park, New York, for a reception in his honor given by Eleanor Roosevelt. There he made the acquaintance of a man whose family had once been extremely important in Moscow—Victor Hammer. This meeting marked the beginning of the Hammers' return to the peculiar status they had once enjoyed.

It was most convenient that Victor knew Mrs. Roosevelt well enough to be invited. He and his brother Armand had cultivated the relationship over the course of many years, and it had paid off. The relationship had, in fact, been advantageous to the Hammers for years. Armand had seen Franklin Roosevelt only once, and despite a steady stream of letters and gifts, knew Eleanor Roosevelt only slightly until he and Victor struck up an acquaintance with her son Elliott. Friends of the Roosevelt family tell that Elliott was often short of money, and Armand Hammer came to his aid several times with loans or outright gifts. At the same time, he and Victor made it clear to Elliott that the Hammer Galleries would be the ideal agent to dispose of whatever Roosevelt family items Elliott wanted to sell.

Elliott took up the offer several times. In the early fifties, he arranged with Victor to sell a precious family heirloom with which his mother had entrusted him, a silver Livingston bowl that had been crafted in Paul Revere's workshop. The bowl had been in

Eleanor's branch of the Roosevelt family for generations. Victor told Elliott that he would sell it for $22,000, keep one-third of that as commission, and pay Elliott $14,000.

When Eleanor learned that he was selling the bowl, and at such a ridiculously low price, she was incensed. She called her personal physician and close friend, Dr. David Gurewitsch, who lived in the upper two stories of her town house on East Seventy-fourth Street, and asked whether she could come up and try to figure out with him some way to block the sale.

Mrs. Roosevelt, Dr. Gurewitsch, and his wife, Edna, talked the matter over. After a while, Mrs. Roosevelt, who appeared more distressed than the Gurewitsches had ever seen her, realized that there was a technicality that might keep the bowl in the family: she had never formally recorded the gift in her income tax returns, and so had legally never given it up.

Edna Gurewitsch, an art dealer, immediately set about determining the bowl's real value. A silver expert in London told her that a Livingston bowl—he did not know it had belonged to the Roosevelts—would sell for about $60,000. Edna went for a second appraisal to a friend of hers in New York who specialized in silver. When she described it, the dealer reddened and blurted out, "Why, I'm buying that with Victor Hammer!"

Victor had arranged to purchase the bowl with this dealer and, keeping this secret from Elliott, to collect a commission on top of it. Mrs. Roosevelt, upon hearing of Victor's ruse, was even further enraged. She managed to block the sale but thereafter spoke of the Hammers with the mingling of sadness and contempt that only Eleanor Roosevelt could express.

A previous incident had raised Mrs. Roosevelt's distaste for the Hammers. In 1952 she had gone on a trip to Europe and granted Elliott power of attorney in her absence. She returned to find that Elliott had sold the Hammers her ancestral home on Campobello Island in Canada for the grand sum of seven thousand dollars. She was shocked—but since the deal had been signed, she resigned herself to the loss.

The house had been bequeathed to Eleanor by her side of the family, and it had enormous sentimental value to her. There she and Franklin had spent their honeymoon; there, in the icy waters, Franklin had been stricken with polio; and there she had often found retreat after her husband's death. She found giving it up—at any cost, and especially for seven thousand dollars—a devastating thought.

Several years later she decided she wanted to visit Campobello once more, and the Hammers gladly consented. When she arrived, she was appalled to see that the Hammers had turned it into a shoddy tourist trap—they were now charging admission and selling such souvenirs as sugar bowls and creamers emblazoned with a picture of the homestead and the legend, "The Home of President and Mrs. Franklin D. Roosevelt at Campobello."

Not only had the house been preserved exactly as she had left it, but it was now full of trophies from Franklin's past that the Hammer brothers had scrounged, things like the rowing oars from his Harvard days. Every single item in the house was labeled with tags that read, "Collection of President and Mrs. Franklin D. Roosevelt." Eleanor walked about the house, stunned, lifting up corners of carpets and looking at the backs of chairs and sofas, all of which bore the odious tags.

Later, Armand tried to sell Campobello to the U.S. government as a memorial to President Roosevelt—he even persuaded Mrs. Roosevelt to urge the Kennedy administration to purchase it—but President Kennedy was uninterested. Instead, Armand donated it to both the Canadian and the U.S. governments (a tax write-off) and presented it at an elaborate ceremony on the island in 1962. Armand, Victor, Harry, and their wives planned to stay at the homestead for the occasion, and asked Mrs. Roosevelt to come for the dedication and stay with them.

She agreed to come to Campobello, but on one condition: that they not stay in the house with her. They were to stay somewhere else and let her spend the few days there with the Gurewitsches.

Armand agreed to the condition, but when she arrived he sent over a message that the Hammers would be honored to have tea with her at the homestead. Although Mrs. Roosevelt was seriously ill (she died a few days after leaving the island), she consented. Barely strong enough to entertain, she felt obliged to receive the Hammers, since she regretted having made her dislike for them so plain. But she asked the Gurewitsches to stay away. The fewer the people, she said, the faster the visit would be.

By the early 1950s, Armand Hammer's business career had entered a decline. He was a multimillionaire, but his corporate empire was small, shaky, and owed much to his wife's assets. When in 1952 Angela demanded to see her husband's account books, the marriage rapidly began to deteriorate. It ended viciously on a July night in 1953, and a lengthy divorce trial ensued. Armand testified that on their last night together he was lying in bed, half asleep, when Angela entered the bedroom. He awoke in time, he said, to see his wife standing over him with a lit cigarette, muttering that she was going to burn his eyes out.

The next morning, Armand further charged, Angela accused him of having had "improper relations" with his employee's wife, and the two began to quarrel. She slapped his face, knocking his eyeglasses to the floor. Armand left their home in Red Bank, New Jersey, and moved into his Greenwich Village town house.

Although Armand has always maintained that he is a Unitarian, his wife apparently considered him Jewish. He charged that Angela had repeatedly called him a "dirty Jew," a "damned Jew," and a "double-crossing Jew." Once, Hammer claimed, she said, "It is too bad Hitler didn't take care of all the Jews."

Angela said that her husband had had so many affairs with other women that she was known as "The Madam of Shadow Isle." Armand charged that these and other wild accusations, and his wife's alcoholism, had so humiliated him that he had become "highly nervous, and suffered from sleeplessness and anxiety to such a degree as to require medical attention and sedation."

Angela's sister claimed that Armand could never have suffered physical illness as a result of his wife's conduct. He is "a man of boundless energy, possessed of an iron will and strong determination," she said, "and is not one whose mental and physical condition can be easily affected by other persons."

The sister recalled that once she had been with them aboard their yacht, when suddenly she heard Angela scream.

> I saw that she had been assaulted. Her eyes were blackened and her nose and face were injured. When I asked her what happened, she told me that Armand Hammer had attacked her because she had recently chided him about his undue attention to one of the female guests at a social function.

Another time, there was a violent quarrel over a "little black book"—Hammer's book of secret addresses and phone numbers connected with his business dealings—that Hammer accused his wife of stealing. Angela alleged that in an effort to force the return of the book, Armand brandished a metal pipe and threatened to "beat her brains out."

In her affidavit, Angela told that her husband had warned her not to sue him for divorce, and that if she did, Armand was prepared to "use all of his wealth and all of his power and influence to ruin and destroy me." She depicted him as devious:

> My husband possesses a cold and calculating brain. He is a master of psychological warfare. His nine years in Russia, at a time when that country was in a post-revolutionary state, replete with purgings and liquidations, together with his medical training, causes him no pain to see the suffering of others. This has been adequately illustrated to me by the hard, cruel manner in which he dealt with people in the year or two before he left me. In many conversations intimate to us, my husband would boast about the way he handled people and organizations who sought in any way to block him in his desires.

Angela sued her husband for ten million dollars, which she claimed were profits derived from her estate and livestock. But Armand insisted that he was worth no more than two million.

"My husband is a man of tremendous personal wealth," she challenged, "and [even] I have no personal knowledge of the magnitude of his fortune, his vast holdings, his security interests, and all of his other resources and the value thereof." Armand's wealth was a major issue. By the time of the trial in 1955, he had sold all of the distillery operations for more than six million dollars and sold all his cattle at auction. But he submitted copies of his income-tax returns for the years 1949 to 1952, which showed an income of no more than $25,000 a year. Dun and Bradstreet was asked to assess his fortune and could only determine vaguely that "Dr. Armand Hammer is reported to be a man of substantial personal means."

Hammer engaged some of the most expensive legal counsel in the country, including Louis Nizer, and he was able to see that Angela received a meager alimony settlement. Yet Angela was able to strike at her husband in one way that hurt deeply. She knew that he valued perhaps more than anything his handwritten letters from Lenin, now fragile and yellow with age. She hid them, and he was unable to force her to return them. Angela died on March 15, 1965; perhaps the Lenin letters were passed on to heirs. Hammer offered Angela's lawyers substantial rewards if they could track them down, but to this day the letters have not been found.

With United Distillers sold, Hammer moved from his office in the Empire State Building to the mezzanine of the Hammer Galleries on West Fifty-seventh Street. He had failed as an entrepreneur, and he was humiliated and exhausted from a long and public divorce trial. But he was only fifty-seven and, as his ex-wife's sister had said, a man of iron will.

Late in 1955 he received a letter from a wealthy widow named Frances Barrett Tolman who had read about the divorce in the lurid tabloid *Police Gazette.* Years before, when the Romanov treasures were being sold at Marshall Field's in Chicago, she had met Hammer. Now she wondered if he needed any help. Hammer took her to dinner; they were married in January 1956 and moved into the house she had just bought at 10431 Wyton Drive in Westwood, California. Hammer began casting around for a new business career.

Soon after arriving in California, Hammer heard that there was a failing oil company in which he might invest as a tax shelter. The company was Occidental Petroleum, chartered in 1920; it had not paid dividends since 1934 and was now almost bankrupt. Its stock was selling on the Los Angeles Stock Exchange for eighteen cents a share. He and Frances agreed to loan the company $120,000 to finance the drilling of two wildcat wells in Bakersfield. In exchange they would receive a 50 percent interest in the company.

The wells gave forth oil. Hammer then invested one million dollars so that Occidental could acquire leases on eleven oil fields near Los Angeles. In 1957 he negotiated for control of the company. He became president and majority stockholder of a company that still had only three employees.

He engaged the services of one of the most famous oil drillers in California, Gene Reid, and along with several other investors, he sank tens of millions of dollars into an extensive exploration program. Nothing turned up. Occidental remained a faltering company. Hammer realized that if he wanted to make real money, he would have to turn his firm into something other than an oil company. And if he built a giant multinational corporation, he knew he would be able to return in triumph to the land in which he had once enjoyed such wealth and power. For he and his brother had kept close ties with the Soviet Union.

From 1957 to 1958 Hammer owned the Mutual Broadcasting System. It proved to be moderately profitable but, perhaps more important, it brought him in contact with both Russia and Eleanor Roosevelt.

Mrs. Roosevelt had gone to Russia in the fall of 1957, accompanied by Dr. Gurewitsch, who was fluent in Russian. She arranged to meet with Nikita Khrushchev at Yalta. When the Hammers heard about the planned visit, they took marked interest.

Dr. Gurewitsch brought a portable tape recorder to the Khrushchev interview and recorded the entire two-and-a-half-hour talk. He also translated Khrushchev's Russian, while Anna Lavrova, who had served as Franklin's interpreter at Yalta twelve years earlier, translated Eleanor's English into Russian for the Premier.

When they returned, Gurewitsch was contacted by Hammer, who wanted a copy of the recording to broadcast on MBS radio. "Make sure he pays you for it," Mrs. Roosevelt told Gurewitsch. Hammer offered five hundred dollars for the use of the recording and agreed to pay an additional sum if Gurewitsch would rerecord parts of his English translation that were inaudible.

Gurewitsch took time from his medical practice to help prepare the interview. The studio sessions ran late into the night. When he had finished, Hammer refused to pay anything more than the five hundred dollars he had offered. Gurewitsch, angered, told Hammer that they had made an oral agreement "just as I do when I take on patients without contract or any other to-do."

Hammer again refused to pay anything more. When Mrs. Roosevelt heard about it several months later, she sent Hammer an angry letter that fairly oozed indignation. "I believe that you would not like to have made an arrangement which you did not fulfill," she wrote. "I am sure this has been an oversight on your part." Hammer responded that "because of my deep respect for you and my appreciation of your many kindnesses to me and to my family, I will be glad to send Dr. Gurewitsch an additional check for $100 if you feel that this is the right thing to do." Mrs. Roosevelt rejected this paltry sum, with the implication that he owed a good deal more.

Later in 1958, the Internal Revenue Service sued Hammer for $750,000 in back taxes that it claimed he owed from income received from the sale of United Distillers. Armand needed a prestigious character witness for the trial, and asked Mrs. Roosevelt, who was the most famous person he knew. She told him pointedly that she would not testify until he paid Dr. Gurewitsch—which he did. In return, Mrs. Roosevelt testified on his behalf in generous terms. "Not only do I admire him for his great service to our country in the late war," she said, "but my husband, the President, esteemed him greatly." The government reduced its demands.

Mrs. Roosevelt was nonplussed when, in June 1958, she received a peculiar call from Victor Hammer. He had an unusual favor to ask. Victor explained that he had a thirty-one-year-old son living in Moscow as a Soviet citizen, who wanted to visit the United States. But he would only be granted permission by the

Soviet authorities if he was invited by someone like Eleanor Roosevelt, whom the Soviets held in high esteem. Would she be willing to write a letter of invitation?

On June 26, 1958, she wrote to Armand Victorovich Hammer at his apartment on Krasnaya Presnya in Moscow:

> Your father tells me that you would like to visit this country and I want to invite you to come and stay with me. It would be the greatest pleasure to have you visit me and I think you would find the memorial to my husband interesting and well worth seeing.

Victor had the letter translated into Russian, certified by the Soviet embassy in Washington, and had a copy sent to Nikita Khrushchev.

Armand Victorovich's life had changed markedly since his early years as a child of American royalty in the Brown House in the late 1920s. Because he had an American father and thereby dual citizenship, he recalls, he was regarded with suspicion in the Russia of Stalin's time. His world of wealth had been shattered when the rest of the Hammers left Moscow, and he and his mother were reduced to the standard of living of ordinary Soviet citizens.

"I lived my life as if under a microscope," he says, "and I was considered a second-class citizen." It is difficult to understand why he should have been treated poorly while his father, uncle, and grandparents were doing business with the Soviet Union—for the Hammers were among the Soviet government's few links to the capitalist world—but this is the story that Armand Victorovich tells, and it is confirmed by Russian émigrés now living in the United States who knew him.

Victor continued to support his son by sending over fur coats and other items that could be sold. They were conveyed by ambassadors and other diplomats, as well as friendly newspaper correspondents. Armand Victorovich entered the Institute of Foreign Languages in Moscow in 1949 as a student in Spanish, while receiving a monthly stipend from his American father of seven hundred dollars, by Moscow standards a princely sum.

Handsome, fun-loving, and gentle, he acquired a reputation as a gilded youth. He liked to smash cars, in imitation of the daredevils in American movies whom he and his friends admired. Fellow students recall hearing rumors that Armand Victorovich was a child of the famous Hammer family that made pencils and had once lived in Moscow like landed gentry. One acquaintance remembers asking him once why he had lived through the purges of the thirties when anyone with even the remotest affiliation with foreigners was executed. "With all of your American relatives," the friend asked, "why were you spared?" Armand Victorovich seemed not to want to discuss it. "Oh, they knew about it," he said simply. "It was all right."

For some reason, he had entered the Institute at the unusually advanced age of twenty-two, while most other entering students were eighteen. There were rumors that he had spent four years in a labor camp during the war because of his uncle Armand's support of Lend-Lease. This theory is supported by high-level executives of Occidental Petroleum—perhaps to emphasize that Hammer had once broken away from the Soviet Union. Russian friends of Armand Victorovich's point out that he wore dentures even at that early age; the gossip at the Institute held that he had lost his teeth in the camps. But Armand Victorovich denies that he was imprisoned.

Upon graduation in 1953, he was assigned, like most of the Institute's graduates, to live and teach somewhere outside of Moscow. He chose a region as far from Moscow as there was: Kirghizstan, in Central Asia. There he taught in both a Russian and a Kirghiz national school and became a prominent citizen. A woman with whom he had studied at the Institute had fallen in love with him and joined him there. They were married, built a house, and bought a car.

In 1956 Nikita Khrushchev delivered his now-famous Secret Speech to the Twentieth Party Congress, denouncing the "errors" of Stalin (though omitting to mention the many "errors" with which he had himself been closely associated), and a limited thaw in the Soviet political climate began. Armand Victorovich and his wife returned to Moscow, where he got a job as an editor for a technical journal of automatic vending machines, and his wife gave birth to a girl.

Victor Hammer was overjoyed at becoming a grandfather, and he threw a party for his son and daughter-in-law in July 1956 at the Savoy Hotel in Moscow—the same hotel in which Armand had spent his first days in Moscow in 1921. If reports that Victor has had an apartment in Moscow since the war are true, this was certainly not his first meeting with his son since 1934. He made plans for his son to visit the United States. A letter from Eleanor Roosevelt, he surmised, would do it.

But it did not. There was no response to Mrs. Roosevelt's letter. Armand Victorovich remained in his small apartment in one of Moscow's working-class districts while his father tried to find another way to bring him to America.

The opportunity came in 1960, when Khrushchev traveled to

New York. A year before, the Russian leader had been received in the United States with politeness if not always hospitality; now he was met everywhere with open hostility. He welcomed the chance to see Mrs. Roosevelt again and enjoy the lavish luncheon she had prepared for him and his party on October 6.

The State Department, however, disapproved of the jaunt to Hyde Park and saw to it that it was as uncomfortable as possible. They would not let Mrs. Roosevelt know how many to expect for lunch, and they scheduled an appearance at the United Nations in the early afternoon so that the Premier would not be able to enjoy Mrs. Roosevelt's buffet.

Khrushchev placed a floral wreath on FDR's grave that bore the inscription, "To the outstanding statesman of the United States of America—the great champion of progress and peace among peoples," and stood by the gravesite for a few minutes in solemn silence. After leading Khrushchev through the library, Mrs. Roosevelt brought him and the others to her cottage for an exchange of champagne toasts.

She proposed a toast of friendship between the two nations. Khrushchev accepted it and, noticing a champagne glass in his wife's hands, remarked, "They call me a dictator. You see how little power I have? I told my wife not to drink any alcohol and in front of me she takes champagne."

Victor Hammer had pressed Mrs. Roosevelt for an invitation to this affair, which she extended. He would not have missed it for anything, for he hoped to ask Khrushchev a favor.

After the round of toasts, Mrs. Roosevelt brought Victor up to the Premier and said, "I would like to introduce Victor Hammer." They shook hands. The name meant nothing to Khrushchev. Victor gave him a small jade key ring and said in Russian, "Do you remember Hammer pencils?"

"Of course," Khrushchev replied.

"Well, that's me. I'm one of those Hammers." He rapidly explained that he had a son in Russia named Armand Hammer who very much wanted to see the United States. "You may remember that Mrs. Roosevelt sent you a letter inviting him," he said.

Khrushchev said he had never seen such a letter and that if Hammer wanted his son to visit it could be arranged. He walked over to the nearest telephone, picked it up, and asked to be connected to Ambassador Menshikov in Washington. When Menshikov got on the line, Khrushchev barked an order for a visa to be issued without delay for Armand Victorovich Hammer. Then he slammed down the receiver. Victor thanked him profusely.

After Khrushchev went on to talk to others, Victor slipped away and entered Mrs. Roosevelt's private study, believing that he was unnoticed—although, out of his view, Edna Gurewitsch was lying on the couch resting. He dialed a long-distance telephone number and asked for *New York Post* columnist Leonard Lyons. Victor described Khrushchev's visit to Hyde Park, with a special emphasis on Khrushchev's conversation with both Mrs. Roosevelt and Victor Hammer. Lyons's column, "In the Lyons Den," featured the item that evening. From then on, Victor realized, he and his brother were going to be known as special friends of the Soviet leader.

Within two days, Armand Victorovich received permission to leave Russia for a brief visit to the United States. He could leave anytime until October 16, 1960.

But the American Embassy refused to grant him a visitor's visa, Armand Victorovich says, because of the tensions that had arisen after the American U-2 spy plane was shot down over Russia on May 1. The United States would not permit Soviet citizens to visit. Instead, it would grant a permanent, emigration visa. Armand Victorovich would be allowed to come to the United States only if he planned to take up residence here. The days remaining on his Soviet visa slipped by, and the Americans were still intractable. Finally, on October 16, the embassy relented. It was too late, however; the Soviet visa had expired. But Armand Victorovich went to the Ministry of Foreign Affairs, explained the situation, and they agreed to extend his visa.

In a few days, Armand Victorovich, who had recently divorced his wife, left Moscow for Copenhagen and then Idlewild Airport in New York. He was met by his father and, as he recalls, "a tremendous crowd of my father's friends."

"It was the most exciting day of my life," he says. "After so many years of hearing about my father's country, to set foot on American soil was an enormous thrill."

Victor took his son to his large and expensively furnished Fifth Avenue apartment, and treated him to an extravagant whirl around the city—dinner at the 21 Club, flashy parties, and Broadway plays. Armand Victorovich was awestruck by America. At tea at Mrs. Roosevelt's, Victor boasted enthusiastically about the upper-crust New York life he had shown his son. "How can you compare this to Moscow?" Victor asked. At length he confided to Mrs. Roosevelt that he was trying to persuade his son to defect—simply to remain in the United States.

Armand Victorovich admits that he considered defecting and that both his mother and Victor urged him to stay in New York. But he maintains that life in the United States did not appeal to him. "I was born in Russia. My heart is in Russia; I am a Russian. Whenever I am in America I feel uncomfortable, and you cannot live like that. And I am not a *kommersant,* a businessman."

He told a friend in Moscow that living in the United States was an exertion he found unpleasant. "In America you have to work in order to get by," he said, "and in Russia you can live without working at all."

He came back from New York with a new American car and an expensive set of dentures his father had bought for him, as well as stories of how aggressive Americans all seemed to be. This type of pushy and ungenerous American alien to his nature was symbolized, he said, by his uncle Armand, whom he had come to dislike. He regaled his Russian friends with tales of Armand Hammer. Once, he said, Armand was trying to persuade Victor and him to go out somewhere in New York. It was a Sunday. But Armand Victorovich did not feel like going out, and said, "Oh, no, I'll go tomorrow instead." Armand was angry. "We have to go today," he said. "On weekends the subway fare is half-price." Here was a man with millions of dollars, Armand Victorovich would say, who was stinting on a few pennies. He could not understand that kind of mentality. No, he said, he did not want to live in the United States.

Indeed, his life in Moscow noticeably improved after his visit to America. Suddenly he had elegant American clothes and a new car, along with the fancy new teeth. He began to live as only a Russian can who has direct access to the West.

Yet there are questions about the visit that remain unanswered. Despite his disparaging comments about American life, it is likely that he could have lived a similar life of luxury working for his father in New York, and he would not even have had to work very hard. As he admits, he had no family ties to keep him in Russia.

There is a theory—admittedly unsubstantiated—advanced by some of Armand Victorovich's Russian friends that he did want to defect but Uncle Armand forbade it because a defection would damage Hammer's potentially rewarding business relationship.

"From 1930 on, I had no international business, no connection with the Russians for thirty-one years," Armand Hammer once told *Forbes* magazine. It is curious that he would disregard his Russian beer-barrel business of the thirties, his steady import of Soviet art, and his work for the Russian War Relief and the UNRRA. At least until World War II, Hammer had an *unbroken* connection with the Soviet Union. There is no evidence, however, that he had any business dealings with Russia in the immediate postwar period.

But there are clear indications that he began building Occidental Petroleum, almost immediately after taking charge of it, into a company that would be ideally suited to trade with the Soviet Union. Oil obviously was not going to save the company. Despite the millions he sank into oil exploration in 1957 and 1958, Occidental continued to lose money. In 1959 its net loss was $684,897, which Hammer blamed in the annual report on a drop in the demand for crude oil. He informed his stockholders that the company was engaged in "an effort to decrease the extent of its reliance on its oil wells" by prospecting for natural gas. The same explanation was furnished in 1960, when the loss was $127,459.

At last, in 1961, Occidental discovered gas in the San Joaquin valley, east of San Francisco. Several major oil companies, including Texaco and Standard Oil of California, had abandoned the field, but Hammer's engineer, Gene Reid, was convinced that there was gas to be found, and he was proved right.

It turned out to be the second largest gas field in California. Oxy (as the company was called on the stock exchange) stock shot up to fifteen dollars a share, and the firm was finally in the black. Hammer signed a contract to supply gas to Los Angeles's major energy company, Pacific Gas and Electric.

Natural gas, however, was then a minor source of energy. But it was used to produce ammonia, which in turn makes fertilizer. In short order Occidental acquired several major fertilizer companies. Suddenly it was a major producer and exporter of fertilizers.

Russia, with one-sixth of the world's land (much of it barren), a dismal climate, and millions of mouths to feed, desperately needed fertilizer. The Soviet leadership was making fevered attempts to reduce the country's dependence on imported grain. Hammer, who followed events in Russia closely, knew this well.

The year 1961 seemed to herald a new era in Soviet-American relations. The Kennedy administration was now in power, replacing the old Eisenhower administration, which had restricted almost all trade with Russia. The time seemed ripe for Hammer to return to Moscow.

But these were not the old days, when a Westerner could simply go to the Soviet Union and start a company. A multinational businessman who wished to do business with the Russians needed government permission. Hammer, who understood the importance of knowing the President, did not know Kennedy. This was a problem.

Years later, he told the Foreign Policy Association, "It was not until 1961, thirty-one years after I left, that my friendship with Jack Kennedy afforded me the opportunity to return to Moscow. It was three days after the President's inauguration. President Kennedy asked me to see what could be done to establish better trade relations with the U.S.S.R."

That is not how it happened. Kennedy did not know Hammer. But Hammer had a friend in the Senate with ties to the Kennedy administration: Albert Gore of Tennessee, whom he had met under a tent at a cattle auction in the early fifties. Hammer had sold him semen from his prize bull, Prince Eric, with which Gore was able to enlarge his herd of Aberdeen Angus cattle. When Gore ran for office, Hammer provided generous campaign contributions.

In January 1961, Hammer contacted Gore and told him that he planned to make a tour of eight countries, including India, Libya, and the Soviet Union, and asked if he would be willing to talk to the new Secretary of Commerce, Luther Hodges, to arrange for government endorsement. Gore agreed, and it was arranged. Not exactly a presidential imprimatur, but close enough for his purposes.

Hammer also secured several letters of introduction to the Soviet leaders. One was from Gore to Mikoyan, dated January 27, 1961. "Perhaps you may recall that Dr. Hammer was in business in the Soviet Union from 1921 to 1930," Gore wrote. "At my suggestion, Dr. Hammer is going to inquire into the opportunities for increased peaceful trade between our two countries."

Victor Hammer asked Eleanor Roosevelt to send a letter on his brother's behalf to Khrushchev. He prepared a "suggested draft" to which she could simply sign her name. She agreed to send a letter, but made a few emendations—emphasizing her sons' esteem for Hammer rather than her own.

When Hammer arrived in Rome in early February, he found Mrs. Roosevelt's letter awaiting him at the Grand Hotel. He wrote to thank her warmly: "I shall be very glad if I can be of some help to our government, remembering President Kennedy's words that we should ask what we can do to help our government and not what our government can do to help us."

Traveling as a tourist without Frances, Hammer arrived in

Moscow and on February 14 met with several ministers of foreign trade, including V. M. Vinogradov and M. N. Gribkov. He did little more than to acquaint them with "my previous experiences in the Soviet Union."

The next day, Mikoyan sent a car to take Hammer to the Ministry of Foreign Affairs. There they spoke for an hour and a half in Russian. (Hammer later said that he had "brushed up" on his Russian by seeing Russian movies in New York.) "It was a nice meeting," Hammer later told *The New Yorker*. "He got kind of sentimental." Hammer reported that they discussed Soviet repayment of the Lend-Lease debt to the United States, which was then estimated at eleven billion dollars, and spoke about whether Soviet crab meat was produced by "slave labor." Mikoyan told Hammer that he had just placed a large order for steel with the Swedish and Italian governments because the United States refused to permit the sale of steel to Russia.

Mikoyan and Hammer agreed that the Soviets should loan a group of paintings from the Hermitage in Leningrad to the National Gallery in Washington. Hammer suggested that Eleanor Roosevelt should be appointed chairman of a committee to supervise the undertaking, "in order to make it strictly noncommercial and nonpolitical," and that proceeds from admission should go to the Eleanor Roosevelt Cancer Foundation. Unfortunately, Mrs. Roosevelt did not take to the idea; when Victor had dinner with her a few weeks later to discuss it, she demurred, explaining that her association with the United Nations—she was then a delegate to the U.N. General Assembly—precluded a political undertaking.

On February 17, two days after the meeting with Mikoyan, Hammer received notice that Khrushchev would see him. He arrived at the Kremlin at six o'clock in the evening for a talk that lasted two hours and five minutes. Hammer proudly noted that he was the first American to meet with Khrushchev after Kennedy's inauguration.

They were joined by Anatoly Dobrynin, then the chief of the American Countries Division of the Ministry of Foreign Affairs and later Ambassador to the United States. The conversation was conducted entirely in Russian, Hammer claims.

A photographer snapped a picture of Hammer and Khrushchev shaking hands—Hammer, in a natty dark suit, appears to be laughing heartily, while Khrushchev, only slightly shorter though considerably wider, is smiling broadly. Later, Khrushchev gave Hammer a copy of the photograph, which he inscribed: "To Mr.

Hammer, the first concessionaire who talked to Lenin." As Hammer has repeatedly pointed out, Khrushchev never met Lenin.

The only record of the talk is a five-page memorandum that Hammer assembled from "my best recollection assisted by rough longhand notes," and later sent to the President, Mrs. Roosevelt, Albert Gore, and Luther Hodges. It is far from complete, of course. For example, Hammer does not record exactly how he described his past association with Russia to Khrushchev.

They discussed a wide range of subjects, mostly political, although Khrushchev did express his admiration for Hammer's success in breeding cattle. Good food, and especially steak, was important to Khrushchev. The Premier rhapsodized about the first steak he had seen on his visit to America. "It was so large," he said, "I thought it was for three people." He was envious. "Unless Russia can bring its steak up to American size and quality," Hammer recalls Khrushchev said, "Communism is sure to fail." Hammer explained to *The New Yorker* a year later, "He sounded to me more like a capitalist than a Communist."

Khrushchev boasted about Soviet accomplishments. They had produced from natural gas, he said, an alcohol "so pure that it can be used for drinking." He insisted that Soviet steel production was quickly outpacing American. "If some people in the U.S. think that by not trading with us they can crush us," he warned, "they are mistaken."

The Premier mentioned the U-2 incident of 1960, in which an American spy plane was downed deep in Russian territory, and after which Khrushchev had canceled the Paris summit meeting with Eisenhower. "I tried to give Mr. Eisenhower an opportunity to apologize," he said, "but when he refused I would not speak to him in Paris. Mr. Kennedy said, during the campaign, that he would have apologized. This shows that he is an honorable and clever man. However, the matter is now forgotten and we do not require an apology." After more talk of politics—and, though Hammer did not record it, probably of business—Khrushchev invited Hammer to return in the summer, to which Hammer gladly consented.

At the end of the talk, Khrushchev presented Hammer with an engraved gold automatic pencil, "in return for what you have done in establishing the first pencil factory in the U.S.S.R." The pencil was adorned with a portrait of the Kremlin and a red star that contained a small red ruby. Hammer then mentioned that he had tried to visit his old pencil factory, but Intourist would not allow it. Could the Premier do anything? he asked. Khrushchev told Dobrynin to arrange it at once.

In exchange for the automatic pencil, Hammer gave Khrushchev a copy of *Quest of the Romanoff Treasure.* He apologized for the title, which made the book sound like the story of an American's exploitation of Russia. He claimed that the publisher had chosen the title. Khrushchev complimented Hammer on the book, saying it showed "considerable understanding and farsightedness." As they parted, they wished each other *"mir i druzhba,"* peace and friendship.

At 9:30 that evening, a Soviet limousine picked up Hammer at his hotel and took him to the Sacco and Vanzetti Pencil Factory. "It was just as it was when I left it," Hammer later remarked. "The snow was falling on the factory, falling on the schoolhouse, the recreation hall. . . . It was the most romantic setting you can ever imagine."

He noticed that most of the equipment in the factory was the same that he had brought from Germany over thirty years before. Hammer was taken on a tour and then honored with a champagne, vodka, and caviar reception in the boardroom. A few of the old employees were still there, including an old woman who tactlessly pointed out that he had so aged that he was practically unrecognizable. "It was just like a prodigal son coming home," Hammer recalled.

Back at the hotel, Hammer was met by reporters from *Moscow News,* the English-language newspaper that the Soviet government publishes for foreign visitors. "Since they already knew about my visit, I felt obliged to speak to them," Hammer cautiously reported in his memo, "although I was careful to point out that I was in the U.S.S.R. as a tourist and in no official capacity whatsoever."

Hammer was extremely defensive about this trip, evidently worried that information about his lengthy involvement with the Soviet government would be dragged out. When *The New Yorker* did a "Talk of the Town" piece on him in 1962, Hammer recounted that Mikoyan had asked him, "What have you been doing since 1930, when you sold your pencil factory?" If anyone in the Soviet Union would have known the full extent of the Hammers' dealings with Russia throughout the thirties, it would have been Mikoyan. In the same interview, Hammer proudly produced a clipping from *Pravda* that reported on a speech by Khrushchev that mentioned Hammer. "When I received this American," Khrushchev is quoted in the article as saying, "he asked permission to visit the factory and look it over. He left satisfied with the factory, and several of the old workers remembered Hammer and said, 'See how our former boss is pleased!' [*Laughter in the hall.*]"

Understandably, Hammer omitted the remainder of the clipping, dated June 30, 1962. "Old timers remember," Khrushchev continued,

> that the Soviet authorities decided to lease land. . . . Now everyone sees where our leader V. I. Lenin led the country and the party! [*Tumultuous applause.*] The party correctly understood Lenin, it followed Lenin. The measure which our government took under Lenin's initiative yielded good results: it contributed to the success of socialism in our country. Was the New Economic Policy a retreat? Now it is clear to all that it was an attack by socialism on capitalism!

This would not have made good press for Hammer in the United States.

Eleanor Roosevelt was once asked whether Nikita Khrushchev would meet with her when he came to America in 1959. "He has no interest in me whatsoever," she responded. "I have no power. That gentleman likes power." She was partly wrong; she did have political influence in the United States, and Khrushchev, who appreciated that, did meet with her. But her main point was correct: Khrushchev preferred powerful friends.

Hammer knew this, and so, immediately upon returning to the United States, he set about obtaining an appointment with the President. At first he attempted to arrange it through Senator Gore; on February 25 Gore called Kennedy's personal secretary, Evelyn Lincoln, and reported that "a personal friend" of his had just returned from Russia, where he had had a two-hour visit with Khrushchev. He asked whether Kennedy would see this friend. But Kennedy would not. On March 6 Hammer sent the President a telegram:

> I HAVE JUST RETURNED FROM A PRIVATE TRIP TO THE USSR TO FIND OUT IF ANYTHING COULD BE DONE TO IMPROVE TRADE RELATIONS IN PEACEFUL GOODS MADE AT THE SUGGESTION OF SENATOR ALBERT GORE AND AT THE REQUEST OF SECRETARY HODGES WHO THOUGHT I COULD BE OF HELP TO OUR GOVERNMENT BECAUSE OF MY NINE YEARS EXPERIENCE DOING BUSINESS SUCCESSFULLY AS AN AMERICAN IN THE USSR.

He suggested that Kennedy read the memorandum he had sent.

Not until September 15, 1961, was Hammer able to arrange an interview with Kennedy, and then with the help of California congressman Jimmy Roosevelt. That afternoon, at four o'clock,

Roosevelt took Hammer to the White House family headquarters for an off-the-record meeting. They spoke with the President for less than fifteen minutes. It was the only time Hammer would ever see Kennedy.

Hammer stayed in close contact with Khrushchev and sent him a gift of two Angus breeding bulls and two heifers to improve Soviet beef-cattle herds. He also tried to arrange another meeting with Khrushchev later that year, but Ambassador Menshikov wrote that the Premier was sorry, but he was occupied with the Party Congress. As compensation, Menshikov gave a private dinner for Armand and Frances and Mr. and Mrs. Jimmy Roosevelt at the Soviet Embassy in Washington.

Although Hammer may have returned to Moscow the next year, not until two years later was the real substance of Hammer's February 1961 talk with Khrushchev revealed. They had made plans for a billion-dollar deal to build fertilizer plants in Russia—forty years after Hammer's similar business meeting with Lenin.

Throughout the early sixties Hammer was engaged in turning Occidental Petroleum, its name notwithstanding, into a gigantic fertilizer conglomerate. On July 1, 1963, he acquired the Best Fertilizer Company of California, which produced nitrogen fertilizers from ammonia and superphosphoric acid—one of the most effective fertilizers ever invented—out of phosphate ore. Soon Occidental bought the Jefferson Lake Sulphur Company, the third largest producer of sulphur in the country. In December 1963, the International Ore and Fertilizer Corporation, the world's largest exporter of fertilizer, became part of Occidental. Known as Interore, it distributed to fifty-nine countries such chemical fertilizers as ammonia, phosphoric acid, and anhydrous sodium sulphate.

With this production and distribution network established, Hammer acquired several giant phosphate tracts in northern Florida. In Occidental's Annual Report for 1963, Hammer hinted, "Occidental intends to expand Interore's operations and to take an active part in creating future profitable and industrial joint ventures abroad." He added that the world price of sulphur was increasing, "since the Iron Curtain countries, formerly exporters of sulphur, are now buying sulphur on the world markets." By the end of the year, sales of oil and gas earned Occidental Petroleum only $2.7 million, while fertilizer brought in $22.3 million.

Now a fertilizer king, Hammer cabled President Kennedy on

September 21, 1963, and tried to arrange an appointment to discuss an ingenious plan he had devised:

> I BELIEVE OUR ORGANIZATION WILL BE ABLE TO FURNISH AMERICAN KNOW-HOW TO HELP HUNGRY PEOPLE THROUGHOUT THE WORLD TO RAISE THEIR STANDARD OF LIVING WHICH IS THE BEST ANSWER TO COMMUNISM AND OTHER OPPRESSIVE SYSTEMS ENDANGERING PEACE. HAVE ASKED JIMMY ROOSEVELT TO REQUEST MEETING WITH YOU IN WASHINGTON NEXT WEEK TO EXPLAIN MY PLANS MORE FULLY.

Khrushchev would have been dismayed to learn that Hammer was calling Communism an "oppressive system endangering peace," but it was a transparent bid to secure Kennedy's approval for the great Soviet fertilizer enterprise he envisaged. Kennedy, however, was not persuaded, and there was no meeting.

A week after Kennedy was assassinated, Hammer sent a telegram to President Lyndon Johnson. "You can count on my support in the trying times that will be ahead of you," he told the President.

In January 1964, Armand, Harry, and Victor were invited to lunch at the White House by Johnson's assistant George Reedy to commemorate the President's signing a treaty between the United States and Canada declaring Campobello a monument to Franklin Roosevelt. Again Hammer attempted to finagle a meeting with the President to discuss his project, but it seemed impossible. On May 5, 1964, Hammer had Jimmy Roosevelt call presidential assistant Jack Valenti. "I have a very good friend," Roosevelt told him.

> He formerly owned Campobello and gave it to the Government. Two or three years ago President Kennedy sent him as a private citizen to Russia to negotiate the crabmeat controversy with Khrushchev.
>
> He has now been asked by Khrushchev to come back, and it has been approved by the Commerce Department. He is to leave at the end of May and would like to have a few minutes with the President before he goes—both to be sure it is all right to go and also for a few suggestions.

Valenti firmly replied that the President's schedule was "very pressing right now, and we do not foresee a time to arrange this." Although Hammer sent copies of *Quest of the Romanoff Treasure* to the President and several other White House staff members,

Lyndon Johnson steadfastly refused to see him. Hammer, however, would not give up.

Armand and Frances went off to Russia in early June 1964, and, accompanied by Robert Jellison of the American Embassy, met with the Minister of Culture, Yekaterina Furtseva. Hammer arranged a private art exchange. The Hammer Galleries had recently purchased the rights to exhibit the works of Grandma Moses, a painter of brightly colored "primitives" who was then 101 years old. The Pushkin Museum in Moscow would show the paintings of Grandma Moses, and in return the Hammer Galleries would exhibit the icons of a Russian painter, Pavel Korin.

On the afternoon of June 12, a Soviet limousine took Armand and Frances to meet Khrushchev at a reception for Walter Ulbricht of East Germany at the Palace of St. George in the Kremlin. Mrs. Khrushchev chatted with Frances while Hammer joined Khrushchev and Mikoyan in a corner of the room to discuss briefly the fertilizer plants. "If you are successful in this," Hammer says Khrushchev told him, "it will be much bigger than building the first pencil factory in Russia." When they had finished, the men joined their wives and Khrushchev joked that he now realized why Armand did not bring Frances in 1961: "Your husband was afraid I would steal you away from him."

Hammer then went on a tour of Lenin's office. A female guide pointed out the bronze monkey, Hammer says, and when she discovered that Hammer had presented it, the woman wept.

Hammer returned to the United States at the end of June and renewed his efforts to see President Johnson. Again he asked Jimmy Roosevelt to call Jack Valenti, but the answer was still no. Valenti called Commerce Secretary Luther Hodges to ask about Hammer, and Hodges admitted that he was "not too high on Dr. Hammer having an appointment with the President."

But Jimmy Roosevelt continued to badger Valenti, who in desperation asked LBJ's National Security Adviser, McGeorge Bundy, "What should the President do about this? Congressman Roosevelt keeps calling. This man is obviously a big contributor to him." Bundy responded with a curt note: "Pass Hammer to one or another of us on staff. P. [the President] should *not* have to see him."

Hammer did not want to see Johnson merely to collect an inscribed photograph—Jimmy Roosevelt had already taken care of that. He needed presidential approval for the government financing of his big Soviet deal. By now, though, it seemed hopeless, and he was forced to turn to the British government.

On September 26, 1964, on his way back from Moscow, he called a press conference in London. "Relatively soon," he announced, he would be signing an agreement with the Soviets to build ten chemical-fertilizer plants in Central Siberia that would produce ammonia fertilizer from Soviet reserves of natural gas in Kamchatka. Having bought several leading American fertilizer companies, he now owned the patents for this process.

The undertaking was to be financed by the British government on exceptionally easy terms—five-to-eight-year credits. The Soviets were to pay the British construction companies, Newton Chambers and the Woodall-Duckham Construction Company, 10 percent on order, 10 percent on delivery, and the rest in ten half-yearly installments. The total value of the undertaking was one billion dollars.

Strangely enough, the output of these proposed fertilizer plants would not all go to improve Soviet agriculture. As British government documents reveal, the Soviets planned to export the fertilizer in order to raise hard currency. Hammer had merely supplied the technology for the Soviet Union to turn its natural gas into gold.

A reporter asked Hammer whether there would be American objections to this deal. "I am a businessman, not a politician," Hammer replied, "and this is business." If the reporter had been around in 1922, he might have recognized this scene. Twenty-four-year-old Armand Hammer returned from Moscow that spring to announce the Allied American concession in Moscow, while insisting that he had no love for Communism.

But the American journalists did not overlook the parallel with the Lenin years, for the Soviet press had been fastidious in calling it to the West's attention. *The New York Times* correspondent Theodore Shabad noticed an article on page six of the September 26, 1964, *Izvestiya,* which described Hammer as "a man who may break the ice in trade relations between the Soviet Union and the United States." It went on:

> Soviet people of the older and middle generations probably remember the name Hammer. He was probably the first businessman from the other side of the ocean to understand the advantages of developing trade relations with the young Soviet Russia.

Lenin's suggestion to Hammer—"Someone must break the ice. Why don't you yourself take a concession?"—was quoted, followed by a thousand-word excerpt from *Quest of the Romanoff*

Treasure that described the Lenin meeting. It was clear that the Soviet government wished to point out that Lenin himself had sanctioned trade with the West.

And so it was that Armand Hammer was almost restored to the status of Russia's most favored Westerner. Were it not for turmoil in the Kremlin, it would have happened. Two weeks later Nikita Khrushchev was removed from office, replaced by Leonid Brezhnev and Alexei Kosygin, men who did not share his idea of what was best for Communism.

"I didn't see Khrushchev after he lost his job," Hammer recalled. "There's no question that the deal was scotched by his ouster." Hammer would have to wait almost eight years more to sign the deal. As usual, he was determined not to let a power struggle in the Kremlin interfere.

10

THE LAST OF THE GREAT TYCOONS

On May 19, 1960, at a press conference in Paris, Nikita Sergeyevich Khrushchev told President Dwight Eisenhower to go soak his head in a pail of milk. He railed similarly against British Prime Minister Harold Macmillan and French President Charles de Gaulle, who were waiting to meet with him in the Elysée Palace for a long planned, much vaunted summit meeting.

Eighteen days earlier, the American U-2 spy plane had been shot down above Sverdlovsk. Khrushchev demanded that the Americans formally apologize, and when Eisenhower refused, Khrushchev called off the summit, canceled Eisenhower's invitation to visit Russia, and stormed off with the rest of his delegation to their plane at Orly Airport, en route for East Berlin.

The quickly arranged festivities that greeted the Soviet delegation at Orly gave no indication that the Premier had just created an international incident. A band played as the huge crowd awaited Khrushchev. Beneath a clear blue sky, Soviet flags waved, and across the glistening expanse of white cement pavement ran several hundred feet of broad red carpet straight up the ramp of the Premier's jet.

Khrushchev arrived, and after a brief parting speech he strode down the carpet, clutching a large bouquet of red roses he had received from children of the Soviet diplomats in the French embassy. He was followed by fifty members of his party. Suddenly Khrushchev veered off the carpet, and so did his entourage.

Waiting for him beside the carpet were Cyrus and Anne Eaton. Khrushchev's face lit up, and he thrust the bouquet of roses into

Anne's arms. Dozens of flashbulbs went off as newsmen asked each other why those two Americans were there.

Cyrus Eaton was on his way to Eastern Europe, and three days earlier—before the collapse of the summit—he had received a message from Khrushchev inviting him and his wife to stop by and see him in Paris. Eaton replied that he would be delighted. But after his tirade at the Paris summit, Khrushchev radioed a dispatch to the Eatons, who were aboard an airplane over the Atlantic: if they wanted to forgo the meeting, in light of what had just happened, he would understand. Eaton replied that of course he still wanted to see Khrushchev; a spat between heads of state was not going to come between them.

The wrath of the Soviet leader that morning had mysteriously disappeared. Instead, Khrushchev was jovial and exuberant. He smilingly assured Eaton, "When Communism has triumphed in the whole world, I shall put in a good word for you." They spoke for only ten minutes. Khrushchev warned that the United States "must never permit its foreign policies to be based on prejudice or hatred of another nation"—a clear reference to George Washington's Farewell Address, which Mikoyan had been handed a few months before by the American Secretary of Commerce. Speaking of George Washington, Eaton explained that the founder of his corporation, the Chesapeake & Ohio Railroad, was in fact Washington—he had organized the Potomac Company, which built a route that later became part of the Chesapeake and Ohio Canal, whose work was taken over by the C & O. This brought Eaton to the parable about George Washington and the cherry tree. Eaton made the point that Eisenhower, thirty-three presidencies after Washington, *had* told a lie by at first denying American responsibility for the U-2 incident.

Had Cyrus Eaton been just any American, this airport rendezvous would have been dismissed as merely bad form. But Eaton was a rich, powerful businessman with an immense empire. This amicable meeting immediately after Khrushchev had wrecked the summit rankled a good many Americans.

As Eaton visited Czechoslovakia, Hungary, Poland, and East Germany, he was attacked in the United States as never before. Senator Thomas J. Dodd of Connecticut proposed that he be prosecuted under the Logan Act, a 160-year-old law, never invoked, which forbids attempts by private American citizens to influence foreign policy. "I believe this man is violating the law," Dodd said in the Senate. "I think the Attorney General ought to prosecute." Eaton, he insisted, was a "materialistic, meddlesome, evil old man."

Another Senator, Bourke B. Hickenlooper of Iowa, took the floor to agree. Eaton's "strange aberrations," he said, showed "how far the tolerance of the American people can go in the field of freedom of speech." The *Cleveland Plain Dealer* called Eaton's action "brazenly unpatriotic."

After Eaton's loud pronouncements and unseemly trysts with Soviet leaders of the past few years, the airport rendezvous seemed outrageous. When Khrushchev had come to the United States the year before, Mrs. Eaton had given a luncheon for his wife at the Sheraton-Carlton Hotel in Washington; while at the Soviet Consulate in New York, Cyrus and Nikita engaged in a private twenty-minute talk, after which Eaton proposed a toast to eternal Soviet-American friendship. On his seventy-sixth birthday on December 27, 1959, Eaton received congratulatory telegrams from several Soviet officials, including Khrushchev, who thanked him for his work toward disarmament, "the most urgent task of our time." Eaton seemed to entertain the Soviet ambassador, Mikhail Menshikov, all the time. Early in 1960, Menshikov returned to Acadia Farms to catch up on old times, see a performance of the Moscow State Symphony, and be honored at a lunch at the Union Club once again. Communists began coming to lunch at the Union Club so often that some of the more staid members griped that it should be renamed the Soviet Union Club.

Eaton was also unrestrained in his attacks on the Federal Bureau of Investigation, which set about compiling a three-thousand-page file on him. It described Eaton—"industrialist and Soviet apologist"—as "unethical and opportunist," a man "widely publicized . . . re critical statements concerning FBI and other Federal law enforcement agencies."

One secret FBI report portrayed him as

> a classic example of one who has traveled abroad under the protection of a United States passport and while abroad has made numerous statements which undoubtedly have painted a false and damaging picture of his adopted land for our foreign friends and cold war enemies. Eaton, a naturalized United States citizen and a consort of the Soviets, under the pretense of being an apostle for peace and coexistence has been most blatant in his criticism of United States foreign policy . . . and has heaped praise upon the Soviets, satellites, and their leaders.

Another FBI document reported on Eaton's meeting with "the world's top Communist, the blustering, shoe-waving Nikita Khrushchev," at Orly Airport in May 1960:

> Eaton greeted Khrushchev as the "brilliant leader of the great Soviet people" and Eaton was quoted as saying Khrushchev informed him he would put in a good word for Eaton when communism dominated the world. . . . Eaton made a statement relative to the principles of truth and integrity practiced by George Washington. . . .

After this meeting, the report continues, Eaton told *Pravda,* "I understand well Khrushchev's firm protest against many provocations and provocationary statements by irresponsible small time bureaucrats from the State Department and Pentagon." And then, in Poland a few days later, the report fumed, Eaton denounced the "folly of the United States in sponsoring general campaigns of propaganda and military moves against the communist bloc countries."

Khrushchev had undoubtedly found it convenient that Cyrus Eaton was willing to meet with him on the landing field. Having just stormed out of Paris, he needed some way to convey the message that, although offended by Eisenhower's duplicity, he was really not as bellicose as the West believed. What better way than to have a pleasant chat with a friendly American couple?

But Eisenhower believed that Khrushchev wanted an opportunity to cancel Eisenhower's visit to Russia. In his memoirs, Eisenhower asserts that the Premier feared the great popularity the American President would surely enjoy on a Soviet tour—after all, Eisenhower writes, look at how the Russians had flocked to see *Richard Nixon* in 1959! In their talk at Orly, however, Khrushchev confided to Eaton that he and a majority of the Politburo were so eager for Eisenhower's visit that they had constructed great dachas all across Russia expressly for him. General Eisenhower, Khrushchev lamented, was a war hero, and he would have received a hero's welcome. Perhaps Eisenhower would have been so charmed that he would have been converted to an apostle of "peaceful coexistence." Yet that was now dashed to pieces. Clearly, Khrushchev did not want to meet with Eisenhower, de Gaulle, and Macmillan—but he did want the rest of the world to think that he was peaceloving, the Paris incident notwithstanding.

And Eaton did his part. After returning from Eastern Europe, he told reporters at Claridge's in London that he knew Khrushchev well, and that he genuinely wanted peace. Khrushchev's scene in Paris, he told one newsman, was not intemperate, just "emphatic." "I don't feel he ever lost control," Eaton insisted. "I never saw a man more in control of his feelings and manner of speaking." He had dinner with the owner of the London *Evening Standard,* Lord Beaverbrook, and a reporter from the paper came by the next day for an interview. Khrushchev, he told the journalist, "impressed me right from the start. . . . He astonished me by the width of his information. He is hard working and widely read. I told him that if he had come to America as a boy he would have been the head of one of our greatest corporations."

Eaton returned to the United States on June 10, 1960, carrying with him his now accustomed storm of controversy. A few weeks later he flew to Pugwash to participate in a ceremony that further vexed his many opponents and may have damaged whatever remained of his public reputation as an acceptable capitalist.

Amid the skirl of bagpipes at Eaton Park on July 1—it was Canadian Dominion Day, time for the gathering of the Scottish clans in Nova Scotia—more than 2,500 people gathered to watch Cyrus Eaton be awarded the Soviet Union's greatest honor: the Lenin Peace Prize. The citation hailed him as "a public figure whose deeds are an example of courageous dedication to the lofty idea of peaceful coexistence between the peoples." Three Russians were on hand to make the award: Dmitri Skobeltsyn, the courtly physicist of the Pugwash conferences; Mikhail Menshikov, the Soviet Ambassador to the United States; and Amazasp A. Arutyunyan, Soviet Ambassador to Canada.

The gold Lenin medal glinting on his lapel, Eaton declared this was "a proud and happy moment in my life." For the world's leading Communist state to so honor "an acknowledged apostle of capitalism from the U.S.A.," he said, was "a hopeful omen for brighter days ahead." He proceeded to attack American foreign policy.

"Honored" with the Lenin Peace Prize! scoffed the *American Mercury*. At last, it said, Eaton, that "obedient and docile stooge of the Kremlin hooligans," had received "his symbolical thirty pieces of silver from the Kremlin thugs."

It was official: Cyrus Eaton was Khrushchev's favorite capitalist. The FBI noted in his file that "a confidential source" had learned two years earlier that Eaton was then "attempting to obtain official recognition in the form of an award from the Soviet Union for his contribution to world peace and understanding." According to the FBI source, Eaton, in lobbying for the prize, told the Soviets that it would "greatly strengthen his influence, especially in Canada."

When Khrushchev came to New York in September 1960, the only Americans on hand to meet his ship were the Eatons. Since the collapse of the Paris summit, official U.S. policy was to give Khrushchev the cold shoulder, but Eaton was as usual the renegade. Khrushchev attempted to secure permission from the State Department to visit Acadia Farms but was rebuffed. Instead, Eaton gave a lunch in his honor at the Hotel Biltmore in New York (Eaton was a Biltmore director).

Khrushchev rose to toast "my good old friend" and added, for the benefit of the hundreds of businessmen at the lunch: "Just as I have no intention of converting Mr. Eaton to the Communist faith, so, I hope, Mr. Eaton would not waste his time trying to turn me into a supporter of the capitalist point of view."

The crowd outside carried signs that read CYRUS EATON IS A TRAITOR. Eaton was convinced that this and other demonstrations against him were "organized and paid for by our own government. It's humiliating that this great country has to stoop to that kind of conduct." The Social Register retaliated against his untoward kindness to the leader of the Soviet Union by expunging his name from their list.

Even the Pugwash scientists turned against him. In October 1960, Eugene Rabinowitch's *Bulletin of the Atomic Scientists* published notice of the upcoming Pugwash Conference in Moscow in December, and thanked Eaton for his generosity, but noted that "As Mr. Eaton has come to play an increasingly active and controversial role in political affairs, the scientists felt that his exclusive support of their conferences may place them in the wrong light." Eaton would be welcome at the Moscow conference, the *Bulletin* continued—but not as a sole sponsor. The Pugwash scientists had fired their patron. This declaration, however, was largely fluff. Eaton did not reduce the amount of his contribution; the conferences had grown so large that other groups, chiefly the American Academy of Arts and Sciences, had assumed most of the financing.

Hurt but undaunted, Eaton took the scientists up on the offer and went to Moscow on the first of December. Although most Americans assumed that he went all the time, it was only his second visit to the Soviet Union. Eaton was an official guest of the state. He and Anne were met at Sheryemetyevo Airport by two Soviet officials, Minister V. V. Matskevich, and Yuri Zhukov (the editor of *Pravda* and chairman of the State Committee for Cultural Relations with Foreign Countries) and three leading Pugwash participants, Sir Robert Watson-Watt, A. V. Topchiev, and Dmitry Skobeltsyn (who also chaired the committee that decided on the Lenin prizes).

"Mrs. Eaton and I are happy to visit Moscow again," Eaton said at the welcoming ceremony. "We have many good friends here whom we wish to see again." Among his friends were Andrei Gromyko, whom he met in the Kremlin, Zhukov, who gave a luncheon in his honor, and Frol R. Kozlov, Secretary of the Central Committee. Mrs. Khrushchev gave a tea party in their honor, and Mrs. Eaton presented her with a Raggedy Ann doll for the Khrushchevs' new grandchild.

Khrushchev was ill and could not see Eaton, but he nevertheless ordered Eaton's photograph to appear on the front page of *Pravda* for two days in a row—an unprecedented accolade. The first photograph, on December 1, showed a pleased Eaton holding his hat and looking heavenward. "Moscow cordially welcomed as a dear friend the indefatigable American champion of peace and friendship between the peoples of the U.S.S.R. and the U.S.A.," the accompanying article said, "the most distinguished public figure in the United States."

A lot of people decided that Eaton was a crackpot. Some came to this conclusion after the Mike Wallace interview in 1958, some not until he received the Lenin Peace Prize in 1960. He lambasted J. Edgar Hoover at a time when one did not do so publicly and called John Foster Dulles an "insane fanatic" when a *Forbes* Business Leader of America would do so only privately.

Yet he was rich and well connected, and so people tended to pay attention to him. Unlike the Social Register, Cleveland's Union Club, for example, never threatened to revoke his membership, for he was the member who would from time to time bring by friends like the Duke of Windsor ("The Duke had a beautiful voice and charming manners," Eaton once said, "and he got along famously with the business people I invited to meet him").

From 1960 on, though, much of America came to consider Eaton eccentric. This change is demonstrated in the long and copious correspondence he conducted with the eminent journalist Walter Lippmann, whose thinking Eaton tried, and failed, to influence.

Shortly after the 1957 Pugwash Conference, Eaton sent Lippmann a "confidential" letter with information he had just learned about the great expansion of Russian industry. He asked whether the two might get together. "I should be only too happy to talk with you," Lippmann responded. "In fact, it would give me great pleasure to be able to meet with you." This set Eaton off on a flurry of letters to Lippmann, always enclosing one newspaper clipping or another on or about himself. It was as if to say that not *all* of his press was bad.

Some letters concerned John Foster Dulles. "I may be wrong," he wrote on April 17, 1958, "but it seems to me that Mr. Dulles visualizes himself as setting the stage for Armageddon rather than earnestly trying to work out an agreement that will enable East and West to live on the same planet in peace." Another time he declared simply, "He is misplaced as Secretary of State." Lippmann noted at the top of Eaton's letter: "No answer."

In April 1960, Eaton pressed Lippmann on the importance of coming to an "understanding with the Soviet Union, a proud and powerful country." Lippmann did not reply. A few months later, Eaton sent a copy of a letter he had mass-mailed to newspaper editors around the country. "If you were Khrushchev," it asked, "what would you say in your address to the General Assembly of the United Nations? . . . Put yourself in Khrushchev's place . . . realize that every word you utter will be suspiciously seized upon, and twisted and distorted, in the United States. . . ." Again, Lippmann gave no response.

At the end of September 1960, after his lunch for Khrushchev at the Biltmore, Eaton sent Lippmann a long, angry letter concerning the heckling he always seemed to receive. Much of it, he said, was obviously "financed by someone with ample funds, reputedly Uncle Sam." Lippmann had his assistant note at the top of the letter, perhaps for the record, "W. L. did not read this letter and said he did not want to see it." When, a week later, another Eaton missive came in, Lippmann ordered, "Don't bother to open it." He would have nothing more to do with Eaton, and eventually the letters came to a halt.

When John Kennedy came into office, Eaton sent him a letter of felicitation. Impressed by Kennedy's new President's Council on Physical Fitness, Eaton sent clippings on the fitness and all-around enthusiasm of "socialist youth." He urged Kennedy to see at first-hand their "zest for living."

Angered by State Department statements on the Soviet Union, Anne Eaton complained to the President. Kennedy's assistant, Kenneth O'Donnell, sent her letter on to State for a routine response, cautioning, "I presume this is *the* Mrs. Cyrus Eaton and the reply we make will most likely be published."

The Eatons' letters to Kennedy all received courteous, bland responses, although as time went on they were answered by staffers further and further down in the White House hierarchy. Occasionally, a baffled White House staffer would scribble across the top of an Eaton letter, "Who *is* this character?" At the same time, the White House received dozens of letters from indignant Americans, labeling the Eatons as "traitors" and demanding that they be "put out of the country."

In general it was considered politically dangerous to be associated with Eaton. But not everyone felt this way. Adlai Stevenson, while U.S. Ambassador to the United Nations, made a point to lunch with Eaton whenever Eaton returned from a visit to Russia, saying that he got far more information that way than from the entire American diplomatic corps. "Adlai thought the Russians were franker with me than with any other American," Eaton recalled.

Much of Eaton's power-brokering doubtless involved an element of vanity: he was proud of being the Russians' favorite capitalist. As a result, he disparaged any rivals to this claim. Early in 1961, he contacted a longtime acquaintance, Chester Bowles, who was Kennedy's Under Secretary of State, and urged that the Kennedy administration send someone to the Soviet Union immediately after the inauguration. Adlai Stevenson, he suggested, might be the right one, or perhaps Lyndon Johnson. He cautioned that

> it would be a serious mistake to have Averell Harriman undertake this assignment. While he could obtain admirable results from special missions to some nations, he would not be useful with the socialist countries. I could furnish convincing reasons why he is disqualified for the Soviet task, if you wanted them.

This was, of course, at the precise time that Khrushchev was urging that Harriman be named Secretary of State.

The Eatons returned to Eastern Europe in 1961, where they met with all the heads of state and experienced their customary VIP treatment. Eaton reported to Chester Bowles, "It is abundantly clear to an objective observer that Czechoslovakia, Hungary, and Bulgaria are completely committed to Communism, and that their relations with the Soviet Union are cordial and every year more mutually advantageous." Not only was it curious that he called himself an "objective observer," which he no longer seemed to be, but his assessment of the Communist world was entirely without reservation.

This latest sojourn fanned the old embers. Senator Thomas

Dodd led an attack on the Pugwash conferences, which he termed a Soviet "propaganda device." Eaton, a man of "strong and unconcealed sympathy for Soviet policies," he said, was the main conspirator. The *Toronto Financial Post,* Eaton's staunch defender, lamented this attack. "It's very sad indeed," the paper said. "It's enough to make the angels weep. It makes one doubt if the human race has sufficient brains to save itself."

Still, Dodd's opinion was widely shared. Warren Weaver of the Rockefeller Foundation once reminisced:

> I have been invited to every one of the Pugwash Conferences since the first one, and I have never gone to one and I never will go to one. . . . I was convinced that this was going to be an odd lot of people . . . and this has turned out to be a very odd lot of people.

Sir Robert Watson-Watt remembered Pugwash as "a very good idea" that "didn't work."

But there were definite, significant results of the conferences. One was the development of a specialized jargon, formulated by the American participants and picked up by the Soviets, that would make up the vocabulary of all future arms-control talks. The terms included "first strike," "second strike," "stability," "accidental war," "counterforce," and "countervalue." The leading Chinese delegate, Dr. Chou Pei Yuan, once said, "I came across the word 'deterrent' the first time at Pugwash, and I must admit that it sounded very repugnant to my ears." After Pugwash began, Soviet military and scientific journals began to employ the new terms. Soon Russians and Americans were at least speaking the same technical language—the first step in coming to any arms agreement.

A more significant result of Pugwash was that by the mid-sixties, Soviet proposals began to shift from *disarmament* to *arms control.* In his book *The Giants,* Richard Barnet of the Institute for Policy Studies writes:

> The difference is fundamental. The idea of disarmament is that both sides agree to reduce their capability to make war on each other. The theory of arms control is that both sides try to make the military environment safer—by eliminating particularly dangerous weapons, reducing the danger of accidental war, cutting costs by eliminating weapons that both sides would prefer not to build, or removing the temptation of either side to "preempt" a nuclear war by starting one.

Of course, the impassioned statements put out by the Pugwash scientists greatly encouraged forces opposed to the nuclear arms race. The 1957 manifesto attracted wide attention, as did one issued the following year, which became known as the "Vienna Declaration." The Geneva Conference of 1958, which gathered technical experts to discuss detection of nuclear weapons tests, was generally credited to Pugwash.

Bertrand Russell writes in his memoirs that "The most obvious achievement of the Pugwash movement has been the conclusion, for which it was largely responsible, of the Partial Test-Ban Treaty which forbade nuclear tests above ground in peace time. . . . It showed that East and West could work together to obtain what they wished to obtain."

Eaton's office on the thirty-sixth floor of the Terminal Tower in Cleveland looked, at first glance, like that of any other powerful industrialist. A closer inspection revealed adornments only Eaton would display. On the walls hung framed covers of such magazines as *Forbes* and *Fortune*—but alongside them hung covers of *The New Republic* and *Soviet Union.* Above the fireplace was a landscape presented by Nikita Khrushchev. In fact, all of the paintings in the room were gifts of Communist leaders. Inside the front door of his house at Acadia Farms was mounted the stuffed head of a boar that Khrushchev himself had shot.

In 1962 *Pageant* magazine listed the ten most controversial people in America. Cyrus Eaton was number eight. First was Jimmy Hoffa, although the *Cleveland Plain Dealer* insisted that Eaton should be first instead. For surviving the Depression financially, unlike many of his colleagues, Eaton was already widely disliked in Cleveland. When he became visibly identified with Khrushchev, this dislike turned to hatred. Angry Clevelanders, many of them refugees from Eastern Europe, expressed their disapproval by dumping garbage on the lawns of Acadia Farms. So much would occasionally accumulate that Eaton had to call in garbage trucks to make extra pickups.

A friend of theirs, the writer Kay Halle, remembers having lunch with Eaton at a club in Washington and overhearing acquaintances remark a bit too loud, "Look at Kay Halle with Cyrus *Eaton,* that *Communist*!" Anne Eaton, once a Cleveland socialite, was somewhat estranged after she adopted her husband's political views. "I suppose I've had more Communists to dinner than any other woman in the Western Hemisphere," she once said. This is not to say that the Eatons were exactly social outcasts. "People would criticize them, make fun of them, and say they'd have nothing to do with them," a friend in Cleveland recalled, "but no one ever turned down an invitation to the Eatons'. Their dinners were always lavish and fascinating."

But only the Soviets remained steadfast friends. When Andrei Gromyko wanted some political advice in October 1961, he invited two Americans to the Soviet U.N. Mission: Eaton and Bernard Baruch, the park-bench sage. No one thought anything of Baruch's remark that he and Gromyko were "old friends."

Eaton returned to Moscow at the age of eighty in February 1964, for his fifth and last meeting with Nikita Khrushchev. He and Anne were met at the airport by Foreign Trade Minister Nikolai S. Patolichev; he had lunch with Gromyko and met with Anastas Mikoyan for two hours. On February 17, he met with Khrushchev and the next day was interviewed for an hour on Soviet television by a panel of five journalists. Forty million Russians watched the elderly American industrialist predict that it would not be long before the United States "climbs on the bandwagon" and begins trading with Russia. At the end of the visit, excited by the attention paid him, he wrote to Chester Bowles from his suite at the Sovietskaya Hotel, "The Soviet Union is moving!"

Eight months later his friend the Premier was ousted, but Eaton maintained that he was not terribly surprised. "He had once told me, 'Your people call me a dictator. Why, my Cabinet could turn me out of office tomorrow,'" Eaton recalled. "And that's of course what happened." Like Armand Hammer, Eaton made a point of not attempting to see Khrushchev in later visits to Russia, explaining, "I wanted to keep my position with the men in power."

He did, however, stay in touch with the deposed leader. When a Soviet delegation came to Acadia Farms a few weeks after the shake-up, he asked after his old friend and was told that Khrushchev was in fine shape. In his typically outspoken way, he took the occasion of an interview with the Associated Press on his eighty-first birthday to remark acidly that at least Khrushchev was having an easier time than the defeated Republican candidate for President, Barry Goldwater.

A year after the famous interview with Mike Wallace at which the House Un-American Activities Committee took such umbrage, Eaton was again interviewed by Wallace. He was no less tendentious, though by 1959 people had ceased to be amazed by his proclamations.

Yet anyone who listened closely would have gained an enormous insight into his real views of the Soviet Union. Wallace called him "the last of the great tycoons," and then went on to ask what Mr. Eaton thought of Communism. "I have no doubt that in the beginning the Soviets had the enthusiasm that all new converts have," Eaton replied. "They thought they could sell their doctrine to the world. But as far as the Soviets are concerned today, I think their objective is to upbuild their own country and not to take on enterprises in remote parts of the world."

Wallace was not satisfied with that response, and he read from a sheet of notes:

WALLACE: Mr. Eaton, back in 1923, Nikolai Lenin announced: "First we will take Eastern Europe, then the masses of Asia, then we will encircle the United States, which will be the last bastion of capitalism. But we will not have to attack. It will fall like an overripe fruit into our hands." Would you say that history so far has proven Mr. Lenin wrong?

EATON: [*Laughing*] . . . The people who rule Russia today . . . have no such idea as Mr. Lenin entertained at that time. He was a fanatic. Stalin was a fanatic. Those years are behind us.

WALLACE: But was it not just last year that Khrushchev referred to East and West saying, "One of us must go to the grave. We do not want to go to the grave. They do not want to go to the grave. We must push them"? [*Eaton laughs*]. And was it not Mr. Khrushchev that said, "We will bury you"?

EATON: . . . We try to read into it terrible meanings to *terrify* our people, and I think one of the greatest problems in this country is the fear and terror we have of Communism because we don't have faith in our system. I have faith in our system!

Wallace asked Eaton to describe the Soviet leaders he knew well, beginning with Khrushchev:

EATON: A powerful personality, strong in body and in intellect and in will. A blunt, direct man.

WALLACE: An honest man?

EATON: I think he's not a devious man. He'll tell you what he has on his mind. And I think we can deal with him.

WALLACE: Mikoyan—who visited you at your home outside of Cleveland?

EATON: An extremely clever man with very wide experience with humanity, tremendous understanding of history.

Wallace asked whether these men were not "international cutthroats":

> EATON: I don't regard them in that light. They are trying to defend a great area which they think is subject to possible attack. . . but I think we can get along with them if we try.
>
> WALLACE: Before the Second World War, would you have been equally friendly, would you have exchanged gifts, let us say, with Adolph Hitler and Hermann Goering?
>
> EATON: Oh, no.
>
> WALLACE: What do you essentially understand is the difference between the two regimes, Mr. Eaton?
>
> EATON: I think that Hitler was an insane man. These other men, I think, are rational, and that they will be guided by reason. Whereas Hitler was a completely mad man.

But Wallace's analogy was interesting, and not entirely inappropriate. The Soviet leaders who showed Eaton such hospitality were important henchmen of that "fanatic," Stalin. When the Soviet secret police, the NKVD, held a ceremonial meeting in the Bolshoi Theatre in December 1937, Mikoyan was the main speaker. He hailed the head of the NKVD, Nikolai Yezhov, as "a talented faithful pupil of Stalin . . . beloved by the Soviet people." He continued his shower of praise by exhorting his audience: "Learn the Stalinist style of work from Comrade Yezhov, as he learned it from Comrade Stalin!" The same year, when G. K. Ordzhonikidze, a top Soviet leader, was murdered or forced to commit suicide by Stalin's agents, Mikoyan posed for a photograph with the rest of Stalin's cabal around the corpse of Ordzhonikidze, looking, as Robert Conquest writes in *The Great Terror,* "overcome with comradely sorrow." In 1950 an assistant minister was arrested and sentenced to execution; when he protested that Mikoyan would intercede on his behalf, he was shown the warrant for his arrest, signed by the entire Politburo, including Mikoyan. Khrushchev, who rose rapidly to power during Stalin's purges, was the First Party Secretary of the Ukraine, in charge of cleansing the ranks of the Party; he came to be known as the "butcher of the Ukraine." These men, accomplices in the Soviet purges of the thirties that resulted in some six to ten million deaths, were not terribly dissimilar to Adolph Hitler.

In the Wallace interview, Eaton went so far as to assert that in the nuclear age, the United States was powerless to combat Soviet aggression—and that, in fact, it *should* not do so:

WALLACE: Adlai Stevenson has warned, and I quote him, "After our experience with Communist methods in Korea, Indochina, Malaya, the Middle East . . . we should be militarily prepared to prevent the enemy from nibbling into the free world." Don't you consider this a necessity?

EATON: No. I don't think we have the military capacity to interfere with the spread of their doctrine.

WALLACE: . . . Should we sit back and let the fear of atomic war paralyze us as we constantly lose ground?

EATON: Well, anyone who has studied atomic warfare knows that in one day of all-out nuclear war, ninety percent of the people of the United States would be killed or hopelessly wounded. So that we're not going to, if we can help it, ever resort to the use of arms. . . . And it's idle to talk of anything that we might do in any country any more if Russia wants to go forward, so far as the military defense is concerned. . . . We're *gone* if we, in a military spirit, think that we can handle any other part of the world. The intercontinental missile—the hydrogen bomb—has put an end to all of that . . . if we ever carry it to the point where war starts, we're all gone. There's nothing left but dust and ashes.

Throughout the interview, whenever Wallace asked about combating the Russians, Eaton returned to this nuclear threat.

EATON: The hydrogen bomb will not convert them. All the hydrogen bomb can do is to obliterate them—

WALLACE: Well, Mr. Eaton—

EATON: —no one left to enjoy either system.

Perhaps most amazingly and—to observers of the Soviet system who believe much of Russia is oppressed by the Communist leadership—perniciously, Eaton assured Wallace that under Communism, the people of the Soviet Union are entirely contented. "I saw no signs in the Soviet Union when I was there of any pronounced objection to that form [of government] among the people. *They were happy,*" he said. "I was amazed at their happiness and their dedication to the system."

How had he come to this conclusion? As a guest of the state on all of his visits to Russia, he was flattered by long visits with the Premier and cordial receptions with Soviet officials in the Kremlin. Whatever minimal contact he had with ordinary citizens was carefully arranged. No one with the slightest complaint about Soviet life was ever allowed to disturb his happy perception; the

Russia he saw bore little relation to the land of the Soviet proletariat.

Khrushchev kept Eaton cheerfully ignorant.

Eaton infuriated much of America precisely because he was such an impeccable example of the successful capitalist, a paragon of American free enterprise. Yet he believed and affirmed the official Soviet propaganda line: the Soviet people love their system; the Soviet leaders are peace-loving and protective of their endangered bulwark; Soviet expansionism, in this nuclear age, should be met by American passivity; the triumph of Communism in at least many countries of the world is inevitable.

Certain irate Americans, including bellicose House Un-American Activities Committee members and FBI agents stung by Eaton's attacks on J. Edgar Hoover, were convinced that he was a Communist. Eaton's response was pat and unanswerable. "With my record," he would say, "I find the notion that I might be a Communist rather astonishing."

It is true that he profited from his ties with the Kremlin. Preferring to have his visits to Moscow seen as purely humanitarian, Eaton kept his business dealings secret. But throughout the fifties and sixties, the company he had founded, Tower International, which was run by his son, Cyrus Eaton, Jr., did business with such Communist nations as Hungary and Rumania, trading in textiles, leather goods, and pharmaceuticals, and constructing hotels in association with Hilton and Intercontinental.

Cyrus, Jr., explains that the role of the Eatons "is one of the best-kept secrets as far as East-West trade is concerned, and there's a very good reason for that. In the early days, before it became fashionable, none of the big companies wanted to admit that they were doing business with the Communist countries, so it was always disguised through an organization like ours. Part of the arrangement with major companies was that we kept it strictly hush-hush. But I think the Eaton group was probably the real pioneer in East-West trade in North America."

As far as the American press knew, the only business Cyrus Eaton, Sr., ever did with the Soviets was in 1971, when he sold them 350 head of Angus, Shorthorn, and Brown Swiss cattle. Though there was a good deal of other trade, it was on the order of a few million dollars a year—small change to an extremely wealthy man. It should have been expected, though, for the consummate businessman who preached the merits of East-West trade to do some of his own.

Neither the lure of money nor an affection for Communism explains Eaton's attraction to the Soviet Union. Undeniably he had good intentions, though his was the social conscience of a man who had made a spectacular fortune in ways sometimes underhanded. An inveterate iconoclast, he was sincerely concerned about the state of the world and was determined to do whatever he could about it. The more feathers he ruffled, the better.

He had, too, a strong element of vanity, which the Soviet leaders artfully played to with front-page photographs in *Pravda* and *Izvestiya,* national TV interviews, the Lenin Peace Prize, and long sessions at the green-baize-covered tables of the Kremlin. His sojourns to Moscow usually made the front page of newspapers in the United States too. He had a cause and received the attention the cause aroused.

Yet his vanity had its darker aspects. Throughout his life, for example, he campaigned actively to win the Nobel Peace Prize by sending cables to influential friends, asking them to nominate him. "I don't think he had principles, frankly, at all," recalls a recipient of such telegrams. "He masqueraded as a do-gooder. But he wanted the Nobel Peace Prize. It never occurred to me that people *campaigned* for that sort of thing, but he did. And I think Pugwash was designed for that purpose. So he wound up getting the *Lenin* Peace Prize instead. And that really bitched him: it was the only thing he could get."

In the last years of his life, as he grew deafer and more cantankerous, he became increasingly stubborn in his insistence that he was right and that everyone else around him, with the exception of his wife, was wrong. "My father was always outspoken," Cyrus, Jr., recalls, "making speeches all over the country. It reflected on the entire Eaton family, on everything I was doing, and on my children. But of course that didn't bother my father in the slightest. It made him talk all the louder and longer. And I think it's been proved that his position was correct."

He continued to travel to Communist countries almost until his death. He maintained a close friendship with Fidel Castro and spent his eighty-fifth and ninety-second birthdays in Havana. Raul Castro once spent a week with the Eatons at Deep Cove and demanded Scotch and steak at every breakfast. In November 1969, Eaton went to North Vietnam, conferred with Pham Van Dong and Le Duc Tho, and attempted singlehandedly to effect a settlement. They shared with him, somewhat reluctantly, the terms on which they would negotiate; when Eaton tried to notify the Nixon administration, Secretary of State William Rogers brushed him off. Gone were the days of influence Eaton had enjoyed when Khrushchev occupied the Kremlin, and before old age had taken its toll.

Yet the deposal of Khrushchev did not completely spell the end of Eaton's involvement with the Soviet Union. It was, in fact, seven months after the ouster that Eaton experienced the final great storm of controversy of his long and controversial life.

He had told the Associated Press on his eighty-first birthday the December before that he was planning another jaunt to Russia. The Soviet leadership, shaken by the power struggle that had removed Khrushchev, welcomed the constancy of Cyrus Eaton's friendship and, with the war now raging in Vietnam, decided to use the crusty old millionaire's visit to make a major statement.

The Eatons arrived in Moscow in the middle of May, as usual guests of the government, but unsure as to whom in the new leadership would receive them. Two Deputy Foreign Ministers asked them separately to their offices and discussed Vietnam. One of them explicitly said that the Soviets planned to increase their military involvement.

But it appeared that the top leaders were uninterested in meeting with the Eatons, and so Cyrus and Anne booked their flight home. Suddenly, the day before they were to leave, a message came from the Kremlin: Premier Alexei Kosygin would see them. Apparently, a high-level policy decision had just been made.

On Thursday, May 20, 1965, at 10:00 A.M., the Eatons arrived at Kosygin's office. Kosygin seemed extremely anxious. There was no small talk.

During the ninety-minute talk, Kosygin smiled only once: Anne was taking notes, and Kosygin complimented Cyrus on his "attractive stenographer."

"I've never been in the presence of a man so serious, so wrought up," Eaton later recalled. Kosygin spoke angrily. "We had planned to develop the relations between our countries differently from what unfortunately has happened," he warned. "We had assumed that relations would develop normally. We did not expect overnight improvement, but we did not expect deterioration."

Lyndon Johnson was a sore disappointment, he continued. The Soviets had expected peaceful trade to increase, and instead there was war in Vietnam. "We have searched for ways to avoid trouble," he said. "Countries with different systems can live without war. This is a Lenin principle." But Lyndon Johnson "is asking for war."

Kosygin told Eaton that Vietnam is only "a small, poor nation, but one that will fight until they oust the last invader." And "behind small Vietnam stand the U.S.S.R., China, and the entire socialist camp." We are not afraid of Johnson, the Russian said, "with all of his military and bombs." If Johnson did not withdraw American forces, there would be a long and awful war, and "the U.S.A. will never forgive their President."

Eaton asked whether it were true that a rift had formed between China and Russia. Kosygin angrily denied it. "That theory is completely wrong," he said. "There are some internal differences with China, all of which will be ironed out."

That afternoon, the Eatons spoke with Mikoyan for two hours. Again the topic was Vietnam. "President Johnson ought to hear from Americans who disapprove of his policy in Vietnam," Mikoyan suggested. "Suppose you make him aware of your views. He should grasp the situation himself." Eaton expressed his agreement in a typically capitalistic analogy: "We capitalists are supposed to know the difference between an asset and a liability on a balance sheet."

At the end of the talk, Mikoyan had some bad news for the Eatons that puzzled them: they were not going to have their picture on the front page of *Pravda* as was once customary. He explained that the Soviet leadership did not want to anger China by showing an "undue devotion to American capitalists." "We hope that you, as an old friend, won't take it amiss," he said. Mikoyan's explanation was something of a mystery—was it really "internal difficulties" with China that were depriving the Eatons of their niche, or was it a change in official Soviet attitude? Eaton's days as a state hero were clearly over, as a new, hard-line Politburo apparently decided that they would talk to American capitalists but not yet celebrate them openly.

On May 24 the Eatons were in Detroit, where Cyrus reported before the Economic Club on his unsettling visit. There, and at a news conference, they related the dire news about the threatened Soviet escalation. Anne seemed more upset than her husband, interrupting the news conference several times to warn that the Soviets were committed to protecting North Vietnam, and to castigate the United States for returning to the policies of Dulles "and all of that hash."

Virtually every newspaper in the country carried the Eatons' story on the front page. In response to charges that he had distorted Kosygin's remarks in order to influence U.S. policy, Eaton published Anne's transcript of the meeting. Nettled by accusations that the Soviets were using him to stir up American sentiment against the war, he fired off a letter to Walter Lippmann. "More intimately than any other American," he wrote, "I believe I know the Soviet leaders, political, military, academic, and industrial. I am sure I know what is in their minds." Lippmann never answered.

Wearily Eaton announced to reporters, "I must tell you with sadness that my life is a failure. . . . In my somber judgment, we are on the brink of a catastrophe, and unless some miracle occurs in the next month, I fear that mankind is doomed."

There was a peculiar sort of irony to Cyrus Eaton's life. Few men in America have ever been so reviled and scorned. Certainly, few men of his wealth have ever received such abuse. Had he been born twenty years later—had he become outspoken during the détente period of the seventies instead of the more tense preceding one, his life would have been far less controversial. Much less would he have seemed a dangerous freak of capitalism. But then, Cyrus Eaton relished controversy.

11

THE PRINCE OF CAPITALISM

IN THE ARCHIVES of the Chase Manhattan Bank there is an old black-and-white photograph of a youthful-looking David Rockefeller posing with Nikita Khrushchev in the Premier's wood-paneled Kremlin office. The photo is dated July 31, 1964.

The men are smiling so civilly, the encounter seems so cordial, that at first glance one would not realize that it is a historic meeting—the first appearance ever in the Kremlin of a Rockefeller, a man whose name had come to be synonymous with capitalism and had therefore been reviled by Soviet propaganda for decades. To the Soviets, the Rockefellers are not a family but a line of bloody tyrants, "the Rockefeller dynasty." They are the real rulers of the Western world. In 1957, for instance, Pravda Press in Moscow published a book on the five Rockefeller brothers—John III, Nelson, Laurance, Winthrop, and David—with the awkward title, *Ever Knee-Deep in Blood, Ever Trampling Corpses.*

David Rockefeller was forty-nine in 1964, the youngest of five famous brothers and the new president of the Chase Manhattan Bank. His temperament was noncontroversial; friends and associates characterized him as bland. His grandfather, John Davison Rockefeller, the "robber baron" who founded Standard Oil, had come to be known and widely hated as the richest man in the world who made his fortune by dint of enormous ruthlessness. To spruce up his image, he took the advice of his public-relations man, Ivy Lee, and gave out dimes to children on the street. He made a billion dollars in his lifetime and gave away half of it, leaving his only son, John D., Jr. (known as Junior), $465 million. Junior set about building a new family image in earnest by pouring an estimated $500 million into philanthropic causes. The Rockefeller name came to be an almost magical symbol of wealth, power, and largesse.

From birth David was inculcated with his father's stern ethic of the obligations of great wealth. The family was devoutly Baptist, and at breakfast David and his siblings were led by Father in prayer and were lectured in responsibility. Born on June 12, 1915, David was raised in the family's several homes. One was a town house at 10 West Fifty-fourth Street—nine stories, with a squash court, private playground, and family infirmary. There was also the family estate at Pocantico Hills, and a ninety-room "cottage" at Seal Harbor, on Mount Desert Island, Maine.

He attended the progressive Lincoln School in Morningside Heights, which had been built with Rockefeller money. There, possessed of a quiet, diffident exactness that his brothers lacked, David became interested in collecting beetles. Joseph Persico, an aide to Nelson Rockefeller, contrasts David with his brasher, political brother:

> No one associated with Nelson Rockefeller could imagine him crouched for hours over a magnifying glass and shivering inwardly at the discovery of a new species of beetle. Yet entomology was David's passion. His pleasure in identifying, organizing, classifying, seeking to find an essential order and thus a predictability in things was wholly at odds with Nelson's freewheeling improvisations.

The Rockefellers' groundsman at Pocantico, Tom Pyle, recalls several incidents that illustrate David's fussiness. Once David was escorting his future wife, Peggy McGrath, along the footpaths at Pocantico. Peggy was eating an orange and dropping the peels on the ground as they walked. When David saw what Peggy was doing, he immediately set about picking up the peels and putting the pieces in his pocket, explaining, "We never leave any litter on the grounds." Another time, shortly after they were married, Peggy asked one of the estate guards to get her a certain type of seat for her bicycle. The guard went out and got it the next day on his own time, and installed it. Peggy asked David to come out of the house, admire the seat, and reimburse the guard. It cost $2.63, and David had only single bills. He returned to the house to get the exact change.

In the fall of 1932, David entered Harvard, where he led an unremarkable undergraduate life. His only A as an undergraduate was in a graduate course in entomology he took as a freshman: a seminar on ants. Each of his four elder brothers had already entered the family business, so there was no pressure for him to do so. He was uncertain as to what to do next.

A friend of his father's, W. L. Mackenzie King, the Prime Minister of Canada, suggested that he start off by getting a Ph.D. in economics, with which he could do just about anything. David agreed, and attended the graduate school at Harvard for a year, the London School of Economics for another year, and finally the University of Chicago—which his grandfather had founded. His dissertation, "Unused Resources and Economic Waste," was remarkable because it criticized, albeit in the most desiccated academic language, monopoly—the basis of his grandfather's fortune—as "a social evil."

His mind still not made up, David went to work in the spring of 1940 for New York's Mayor Fiorello La Guardia as a factotum and eventually a fund raiser; a year later he joined the Office of Defense, Health and Welfare Services in New York, which was run by Mrs. Anna Rosenberg. In May 1942 he enlisted in the Army as a private. After a year as a file clerk, he attended Officer Candidate School, and then went to Algiers in 1943 as an intelligence officer. By the end of the war, a captain, he was an assistant military attaché in Paris, and there he polished his French and acquired an appreciation for French cuisine.

After V-J day, his uncle Winthrop Aldrich arrived in Paris and urged him to join the family bank, Chase National. In April 1946 David became assistant manager in the Chase foreign department in New York. Ironically, the desk in front of his was occupied by a man named John McLean, who was in charge of Chase's business dealings with the Soviet Union.

David's rise to the top, unsurprisingly, was swift. He became an assistant cashier, a second vice-president, and vice-president. From 1950 to 1952 he headed Chase's Latin American business and opened branches in Panama, Puerto Rico, and Cuba. In 1955 Chase National merged with the Bank of Manhattan, and Rockefeller became an executive vice-president in charge of development of the new Chase Manhattan.

On the first day of January 1961, at the age of forty-five, he assumed the presidency of the bank and chairmanship of the executive committee of the board of directors. He divided chief executive duties with the bank's chairman, George Champion. "He was, by then, totally aware of the unique power he wielded," Joseph Persico notes. "He enjoyed an access to world leaders perhaps unrivaled by any other private citizen."

"I can't imagine a more interesting job than mine, to tell you the honest truth," Rockefeller once remarked. "The bank has dealings with everything. There is no field of activity it isn't involved in. It's a springboard for whatever interests one may have in any direction—a very good platform from which to participate in the economic advancement of the world."

He rapidly became, as the *Christian Science Monitor* described him at the time, "a businessman who is listened to all over the world." In a 1965 profile in *The New Yorker,* E. J. Kahn, Jr., writes that the crowds that would greet Rockefeller when he arrived at airports "are sometimes large enough to make bystanders wonder what movie star is approaching." Whenever he visited a country, he was sure to pay a call on the head of state. "Such a gesture is expected of him," Kahn writes, "much as if he were a head of state himself."

His affinity for hobnobbing with world leaders angered some fellow bankers whose names bore less cachet. "David's always got an Emperor or Shah or some other damn person over here, and is always giving him lunches," a banker once complained. "If I went to all the lunches he gives for people like that, I'd never get any work done."

In 1961 President Kennedy—whom Rockefeller had met in London in 1938—offered him the job of Treasury Secretary. David refused, maintaining privately that as president of the Chase he had more influence than he would have in the Cabinet. Kennedy repeatedly turned to him, however, for advice on the national balance of payments and the federal budget; as a result, David became an unofficial high-level spokesman for the American business community.

Father had built Rockefeller Center, and John III had built Lincoln Center. David, too, was intent on doing his share to change the face of Manhattan; it was by now a family tradition. Among his many contributions were One Chase Manhattan Plaza, which was designed by Skidmore, Owings & Merrill and which revitalized the Wall Street area in the early sixties. Another was the World Trade Center. When that was completed and unnervingly lacking occupants, his brother, Governor Nelson Rockefeller, came to the rescue by moving a large chunk of the state bureaucracy into his brother's building complex.

The nerve center of the Rockefeller family fortune is located on the top three floors of 30 Rockefeller Plaza, known, a bit misleadingly, as Room 5600. He and his four brothers had offices there, and their staff, to avoid confusion, would call them Mr. David, Mr. Laurance, and so on. Joseph Persico was once at a Room 5600 Christmas party. He pointed to his name tag, which read, "Mr. Persico—Mr. Nelson's staff," and joked, "Ah belongs to Massa Nelson." It was an unthinkable breach of decorum. "Cold stares were turned on me," he writes. "That was not the 5600 style."

When Junior died in 1960, his office at Room 5600 was preserved as a shrine, everything left just as Father had kept it—as a reminder of the awesome responsibilities of their fortune, they said. Not only is Room 5600 the headquarters of the family's assets, but it is also where the endowments of Rockefeller University, the Rockefeller Brothers Fund, and the Rockefeller Foundation are managed.

Room 5600 also contains an index-card file of David Rockefeller's friends around the world. In 1965 they numbered twenty thousand. Among them were some of the most powerful people on earth.

Since 1954 Rockefeller had participated in a mystery-enshrouded parley of the leaders of the Western world called the Bilderberg Conference, the purpose of which was to discuss, in secrecy, international misunderstandings and problems in an unofficial setting. The founding session took place that year over a long weekend at the Hotel de Bilderberg in the Netherlands. Prince Bernhard presided over a meeting of several dozen political and business leaders. The U.S. delegation included Dean Rusk, Dean Acheson, and Christian Herter.

Less high-powered is the Dartmouth Conference, a conclave of eminent citizens of the United States and the Soviet Union founded by Norman Cousins. Then the editor of *Saturday Review,* Cousins had visited Russia on a cultural exchange and there decided that it might be useful to establish regular conferences of Americans and Russians to discuss problems of Soviet-American relations in a private and informal setting. Each side could float ideas and obtain an unofficial reaction; perhaps some of the discussion would even filter upward. President Eisenhower granted his approval, and the first meeting was held at Dartmouth College in Hanover, New Hampshire. The next year it took place in the Crimea.

The Soviet participants were, of course, not mere private citizens; in fact, they were under instruction from their government.

Similarly, the American delegates were often asked by the U.S. government, sometimes even the President, to raise certain topics discreetly and to take note of the Soviet reaction.

Cousins selected prominent Americans of high respectability, including Norton Simon, Arthur Lawton, Paul Dudley White, and John Kenneth Galbraith. Yet he needed a "kingpin," Cousins recalled. He knew Rockefeller socially (and also as *Saturday Review*'s banker), and asked him. "We wanted an outstanding businessman who was not necessarily identifed with a viewpoint towards the Soviet Union," Cousins says. He was surprised when Rockefeller said yes; it was quite a coup for the Dartmouth Conference.

"Nothing impresses a Russian more," observes Marshall Shulman, whom Cousins also selected, "than a Rockefeller as a Dartmouth participant." Soviet officials would listen closely to everything David Rockefeller had to say. "The Russians respect power," Cousins once remarked, adding:

> The epitome of capitalism is the millionaire. The Rockefeller family is the world symbol of family wealth and station. As far back as the 1930s, Joseph Davies, the U.S. ambassador to the Soviet Union, observed that Moscow loves millionaires. Some Russians tend to feel the same way about millionaires that we do about movie stars.

Moreover, Cousins feels, Rockefeller was an ideal diplomat. "David is poised, balanced, and knowledgeable," he says. "He doesn't bristle very readily. He's effective in debate. When he makes his points he does so with a minimum of rhetoric. And he has very warm human qualities."

In 1962 Rockefeller attended his first Dartmouth Conference, which was held at Andover, Massachusetts. He thought it had gone well and was a good thing. Then, in 1964, the Conference was scheduled to meet in Leningrad, but the plain fact was that no Rockefeller had ever set foot on Soviet soil. He admits that he gave a good deal of thought to whether it would be "appropriate" for him to go to Russia, and at last decided that it was, that this was a new era.

As a political force and as rulers of a financial empire, the Rockefellers had had a long and ambivalent relationship with the Soviet Union. The Chase National Bank was the

Soviet government's leading lender almost from the time of the Revolution. During the twenties, it financed Soviet imports of American cotton. When Amtorg was established in 1924, Chase agreed to handle its promissory notes and letters of credit to aid the import from Russia of fur, timber, and precious metals. In 1926 Chase advanced the Soviet government revolving credit of thirty million dollars. David Rockefeller has remarked that the Chase was "witness to the punctiliousness with which the Soviet Foreign Trade Bank honored its commitments."

A Chase vice-president, Reeve Schley, was president of the American-Russian Chamber of Commerce during the twenties. He pressed for recognition of the Soviet state and increased Soviet-American trade. Schley and Chase were widely accused of engaging in propaganda on the Soviets' behalf. During the Second World War, Chase was Amtorg's principal American bank in Lend-Lease transactions. Chase even offered to lend the Soviets money to purchase grain abroad after the war, an offer the Russians declined.

Another mighty Rockefeller institution had a more complicated involvement with the Bolsheviks. Immediately after the Revolution, Walter Teagle, a Standard Oil officer and associate of John D. Rockefeller, Jr., secretly purchased from the Nobel brothers a vast oil field in Russia for $11.5 million—even after the Red Army had expropriated the field. Teagle and the rest of the Standard Oil board waited patiently for the collapse of the Bolshevik regime. When it did not happen, and it was clear that the company was out a lot of money, Standard Oil protested. The Soviets ignored them.

Then, in 1926, there was a defection within the Standard Oil family. The Vacuum Oil Company, a subsidiary, and the Standard Oil Company of New York (which later combined to form Mobil), began buying large quantities of Soviet petroleum.

Furious, Standard Oil of New Jersey accused the two firms of being traitors. "Is it more unrighteous," the president of Vacuum Oil responded, pointing out that the United States was at the time selling cotton to Russia, "to buy from Russia than to sell to it?" For all of Standard Oil's indignation, there was a change, literally overnight, in its attitude. The day after the two renegade companies signed the contract with the Soviet government, the American press published reports that Ivy Lee, public-relations counsel both to the Rockefellers and to Standard Oil, now favored recognition of Russia. Soon after a trip to the Soviet Union, Lee published *USSR: A World Enigma,* in which he urged recognition and trade.

After the war, however, the Rockefellers came to be known as advocates of armament against the Soviet threat; in fact, they were among the leading proponents. Nelson, as an assistant to President Eisenhower, in 1955 gathered academics, including Henry Kissinger, from around the country to draft a position paper for the President that spoke of a "global" and "total" way for the United States to "seize the initiative in international affairs and articulate its long-range objectives." Only one of its points, an "Open Skies" proposal for mutual Soviet-American aerial inspection of missile sites, was accepted by Eisenhower, and by the end of the year Nelson resigned.

The following year the Rockefeller brothers assembled more than a hundred prominent Americans as a task force, "America at Mid-Century," to define the "major problems and opportunities" facing the United States. It was an illustrious group, with such celebrities as Chester Bowles, Arthur F. Burns, John W. Gardner, Theodore M. Hesburgh, Henry R. Luce, Dean Rusk, David Sarnoff, and Edward Teller.

The result was *Prospect for America,* a volume of six reports, the most important of which was Henry Kissinger's "International Security: The Military Aspect." It was published in December 1957, a few months after the Soviets fired the Sputnik artificial satellite into orbit, alarming America. The American public was prepared to be shaken by doomsday predictions, and the Rockefellers' report was rife with them:

> Ever since World War II, the United States has suffered from a tendency to underestimate the military technology of the U.S.S.R. . . . In the military field, the technological capability of the U.S.S.R. is increasing at a pace obviously faster than that of the United States. If not reversed, this trend alone will place the free world in dire jeopardy. . . . Unless present trends are reversed, the world balance of power will shift in favor of the Soviet bloc. If that should happen, we are not likely to be given another chance to remedy our failings. It is emphatically not too late, however, if we are prepared to make the big effort now and in the years ahead.

After the television host Dave Garroway discussed the "International Security" report on television, it became a best-seller; over two hundred thousand copies were sold. During the 1960 presidential campaign, the Democrats and the Republicans alike used the report in their platforms. Its influence on American politics was enormous.

The Soviets reacted with a fury so great and so swift that it seemed they had just been waiting for the chance to take aim at America's richest family, who were no longer engaged in trading with them. *Pravda* published in January 1958 a long, vitriolic attack: "The Rockefeller Doctrine—Doctrine of Aggression and War." Later in the year, the Soviet English-language magazine, *New Times,* published a sweeping, historical attack on "the Rockefeller Dynasty." It traced the history of the Rockefeller fortune—curiously omitting all mention of Chase National Bank's and Standard Oil's involvement with Russia. "The age of the decline of capitalism," the article begins, "is marked by the conversion of the leading bourgeois states into what might be called empires of the billionaires. . . . Of all the billionaire dynasties reigning in the world, the most powerful is that of the Rockefellers."

The article charged that because of the gigantic increase in the demand for oil during the Second World War, the Rockefellers made more money than they had made in the preceding fifty years. They invested the money in armaments—"instruments of death"—and thereby became the prime initiators of the Cold War.

Moreover, during the war, the Rockefellers, in concert with the Morgans and the Du Ponts, seized control of the atomic industry. The article quotes *Collier's* magazine: "Lacking Rockefeller help, the United States might have had no A-bomb in World War II or even now." In the arms race, *New Times* concludes, "the main button is pressed at 30 Rockefeller Plaza in New York."

As if these deeds were not heinous enough, *Izvestiya* asserted in December 1963 that David Rockefeller, out of an evil desire to fog the minds of Americans, was fostering the spread of abstract art through his chairmanship of the Museum of Modern Art. "At home the Rockefellers are admirers of classical art," the article said. "They pursue another policy outside their imperial palace." The reason for this was clear: "Under the Rockefellers' tutelage, abstract art is summoned to play a definite political role, to distract the attention of thinking Americans from real life and to make them stupid. If millions, or hundreds of millions, of dollars are necessary, the bosses will shell out in order to achieve that goal."

So David Rockefeller knew that he was visiting a country that was decidedly hostile to him. What might happen? Who could know, with Khrushchev in the Kremlin? "I wouldn't want to do anything disadvantageous to the country or the bank," he told a friend. "I want to make sure I do what's appropriate."

In July, shortly before the Dartmouth delegation flew to Leningrad, Norman Cousins met with McGeorge Bundy at the White House. Bundy asked Cousins to convey a few points to Khrushchev. What these were is unknown, except that Johnson wanted Khrushchev to "keep out of the election." Johnson wanted to defeat Goldwater soundly and not allow his opponent to boast of being attacked by the Russians.

David Rockefeller took along his second-oldest daughter, Neva, then a twenty-year-old junior at Radcliffe. *Neva* happens to be the name of the broad river that flows through Leningrad. She had been named for a best friend of her grandmother's who was born while her family was on vacation in St. Petersburg at the end of the nineteenth century. All of the Soviet Dartmouth participants were tickled that the daughter of the great Rockefeller was named for their river.

Cousins had been scheduled to meet with Khrushchev but found he was "too busy," he says, when the time for the appointment came. He asked Rockefeller to go in his stead. On Wednesday, July 30, David and Neva boarded the overnight train to Moscow.

Rockefeller had met Anastas Mikoyan at Averell Harriman's house in January 1959, but he was not the first Rockefeller to have met Khrushchev. That distinction belonged to Nelson. In 1955 Nelson had traveled with President Eisenhower to the Big Four Foreign Ministers Conference in Geneva, where he was introduced to Khrushchev. "So this is Mr. Rockefeller himself!" Khrushchev had exclaimed, and playfully poked his fists into Rockefeller's ribs. Nelson took it all in good fun and returned the poke. "There was nothing special about him as far as I could tell," Khrushchev observed seriously in his memoirs. "He was dressed fairly democratically."

Nelson and Nikita met again when Khrushchev visited New York in September 1959. As Governor of New York, Rockefeller paid his respects to Khrushchev in his suite at the Waldorf-Astoria.

"I went in alone," Nelson recalled. "He must have had seventeen people with him, his children, two psychiatrists. They sort of wanted to study me." Knowing that Nelson did not drink hard liquor, they had provided him with soft drinks.

"I want to propose a toast of coexistence," Khrushchev had declared.

"I won't drink to that," Rockefeller replied. "I don't believe in it."

"What do you mean you don't believe in it?"

Rockefeller replied with an attack on Soviet domestic and foreign policy, and said that in New York alone there were half a million Russians who had escaped the Soviet Union for the freedom of the West.

"Don't give me that stuff," Khrushchev retorted. "They only came to get higher wages. I was almost one of them. I gave very serious consideration to coming!"

"If you had come, you would have been the head of one of our biggest unions by now."

Recalling that they had first met in 1955, when Rockefeller was a lowly assistant to the President, Khrushchev asked with barely concealed sarcasm, "How did you happen to be Governor?"

"I guess you didn't expect to find me in this spot," Nelson said.

"It could happen only in America," Khrushchev scoffed.

In Moscow, David met with the chairman of the State Bank, A. A. Poskonov, the chairman of the Bank for Foreign Trade, M. N. Sveshnikov, and the Minister of Finance, E. Pekola. The talk concerned business.

Later that day—Thursday, July 31, 1964—David and Neva were escorted to the Kremlin for what Rockefeller later remarked was "the most intensive conversation I've ever had with anyone." Khrushchev greeted them with an almost childlike eagerness, and then they, with the interpreter, Valentin Kuznetsov, posed for a picture, as was the custom. Since the meeting was so significant, it was worth displaying in *Pravda.*

David asked whether he would mind if Neva took notes, and Khrushchev replied that he would not mind at all. He took the Americans into his large office, and guided them to seats at the inevitable green-baize-covered table. They drank mineral water, Neva feverishly scribbled notes, and for the next two and a half hours, the leader of world Communism debated the prince of capitalism.

To Khrushchev, accustomed to loud and heated exchanges—shouting matches—the bland, unexciting David Rockefeller must have been a tremendous frustration. The Premier repeatedly tried to unsettle his visitor with insinuating and provocative statements, only to be deflected by annoyingly cordial, polite demurrals. When soft words did not work, Rockefeller would simply change the subject.

"My brother Nelson has told me of conversations he has had

with you several times, and how much he enjoyed them," David began. He explained that while he was the first family member of his generation to visit Russia, he was not the first Rockefeller; his mother had visited in 1893. "I am sure she would have found many changes now." He thanked Khrushchev for the hospitality Dartmouth Conference participants had received and offered, "as a little souvenir of our appreciation," two etchings by the American artist Grant Wood. Nothing abstract, he was aware, would be appreciated here.

One of the messages the White House wanted to send to Khrushchev was apparently a vague offer of conciliation. "I hope it will be possible for the Chairman and President Johnson to establish closer relations," Rockefeller said, "—relations of the sort which you had with President Kennedy, and which are very useful in times of conflict." In case Khrushchev had not understood that this was a clear message from the White House, Rockefeller added, "I suspect—and I am speaking with confidence—that this is also in President Johnson's wishes."

But Khrushchev was not in a conciliatory mood. He informed Rockefeller that the Soviet Union conducted its relations with all nations of the world without interference in "internal matters."

Rockefeller ventured: "That is one of the areas which gives me cause for concern." He and Nelson were influential in expanding Rockefeller enterprises in Latin America, a region constantly threatened by Soviet incursions. "In recent cases, particularly in Latin America, we feel that you make use of the Communist parties to seek to bring into power governments favoring the Soviet," he said. He wryly conceded that Khrushchev had denied any Soviet sponsorship of revolutionary activity in the area and said, "I am very pleased to hear that this is not your policy."

Khrushchev exploded with rage. *"Nyet!* A revolution cannot be organized or instigated just at anybody's will. The people of the country must accomplish it themselves." After all, he explained, Lenin was not even in Russia at the time of the Revolution. "Our people accomplished it themselves. Hungry women went out into the streets in Leningrad, and the government fell." It was that simple: "hungry women" and no Bolshevik coup. "This is the case in other countries," he continued. "It is the people who cause a revolution; it can never be accomplished by another state or party." Revolutions in Vietnam, Korea, and Cuba were proof, he said, that "revolutions will occur in all countries, even in the United States."

When the conversation came around to the subject of Vietnam, and Rockefeller chided Khrushchev on Soviet actions there, Khrushchev, who had been playing with a paperweight, began to thump it on the table. "You're mistaken," he said.

"I'm afraid I can't agree with the Chairman in his interpretation of the case," Rockefeller said.

Again, Khrushchev burst out in anger, and launched into a defense of Soviet foreign policy. Rockefeller interrupted: "I think that our basic differences are such that nothing will be gained from pursuing this particular subject." He brought up another topic that enraged Khrushchev still further: Cuba.

Khrushchev denied that he had had any aggressive designs against America when he had placed forty-two rockets, aimed at the United States, on Cuba two years before. "It was only in order to deter the United States from attacking Cuba," he said. "Cuba has nothing we don't have in our own country—"

"Except," Rockefeller interjected, "perhaps, proximity to the United States."

"What does that give us?" Khrushchev asked loudly. "Do you really believe all that rot, that we want to seize the United States? If you think that is possible, tell me how, tell me by what means. We *can* destroy the United States, but why?"

"I suppose, judging from what I've seen, that you use Cuba as a base to activate the Communist movements in other parts of Latin America," Rockefeller said. "There is no thought of landing an attack in the United States—serious thinking Americans don't feel you want to take us over by force. Our fear is that by the kind of activity I have suggested to you, you would cripple the United States, weaken our position."

On the subject of trade, though, Khrushchev grew calmer. "We think it would be very useful if our two countries were to establish broader ties, particularly in the field of trade," he said. He explained that trade "leads to growing confidence between states." He added that he knew American businessmen were eager to "establish ties with us. . . . We have partners of long standing with whom we have had very good relations," Khrushchev said. "In 1962, I met with the president of Westinghouse International—"

"—Bill Knox. He sends you his best."

"I am sure that he would like to continue our business relations if there were no Congressional restrictions," Khrushchev told Rockefeller. "We have relations with Du Pont—"

"—and with our bank," Rockefeller said. Chase had maintained a small but uninterrupted business relationship with the Soviet Union and the Eastern Bloc nations since the twenties.

Rockefeller undoubtedly wanted to expand the relationship, and he admits that, while the primary purpose of his visit to Leningrad was the Dartmouth Conference, "I did establish some initial contacts for the bank at that time."

"Ours is a firm that will never collapse," Khrushchev boasted. "We are careful with our payments."

"You have always been extremely good in dealings with the Chase Manhattan Bank," Rockefeller agreed.

The problem with increasing trade, Rockefeller explained as Khrushchev listened intently, was a lack of "confidence" between the superpowers. But it seemed that the situation was improving under Khrushchev's leadership. "Knowledgeable people in our country," Rockefeller said, "feel that you personally, Mr. Chairman, have been largely responsible for the lessening tension. And for that I assure you that we are very grateful." Considering that in barely two months Khrushchev would be living as a pensioner in a cottage outside of Moscow, the *personal* aspect of this compliment is intriguing. But Rockefeller, of course, could not have known that Khruschev's power was soon to be eclipsed. "He seemed extremely confident," Rockefeller recalls. "I didn't get any impression at all that he had any inkling that he might be out two months later."

Speaking with the assurance of one who has been briefed, indirectly, by the White House, Rockefeller assured him that "Before I left the United States a short time ago, I talked with various people in our government. . . . It appears to me that our trade relationships can improve." But, as a banker, Rockefeller informed Khrushchev that Russia must first settle its Lend-Lease debts.

Khrushchev became solemn. "We paid for that with our blood. Do you know how many soldiers we lost in the war? Twenty million."

It was not a question of human sacrifice, Rockefeller protested, but a contract. "The transactions took place subsequent to hostilities," he said, although in fact the United States furnished Russia with equipment after the Nazi invasion of June 1941.

Speaking slowly and quietly, with his eyes downcast and at times closed, Khrushchev began an emotional lecture. "We must proceed from the major issues," he said. "You are a capitalist and a Rockefeller. I am a Communist. You are a banker. I was a miner. You represent a capitalist nation, while I speak for the Soviet Union. Whatever you say or do, you sympathize with the strengthening of capitalism. Whatever I say or do, I sympathize with the cause of Communism, which I believe to be the strength of the future, the up-and-coming philosophy. We believe that capitalism has reached its sunset. The time will come when she"—and here he waved a hand at Neva—"will be allied with me and my ideas."

At last the conversation drew to a close. "Actually, in the end I sort of brought it to a close," Rockefeller remembers. "He seemed willing to go on indefinitely. It seemed to me that for the head of one of the great countries in the world to have no interruptions of any kind, and to be willing to talk on this basis for that long, was extraordinary."

David's daughter did not find it all that extraordinary. "Khrushchev assumed my father represented the Establishment," Neva says. "He made it clear that he thought he represented American capitalism. He assumed that American capitalists thought that what was good for the Rockefellers was good for them, and vice versa." There seemed to be a peculiar sort of camaraderie between the two men, Neva recalls. "Just as Khrushchev represented the interests of the Russian people, he thought David Rockefeller represented the interests of Americans."

As the Rockefellers got up to leave, David said he would be interested to receive a copy of Khrushchev's official transcript of the meeting. Khrushchev said he did not understand what Rockefeller was talking about.

"Surely you've tape-recorded this session?" Rockefeller asked hesitantly.

Khrushchev was indignant. "Oh, we don't do such things," he said.

But when David and Neva returned to Leningrad the next day, they were astonished to hear the Soviet delegates to the conference quoting verbatim Rockefeller's statements of the previous day: "Now, as you told Nikita Sergeyevich yesterday . . ."

The New York Times gave the Rockefeller-Khrushchev meeting scant notice, but *Pravda* considered it front-page news: "The guest told N. S. Khrushchev that at present opinion in America is moving in favor of expanding trade with the U.S.S.R. He became convinced that 'N. S. Khrushchev sincerely desires peace.' . . . David Rockefeller emphasized that the meeting with N. S. Khrushchev had proceeded in a very unrestrained and friendly atmosphere."

At the beginning of August, when Rockefeller returned to the United States, he called Jack Valenti at the White House to set up an appointment with President Johnson. He also sent a copy of Neva's notes on the interview, which, he said, recorded the most important aspects of the conversation. "There are, however, one or two other interesting sidelights which I did not feel it advisable to include in the report (copies of which I am sending to the State Department)," he wrote, "which I should be glad to mention to the President if he could spare a moment."

President Johnson thanked him on August 24 for his "excellent work" and invited him to meet with him at the White House. "I understand that you conveyed most effectively the American viewpoint on the key issues you discussed," Johnson added.

The appointment was scheduled for September 11. Since it was so near election time, Jack Valenti urged the President to make full use of Rockefeller's appointment for public relations. "I would recommend that we put him on your schedule on the record," he urged. "I think this would be very helpful to us in the business community."

The morning of the appointment, Bundy prepared a memorandum for the President. Rockefeller had given Khrushchev "one important message," Bundy wrote: "namely, that it is important for the Chairman to keep out of the election. Khrushchev indicated to Rockefeller that he understood the point and would behave himself. Rockefeller of course did not bring the White House into his comment.

"Somewhat more interesting is Rockefeller's discussion with Khrushchev on trade," Bundy noted. They discussed the Lend-Lease debt, but Khrushchev had refused to settle unless the United States extended to Russia the same long-term credits it does to its allies. "From this and all other evidence," Bundy wrote, "I conclude that Nikita simply does not understand the politics of East-West trade in this country."

The only question was, Should the President send a short, informal note to Khrushchev, saying he had heard Rockefeller's report on the talk? "I would be in favor of it," Bundy said, "but my bet is that the State Department experts would be cool. This is exactly the sort of thing which created a sense of personal communication between Khrushchev and Kennedy, and I believe that such a sense of connection can be useful to us as time goes on." Bundy added that "Rockefeller's bank is also having some trouble with the Arabs, but the State Department has been helping him all the way, and I am urging him not to raise this with you."

The meeting was duly noted in the press. Circumspect as always, Rockefeller described it only as "interesting."

From being a messenger between the two heads of state, Rockefeller swiftly became an apostle of East-West trade. On October 21, exactly a week after Khrushchev's ouster, he told a group of businessmen in Paris that trade was "an excellent proving ground" to discover whether the Russians are "ready to match declarations with deeds." But he cautioned that credits should be limited to five years. "Anything more than that would amount to aid," he said, "and I don't believe we should give aid to countries trying to subvert or overthrow friendly governments."

In mid-November he was back in Moscow for a trade conference sponsored by Business International and the National Foreign Trade Council. Ninety-two American businessmen attended the three-day convention, which included meetings with Soviet President Anastas Mikoyan now Chairman of the Presidium of the Supreme Soviet, Foreign Trade Minister Nikolai S. Patolichev, and Foreign Minister Andrei Gromyko. The group presented Rockefeller with the Captain Robert Dollar Award for his "distinguished contribution to United States trade."

American attitudes toward doing business with Russia had begun gradually to change, and Rockefeller's public advocacy probably contributed to the change. That year the Senate Foreign Relations Committee surveyed businessmen and found that a majority favored increasing trade with the Soviet Union. Rockefeller himself initiated a survey of economics professors in American universities, and discovered that 82 percent of the 375 who responded favored the easing of restrictions on East-West trade. Two years later, on October 13, 1966, President Johnson removed restrictions on the export of over four hundred commodities to Communist countries.

William Hoffman, the author of an unfriendly biography of David Rockefeller (in fact, the only biography), notes that the widening of trade relations, coming just two years after Rockefeller's meeting with Khrushchev, clearly seemed "a direct result of agreements reached between the two men." It is difficult to believe that the prince of capitalism could have reached any substantive agreement with the leader of world Communism, especially since Khrushchev was removed so soon after the talk. What was probably more significant about the July 1964 meeting was that it occurred at all—that American attitudes toward doing business with the Soviet Union had become so favorable that the leading envoy of capitalism felt it was "appropriate" to discuss the matter with the Premier of the Soviet Union.

Does Rockefeller think his talk contributed in any way to the shift in American policy? "It certainly contributed to my knowledge," he says carefully. "It was an absolutely fascinating talk."

Times had indeed changed. In 1932 *Vanity Fair* published a drawing depicting two men against a backdrop of the skyscrapers of New York. One was Marshal Joseph Stalin in his familiar military tunic and boots and a walrus moustache, his hand extended in greeting. Dropping a dime into his palm was the stooped, wizened, patriarchal figure of John D. Rockefeller, Sr., with a wide grin. The cartoon was entitled "Impossible Interview."

UNITED PRESS INTERNATIONAL PHOTO

Armand Hammer, age 24, arrives in New York aboard the S.S. *Majestic,* June 13, 1922, to publicize his family's Soviet concession.

The Brown House, Sadovo-Samotechnaya 14, Moscow, as it appears today. Now the Lebanese Embassy, it was the residence of the Hammer family from 1923 to 1931.

DOUGLAS KIRKLAND/CONTACT

An American congressional delegation visits the Brown House in 1923. *Front row, left to right:* Julius Hammer, Congressman James Frear, Senator William King, Rose Hammer, Senator Edwin Ladd. *Second row, second from right:* Armand Hammer; *third from right:* Victor Hammer. All others are Soviet political and trade officials.

Anastas Mikoyan presents Cyrus Eaton (in light hat with black band) with a troika at Acadia Farms, January 7, 1959.

UNITED PRESS INTERNATIONAL PHOTO

COURTESY PEPSICO, INC.

Nikita Khrushchev and Richard Nixon sip Pepsi-Cola at the American National Exhibition, Moscow, July 26, 1959. At left, Donald Kendall displays a Pepsi bottle for the cameras. Behind Nixon, Anastas Mikoyan looks on.

Averell Harriman escorts Khrushchev from the Harriman town house, New York, September 17, 1959.

UNITED PRESS INTERNATIONAL PHOTO

At a luncheon in his honor given by Eaton (*right*) at New York's Hotel Biltmore, September 26, 1960, Khrushchev admires the glittering tableware.

WIDE WORLD PHOTOS

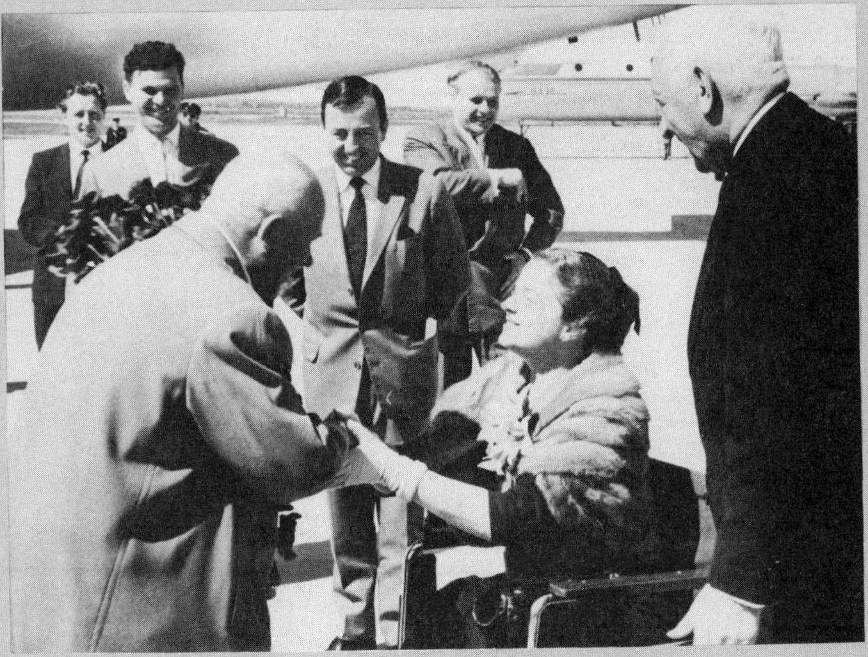

WIDE WORLD PHOTOS

Just after canceling the Paris Summit, Khrushchev presents Mrs. Eaton with a bouquet of roses at Orly Airport, May 19, 1960. Eaton is at right.

Khrushchev and Harriman at a U.S.-U.S.S.R. track meet, Moscow, July 1963. At far left is Leonid Brezhnev.

UNITED PRESS INTERNATIONAL PHOTO

UNITED PRESS INTERNATIONAL PHOTO

Hammer meets Khrushchev in the Kremlin, February 17, 1961.

David and Neva Rockefeller, interpreter Valentin Kuznetsov, and Khrushchev, Moscow, July 31, 1964.

NOVOSTI PRESS AGENCY

UNITED PRESS INTERNATIONAL PHOTO

Ambassador Anatoly Dobrynin, cruising with Hammer off Palm Beach in August 1973, describes the size of the fish he caught.

WIDE WORLD PHOTOS

Rockefeller and Alexei Kosygin, Moscow, April 25, 1974.

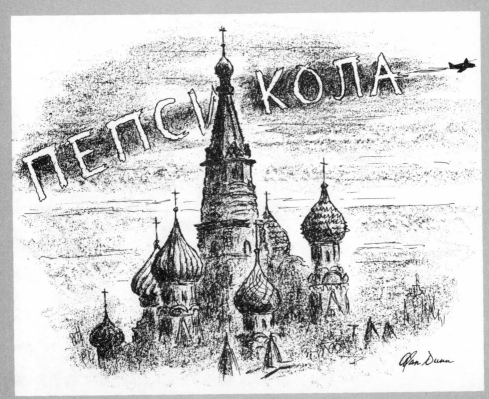

DRAWING BY ALAN DUNN; © 1972 THE NEW YORKER MAGAZINE, INC.

BURT GLINN/MAGNUM PHOTO

The PepsiCo board of directors meets in Novorossisk, June 1974. Don Kendall gestures at center.

Brezhnev tries, unsuccessfully, to open the first bottle of Pepsi-Cola bottled in the Soviet Union, by smacking it. Kendall is at right.

COURTESY PEPSICO, INC.

COURTESY OCCIDENTAL PETROLEUM CORPORATION

Hammer and Leonid Brezhnev, October 1976.

Hammer and Brezhnev at Yalta, August 1978.

COURTESY OCCIDENTAL PETROLEUM CORPORATION

PART THREE

"Let's get them all a little pregnant."
—RICHARD NIXON to Leonid Brezhnev,
June 27, 1974, on supporters of détente

THE RISE AND FALL OF DÉTENTE

12

THE PEPSI GENERATION

THE DÉTENTE of the 1970s between Russia and America can be said to have begun—in a technical sense, at least—when Commerce Secretary Maurice Stans received a phone call in early October 1971 from National Security Adviser Henry Kissinger. Almost from the day he had taken office, Stans had been urging Nixon and Kissinger to expand trade with Russia, but the answer had always been: "Not yet; the time isn't right."

During the summer of 1971, Kissinger sounded more hopeful on the subject. "It's almost time to make the move," Kissinger had said. "Just about every member of the Cabinet wants to go to Moscow and open the talks, but you'll be the first." Some sort of agreement between the White House and the Kremlin had apparently been reached by the beginning of October 1971, for Kissinger called Stans to say, "Get ready to go. We have everything worked out." On Kissinger's instructions, Stans invited Ambassador Dobrynin to lunch at the Commerce Department for a secret planning session.

A month later Stans set off for the Soviet Union, accompanied by his Assistant Secretary for Domestic and International Business, Harold B. Scott; one of Kissinger's aides, Helmut Sonnenfeldt; and seven others from Commerce. They arrived in Moscow on November 20, 1971, and were immediately brought to the office of Premier Alexei Kosygin, the number-two man in the Soviet hierarchy. The Moscow correspondents of the American and European newspapers and wire services gathered in Kosygin's office and heard him announce crisply, "We don't expect this one visit to yield momentous decisions, but we feel that we can reach an understanding in preparation for future important decisions."

One week later, one hundred chairmen of multinational corporations, including IBM, General Electric, Du Pont, and Westinghouse, arrived in Moscow for a trade conference. Business International, a corporate consulting group, had skillfully planned this meeting to overlap by a few days the visit of the Commerce Secretary. This was Business International's second try at such a conference. The first, in 1964, had not really led to anything primarily because the U.S. government was opposed to such trade. This time, though, conditions were right; the Nixon administration was clearly favorable. "There is a real thaw," one of the Business International organizers said upon arrival. "You can hear the ice cracking."

One of the leaders of the conference, and the chairman of the commercial discussions, was the fifty-year-old, white-haired, pugnacious chairman of PepsiCo Inc.—Donald McIntosh Kendall. Few people could claim to be as conservative and as Republican as Don Kendall. "I am a Republican," he had once boasted, "and I happen, in addition, to be an absolutely dedicated Nixon man." Pepsi-Cola was the company that had backed Joe McCarthy in the late forties; although Kendall joined the company after that period, he shared the Cold War sentiments of Pepsi-Cola's management and most of America's business community. His rise to the top of the company was due in large measure to a friendship he had struck up with one of the leading Cold Warriors of the fifties, Richard Nixon. Their relationship had begun, curiously enough, twelve years before, in Moscow.

Kendall was born in 1921 on a dairy farm in Sequim, Washington, and attended Western Kentucky State College on a football scholarship. He boxed in the Golden Gloves. During his sophomore year he dropped out of college to join the navy as an aviator in 1942. While in the navy he won two Distinguished Flying Crosses and three Air Medals, and married his first wife, Ann McDonnell.

After he left the navy he began to look for a job. A friend recommended a small soft-drink company called Pepsi-Cola, which, despite its famous radio jingle "Pepsi-Cola Hits the Spot," was a distant second in business to Coca-Cola. Pepsi-Cola's management was notoriously inept; a fellow with drive and ability could rise quickly through the ranks, and Kendall had both.

He joined the company in 1947, and, sure enough, his advance was amazingly swift (his official company biography called it "meteoric"); by 1957 Pepsi chairman, Alfred Steele, had made Kendall president of the company's international division. Kendall was then thirty-six, but he had prematurely gray hair, and he is convinced Steele would never have given him the job if he had known how young Kendall was.

Kendall's aggressive temperament clashed violently with that of Steele's wife, the actress Joan Crawford, whom Steele had married in 1955. Crawford, who became Pepsi's glamorous huckster, was a threat to Kendall, who considered himself the company's greatest salesman. Once, on a badly organized, unsuccessful business trip in Kenya, Crawford took Kendall aside and angrily blamed him for the fiasco. But Kendall would not take her lashing. "Why the hell should I take orders from a goddamn actress?" he exploded. From then on, their relationship was glacial. Crawford took to calling Kendall "Fang," and occasionally "White Fang." When Kendall became chairman in 1963, four years after Steele's death, he managed to have Crawford deposed as the Pepsi-Cola Lady. Her hate for him, of course, grew. Shortly before her death, Crawford is said to have told friends that she felt so good she could *even* think good thoughts about Don Kendall.

Kendall's greatest career gamble came in 1959, when the U.S. government announced plans for an American trade fair in Moscow. Kendall, always alert to sales opportunities, was interested in participating. Dispensing cola in Moscow was actually Al Steele's idea; he had suggested to the State Department that both Coke and Pepsi be allowed booths in Moscow as a demonstration of American-style competition. But three months before the exhibition, Steele died. Coke vetoed participation, perhaps because it was discomfited by the idea of giving free drinks to Communists, perhaps because it did not care to share billing with the parvenu beverage company. When the State Department informed Kendall, as head of Pepsi's overseas operations, that Pepsi would be the only cola in Moscow if the company participated, he promptly agreed to go.

But this was not an expense for the small company to take lightly. To send tanks of cola syrup, carbonating machines, and bottling equipment to Russia, let alone hire a team of Russian-speaking American hostesses to serve the product, would cost over a quarter of a million dollars. And there were several people in the Pepsi hierarchy apart from Joan Crawford who had it in for Kendall. His main enemy was an executive vice-president named Emmett O'Connell, who was extremely influential with the new company chairman, Herbert Barnet. O'Connell made it known that he considered the notion of a Pepsi booth in Moscow frivolous, extravagant, and stupid. Kendall believed that if the Moscow venture did not lead to a dramatic public-relations success for Pepsi-Cola, he would lose his job.

The American National Exhibition in Sokolniki Park in Moscow was a major production because President Eisenhower wanted it to be. To open the exhibition he had sent an official delegation consisting of Vice President and Mrs. Nixon, Milton Eisenhower, and Admiral Hyman Rickover.

Nixon met with Khrushchev on July 24 and the next evening was the guest of honor at Spaso House, the American ambassador's residence, where Ambassador and Mrs. Llewellyn Thompson gave a reception for the American participants. Kendall, who had known Nixon casually for two years, approached the Vice President on the receiving line and said, "I'm in trouble. I need some help. I've got to get a Pepsi into Khrushchev's hands." Nixon, who was to lead Khrushchev around the exhibition the next day, replied, "Don't worry. I'll bring him by."

July 26, 1959, was stiflingly hot, unusually hot for Moscow, and the crowds that jammed Sokolniki Park were sweating profusely. Nixon and Khrushchev appeared before color videotape cameras in the RCA and Ampex sample studio to engage in an intemperate "debate" that the Russian—who was louder, funnier, and a better debater—appeared to win.

Nixon was determined to engage his Soviet opponent in another argument in order to make up for the embarrassment at the TV studio. He led Khrushchev to the model of a fourteen-thousand-dollar American home, which he accurately predicted would arouse Khrushchev's sarcasm. (Soviet newspapers had sarcastically labeled the American display, which featured some of the finest of American consumer goods, as "Taj Mahal"—an unrealistic piece of propaganda.) Nixon and Khrushchev argued beside the dishwasher and the box of S.O.S. scrubbing pads; the spat became famous as the "Kitchen Debate." Nixon did better than he had before.

After lunch, Nixon continued as tour guide and led the official Soviet party in the direction of the Pepsi-Cola booth, just as he had promised Kendall he would. Khrushchev saw where he was being taken and attempted to veer off in another direction. After all, cola was the Soviet symbol of decadent capitalism. Postwar Russia had seized upon cola as an anti-American totem because of Coca-Cola's popularity as the "global high sign" of the Second World War. Besides being a useless syrup, cola was, to the Russians, identified with American dominance in Western Europe. Khrushchev would have none of it.

But Khrushchev's colleague Anastas Mikoyan, who had tasted and liked cola when he visited America in 1959, pushed to the front of the group and helped Nixon steer it to the Pepsi display. Though visibly reluctant, Khrushchev came along. It was an exceedingly hot day, after all, and the sight of all those free cups of cold drink must have been tempting.

As the group approached, Kendall took over. He was Pepsi's great salesman, and this was the do-or-die chance to make headlines. He gave Nixon and Khrushchev specially designed souvenirs: Plexiglas squares in which Russian and American coins and a Pepsi bottle top were embedded. As cameras snapped away, Kendall took a full cup from one of the hostesses and presented it to Khrushchev, while holding up in his other hand a bottle of Pepsi, its label in full view of the cameras. Khrushchev downed the drink in an instant.

Kendall suggested that Khrushchev might want to compare it to a sample bottled on location, which Khrushchev pronounced infinitely superior ("Very refreshing," he said). Mikoyan smiled and raised his glass in a toast. The Chairman of the Presidium of the Supreme Soviet, Kliment Voroshilov, said, "Not bad." A reporter asked the dour Minister of Culture, Yekaterina A. Furtseva, how she liked the American soft drink. "Look for yourself," she responded. "I'm drinking it."

"Do you think that the Soviet Union will now have a cola drink?" asked one American journalist of a Soviet bystander. The man shrugged his shoulders. "What do you think?" he said. "You saw who was drinking it and you saw how they liked it, didn't you?" Pepsi-Cola, the forbidden and disparaged American beverage, was a hit with the Russians.

Khrushchev was charmed by the young American women who served the drinks. Some of them, the children of Russian émigrés, spoke Russian almost without accent, and he insisted they could not really have been born in America. He flirted with and accepted a cup from each one. By the time the brief episode had ended, he had quaffed seven or eight papercupfuls of Pepsi.

The photograph of Khrushchev, Nixon, Kendall, and, off to one side, Leonid Brezhnev, all enjoying Pepsi ran in newspapers around the United States. Playing on the latest Pepsi slogan, "Be Sociable—Have a Pepsi," the *Philadelphia Inquirer* printed the picture under the headline, "KHRUSHCHEV LEARNS TO BE SOCIABLE." The tableau fascinated Americans; if the threatening Soviet Premier was really drinking Pepsi, a new era in Soviet-American relations seemed to have been born. *The New York Times,* announcing that "COLA CAPTIVATES SOVIET LEADERS," speculated: "Not only did this refreshing pause symbolize a reversal in Communist propaganda, it supported a conviction that many observers of the Soviet scene have long held. The conviction is that the way to do business with Mr. Khrushchev is to let him see things and taste things at first hand for himself." Don Kendall was quite pleased with what Nixon had done for him. The publicity that Pepsi had received from the Moscow exhibition proved to be an enormous boon to his career. His enemies in the Pepsi management were silenced.

By 1963 Kendall had doubled the number of countries in which Pepsi was sold—from 53 in 1957 to 102. The profits from the international division now comprised 41 percent of Pepsi's income. The gap between Pepsi and Coke began to narrow. In September 1963, Herbert Barnet was stripped of his executive duties, and Kendall was made president and chief executive officer. He broadened the soft-drink line by adding Diet Pepsi and Mountain Dew, and acquiring the Frito-Lay Company, makers of snack foods. PepsiCo became a mighty conglomerate.

PepsiCo's—and Kendall's—success was aided tremendously by Kendall's friendship with Richard Nixon, which had really begun on that sweltering day in Moscow. When Nixon lost the 1960 presidential election, Kendall, mindful of the value of having someone as well known as Nixon in his company, offered him the chairmanship of Pepsi International. But Nixon, who wanted to run for the governorship of California, turned the offer down. After Nixon lost that election as well, and concluded his "last press conference," Kendall repeated the offer. Nixon's other close friends, especially Elmer Bobst of Warner-Lambert, advised him not to take a job in industry. Bobst warned that those who offered such jobs were merely "people who wanted to use him." Nixon decided to return to his long-dormant career as a lawyer for he believed it had greater prestige and would enable him to make more useful contacts should he decide to make another run for the presidency.

Bobst talked to Milton Rose, the senior partner in the old New York law firm that handled Warner-Lambert's business, Mudge, Rose, Baldwin and Todd. What the old law firm needed to achieve national prominence, Bobst said, was to make Richard Nixon its senior partner. When Kendall learned that Nixon was thinking of joining Mudge, Rose, he told Nixon that whichever firm hired him would automatically receive the lucrative PepsiCo account.

Mudge, Rose realized the benefits, both political and financial, of hiring the former Vice President and immediately offered Nixon a salary of $250,000 to join. Nixon accepted, and moved to New York. The firm became Nixon, Mudge, Rose, Baldwin and Todd.

"One advantage of my New York law practice was that it allowed me to travel extensively abroad to see some of the firm's international clients," Nixon writes in his memoirs. "In this way I was also able to visit old friends from my vice presidential days and make new ones." He became PepsiCo's "goodwill ambassador"—replacing, in a sense, Joan Crawford.

Nixon's most famous PepsiCo world tour was in the spring of 1964. The tour was a skillful mix of business and politics. While commenting on the Republican primary contest between Nelson Rockefeller and Barry Goldwater, Nixon sipped Pepsi at Fiumicino airport in Rome. He held a news conference at the home of a Lebanese Pepsi bottler in Beirut, and announced that he would accept his party's nomination if asked; a waiter stepped into the view of the television cameras to hand Nixon a bottle of Pepsi, label showing. When Nixon returned to the States from a meeting with Ambassador Henry Cabot Lodge in Saigon, reporters asked him whether he had talked politics with Lodge, his running mate in 1960. "We had a very interesting discussion and actually made a deal," Nixon answered. "He is going to put a Pepsi-Cola cooler in the embassy in Saigon." Lyndon Johnson, who thought the idea of Richard Nixon's being the Pepsi ambassador ridiculous, once referred to him derisively as "a former Vice President" who "drinks Pepsi-Cola."

Nixon and Kendall became fast friends. When Kendall was married for the second time, to Baroness Ruedt von Collenberg at the Hotel Pierre in New York in 1965, Nixon played the piano at the reception. When Nixon decided to run for President in 1966, Kendall was one of his earliest contributors. He gave large parties to rally support for Nixon in the business community. Nixon would give a rousing speech and then depart, leaving Kendall to do the dirty work of asking for money.

In 1968, when Nixon was elected, Kendall's influence increased appreciably. Although the general public did not know Kendall's name, business leaders did. On January 2, 1969, he was elected chairman of the nation's most powerful lobbying group for multinational corporations, the Emergency Committee for American Trade (ECAT), which had been founded in 1967 by David Rockefeller to combat protectionism.

Kendall went frequently to the White House on social visits.

On March 17, 1969, there was a black-tie dinner in the East Room—a surprise birthday party for Pat Nixon. When the President rose to toast his wife, he also hailed Kendall, whose birthday it also happened to be.

Kendall was part of Nixon's inner circle of business friends; the others included Bobst, Bebe Rebozo, and Robert Abplanalp—all self-made nouveaux riches. They shared Nixon's distrust of the Eastern Establishment and financed his campaigns generously. When the secret "Town House" fund was established in 1970 to fund Republican congressional candidates sympathetic to Nixon's policies, Kendall pledged $250,000. The pledge was later declared illegal.

Of course Kendall received help in return, as well as the newfound prominence his friendship bestowed. In September 1972, for example, a Pepsi bottler from Chile named Augustin Edwards flew to see Kendall at the new Pepsi headquarters Kendall had built in Purchase, New York. Edwards warned that Salvador Allende, the new socialist president-elect of Chile, was planning to nationalize all Chilean industries—including the Pepsi bottling franchise. He asked Kendall to help. Kendall in turn called Nixon, who arranged a meeting between Kendall, Kissinger, and John Mitchell, and then a session in the Oval Office with Mitchell, Kissinger, and CIA Director Richard Helms. Nixon ordered Helms to prepare a "major effort" to prevent Allende from assuming power and he assured Helms he could have ten million dollars for the project if needed. Allende was eliminated, allegedly assassinated by the CIA. Three years later, Kendall told an audience at the Waldorf-Astoria in New York that the fact that Communism was not restored in Chile after Allende's demise demonstrated that détente was working; the Soviets were restrained. Several Soviet trade officials at the Waldorf agreed. "I think he knows what he's talking about," one of them said.

Now that Richard Nixon had sent a Commerce Department team to Moscow in November 1971, it made sense for Kendall to be one of the leaders of the Business International conference in Moscow: he spoke with the self-assurance of one who had had many long talks over drinks with the President of the United States. Kendall had also prepared well for the trip. He had spoken with a friend from the board of Investor Diversified Services, Llewellyn Thompson, the former ambassador to the Soviet Union (Kendall had taken Richard Nixon's old seat on the IDS board in 1968).

Thompson suggested to Kendall the idea of trading Pepsi-Cola for Soviet vodka. The Russians, he said, had always been irritated that Smirnoff vodka was purchased in the United States under the misconception that it is made in Russia. Although Pierre Smirnoff had made vodka for the czars in the nineteenth century, after the Revolution Smirnoff moved its operations to America. Most Americans did not know that Smirnoff vodka was really distilled in Hartford, Connecticut. Another well-kept secret was that the Soviets were marketing their top-grade vodka, Stolichnaya, in the United States through a small importing firm, Monsieur Henri Wines, Ltd. The deal had been arranged by Cyrus Eaton, Jr. Thompson said that the Russians were dissatisfied with the arrangement, that Kendall could do better. Thompson urged, "Make them an offer. Go see Dobrynin in Washington."

"I didn't know Anatoly at that point," Kendall says, "although today he's a very close friend of mine." Kendall made an appointment to see the Soviet ambassador, and when he saw him put forth his proposal. Kendall said he would be in Moscow in November, and would like to talk further about it if the Russians were interested.

The one hundred businessmen of Business International met with Trade Minister Patolichev, and then a smaller group of seven went to Kosygin's office to hear about the latest Soviet Five-Year Plan. Kosygin amazed his listeners by reciting the smallest details without notes. Kendall had brought with him a souvenir to present to Kosygin—shades of 1959—a transistor radio in the form of a Pepsi can, tuned to Radio Moscow (there are not many radio stations in Moscow from which to choose). Kendall had brought it in his briefcase, which to his amazement was never searched.

"You're the man who wants to trade your Pepsi-Cola for our vodka," Kosygin said when they shook hands. Kendall said yes, and then opened his briefcase and drew out the radio. Kosygin, thinking it was a sample of Pepsi, laughed uproariously, and laughed even louder when Kendall switched it on. "He just thought that was funny as hell," Kendall says.

That evening, in the Grand Hotel–style ballroom of the Sovietskaya Hotel, the Soviets entertained both the visiting businessmen and the Stans delegation. The tables were crowded with meats, fish, and sturgeon, and one very long table of vodka, wine, champagne, and brandy. The Americans mixed convivially with Soviet officials. Kendall and his wife were explaining to the heads of Quaker Oats and Kraft how he had set the Pepsi-radio down on Kosygin's desk and then made his bold pitch, when Kendall was suddenly tapped on the shoulder by an official-looking Russian. "Prime Minister Kosygin wishes to see you," the man said.

Kosygin entered the room, spotted Kendall, and approached. "Are you serious about trading Pepsi for our vodka?" he asked.

"Yes, sir, I am."

"On a liter-for-liter basis?"

Kendall, somewhat inebriated, joked, "I can see why you're not Minister of Trade. If we traded liters of Pepsi-Cola for liters of vodka, we'd be making a lot more money than you would."

One did not joke with Kosygin. He stared for a moment and said dryly, "Mr. Kendall, I'm talking about Pepsi *concentrate*." He motioned for Minister Patolichev to join them. "I want you to meet with Mr. Kendall in the morning. What time can you make it?"

"Ten o'clock," Patolichev answered.

"Please be in Mr. Patolichev's office at ten o'clock tomorrow morning," Kosygin said to Kendall. They shook hands, and Kosygin said, "You have a deal."

At that moment, Maurice Stans noticed that Kendall was shaking hands with the Premier of the Soviet Union; he walked up to them and cracked, "What's Kendall trying to do, sell you a Pepsi?" Stans's witticism was too close to the truth. "I could have kicked Stans' ass," he recalls. Kosygin turned to Stans and said, a touch defiantly, "I know you don't like monopolies in your country. Let me tell you what I'm doing. I'm going to give Mr. Kendall an *exclusive* on our vodka in your country, and an *exclusive* on cola here." He turned and left, but when he got no more than twenty feet away, he returned and asked Kendall, "Have you tried our champagne?" When Kendall said no, Kosygin summoned a waiter and ordered several glasses of *shampanskoye*. Kendall sampled it, enjoyed it, and was told, "You've got an exclusive on that, too." They shook hands again, and Kosygin left. He returned immediately. "You have not, by any chance, tried our Armenian brandy, have you?" Kendall had not. After two glasses each, Kosygin included that in the deal too.

Early the next morning, Kendall was awakened by a call from the Ministry of Trade. In the excitement of the night before, Patolichev had forgotten that he had to see the Secretary of Commerce off at the airport. The appointment with Kendall was moved to eleven.

When Kendall arrived at the Ministry to begin secret negotiations, he found that the besotten cordiality of the Sovietskaya reception had evaporated. Now the Russians were grim and serious, relentless negotiators. Several times Kendall was forced to get up and declare, "That's it. We just can't work this out." But Kendall realized that a deal would indeed be worked out, for the decision to trade Pepsi-Cola for vodka had already been made at the top of the Soviet hierarchy.

Negotiations took eleven months; Kendall came to Moscow three more times. After the initial session with Patolichev, Deputy Foreign Trade Minister Vladimir S. Alkhimov took over the Soviet side. For some reason, the Pepsi negotiations went on longer than discussions over far larger and more significant projects. There were a number of difficulties. The Ministry of Health asked some hard questions: Is Pepsi bad for the teeth? Does it damage the nervous system? Does it *really* dissolve metal? And what about its shelf life—how far could it be shipped? Although the talks were confidential, an astute observer might have suspected that something was going on. On April 5, 1972, PepsiCo announced that it had acquired a wine-and-liquor-importing house, Monsieur Henri Wines, Ltd., of Brooklyn, New York, for 367,776 shares of PepsiCo stock.

It developed that the Soviet Minister of Food, Voldemar Lein, was "not too happy" about the idea of selling Pepsi-Cola in Russia. Alkhimov recommended that Kendall "get to know Lein better" by inviting him for a visit to the United States. This was Soviet craftiness at its most droll. If Alexei Kosygin had shaken hands with Don Kendall, no Minister of Food was going to get in the way. But détente had begun, and Soviet trade officials had become regular patrons of America's better hotels; one of the greatest perquisites of being a high-level Soviet bureaucrat was the privilege of leaving the country once in a while. The most treasured tour was America, land of plentiful consumer goods. One could only make the trip, however, if one was invited. And, besides, now Lein would be able to take a good, close look at all the sophisticated American food-processing equipment he had heard so much about.

Kendall took Minister Lein across the United States, to receptions and dinners, and on tours of such plants as Kraft's in Denver and Sara Lee's in Chicago. Lein's eyes bulged at the high technology of the American food business. "He got excited as hell," Kendall says. Before the visit to the Sara Lee factory, Kendall gave Lein a PepsiCo tie, and Lein gave Kendall his Soviet-made one. During the tour, a Russian-speaking employee came up to Kendall and, determining from the tie he was wearing that *he* was the visiting Soviet dignitary, began speaking excitedly to him in Russian. Kendall played along, muttering, *"Da, da, da."*

As a final, masterful stroke, Kendall brought his guest to see the President at San Clemente. "Ever since then," Kendall says, "Lein was one of the biggest advocates of détente."

In late May 1972, Richard Nixon and Henry Kissinger sat across from General Secretary Leonid Brezhnev, Premier Kosygin, and President Nikolai Podgorny at a long rectangular table covered in beige felt in the Kremlin's impressive, gilded St. Catherine's Hall. This was the first time an American President had ever set foot in Moscow.

They ran quickly through the topics for discussion—global politics, nuclear arms control, and then economic relations. Brezhnev remarked, half seriously, that relations would be greatly improved if the United States would agree to grant credits of three or four billion dollars a year for twenty-five years at 2 percent interest. Kosygin agreed; then, he said, it would be possible to sell the United States great quantities of Soviet vodka, which was infinitely superior to the "émigré vodka" (by which he meant, of course, Smirnoff and the other brands). Brezhnev joked that Nixon and Kissinger could set up a trading company for the purpose. But Nixon was not in the mood to joke, and he dismissed the banter.

Brezhnev's facetious suggestion was clearly unnecessary. A few months later—two weeks after the presidential election—Kendall announced that he had reached an agreement to make and sell the first American "consumer product" in the Soviet Union. It was a ten-year contract, renewable if both parties were satisfied, in which PepsiCo bought Stolichnaya vodka for dollars and the Soviet government bought Pepsi concentrate made in America, also with dollars. Over a five-year period, purchases on both sides were to balance out. The Russians were not given the secret Pepsi formula. PepsiCo also agreed to spend about a million dollars renovating a Soviet bottling plant in Novorossisk, the resort on the Black Sea, installing a high-speed bottling line, and training Soviet personnel. Within two years the plant was to be turning out seventy-two million bottles a year. (To discourage people from keeping the bottles, ordinary Soviet beverage bottles were used instead of the special Pepsi ones. Customers could keep the foil labels instead.) Within seven years there would be Pepsi bottling plants in Moscow, Leningrad, Tallinn (the capital of Estonia), Kiev, Tashkent, Novosibirsk (the largest city in Siberia), Alma-Ata (in the Kazakhstan Republic), and Sukhumi (a Georgian resort town on the Black Sea). A Soviet bottle of Pepsi-Cola would be enormously expensive—forty kopecks, or about a dollar, when most Soviet soft drinks sell for a few kopecks. The Soviets even embarked upon a modest advertising campaign, unusual in an economy that generally does not advertise. They decided that Pepsi's American slogan—"Feelin' Free"—was inappropriate. Their less mellifluous ad copy read: "A swallow of cold Pepsi-Cola will put you in a good mood and refresh you." *Cold* was the key word. Russians drink their beverages at room temperature, but this American product tastes unpleasant warm. In an interview in *Izvestiya,* Kendall stressed this point: "But don't forget, it has to be chilled before you drink it. Otherwise, it isn't enjoyable."

America reacted to the news with unrestrained delight. Suddenly, it was "The Pepski Generation." If this was détente, it was *fun. The New Yorker* printed a memorable cartoon by Alan Dunn that showed a skywriter (the advertising device made famous by Pepsi in the thirties) drawing PEPSI in Cyrillic letters in the sky above the Kremlin. Even *Fortune* magazine, though stoutly opposed to trading with the Russians, was taken by the novelty of Kendall's deal. It ran a full-page advertisement in *The New York Times* consisting of a giant photograph of the sour-looking Politburo members on a reviewing stand in Red Square with the caption, "The Pepsi Generation."

Pepsi in Russia became something of a legend, a symbol of the new American rapprochement with the Communists. Once, when a Soviet Tupolev Tu95 fighter jet was intercepted by a British Phantom jet above the North Sea, a crewman in the Soviet blister was spotted holding aloft a mysterious object; when the reconnaissance photograph was enlarged, the object turned out to be a Soviet bottle of Pepsi.

Coca-Cola, of course, was not pleased; executives there were tight-lipped. An internal memo to Coke's top officers assured them that "Coca-Cola, as the world's most popular soft drink, in due course will be available in the Soviet Union" (which almost did occur a few years later). In what Adlai Stevenson once termed "the ice-cold war," Coke was chagrined at being so publicly outdone. Don Kendall, if for no other reason, was thrilled.

The men at the top of Coca-Cola made no secret of their suspicions that something was rotten. Everyone knew Kendall was one of Nixon's best friends; it seemed obvious that the announcement of the deal was held back until after the election to avoid embarrassing the President.

As soon as Kendall returned from Moscow, he was interviewed by Frank Gifford on the "Today" show. The first question Gifford asked was whether Nixon had helped him get the deal. Kendall gave a prepared response he would invariably give whenever he was asked this question, and he was asked it countless times. He said that, yes, Nixon had helped—because he had created the "atmosphere" in which this agreement could be reached.

In reporting the announcement, *The New York Times* was terse: "Mr. Kendall and Mr. Nixon have remained close ever since the 1959 meeting." The *Wall Street Journal* reported:

> Asked if his long and well-known friendship had anything to do with getting ahead of PepsiCo's competitors, Mr. Kendall replied, "I don't know what that would have to do with it." He noted that Pepsi-Cola is sold in 130 countries, "and I opened a lot of those markets," he said. "I've been selling Pepsi-Cola for a long time."

George McGovern's campaign manager, Frank Mankiewicz, reacted with indignation. It was, he wrote, "the first time in our history that a president used his foreign policy power to bestow great financial benefit upon a friend to whom he was indebted."

A few weeks after the announcement, the *New York Post* published a report that a businessman close to the Soviets had revealed that President Nixon had personally asked the Soviets to give Kendall special consideration. Senator Adlai Stevenson received information (through Joseph Califano, the Coke lawyer) that Kendall had actually flown to Moscow aboard *Air Force Two* in May 1972 with Kissinger, carrying a letter to Kosygin from Nixon urging that Kendall be given special dispensation in the interest of détente.

Jack Anderson's investigation concluded:

> There is no reason to believe that Nixon, as President, ever interceded to help his old Pepsi client. But leaders around the world remembered that he had once traveled for the company. This was enough to give Pepsi an edge with world leaders, who thought they might please the White House by keeping Pepsi on tap.

In hearings before the House Committee on Foreign Affairs in May 1974, Stevenson pursued the matter. Did Kendall really carry over a letter from Nixon? Stevenson asked. Kendall replied that these charges were "dirty innuendos." "But I will tell you what the President did do," Kendall said. "Without the President, it would have been impossible to have done what we did. He created the climate in which this could occur. . . . But I don't think I need the President's help or your help or anybody else's help in selling Pepsi-Cola. We have a hell of a fine product. Further, I don't travel around in Air Force planes with Secretary Kissinger."

"You don't?" Stevenson asked.

"No, I don't."

"You didn't in May of 1972?"

"No, sir. There was a wonderful story in a newspaper that was more than a little bit mixed up. The story is that I flew to Japan with Secretary Kissinger and then on to Moscow. The facts are that I was in Japan when Secretary Kissinger was there, but I went there with our entire board of directors. . . . I have never been in Moscow with Secretary Kissinger."

"I am glad to hear it," Stevenson told him. "You apparently travel the way we Senators travel in the Soviet Union. Earlier, you acted as if none of us had ever been to the Soviet Union. I flew by Aeroflot to the Soviet Union."

"The last time I went there," Kendall replied, "I went by Aeroflot."

Kendall's Russian deal turned out to be, financially, far more trouble than it was worth. He had to sell as much vodka as the Soviets were selling Pepsi, and it was not easy for a ten-dollar bottle of vodka to crack a market of five-dollar bottles. Most Americans could not taste the difference between Stolichnaya and, say, Cossack brand. Stolichnaya was sold on the basis of prestige; it cost more, and was considered a luxury item. All this apart, the sales of Pepsi in Russia were minuscule compared to Pepsi's world market—"a pimple on Pepsi's ass," as one Pepsi executive described it. There is no mystery as to why Kendall was so eager to bring Pepsi to Moscow: he made the transaction for the promotional value that it would, and did, receive, and also to "beat the others cold."

The reasons the Soviets wanted the deal are much more complicated. Kendall's Soviet counterparts told him it was to combat the Soviet alcoholism problem, which is one of the worst in the world and a cause of crime and low productivity. They said if there was a prestigious consumer item like Pepsi, Russians would spend their savings on it instead of on vodka. But Pepsi obviously does not help one forget one's problems; Pepsi does not get one drunk. Though their explanation is entirely illogical, Kendall says, "Well, there are a lot of things the Soviets do that don't make sense to us." Once he joked to Kosygin, "Now I understand how this all fits in with alcoholism. You want me to take your vodka to the United States and get Americans drunk, and you'll take Pepsi-Cola." In fact, at resorts on the Black Sea Russians began discovering a new and trendy cocktail—vodka and Pepsi.

But alcoholism was entirely beside the point. The Soviet government never planned to make Pepsi available to the masses. Seventy-two million bottles a year in a country of 250 million people is hardly a mass market. There was enough for the Crimean resorts, for the tourists' hard-currency ("Beryozka") shops, and for hotels and restaurants in the showcase cities: Moscow, Leningrad, Kiev, and Tallin. The average Russian worker, standing in line to buy milk, is unlikely to splurge the equivalent of a dollar for a bottle of Pepsi, particularly when there is a wide assortment of fruit drinks more to a Russian's taste. The privileged Soviet elite, however—about a tenth of the population comprises the most generous definition of "elite"—treasures all things Western. They will spend $250 for a pair of Calvin Klein jeans or a good American ski parka or a pair of "moon boots," a hefty sum for John Irving's novel *The World According to Garp*—in short, for just about anything Western. This includes the syrupy symbol of decadent capitalism, Pepsi-Cola. It is in the interests of the state to keep this Westernophile elite content and feeling prosperous, for they run the organs of the state, edit the newspapers, sing at the Bolshoi, and design the nuclear rockets. And, most important, they mingle with visitors from the West, who then see a Tiffany's-display-window Russia that seems happy and quite Western and therefore not at all threatening.

Tourists can go into any good hotel or restaurant in Moscow or Leningrad and be assured that, of all the items on the menu, the one that is certain to be in stock is Pepsi-Cola. The familiarity is of course reassuring. The Soviets made a brilliant move when they agreed to trade Stolichnaya for Pepsi. "The Pepski Generation," which made such a splash in America, convinced Americans that détente meant a type of convergence. If the Russians were finally drinking our totemic beverage, why, it seemed, they really were becoming almost capitalists. "Pepsi" written in Russian in the sky above the Kremlin came to symbolize trade with the Russians as cultural exchange—sometimes frivolous, but above all safe. The Russians evidently wanted to buy all we had to sell, not just truck factories and microchips. What it really was, though, was a shrewd public-relations gimmick, for they wanted computers from Texas Instruments far more than they wanted Pepsi. And what an extra benefit if Americans with the money to spend began drinking Soviet vodka with their Russian caviar!

There was another, and probably even more important, motive in the Soviet decision to buy Pepsi. Kendall hardly had to carry a letter to the Kremlin from Richard Nixon; they knew well that he was one of Nixon's closest friends. Coca-Cola never had a chance. By signing with Kendall, they enlisted in the ranks of pro-détente, pro-Soviet-American trade forces one of the most influential businessmen in America—a boisterous, energetic, and skilled salesman who was also a drinking buddy of the President. Not that he was duped; Kendall sincerely believed in the cause of doing business with Russia. And in addition to his small vested financial interest, he was now a sort of roving ambassador, and the Soviets treated him as such.

From 1972 on, the old Cold Warrior, who had become, along with his friend the President, a champion of détente, was one of America's leading supporters—in fact, lobbyists—for increased Soviet-American trade. Whatever his attitude, he doubtless would not have been nearly as enthusiastic and forceful if he were not so cordially welcomed to the green-baize-covered tables of the Kremlin. Few people in the world could claim, as did Don Kendall, easy access to both the Kremlin and the White House.

In 1974 Kendall gave a champagne reception in New York for celebrities of the wine industry and Soviet dignitaries. *The New Yorker* called it "Détente at the St. Regis." Kendall announced two varieties of champagne that PepsiCo was now marketing in the United States, Nazdorovya Brut and Nazdorovya Extra Brut (*Nazdorovya* is Russian for "To your health," or "Cheers"). He rose and gave a toast, explaining that this latest transaction was "A milestone between the United States and the Soviet Union . . . sure to lead to better understanding." Ambassador Yakov A. Malik, Soviet Representative to the United Nations, replied, "It seems to me that Mr. Kendall wants to melt away the last remnant of the ice."

In June 1974 Kendall presented Brezhnev with a historic souvenir: the first bottle of Pepsi bottled in the Soviet Union. Brezhnev then attempted to demonstrate the time-honored Russian method for opening a soda bottle, by smacking it hard at the bottom. He gave it a whack, but the bottle, its contents seething furiously, remained sealed.

Later, all of the directors of PepsiCo assembled in the conference room of a winery near the just-opened Pepsi bottling plant in Novorossisk for the first American board meeting ever held in the

U.S.S.R. The board included the retired chairmen of General Motors, IBM, and Chase Manhattan.

Fortune had sent a photographer to record the historic event, and the man roamed about the room snapping shots from different angles. At one point he asked Kendall to move to the other side of the conference table. Visibly annoyed, Kendall asked the reason for this disruption. The photographer gestured at the wall behind the conference table. There, above Kendall's shoulder, was the bearded head of Vladimir Ilyich Lenin in a futurist Soviet mural, floating on block sunbeams emanating from the horizon.

13

"THE BIGGEST DEAL IN HISTORY"

A SHORT, ROUNDISH, seventy-four-year-old man named Armand Hammer flew into Moscow's Sheryemetyevo Airport in early July 1972, aboard his Boeing 727, the *Oxy-1*. This flying luxury suite—with a one-hundred-foot cabin equipped with a Betamax video recorder, a library of Charlie Chaplin films, a cork-lined bedroom, and Muzak—was the first private jet ever to enter Russia. Obtaining the privilege, an all-important symbol to Hammer, had required a great deal of maneuvering.

Earlier in the year he had sought the help of the only person in America who could arrange it, eighty-eight-year-old Cyrus Eaton, whose influence in Moscow at that time was far greater than Hammer's. Cyrus and Anne were staying at Claridge's in London when they received a call from Hammer, who was also in town. They invited him and his wife Frances to join them for dinner in their suite.

Hammer regaled them with stories about his early days in Moscow, his meeting with Lenin, and then asked Eaton whether he might be willing to intercede with Dzhermen Gvishiani or, if necessary, Kosygin, to allow the *Oxy-1* to enter Soviet airspace. Eaton agreed, spoke with Gvishiani, who spoke with Kosygin, and it was done. Flying his own plane into Moscow was "a terribly important thing to Hammer," Cyrus Eaton, Jr., recalls. For such symbols, like visits to the Oval Office or trade missions ostensibly undertaken at the behest of President Kennedy, were part of Hammer's ingenious self-promotion. The glory of a statesman-magnate—which for him meant being, as he was later to brag, "the Russians' favorite capitalist"—still eluded him in 1972 even though he was a very rich man as a result of a decade of shrewd dealings.

On his 1961 "Kennedy mission," Hammer made a side trip to Libya, where oil had recently been discovered. Occidental Petroleum, despite its name, still had very little petroleum, and Hammer was determined to enter the Libyan market, which was then dominated by the so-called seven sisters: the companies we now know as BP, Exxon, Gulf, Mobil, Shell, Socal, and Texaco.

Five years later, when the Libyan oil concessions were being negotiated, Hammer submitted a generous bid wrapped in a ribbon of the Libyan colors, red, green, and black. In February 1966 he was awarded two concessions, totaling two thousand square miles, in the Sirte Basin, a hundred miles from the Mediterranean.

"This extraordinary old walnut of a man," writes Anthony Sampson in *The Seven Sisters,* "had a combination of imagination and ruthlessness that made him in some ways more disrupting to the sisters" than any other independent oil company. Evidence submitted by a New York investment firm, Allen & Company (which Hammer cut out of the deal), in a seven-year lawsuit a few years later revealed that more than eight million dollars—several percentage points of Oxy's Libyan profits—were placed in Swiss bank accounts belonging to at least two Libyan officials. The testimony also contends that in September 1964 Hammer met at Claridge's for two days with a managing partner of Allen & Company, a European middleman, a prominent Libyan businessman, and a "notorious international swindler and Nazi collaborator" who called himself "General de Rovin." This group agreed to help Hammer obtain the Libyan oil fields for two hundred thousand dollars.

A few months later Occidental struck oil in Libya, and one year later hit one of the largest deposits of oil in the world. Hammer hired the giant, secretive construction company, the Bechtel Corporation, based in San Francisco, to build a pipeline from the Sahara to the Mediterranean at a cost of $147 million.

Bechtel, a privately held company, would, if publicly owned, rank about twenty-fifth in the Fortune 500. "Few unnatural forces have altered the face of this planet more than the Bechtel Corporation," notes Mark Dowie in a 1978 profile of the company in the magazine *Mother Jones.* Founded in 1898 by an immigrant mule skinner named Warren Bechtel, it eventually grew so large that in 1931 it headed the consortium of companies named to build the

Hoover Dam. In 1933 Warren Bechtel died in the Soviet Union while inspecting the gigantic hydroelectric dam at Magnitogorsk.

"We will build anything, anywhere, anytime," Steven Bechtel, Sr.—Warren's son, the successor to the dynasty, and one of the five richest men in America—has said. It was for a good reason that Hammer hired Bechtel, a firm with extremely close ties to the Central Intelligence Agency. When America's relations with Libya became difficult in the late sixties, Dowie writes, "Occidental even arranged for Bechtel to conduit 'payments' to Libyan officials so that it could continue working in the country." Dowie also reports that at least two CIA agents operated in Libya undercover as Bechtel managers. When the pipeline was dedicated, moreover, Hammer tried to persuade Lyndon Johnson to send a telegram of congratulations, but Under Secretary of State Eugene Rostow told the President it would be a bad idea.

Now that Libyan oil was flowing through the Occidental pipeline to Europe, Oxy stock shot up; and, with the stock, Hammer acquired several hundred million tons of phosphates, as well as Island Creek Coal and the Hooker Chemical Company.

On September 1, 1969, Colonel Muammar el-Qaddafi seized power and demanded of the twenty-one foreign oil companies in Libya an extra forty cents a barrel. He conferred with each company individually. The seven sisters steadfastly refused to comply, so Qaddafi struck at the company most dependent on Libyan oil: Occidental Petroleum. He ordered Oxy to cut its production from 680,000 to 500,000 barrels a day. It was a strategic pressure tactic, and it had its intended effect.

Hammer told the head of Exxon, Kenneth Jamieson, that he would give in to Qaddafi's demands unless Exxon supplied oil to Occidental at cost. Jamieson said he would agree to sell oil at the normal third-party cost, but would not go lower than that. Hammer then flew to Egypt and asked President Nasser to intercede with Qaddafi; Nasser did so, but with no result. There were also reports that Hammer used Bechtel's connections to offer to underwrite a CIA coup to unseat Qaddafi.

And there is evidence that Hammer may have turned to Moscow in 1970 to seek Soviet help in pressuring Qaddafi. According to a 1981 article in *The New York Times Magazine*:

> The Central Intelligence Agency became concerned with these negotiations when routine interceptions of the secret communications between Moscow and the Soviet Embassy in Tripoli suddenly showed a quantum leap in volume that coincided with turns

> in the oil negotiations. While American cryptoanalysts at the National Security Agency could "count" the messages being transmitted, they could not crack the code itself, and therefore the content of this spurt in volume remained conjectural.

Hammer denied any Soviet intervention. Bunker Hunt's negotiator at the time in Libya, G. Henry M. Schuler, confirms that such speculation was rampant in Tripoli during the negotiations. "But none of the rumors were borne out," he says. Indeed, given the tenuous state of Soviet-Libyan relations in 1970—and Hammer's inability even to get his jet into Moscow without Cyrus Eaton's help—it is unlikely that the Soviets offered any help in Libya.

In any case, Qaddafi showed Hammer no mercy. On September 4, 1970, Hammer acceded to Qaddafi's demands. By the end of the month, most of the other oil companies had also surrendered. The common front was broken, the Organization of Petroleum Exporting Countries instantly acquired enormous power, and a great energy crisis soon befell the United States. If Armand Hammer were at fault, it was obviously not a deliberate action. He had saved his neck, *Forbes* magazine points out, but at "a terrible price to the industrial world."

Just as he had falsely trumpeted his 1961 visit to Moscow as a triumphal return after thirty years, Hammer announced in 1972 that he had had nothing to do with Russia since Khrushchev's ouster. In fact, Hammer may have done business with the Soviet Union steadily, from the early sixties, through his various subsidiaries such as Oxy Metals, Inc., of England. Moreover, he relentlessly tried to revive the giant fertilizer deal he had almost struck in 1964.

In November of that year, after the new regime took power in the Kremlin, Hammer returned to Moscow with the group of one hundred businessmen led by Business International. Although David Rockefeller was the meeting's star attraction, Hammer played a minor role, serving as cochairman of a luncheon for Anastas Mikoyan. The group was received by President Johnson at the White House in January 1965.

Mikoyan retained some influence in the new Soviet leadership, and there were others, including Kosygin, whom Hammer had met four years earlier. Hammer continued his negotiations in Moscow, making several more trips in 1965, but by then the Soviets had hesitated so long that the British government credits had expired, and the deal was called off. But Hammer did not give up.

American credits could only be secured with the agreement of the President, and so Hammer set about trying to cultivate Lyndon Johnson. As Hammer did not know Johnson, he contacted a fellow trustee of the Eleanor Roosevelt Memorial Foundation, Myer Feldman, who was a Washington lawyer and special counsel to the President. King Faisal of Saudi Arabia was to be honored at a state dinner in the White House in June 1966. Feldman spoke with Johnson's appointments secretary and chief of staff, W. Marvin Watson, a longtime Johnson aide who now screened all visitors to the Oval Office and virtually ran the White House staff. Watson arranged for Hammer to attend the Faisal dinner.

Before the dinner, Feldman brought Hammer to Watson's office and introduced the two. Hammer presented Watson with a jade key ring. Hammer may also have made an offer to the President of twenty-five thousand dollars. Perhaps it was an extremely early campaign contribution. "Armand Hammer was in today," Watson reported to the President. "He says he has 25 that he would like to do without." An important member of the Johnson staff privately believes it was a bribe—"Twenty-five thousand dollars sounds like the right amount for someone like Hammer." There is, of course, no evidence that Hammer actually made, or that Johnson accepted, such a payment.

Regardless, Hammer seemed to have had a motive, for the offer was accompanied by a request that the President send him on an official mission to the Soviet Union. A day after the meeting, Watson thanked Hammer for coming in: "Meeting you was my real pleasure. The discussion was most helpful and it's good to have the opportunity to talk of mutual interests." They spoke by telephone a week later, and in response Hammer sent a file of clippings describing his association with the Soviet Union. One of the articles was a flattering profile from the March 12, 1966, issue of the *Saturday Evening Post* entitled "The Man With the Golden Touch." Its only negative remark was that Hammer "has the air of a confidence man."

But Hammer's request received a polite refusal, and Johnson would not meet with Hammer. "Lyndon was unsure of himself, really, until fairly well into his time in the White House," Myer Feldman says. "He didn't want to see Hammer because he was extremely cautious of anyone even remotely suspicious." Still, he sent Hammer a bust of himself as a present for Christmas 1966, a gift he sent to only twenty-seven other corporate chiefs.

At a state dinner for the King of Morocco on April 28, 1967, Hammer approached Johnson and renewed his suggestion. He would "be willing," he said, to visit his old friends in Moscow—

Mikoyan, Kosygin, Gromyko, and others—to improve trade relations. A few days later, he wrote a letter to Marvin Watson, repeating his idea and adding that if he could not go as an official emissary, he could go as part of a group attending the Motion Picture Festival in Moscow in July. "If the President approves I am ready to go," Hammer told Watson. "Even if I fail I will have at least tried my best to serve my President and my country."

Along with the letter he sent a copy of *Quest of the Romanoff Treasure* and a memorandum explaining his reason for wanting a presidential endorsement of his plan to build fertilizer plants in Russia:

> If the offer can be held out to the USSR that with American help they can make themselves self-sufficient in their food needs, perhaps they would be willing, in return, to bring pressure on North Vietnam to come to the peace table with the United States. . . . If the offer is made unofficially by an American businessman and it is turned down, there is nothing to lose.

Watson gave the message to Johnson, who gave it to Walt Rostow, his national security adviser, for his reaction. He told Rostow, "Be very, very cautious about this and do only what you and [Dean] Rusk can justify. It doesn't appeal to me much."

Rostow did some research on Hammer and concluded in a memo to the President that Hammer's request should be denied. In a note to Watson marked "Secret" he stated:

> As you know, the President is uneasy, and a Hammer mission does not appeal to him.
>
> It might be a good idea to get in writing a clear statement that it would be unwise for Hammer to go on a mission of the kind he proposes. There is no objection whatever to Hammer's visiting the Soviet Union as a private citizen, and there is no objection, of course, to his seeing prominent Russians who are his friends . . . the important thing is that he not allow a situation to develop where the Russians or others get the idea he is some sort of emissary.

On May 10, 1967, Rostow informed Hammer and deposited into the White House confidential file the information on what he called Hammer's "rich background" that had caused him to react with caution. Rostow sent the letter special delivery; the day Hammer received it he replied to Rostow that he had now changed his plans and would go in July instead. Without a presidential imprimatur, Hammer knew, the trip would not be worthwhile.

Hammer did finally get to see LBJ in the Oval Office, on Tuesday, June 18, 1968, at 12:30 P.M. A few months earlier he had given Johnson a valuable bronze cast of Frederic Remington's "Bronco Buster" for the Johnson Presidential Library. He managed to see the President to discuss the Library and perhaps to tell him about his contribution. Since Johnson had, in late March, announced he would not seek reelection, Hammer probably did not take the occasion to make another bid for an official mission.

He had set foot in Lyndon Johnson's Oval Office too late, but in a few months there would be another President. Hammer recruited from the Johnson White House a few very well-connected officials: Marvin Watson (perhaps as a reward for his kindness) and Watson's assistant, Bill McSweeny, who was formerly a prize-winning sportswriter. Both were placed in Hammer's lobbying division, Occidental International, in Washington. Watson was named the president; he was succeeded not long afterward by McSweeny. Hammer also hired as his chief of security a former Air Force counterintelligence agent named Charles Sither, who was the head of LBJ's White House Secret Service detail. After acquiring Island Creek Coal in January 1968, Hammer named his old friend from the Kennedy days, Albert Gore, as its president.

When Occidental bought Hooker Chemical that year, Hammer employed Myer Feldman as his attorney in the acquisition. Hooker, a major producer of fertilizers and agricultural and industrial chemicals, enlarged Hammer's fertilizer empire still more.

Between 1966 and 1968, Congress and the President began to lift restrictions on East-West trade. Hammer evidently decided it was the right time to make one last decisive attempt to strike the mammoth deal with Moscow for which he had been striving for most of his life. In an arrangement he understandably has concealed, he flew to Cleveland early in 1969 and enlisted the help of Cyrus Eaton. The ostensible reason was to buy the Eatons' West Kentucky Coal Company. In the course of the negotiations, Hammer told Cyrus and Cyrus, Jr., about his adventures in Russia in the twenties and praised the elder Eaton generously for his role in Soviet-American relations.

Hammer knew all about the Eatons' East-West trading company, Tower International, and proposed that they join forces in one great, concerted attempt to conquer the Soviet market. With Hammer's entrepreneurial ability and the esteemed (in Russia) Eaton name, they would all make a lot of money.

He continued his discussions with Cyrus, Jr., in the Tower International offices in Cleveland. One problem he was facing, Hammer said, was to convince the executives of some of his subsidiary firms of the merits of doing business with Russia. He persuaded Cyrus, Jr., to take a few high-level executives of Oxy Metals and Hooker Chemical on a tour of Eastern Europe.

Young Cyrus told Hammer of a few of his father's pet projects: marketing Soviet natural gas, building a trade center in Moscow, and so on. Hammer thought the ideas were fantastic and arranged to buy a 55 percent interest in Tower International. The Eatons were now formally his employees, and over the course of the next few years they jointly planned these enormous undertakings. Shortly, though, the Eatons would be entirely eclipsed by Hammer in a little-known conflict that would pit Cyrus Eaton and Armand Hammer, two of the Kremlin's favorite capitalists, against each other in acrimonious dispute.

By 1971 Occidental Petroleum, once so profitable because of Libyan oil, was in trouble. Partly because of Qaddafi's demands and partly because of a worldwide glut of oil that year, Occidental stock dropped from its 1968 high of 55 to 10. A stock analyst concluded, "It looks like Hammer is presiding over a disaster." In the third quarter of 1971, Occidental reported the largest loss in its history: $13.5 million.

In the midst of this losing season, Hammer sent the executive vice-president of Occidental International, Tim Babcock, to attend the Business International conference in Moscow in November 1971. At the same meeting during which Don Kendall made his dramatic and successful pitch for Pepsi-Cola, Tim Babcock heard the Soviet Foreign Trade Minister, Nikolai Patolichev, tell the assembled businessmen:

> I know you wonder if a capitalist can do business in a Communist country. I'll put it to you this way. One of your richest men is Armand Hammer. When I was a little boy in the 1920s I learned my mathematics using a pencil bearing the imprint "Hammer." I would wear it to the nub and then turn it in for another.

Of course, his listeners did not need to be persuaded to do business, since they had already paid their way to Moscow in search of profit.

But Patolichev's nostalgic ancedote hinted at what very few others knew—that Armand Hammer was fast at work on an array of deals, each of which was bigger than any other corporate chief would dare think of suggesting to his board. Besides his alliance with the Eatons, Hammer had hired an unlikely collection of unusually skilled experts. One was Samuel Pisar, the international lawyer and survivor of the Nazi concentration camps who had gotten his start in East-West trade as a negotiator for the Eaton group. The Kennedy administration had named him to a task force on foreign economic policy, which recommended, of all things, that Kennedy lift the ban on Soviet crab meat. Hammer knew the problem well. And in 1970 Pisar had written a landmark book *Coexistence and Commerce,* which urged Soviet-American trade.

Another of Hammer's new associates was Sargent Shriver, who, as U.S. ambassador to France, had become interested in Soviet trade by talking with Dzhermen Gvishiani. Shriver, also a lawyer, was a friend of one of the most enigmatic entrepreneurs ever to enter the field of East-West trade—David Karr, whom Hammer had hired in late 1971.

Born in Brooklyn of Russian-Jewish parents, Karr worked at various jobs before entering the world of high finance: Fuller Brush man, reporter for the New York *Daily Mirror,* investigator for the Council Against Nazi Propaganda, penny-a-line writer for the Communist newspaper the *Daily Worker,* and assistant to columnist Drew Pearson. By the late 1950s, he had become an expert in fighting corporate takeovers. When Occidental Petroleum underwent financial difficulties in 1971, Hammer hired Karr to fight any takeover attempts.

Shriver and Karr paved the way in Moscow for Hammer's arrival in the summer of 1972. "Hammer knew who to see to make the trip worthwhile," Shriver recalls, "but we organized it." Karr went further in claiming credit for Hammer's successes. He later said he had told Hammer, "You're always talking about your old friend Lenin. Let's go to the Soviet Union and make a deal." He even bragged that he was responsible for "dragging Armand kicking and screaming to the U.S.S.R." Actually, Karr was well aware of how long Armand Hammer had been planning his return.

In the middle of July 1972, two months after the Nixon-Brezhnev summit, Hammer flew with his retinue to Moscow, stopping only in Copenhagen to pick up the requisite Russian crew—the same one that had navigated Richard Nixon's Air Force One. Then followed five days of meetings with the heads of eighteen ministries.

Much of what Hammer has said about this trip is pure myth. For example, he announced to the press that he had simply flown into Moscow, made a whirlwind tour of the Soviet bureaucracy, and ended up, after five days, with a preliminary protocol covering a host of projects. Since he had probably already decided to cut out the Eatons, he never mentioned that many of the agreements he initialed were not only arranged but actually inspired by the two Cyruses.

Another tale concerned his manner of negotiating with Soviet officials. Concealing his almost yearly visits to Moscow since the early sixties, Hammer said that at "the right moment in a meeting with the chief Soviet planners" he drew from his pocket a yellowed, handwritten note—Lenin's 1922 letter wishing him success on his first concession, which "would be of great importance also for trade relations between our Republic & United States." This gesture, Hammer said, brought the Soviets to tears. This could never have happened, of course; the Lenin letters had been stolen by his second wife.

During the talks, the Soviet officials told Hammer they would require about $180 million in credits from the United States. Hammer assured them the credits would be forthcoming, that he had spoken with President Nixon, and that Nixon had said he would authorize such a loan.

But the Russians did not believe Hammer. Moscow, during the summer of 1972, was crowded with American businessmen, many of whom knew Nixon personally. Vladimir Alkhimov, the head of the State Bank, called one of them.

"We have a problem in our negotiations with Armand Hammer," Alkhimov explained. "Are you friendly enough with President Nixon to ask him a question?" When the businessman replied that he was, Alkhimov continued, "Then I wonder whether you could ask him this. Dr. Hammer tells us that he met with Nixon at the White House before he came here, and Nixon agreed to supply certain credits. Frankly, we don't know whether to believe Hammer. Do you think you could ask the President, when you return to Washington, if he really made such a promise?"

The American agreed, and when he got to Washington he called the White House. "Mr. President," he said. "Alkhimov wants to know if you told Armand Hammer you would grant credits for the deal he's working out in Moscow."

"Who's Armand Hammer?" Nixon asked.

On July 18, 1972, Hammer arrived in London and called a press conference. The air was charged, because there had already been several intentional leaks by Oxy officials. Radio Free

Europe had reported that Occidental Petroleum was about to sign an agreement to develop Soviet oil and gas fields, "the largest deal in the history of Soviet-American trade." An Occidental spokesman in London would only say that at the press conference Hammer would announce something "truly major."

The Soviet government had a compelling reason to have Hammer make the announcement that day. It had just suffered a profound setback in the Middle East: President Anwar el-Sadat had just expelled Soviet military advisors from Egypt that morning. The Soviets probably wanted to offset the humiliation of the Egyptian expulsion by publicizing a significant breakthrough in Soviet-American economic cooperation.

Hammer was suitably exuberant. "In fifty-one years of dealing with the Soviet government," Hammer told reporters, "I have never found the grounds more favorable for the rapid expansion of East-West trade than exists at present." He listed vast planned transactions in which Occidental would supply the Russians with "patents and scientific and technological know-how in five fields" in exchange for Soviet commodities such as oil, gas, nickel, chrome, and chemicals. Oxy was also going to design and contract for the construction of Holiday Inn–type hotels in Russia.

Hammer would not reveal the total value of the deals because, he said, the Soviets had asked him not to. The figure of three billion dollars had, however, been leaked to newsmen, and when he was asked if it was accurate, he refused to deny it. "I wonder where they got that from," he said simply.

The effect of this electrifying announcement was just as Hammer had expected: Occidental Petroleum was, that day, the most active issue traded on the New York Stock Exchange. Its stock price gained almost three points. Within three days, eight million shares of Oxy stock had been traded. The influx of orders was so great that trading had to be halted several times to keep the paperwork under control. At one point, over two million shares of Oxy changed hands in only two hours. Wall Street had rarely seen a stock transformed so rapidly from a loser into a hot property.

Two days after the announcement, on July 20, Nixon's new Secretary of Commerce, Peter Peterson, arrived in Moscow with a trade delegation. The first question he was asked at a news conference was what he thought about the Oxy deal. Peterson responded that it was trumped up: it was by no means a deal but merely "an understanding to cooperate in exploring a variety of deals." Occidental stock immediately dropped.

In Washington that day, Hammer met with Nixon at the

White House. He had requested an appointment to discuss his Soviet ventures, and with the political importance of the matter, he had gotten one at once. Times were clearly different. No longer did he have to send pleading letters to the White House and rely on the help of go-betweens. For once, his grand schemes were in harmony with official government policy. It also helped that he was a major contributor to Nixon's reelection campaign—more generous, as would soon be revealed, than even insiders knew.

Within a few weeks, Hammer's secret negotiations with the Soviet government to build a colossal natural-gas pipeline were going along so smoothly that he decided to shed the Eatons, who were no longer necessary. This took both father and son by surprise. In April Cyrus, Sr., had proudly told a Chesapeake & Ohio shareholders' meeting:

> It will be a memorable day in my life when the *New York Daily News,* our newspaper of largest circulation and the most vigorous denouncer of Communism, uses power produced by Soviet natural gas to run its presses. I will also be delighted when the Cold Warriors of Washington cook their breakfast by natural gas brought in from the Soviet Union.

At the end of August, Hammer called Cyrus, Jr., and asked him to fly out to Los Angeles for a meeting. Eaton arrived at Hammer's house and saw that Hammer was accompanied by the president of Occidental and two company lawyers.

"I think it would be better if we went our separate ways," Hammer said. "I think we should dissolve our relationship."

Eaton had no choice but to buy back Hammer's shares of Tower International. Later, an Occidental executive told Cyrus, Jr., that Hammer suspected Eaton was working for two rival bosses, his father and Hammer, and that he was supplying his father with information on reserves of Siberian natural gas with the intention of breaking away and forming a separate, wholly-Eaton-owned venture. Although Cyrus, Jr., flatly denies any such plans, this was at least the accusation against him that Hammer privately made. "I'd rather smile about it," Eaton says. "That's how he operates, and it's probably how that type of person has to operate in this world."

But Cyrus Eaton, Sr., was furious. He had heard a devastating bit of information about Hammer a few months back, and now he was determined to make it public. It concerned, of course, a major Soviet deal.

By late October 1972, the Soviet natural-gas project in which the Eatons had hoped to participate was taking shape without them. On September 13, 1972, Hammer met with Kosygin and afterward announced that the Soviets had granted Occidental Petroleum permission to open a Moscow office and that he and Kosygin had discussed plans to construct a seventy-million-dollar trade center in Moscow. Then, on October 29, Howard Boyd, the chairman of El Paso Natural Gas, and Hiroshi Anzai, president of the Tokyo Gas Company, jointly announced their intention to develop the giant natural-gas fields in the Yakutia region of East Siberia and construct pipelines to supply gas to Japan and the West Coast of the United States. They projected that by 1978 they would be shipping 525 billion cubic feet of gas.

Naturally, their partner in the deal was Armand Hammer. A number of American and Japanese firms had competed to exploit the gas fields, but Hammer had convinced the Boyd/Anzai group that they would not be selected unless he was in on it. Boyd was once asked why he decided to work with Hammer. "We needed Hammer," he said, "because he's the only man who can get through to the Soviets."

"How do you know that's true?"

"He told us."

As soon as the gas agreement was announced, Cyrus Eaton, a generous supporter of George McGovern, flew to Washington and met with Robert Strauss, head of the Democratic National Committee. Something was suspicious about Hammer's latest project, Eaton said. It involved President Nixon.

The Democrats were eager to publicize as much information as possible on Nixon's financial improprieties. Stories were already being unearthed about the alleged "shakedown" of big business by Maurice Stans of the Committee for the Reelection of the President. Strauss was interested in what Eaton had to say, and he called a reporter he knew in Washington. There were two groups of energy companies bidding for two separate, giant Soviet natural gas projects, Strauss said; because they needed Nixon's support, they were contributing huge, secret sums of money to his campaign treasury. Strauss suggested the newsman see Cyrus Eaton, who was staying at the Statler-Hilton.

Eaton welcomed the reporter cordially and, with a gleam in his eye, related the details. Without explaining his early involvement in the Soviet gas projects, he said that there were two consortia trying to buy the President's favor. One, called "North Star," consisted of Tenneco, Texas Eastern Transmission, and Brown & Root. North Star wanted to bring gas from Murmansk to Boston, New York, Baltimore, and Savannah, and the group had hired as attorneys two friends of the President's: Herb Brownell of Lord, Day and Lord (Brownell had been Eisenhower's attorney general) and John Connally, then head of "Democrats for Nixon." The other consortium, the "Yakutsk group," sought to bring gas from Vladivostok to Los Angeles with the help of the Japanese. This group consisted of El Paso Natural Gas, the San Francisco–based Bank of America, the Tokyo Gas Corporation, and Occidental Petroleum. Maurice Stans was well aware, Eaton said, that all of these companies wanted presidential approval, and Stans had insisted on substantial gifts from all of them.

Eaton continued, with particular relish, that Armand Hammer had given Stans "a big pile of money, a secret campaign contribution," which was flown to Washington just hours before the new campaign financing law, which required full disclosure of contributors, went into effect on April 7.

Eaton had accomplished his purpose. The journalist published the information on the proposed gas venture (while omitting the charges of campaign abuses, for which Eaton was unable to supply documentation) and furnished the information to Congress when the Senate Watergate Committee was formed in February 1973. The Senate committee asked Hammer how much he had contributed to Nixon's campaign, and Hammer claimed $46,000. He did not mention an additional $54,000 he had given in cash just before April 7 because, he says, he thought it had not been received—Stans had never sent a receipt. In fact, Stans did not receive the $54,000 until after April 7, and therefore the contribution was illegal.

The Watergate Special Prosecutor knew this; he accused Hammer of lying to the Senate, and brought the matter before a grand jury for an indictment. Hammer's aide-de-camp Tim Babcock, who had channeled the money, testified before the grand jury that he had received the money after April 7. Babcock pleaded guilty to having assisted Hammer in the crime and was sentenced to four months in prison. (Later, another Oxy executive, Marvin Watson, was found guilty of arranging for the delivery of false documents to hide his boss's contributions and was fined five hundred dollars.)

Hammer then sent the grand jury a letter in which he pleaded guilty but argued his innocence. "Did my intention to make the payment before April 7 become confused with the actual deed?"

he wrote. "In the hectic life I lead, with problems of global scope often engaging me day and night, this matter could conceivably have been overlooked. . . ." But Federal Court Chief Judge William Jones rejected this letter, entered a Not Guilty plea for him, and ordered him to stand trial in Washington.

In addition to his regular lawyer, Louis Nizer, Hammer had engaged the prominent Washington attorney Edward Bennett Williams, who he thought would have the influence to counteract the fervor of the Washington court. Eventually, Williams—who insisted on total control over Hammer's defense—came into conflict with Nizer and another of Hammer's attorneys, Arthur Groman, and resigned.

Believing that the outcome of a California trial might be more favorable, Nizer and Groman began an effort to have the trial moved. When the court rejected the charge of bias, the lawyers argued that Hammer had a heart condition so serious that his life would be endangered if he were away from Los Angeles for any length of time. They produced testimony from several leading cardiologists to support the claim, and the trial was consequently moved to Los Angeles.

Hammer then attempted to enter a plea from his hospital bed at the Cedars of Lebanon Hospital in Los Angeles, insisting that a courtroom appearance would jeopardize his health, but the judge refused to allow it. Was the heart condition genuine? Louis Nizer writes that Hammer had a family history of cardiovascular weakness, and this condition was now aggravated by the stress of the trial. Myer Feldman, who assisted Nizer, recalls seeing Hammer in bed looking "haggard, just terrible. I know it seemed awfully strange," Feldman says, "but he looked like he was about to die."

If this condition had really come upon him suddenly, Hammer used it to maximum effect. On March 4, 1976, he was wheeled into the Los Angeles courtroom in a green-canvas-backed wheelchair, wired to heart-monitoring devices. Several doctors accompanied him in case there was an emergency. His face pale and his hands trembling, he pleaded guilty. "Your honor, this is the first time I've been charged with a criminal offense," he said. "I greatly regret my actions. All my life I have tried to lead a useful life, and I trust, in the time that may be allowed me, your honor will give me the opportunity to be a useful member of society." Hammer was found guilty of a misdemeanor, and his sentence was light: a fine of three thousand dollars and one year's probation. If the dramatic courtroom appearance had been designed to save him from a prison sentence, it had worked.

Later Hammer claimed that he felt no remorse. "As far as I was concerned," he told John Callaway in a television interview in 1981, "it wasn't any worse than getting a ticket for speeding. Misdemeanors are also given for traffic violations. But the newspapers made a big thing out of this thing, as you know."

How had he gotten into this legal tangle? At the end of March, 1972, he had lunch with Maurice Stans in Washington to discuss his contribution to the Nixon campaign. Hammer says he offered $50,000. But Stans knew that Hammer wanted presidential approval for his various Russian deals, especially the natural gas proposal, and may have pressured him for that reason. "Dr. Hammer, $50,000 is not enough," Hammer says Stans told him. "All of your friends in California—Firestone and Justin Dart and others—belong to the $100,000 Club. We expect you to give us $100,000." Hammer does not say whether Stans mentioned the gas project.

Hammer wanted to join the club but had brought with him only $50,000—cash stuffed in a suitcase. The new campaign-financing law was to go into effect in a week, after which time no anonymous contributions could be made. Considering the sensitivity of his Soviet deals, Hammer obviously did not want it to look as if he had in any way bribed the President. Louis Nizer, however, argues that Hammer sought anonymity to avoid pressure from the Democrats for an equivalent sum, since Hammer "was a Democrat."

So on April 3, Hammer claims, he went to his personal vault at Occidental and drew out $54,000 in cash, which he immediately gave to Tim Babcock to take to Washington. He says Babcock did not transfer the funds on time, but instead held on to them for several months. In other words, he had made the questionable donation on time, but Babcock was responsible for missing the deadline. Babcock denied this.

Hammer defended his claim that he had given the cash to Babcock on time by insisting that he had told Nixon, during his July 20, 1972, appointment: "Mr. President, I am glad to tell you that I am a member of the $100,000 Club." The Watergate Special Prosecutor listened to the tape of the conversation, which was not among those the White House had released, and confirmed Hammer's story. While this did not quite prove that he had made the contribution before April 7, it does at least appear to demonstrate that Hammer attempted to make use of his contribution to enlist Nixon's support.

Within a few weeks of the trial, Hammer miraculously

recovered from his heart ailment. In early July 1976, he was once again aboard his private jet, flying around the world and making deals. The sudden malady that had kept him out of jail had just as suddenly and mysteriously vanished.

"The medical reports confirmed what the doctors considered an impossible recovery," Nizer recalls. "They were astounded. Understandably, laymen and readers of his continued exploits became skeptical of the prior prognoses, particularly in the midst of a criminal proceeding." Nizer ascribes the startling recovery to the lifting of stress with the conclusion of the trial.

But Hammer's reputation was damaged. The makers of Arm & Hammer baking soda, the Church and Dwight Company, began to tire of being mistakenly associated with Armand Hammer. Besieged with angry letters after Hammer's trial, they publicly disavowed any relationship with Hammer. "We get letters asking why we're in trouble in the California courts," a Church and Dwight spokesman said. "Some people link Armand Hammer with our brand name, and there's absolutely no connection."

14

ONE KARL MARX SQUARE

If a Muscovite had gotten up very early on the morning of Monday, May 21, 1973, and walked through the empty, cobbled expanse of Red Square, he might have beheld a historical sight. David Rockefeller, accompanied only by an aide, was standing before Lenin's tomb. At a discreet distance were several KGB agents, acting as Rockefeller's security guard.

Rockefeller and his assistant Peter Bakstansky, the Chase Manhattan director of public relations, were there because they did not trust the rooms at the Hotel Metropole, where they were staying. Dignitaries' hotel rooms in Moscow were always bugged anyway, but David Rockefeller's probably had someone listening around the clock.

Bakstansky, who had been in Moscow for ten days already, had come by David's suite early in the morning, as they had arranged, to prepare answers to questions Rockefeller could expect later that day at the press conference he had called. The occasion was the opening of the Chase Manhattan representative office in Moscow—the first American bank in the Soviet Union in over fifty years and Chase's first Moscow office ever.

The press conference—"American style," it was billed, meaning that questions were allowed—was also the first of its kind in the Soviet Union. Some of the questions would be tough, Rockefeller figured, because loaning money to the Communists was still controversial. As the first banker to set up shop in Moscow, he knew he was in for some sharp queries.

When Bakstansky came by that morning, David told him he thought the best way to converse and not be overheard was to take a stroll. Red Square was only two blocks away, and besides, he wanted to see Lenin's mausoleum once again. As they walked, they formulated cautious, bland answers, the kind David preferred.

"This was a major thing," recalls Joseph V. Reed, Jr., Rockefeller's former aide-de-camp, who is as emphatic as his boss is bland. "Imagine—a Chase Manhattan representative office there—a Rockefeller bank in Moscow! It was fabulous. To have the world's preeminent banker-statesman there, well, this is the *big leagues.*"

The Soviet government had provided a room, graced with flowers and a Russian orchestra, in the Hotel Metropole's restaurant for the press conference and the reception. Murray Seeger of the *Los Angeles Times* remembers it as "the greatest spread the Russians had ever seen. There was *real caviar.* Some of these official types had never seen anything like it." Representatives of every embassy and corporation were there, but it was really the Soviets who buzzed with excitement. Some of them had lined up in the street outside the hotel for half an hour just for the chance to shake hands with Rockefeller. The Soviets who specialize in contacts with Western celebrities were there in force to rub elbows with this famous American.

Rockefeller opened the conference with ten minutes of remarks, touting the historical significance of the opening, and then took questions. The American and European reporters were seated with the Soviet ones, and the difference between them rapidly became obvious. The Westerners all asked "hardball" questions, while the Russians asked things like, "What does this mean for the friendship of the Soviet and American peoples?"

The irony of this totem of capitalism being so exalted by the Communists did not escape Rockefeller, but he downplayed it as a creation of Soviet rhetoric. A reporter asked him how he reconciled the royal treatment he was receiving with the Soviet propaganda line that the Rockefellers were the horrid oppressors of the capitalist world. "The world must be changing rapidly," he said. "I have had nothing but the most cordial treatment. I cannot help thinking that Soviet officials do not take their own propaganda too seriously."

Yet he concedes that the address of the new Chase Moscow office, in the Metropole, was a bizarre bit of irony: it was located at One Karl Marx Square. He remarked years later, "Our particular suite of rooms looked out on Karl Marx Square—the *bust* of Karl Marx. So it seemed very appropriate."

Rockefeller's talk with Lyndon Johnson after meeting with Nikita Khrushchev in 1964 seems to have accomplished its purpose. Johnson became convinced by Rockefeller and several White House aides that trade might induce the Soviets to stop backing the North Vietnamese. By 1966, when the Vietnam War was dividing America, Johnson took some steps to ease restrictions on exports to Russia. He announced on October 7, 1966, a shift from "the narrow concept of co-existence to the broader vision of peaceful engagement." A week later, he lifted controls on more than four hundred nonstrategic items, from grain and fertilizers to gas and petroleum. In his State of the Union message at the beginning of 1967, he bade Congress to pass a bill extending Communist nations most-favored-nation tariff treatment and access to American commercial loans.

Exactly a week after Johnson's call, the Rockefellers announced that they were joining with the Eatons to fund investment projects in Communist countries. The declaration was dramatic news—the headline on the front page of *The New York Times* declared, "EATON JOINS ROCKEFELLERS TO SPUR TRADE WITH REDS." The article stated that "an alliance of family fortunes linking Wall Street and the Midwest is going to try to build economic bridges between the free world and Communist Europe."

Specifically, the International Basic Economy Corporation (IBEC), an investment company that Nelson Rockefeller founded to develop Latin American countries, had agreed to cooperate with the Eatons' Tower International to construct rubber-goods plants and hotels in the Soviet Union, Yugoslavia, Hungary, Czechoslovakia, Rumania, and Bulgaria. The venture would combine the Rockefeller firm's money with the Eatons' entrée to Soviet officialdom. Harry Schwartz noted in *The New York Times* that the President, in his attempt to widen Soviet-American trade, "has received what amounts to the backing of the Rockefellers."

But as soon as the deal was made public, it fell through. "It was an unfortunate situation," Cyrus Eaton, Jr., recalls. "The *Times* story was an enormous shock to Nelson Rockefeller's political advisers, who were trying to groom him for the presidency." Although it was Nelson's company, Eaton doubts he knew about it; when the news came out, he ordered the president of IBEC to dissolve the arrangement at any cost. "Nelson's political advisers, who were running the show, said it was the wrong type of image for him to have."

It was probably no coincidence that on the very day the news of the Rockefeller-Eaton enterprise was announced, the Soviet government took out its first trade advertisement ever in an American newspaper. A two-page spread in *The New York Times* headed "FOREIGN TRADE—TWO-WAY TRAFFIC" asked American businessmen to try the Soviet market. The *Times* noted elsewhere that it had solicited advertising from the Soviets for two years and had, until then, received nothing but negative answers. Apparently a political decision had been made in the Kremlin to respond to Johnson's efforts.

Henry Kissinger, in his memoirs, attributes the interest in East-West trade that arose by 1968 to efforts by Theodore Sorensen, John Kennedy's former chief adviser, and former Under Secretary of State George Ball. Sorensen was surprised to read this account, although he concedes that he wrote an article on the subject for *Foreign Affairs* and testified before Congress. Much credit is also due David Rockefeller, who did not fear a public backlash as did his brother. And the Soviets made it clear that they appreciated his help. After the 1968 election, Ambassador Dobrynin conveyed to the Nixon administration that if David were named ambassador to Moscow, the political situation would be greatly ameliorated. David turned down the offer.

Although Nixon did not at first favor expanding trade, he began promoting trade with Rumania after a visit there in August 1969. By the end of 1969, Congress passed a new Export Administration Act that declared it American policy to expand trade with Russia at the President's discretion. The country was coming around to David Rockefeller's point of view.

In October 1970, Rockefeller had the President of Rumania, Nicolae Ceausescu, to lunch at the Chase and afterward urged that Rumania be granted most-favored-nation status. As Rumania's leading correspondent bank, he said, Chase was interested in a large investment in that country.

A good friend and member of the Chase International Advisory Board since 1965 was Giovanni Agnelli, the chairman of Fiat. In 1966 Agnelli signed a contract with the Russians to build a giant, $1.5 billion automotive plant in the Soviet Union. Although Fiat lost money on the transaction because Western inflation pushed the construction costs far above the fixed price the Soviets had paid, Rockefeller was encouraged by his friend's interest in doing business with the Soviet Union.

David began to speak out more often and more forcefully. In March 1971, at a Chase international financial forum at the Cavalieri Hilton in Rome, he chided the United States for falling behind Europe and Japan in building economic bridges to the Communist world. It was time, he said, to replace the Iron Curtain with "a plate-glass curtain."

He happened to be in Kiev for the sixth Dartmouth Conference in July 1971, when Nixon announced he would be visiting China. The day after the announcement that, in Kissinger's words, "shook the world," Rockefeller and three other Dartmouth participants—Senator Frank Church, retired army general James M. Gavin, and Charles W. Yost, the former U.S. chief representative at the United Nations, met with Kosygin for two hours and twenty minutes. Kosygin said nothing about China, so the Americans did not dare bring it up. They discussed trade, disarmament, pollution control, and the U.N. Unlike the 1964 meetings, which were "stiff and formal and not particularly productive," this one, Rockefeller found, was cordial.

Then, on August 10, 1972, two months after the first Nixon-Brezhnev summit, Rockefeller announced that Chase would open a special East-West trade unit in Vienna. Also—as yet a secret—Chase was financing some of the Soviet purchases of grain that were to be called the Great Grain Robbery of 1972. At the end of August, Rockefeller was interviewed on Soviet television for five minutes, introduced as "the number one representative of the American business world." He declared to his Soviet viewers, "It will take some time to develop commerce, but we have brighter prospects than ever before."

On November 14, 1972, Chase announced it had received approval from the Soviet authorities to open a representative office in Moscow. The international financial community took notice. Evidently détente was a serious thing if a giant like the Chase Manhattan Bank was going to invest in it. Rockefeller's aide Joseph Reed admits that it had been a difficult decision for Chase directors to make. "I think there were a lot of people on the board against it," he says. "It was a very controversial issue."

The Soviets made it clear they wanted a high-ranking officer in Chase's Moscow office, one who had earned David's confidence, and specifically one who did *not* speak Russian. Chase pulled a senior vice-president named Alfred Wentworth out of London. At fifty-two, Wentworth was not an up-and-coming officer, but Moscow was hardly a growth field for a bank executive. He was a singularly uncontroversial figure, and after more than twenty years at the Chase he did have Rockefeller's ear.

Wentworth arrived in Moscow at the end of January 1973, with his wife, Nancy, and his dog. He worked on arrangements for the opening and got settled in his new apartment, which was grander than that of any other American businessman in Moscow. The Soviet government, determined to treat Wentworth with the utmost generosity, gave him an immense flat—the size of four—at 86 Leninskii Prospekt. Wentworth recalls it was "the best apartment I ever lived in." Chase spared no expense in fixing it up, and also renovated the lobby of his building, thereby making it clear to the Soviets that it, too, planned to deal with them as genteelly as it did the British, the Austrians, and the French. And the Soviets were thrilled. They had been looking for this kind of prestige since the Revolution.

"This was the beginning of détente, and I was representing David, so they bent over backward," Wentworth remembers. "I demanded the best of everything—the best office, the best apartment, the biggest car—a lot. And I got it." He found a Russian chauffeur at the Italian embassy who spoke English and offered him four times as much as the Italians were paying him. Although he was proud that he had stolen the driver away, he had unknowingly hired an agent of the UPDK (the branch of Soviet intelligence that deals with the foreign diplomatic corps).

Wentworth did not entirely adapt, however. He refused to fly on Soviet airplanes, because shortly after he arrived someone translated for him an article from a Soviet civil aviation magazine about how Soviet planes had a tendency to fall from the sky unexpectedly. From then on, he traveled in Russia only by train.

Before long, the Wentworths were fixtures in Moscow society. They were invited to parties most foreigners never even heard about. They could get tickets to the Bolshoi when almost nobody else could. By the time the Chase office opened, an American then in Moscow observes, "the Wentworths had acquired the color of their surroundings."

Peter Bakstansky came over in early May 1973 to make contact with the Moscow press corps and attract as much attention as possible to the opening. He also brought with him a load of Chase-approved paintings and furniture, so that even the Moscow office on Karl Marx Square would look like a Chase office.

If Armand Hammer could fly his jet into Moscow, why, thought David Rockefeller, shouldn't he also be able to? Although he had used commercial transportation on each of his three previous trips to Russia, this time, for the triumphal opening, he requested clearance for his jet. "I've never worked so hard in my whole life," Joseph Reed recalls. "It was like working out the Vietnamese agreements." Ambassador Dobrynin assured him there would be no problem. But as Rockefeller and his entourage traveled around Western Europe in May, no official word came. Finally, in Nice, twenty-four hours before Rockefeller was to go to Moscow, permission came. They flew from Nice to Copenhagen, picked up a Soviet pilot, and proceeded to Moscow.

While Rockefeller waited at the V.I.P. lounge at Sheryemetyevo Airport for his passport to be approved, he was suddenly hailed by another arriving American: Armand Hammer, who had with him the golf-course architect Robert Trent Jones. The only two people in the world with the privilege of flying into Moscow by private plane had chanced to arrive at precisely the same moment.

The next day, May 20, 1973, Rockefeller and Reed met with Premier Kosygin in the Kremlin for over an hour to discuss, as usual, politics and business. Tass, the Soviet news agency, reported that Rockefeller—"the prominent banker and public figure"—was received by Kosygin "in an atmosphere of mutual understanding."

Rockefeller and Reed returned to their rooms at the Metropole, where Reed typed his notes from the Kosygin meeting. Later he found that Russians, presumably KGB, had gone through his briefcases and taken apart his luggage. "You never saw anything like it," he says. "It was wild. It was right out of James Bond."

That day Rockefeller and ten other Chase executives were guests of Foreign Trade Minister Patolichev and ten trade officials for lunch at a fancy Moscow restaurant. Everything was elegant; the Soviets had gone to great lengths to see that their guest of honor and his assistants were wined and dined royally. The main course was a slab of indeterminate meat, which one of the Americans thought was reindeer steak. The steak knives provided were too dull for the unwary Americans to cut through the meat, and as one of them sawed away in vain, a Soviet official who spoke practically no English turned to him, nodding enthusiastically, and proclaimed the only English word he knew: "Good!"

After the gala, Rockefeller left the country, whisked through customs just as quickly as when he entered. Reed had elected to spend a few days seeing Moscow with his wife. When it came time to leave, however, he realized that his visa had not been stamped coming in, because he had passed through the V.I.P. lounge with Rockefeller. Without the right forms he would not be permitted to leave, and he was unable to explain to Soviet bureaucrats why he was lacking the papers. "Mr. Rockefeller was treated on the way out like a head of state," Reed recalls, "and when I turned around to get any assistance, guess what? The red carpet had rolled up before you could say Jack Robinson, and I was a *nonperson.* It was awful. I spent two days wandering around from bureau to bureau—*'Nyet! Nyet!'* It was a nightmare."

It seemed a peculiarly Soviet blunder that on the very day Chase announced it would open a Moscow office, the Soviet press was attacking David Rockefeller by name. *Komsomolskaya Pravda,* the newspaper for the organization of young Communists, charged that he was linked to activities of the Central Intelligence Agency. *Ekonomicheskaya Gazeta,* the Communist Party's economic weekly, labeled Rockefeller a Zionist who was nefariously plotting to seize Arab oil lands. As soon as the attacks were brought to light in the Western press, they ceased. It was as if a part of the immense Soviet bureaucratic machinery, accustomed to decades of churning out anti-Rockefeller propaganda, had plodded along until the Americans noticed. Yet even a week before the Chase party at the Metropole, the Soviet press denounced the Rockefeller family for its "financial imperialism" in Latin America. The habit was hard to break. "They probably hadn't even read the article," Murray Seeger of the *Los Angeles Times* says of the Soviets at the Chase reception, "or if they read it they didn't pay any attention, and may not have associated it with this charming capitalist banker standing there in the Metropole Hotel."

But, slowly and inconsistently, the Soviet press halted its criticism of the Rockefellers. In February 1973, Yuri Zhukov, a political commentator for *Pravda,* returned from a Dartmouth Conference in Hanover, New Hampshire—one in which Rockefeller participated—and reported, "The most farsighted representatives of American business circles have long advocated such a development [of trade]." He of course had in mind Rockefeller. After that, Rockefeller was routinely labeled by Soviet newspapers as merely "a prominent American public figure."

The shift was startling. When Gerald Ford named Nelson Rockefeller as Vice President in 1974—an occasion that once would have aroused the Soviet press to a foamy wrath—the Russians reacted benignly. Although earlier Soviet propagandists would have been busy pointing out that having a Rockefeller a heartbeat away from the presidency was a confirmation that the Rockefellers really ran America, now *Pravda* criticized those in Congress who opposed Rockefeller's nomination. There had been attempts "designed to discredit Rockefeller," *Pravda* reported, but "these charges, which came from ultra right-wing organizations, were unfounded." Now that the Rockefeller dynasty favored trading with them, the Russians considered them good capitalists after all.

Scarcely had *The Rockefeller Dynasty,* by Soviet scholar A. Fursenko, come out in 1970, than it was removed from many Soviet library shelves. *The Rockefeller Dynasty* today cannot be found in the card catalogue at the Lenin Library in Moscow.

Once in the early seventies, Mr. Fursenko, who is a specialist on the Rockefellers, had the opportunity to meet the object of his study at firsthand. He travels to the United States extensively; before one visit to New York he notified Room 5600 that he was coming. Would David possibly have time to see him? He was surprised when Rockefeller invited him to lunch.

Fursenko was greeted in Rockefeller Center by David and several members of his family. After the introductions, he presented David with a copy of his book, the greatest flattery he could tender. At lunch, David insisted that Mr. Fursenko begin his meal with Oysters Rockefeller. The Rockefellers asked the Rockefeller scholar what he thought of the appetizer. Fursenko confessed, somewhat annoyed, that it really was quite good.

General James Gavin, a regular Dartmouth participant, once had Georgi Arbatov of the Soviet Institute on the U.S.A. and Canada to his home in Cambridge, Massachusetts. "Why the hell do you Russians make such a fuss over David Rockefeller?" Gavin asked. "To us, he's just another businessman."

Arbatov smiled. "Jim, he's a member of the royal family. Some of our leaders think David Rockefeller can walk on water."

Many Americans share this belief. Joseph Reed insists, "David Rockefeller is an institution. He is the most powerful business-statesman in the world."

"The Marxist propaganda," Rockefeller himself observes, "for a long time has said that a few families, such as the Rockefellers, the Fords, the Mellons, and whatnot, rule America. They have repeatedly said this, to a point where they almost believe their own propaganda. To the extent that they do, they like to deal with the people who have the power, and if they think that we have the power, they talk to us." Although some, such as Arbatov, have a more realistic understanding, Rockefeller says, "a lot of people, even in the Soviet hierarchy, ascribe to a person like myself a degree of power which is totally disproportionate with reality. And because they believe it, they're more apt to pay attention to me than they would to someone else."

But are the Soviets wrong? On February 7, 1980, "Bill Moyers' Journal" featured a program, "The World of David Rockefeller," in which Moyers described Rockefeller as "one of the most powerful, influential, and richest men in America . . . the most conspicuous representative today of the ruling class, a multinational fraternity of men who shape the global economy and manage the flow of its capital."

David is shown having breakfast with the Saudi minister of finance, meeting with the most powerful men in Italian finance, paying a visit to the Vatican, asking the president of Germany to receive the international advisory committee of Chase ("Henry Kissinger is the chairman of it," David explains), and conferring with Marshal Tito of Yugoslavia. Moyers observes that every year Rockefeller is named by *U.S. News & World Report* as one of the ten most powerful people in the United States. "Are you conscious of exercising power?" he asks.

Rockefeller's reply, though couched in modesty, was insightful. "The only way . . . I am more fortunate than many," he replies, "is that because people have this perception, I think probably when I pick up the telephone and call somebody, they are a little bit more apt to answer than they might be if they'd never heard my name."

All other considerations aside, it is the magic of the Rockefeller name that carries the most weight. One of David's assistants, a former ambassador named Ridgeway Knight, told Bill Moyers, "I've represented a number of presidents, and I've spoken for a number of secretaries of state, but I've never seen doors open more easily than when I say I'm coming for David Rockefeller—it's fantastic!"

Apart from the almighty aura of power that translates into power itself, there are concrete ways in which Rockefeller is able to exercise influence. Until he retired in 1981, he had the vast apparatus of the Chase Manhattan Bank. The secret of Chase's domestic power lies in the bank's gigantic network of correspondent banks around the country and around the world. If a small bank in Ohio, for example, is asked for a two-million-dollar loan and has a capacity of only half a million, the bank will call on its big brother in New York, the Chase. And then, when Chase wants to effect a political change of some sort in Ohio, it applies pressure on its correspondent bank. This process is replicated around the globe; Chase has more than one hundred branch offices and six thousand correspondent banks.

In a broader sense, much of Rockefeller's influence derives from his chairmanship of the Council on Foreign Relations, which he has held since 1970. He became a member in 1946, a director in 1949, and a vice-president in 1951. The chairman of the Council tends to be a rich man, one who has contributed a lot of money to the organization, and also one who has a good understanding of world politics. His immediate predecessor, John J. McCloy, the postwar High Commissioner of Germany, was also his predecessor as chairman of the Chase. But while the Council's members generally come from the Eastern United States, it is hardly a cohesive force. Among the fifteen hundred members are the "neo-conservative" editor of *Commentary* Norman Podhoretz and the liberal scholar of Soviet affairs, George Kennan, who could not possibly be expected to agree on many of the topics the Council considers in its study groups, gatherings, and dinners.

Rockefeller's selection as chairman was an indication that the Council considered him wealthy, visible, and powerful enough to be its head. Many of the Council directors share his "internationalist" orientation. Therefore, he is chairman because his views are in harmony with others in the Council; as chairman, he does not really shape the group's thinking. Again, though, the prestige of chairing the Council on Foreign Relations—the closest embodiment of "The Establishment" in the United States—is in itself a type of power.

The real basis of his power, of course, is his wealth. At Nelson Rockefeller's vice-presidential confirmation hearings in 1974, information was disclosed that confirmed that the family has colossal and widespread holdings in the largest corporations in America: 2.06 percent of Standard Oil of California, 1.07 percent of Exxon, 1.75 percent of Mobil—all successors to his grandfather's Standard Oil—and significant holdings in General Electric, Eastman Kodak, Texas Instrument, AT&T, IBM, and of course, Chase. The head of Rockefeller Family & Associates and the Rockefellers' senior financial adviser, J. Richardson Dilworth (whom Representative Paul Sarbanes of Maryland called "the chancellor of the exchequer"), testified that Rockefeller holdings in securities and trusts exceeded a billion dollars. While the revelation of this family fortune came as a bit of a disappointment to many who were accustomed to hearing of individual billionaires and equating the Rockefellers with Croesus, this figure does not include the network of Rockefeller-controlled-and-supported foundations. In his book *Rockefeller Power,* Myer Kutz asserts that these foundations generate far more power than the family's raw wealth.

With all these assets and positions, David Rockefeller commands unequaled access to the top leadership of the United States. For example, Richard Nixon, who despised the Rockefellers along with the rest of the Eastern Establishment, offered David the position of Secretary of the Treasury at the beginning of each of his terms as President. Rockefeller recalls that Nixon was never "willing to talk to me about it unless I first accepted. . . . He didn't want to have that direct discussion. To me it was a very strange way of employing a person for a major job in the country."

Nixon's most famous acquisition from the Rockefeller collection was Henry Kissinger, who maintained extremely close relations with David and Nelson Rockefeller. His conception of détente with the Soviet Union meshed neatly with David's belief in the importance of increased trade with the Communist bloc. The Kissinger who warned in 1958 of the Soviet threat had come around, like Nixon, to advocating a web of economic and political ties with Russia.

The information that David persuaded the Carter administration, through Henry Kissinger, to admit the Shah of Iran to American territory—an event that in turn helped to precipitate the hostage crisis in Iran—indicates that Rockefeller may play a larger, though concealed, role in influencing U.S. policy than is generally realized. Since such dealings would occur at the highest levels, it is often impossible to establish whether they have taken place. Rockefeller denies ever having taken messages from Kissinger or Nixon to the Soviet leaders, although before each trip he is routinely briefed by the State Department. But since he did act as an emissary for the Johnson White House, there is reason to believe that he may have played a similar role for the Nixon White House.

When David Rockefeller spoke out in favor of East-West trade, bankers and Presidents alike listened with respect. Yet he is demure on the subject of whether the Soviets' belief in his power is exaggerated. "I have contacts," he admits. "But there's a great deal of difference between having contacts and the ability to tell people what to do and have it happen."

But simply by virtue of being a Rockefeller, his pilgrimages to Moscow were more than the visits of a head of state. They had a great symbolic value. As one Soviet official remarked privately in the early seventies, "the presence of David Rockefeller in the

Kremlin was a symbol of the end of the Cold War. It would never have happened before." David's advocacy of trade with Russia was the very best kind of celebrity endorsement. As soon as Chase announced its Moscow office, Walter Wriston, chairman of Citicorp, left for Moscow to secure permission for a representative office for his bank, too. He met with Ambassador Jacob Beam and told him, "We've applied for a Soviet office. What do you think—is it a good idea?"

Beam was skeptical. "There's no way you're going to make money," he said. "Chase is going to lose an awful lot, and they know it."

"Oh, you don't understand," Wriston said impatiently. "You see, I have to. Chase is there."

Within ten days after Chase's Moscow opening, representatives of the Bank of America, Manufacturers Hanover, Republic National Bank of Dallas, and other American and European banks flocked to Moscow to discuss opening facilities there. In June, the First National City Bank (as Citicorp's Citibank was then called) announced it had received permission for an office.

This led the late Gabriel Hauge, chairman of Manufacturers Hanover, to call a press conference upon his return from Russia and decry the "dubious banking" going on. Eight or ten Western banking delegations a day, he reported, were visiting the Soviet Bank for Foreign Trade and offering their services. Many of the banks were offering the Russians loans at below market rate. Some of Chase's long-term loans, in fact, were at 7 percent—below the cost of offering the loans—making them, as one American banker asserted, "loss leaders."

Chase will not comment on the profitability of its Moscow office, insisting that such information is "privileged" or "proprietary." But with all the money Chase had invested in the Moscow office and Al Wentworth's apartment and limousines—on top of Chase's cut-rate loans to the Soviet government—it seems unlikely that Chase made any money there. As a rival banker in Moscow at the time put it, "Chase couldn't have made a nickel's worth of profit." Once, the Bank of America representative in Moscow was asked how profitable the past year had been. "It was a completely successful year," he replied. "We made no loans."

Although within a few years most American banks pulled out of Moscow, Chase doggedly remained. Certainly it could make loans to the Soviet Union and the Eastern bloc without a Moscow office, but its beachhead in Russia is symbolic. Rockefeller's policy of extending long-term loans contradicted his 1964 declaration that loans given over a period longer than five years "would amount to aid, and I don't believe we should give aid to countries trying to subvert or overthrow friendly governments." Not only had America changed its mind, but so had David Rockefeller.

His "celebrity endorsement" was so valuable to the Russians that, when Jacob Beam retired as Ambassador to the Soviet Union in January 1973, the Russians were keen on having David named. Russia regarded America's emissary to China with envy: he was the wealthy industrialist David K. F. Bruce. *Literaturnaya Gazeta* attacked Bruce as a Cold Warrior, while at the same time referred longingly to his ties to American big business. The implication was clear: if China got an ambassador with influence in the business community, why couldn't the Russians get one too? Dobrynin conveyed the request to Nixon, and in due course Rockefeller was offered the position; no one was especially surprised when he turned it down, for he had more influence in Moscow than any ambassador could have. Although Beam was replaced with another highly capable career diplomat, Walter J. Stoessel, the Soviets were not crestfallen. They had, as one high Chase executive observes, obtained "diplomatic recognition by the Rockefellers" with the Chase office in Moscow.

Some American businessmen who have been involved in East-West trade far longer than he resent the glorification the Russians heap upon him. "He doesn't care about détente at all," one trader complains. "All he cares about is money. He pretends that his main concern is improving relations between Russia and America, but he's just a banker." Another businessman active in business with the Soviets complains about Rockefeller's grandiose, almost theatrical visits to Russia. "He knows his symbolic role, and he loves playing it, but he really goes no further. The Soviets hero-worship him, but frankly it seems like they honor him all out of proportion with his involvement."

Rockefeller protests that his treatment by the Soviets, while generous, is not excessive. "They do roll out the red carpet for me. I haven't been put in one of their dachas, or something like that, but I've been put in better rooms in hotels, probably, than some other people. Also, rooms that were well equipped with sound devices, I'm sure."

At a 1974 Senate hearing on the influence of multinational corporations on foreign relations, Senator Frank Church recalled seeing how well the Russians treated David Rockefeller at the 1971 Dartmouth Conference in Kiev. "He was treated like a celebrity, as we would treat royalty in this country," Church said. "So

I think perhaps American capitalists have special status in the Soviet Union on the basis of some curious reverse principle, just as we turn out great crowds to welcome royalty in this democratic society. It is a curious psychological twist."

By 1973, the most prominent American magnates favored by the Kremlin—Don Kendall and Armand Hammer—had established a personal acquaintance with the undisputed head of the Soviet leadership, Leonid Brezhnev. David Rockefeller, however, was not so privileged.

Joseph Reed considers this fact trivial. "I think they compartmentalize," he says of the Soviet hierarchy. "In China, we didn't meet with Mao, we met with Chou. I think that's the way the Russians do business. If we wanted to see Brezhnev, we would have pushed for Brezhnev. Kosygin's fine—chief operating officer." In Soviet officialdom, though, where protocol is all-important, a meeting with Brezhnev signified the highest approval; perhaps Brezhnev preferred to avoid bestowing his endorsement. Or perhaps, for reasons of pride, he did not care to join the ranks of world leaders who kowtowed to Rockefeller. Moreover, David Rockefeller did not require the prestige of access to the highest levels of the Kremlin in order to be influential in the United States, as Kendall and Hammer did.

Still, the Russian people appear to evince an adoration of Rockefeller that is puzzling. Norman Cousins tells a peculiar story of the reception David received during a Dartmouth Conference in Tbilisi, Soviet Georgia, in April 1974. The Soviets had invited the Americans to visit a subterranean warm spring bath in the Georgian countryside. During czarist times, the cavern had been used as a dungeon, but in the middle of the nineteenth century it had been converted into a luxurious underground spa. The Americans descended into the caves, where the spring was seething ominously, and masseuses stood by, ready to massage the Americans after bathing. Cousins examined the boiling waters and began to feel queasy. He decided simply to observe as the others went in. David Rockefeller, the star attraction, was laid out on a smooth slab of rock, while little old Georgian men walked on his back. When the Georgians had finished, they picked Rockefeller up and flung him into the baths.

Cousins could bear to watch no longer. He discreetly got dressed and walked up to the mouth of the cave. There, awaiting the Americans, was a tremendous crowd of the local people. As soon as they caught a glance of Cousins, they erupted into a cheer: *"Rokfyeller! Rokfyeller!"* Cousins was trapped. He tried to explain that he was not David Rockefeller, but the bystanders did not believe it. They started moving toward him, and he was forced to return to the cave.

When all were done with the bath and massage, the Americans partook of a resplendent Georgian feast in the cavern. Several hours later they departed.

There, still waiting, was the crowd, which seemed to have grown. They cheered as the Americans appeared, again chanting *"Rokfyeller!"*

Rockefeller grinned and bowed modestly. The crowd roared. He got into his Chaika and drove away, as the crowd kept chanting. As George Gilder, the author of *Wealth and Poverty,* observes: "Ironically, nobody knows how to revere, blandish, and exalt a Rockefeller half so well as the Marxists."

15

THE CLASH OF EGOS

LEONID BREZHNEV came to Washington for the first time in June 1973. After spending two days at Camp David recovering from jet lag, he was officially welcomed on the South Lawn of the White House on June 18. He was all ebullience and showmanship: he interrupted the decorous ceremony to shake hands with tourists and kiss babies, and he unnerved the more reserved Richard Nixon by throwing his arm around the President's shoulders and exclaiming, "See, we're already making progress!"

It was strangely reminiscent of Nikita Khrushchev's first visit to the United States in 1959, when he impressed Americans with his splendidly tailored suit and Italian shoes—having left his peasant shirt in Russia, he wanted to show the West how Western he was. Brezhnev vastly improved upon Khrushchev's performance. In 1973 there were neither tantrums nor romps through the cornfields of Iowa.

Brezhnev sported a windbreaker emblazoned with the presidential seal, a gift from Nixon; he swooned over another of Nixon's presents—a dark-blue Lincoln Continental with black velour upholstery. (In return for the automobile, Brezhnev gave Nixon a samovar and tea set, not quite a fair exchange.) He ogled the actress Jill St. John, embraced actor Chuck Connors, and kissed Henry Kissinger. His supply of good humor seemed inexhaustible.

On the evening of the eighteenth, Nixon gave a state dinner for Brezhnev in the White House. Prominent Americans from around the country were in attendance, including Harriman, Hammer, Kendall, Rockefeller, and Eaton. As people departed afterward, Nixon—who had probably waited until he was out of earshot of any reporter—put one arm around Brezhnev and one around the eighty-nine-year-old Eaton and remarked, "For more than twenty years now, Mr. Eaton has been a leading advocate in this country of trade with yours, a belief that I have belatedly come around to myself." Brezhnev laughed and nodded. Eaton, an inveterate Nixon-hater (he had once publicly compared Nixon to Adoph Hitler), only smiled.

A few days later, Brezhnev asked Treasury Secretary George Shultz to invite fifty American business leaders to lunch at Blair House, where Brezhnev was staying. In the receiving line Brezhnev singled out Hammer, holding up the line for a full three minutes while the two spoke in Russian. The group of businessmen was, as the *Washington Post* commented, "a receptive and believing congregation." They listened to Brezhnev hold forth for an hour and a half on the importance of Soviet-American commercial ties, and they agreed enthusiastically.

"The Cold War is over," Brezhnev said. "And I ask you, gentlemen, as I ask myself: was that a good period? Did it serve the interests of the peoples?" He answered his own rhetorical question: "No, no, no, and again no." In his exuberance he was long-winded, and his protocol officers began to glance nervously at their watches. Brezhnev noticed, picked up a piece of paper, and set it afire with his cigarette lighter. "If only I could burn up protocol like that," he boomed, "I would do it." The businessmen laughed and applauded.

After the speech, Kendall told a reporter, "Everybody is convinced that this man is serious about improved relations and increased trade between our countries. There is no doubt about it." The businessmen dined on roast beef and strawberry shortcake and pledged to do everything possible to fight congressional efforts to restrict trade.

For such efforts were considerable. During the summer of 1972, after the Nixon-Brezhnev summit meeting and while the first great rush of business negotiations was under way in Moscow, the Soviet government suddenly and inexplicably announced that anyone who wished to emigrate must pay a tax on the higher education he had received, ranging from $500 to $25,000, depending upon the degree attained. Under Soviet law, Jews were among the few nationalities permitted to leave, because unlike other ethnic groups they lacked a "homeland" within Soviet territory. More

Soviet Jews were allowed out during the first months of 1972 than ever before, which seemed to indicate that détente had really arrived. But this new tax, which may have been Russia's attempt to halt the rise in Israel's population and thereby please an increasingly hostile Egypt, fueled anti-détente forces in the United States and particularly the efforts of one ambitious man, Senator Henry Jackson.

Long an opponent of trade with the Soviet Union, Jackson seized upon the Soviet levy to propose an amendment to the trade reform act that Nixon and Foreign Minister Andrei Gromyko initialed at the White House on October 18, 1972. The bill would grant Russia the "most-favored-nation" status America's major trading partners enjoy—status that meant no restrictive tariffs—in exchange for partial Soviet repayment of its Lend-Lease debts. Jackson's amendment would deny most-favored-nation status to any nation that restricted the emigration of its citizens. Jackson's amendment rapidly gathered support, so that even when the Soviet government lifted the education tax on March 21, 1973, it was too late. A coalition of Jewish groups, labor unions, and conservatives had joined Jackson's campaign.

The 1973 summit, troubled by growing demands for Nixon's resignation in the wake of Watergate revelations, produced almost nothing besides effusive talk. Nixon and Brezhnev signed an empty "Agreement on the Prevention of Nuclear War" and little else. For political reasons, Nixon wanted more visible results than this. Brezhnev, who considered Jewish emigration his own affair, wanted to kill the Jackson amendment. There was a proposal on Nixon's desk that could accomplish both purposes at once: a plan for a U.S.–U.S.S.R. Trade and Economic Council—an organization of leading American businessmen and top Soviet trade officials devoted to the promotion of commerce. Led by twenty-five powerful American corporate executives and twenty-five highly placed Soviet officials, the Trade Council would assemble several hundred of the world's greatest multinational corporations to combat Jackson's legislation—not an official lobby but certainly a de facto one.

The Trade Council was the brainchild of Don Kendall. After his vodka-for-Pepsi deal was signed, he met several times with Brezhnev and, after each meeting, compiled a memo for Nixon. He decided that such an organization would remove Soviet-American trade from the battleground of American politics and provide an important element of continuity. "I convinced Brezhnev that we should form a joint council in which people stayed over long periods of time, to hold the relationship together during times of political problems," Kendall says. "And Brezhnev totally agreed. I came back and told President Nixon the same thing, and he also agreed."

Late in 1972, Kendall invited David Rockefeller, Al Wentworth (who had just been named the Chase representative in Moscow), Helmut Sonnenfeldt of the State Department, and Georgi Arbatov, the Soviet specialist on America, to lunch at the F Street Club in Washington to discuss the proposed Trade Council. As it was his idea, Kendall obviously wanted to be the American chairman, but he asked Rockefeller whether *he* wanted to be in charge. "Well, you know I'm all for this thing," Rockefeller said, "but I honestly can't take one more thing on. Don, why don't you do it?" Kendall responded quickly that he would.

At the summit in June 1973, Brezhnev produced a letter of protocol with Kendall's name already typed in as the American chairman. Nixon, of course, had no objections. When the summit was over, Nixon had Kendall draw up a list of directors, with the assistance of the Commerce Department.

Kendall came up with a star-studded roster of the chief executives of companies both giant and active in trade with the Soviet Union. They included David Rockefeller, Armand Hammer, Reginald Jones of General Electric, C. Peter McColough of the Xerox Corporation, Howard Clark of American Express, Frank Cary of IBM, Samuel Casey of Pullman, Irving S. Shapiro of Du Pont, C. William Verity of Armco, Milton Rosenthal of Engelhard Minerals & Chemicals, William F. Franklin of Caterpillar Tractor, Michel Fribourg of Continental Grain, Richard Gerstenberg of General Motors, Edgar F. Kaiser of Kaiser Industries, and G. William Miller of Textron. These and others constituted a board of twenty-five of the most powerful businessmen in America.

Commerce Secretary Frederick Dent called the men selected and informed them that they were in charge of the new Trade Council. Milton Rosenthal, whose Engelhard Minerals & Chemicals (now part of Phibro, Inc.) buys platinum and other precious metal catalysts from the Soviet Union in exchange for grain and other commodities, recalls the selection process for the Council directors as a sort of "Russian election": "I looked at the briefing book they gave us and there I saw I was a director, and I said, 'Who elected me?'" He recalls looking at the big names on the Council's board and thinking, "Here you have the chief executives of the Bank of America, General Motors, IBM, Xerox, 3M, and so on. Are they kidding? Do they really think they're going to get these people to give up two days a year to be present at the same time? But they turned up."

There was a flap when it turned out that David Rockefeller, whom Kendall had selected, was not asked to be a director. The snub had originated in the Oval Office. When Nixon was presented with the list for approval, he spotted one name he wanted off the board, pulled out a pencil, and scratched out David Rockefeller's name. Although he had begrudgingly offered Rockefeller cabinet positions, now that the election was over, Nixon, who never liked the Rockefellers anyway, wanted to deprive David of the glory.

But one did not leave David Rockefeller off any blue-ribbon board. Predictably, David was outraged. Although he avoided any direct confrontation, he had his associates make a few calls to influential Nixon administration members and intone ominously, "David is *furious.*" Treasury Secretary George Shultz received such a call. At a dinner at the White House unrelated to the Trade Council, Shultz approached one of the newly named directors of the Council and said, "You know, David is quite upset about not being one of the directors. He thinks it was some sort of a deliberate snub."

Rockefeller was called the next day and asked to serve as a director. He promptly said yes. Now, however, there were twenty-six directors instead of the twenty-five both sides had agreed upon, and so the Soviets added another bureaucrat.

Since the Trade Council was Kendall's doing, and Rockefeller was convinced that Kendall had tried to keep him off the board, this contretemps forever poisoned the already tepid relationship between the two. C. William Verity, a good friend of Rockefeller's who is especially diplomatic, observes that "Don Kendall doesn't like to be second. It was a clash of egos. Those are two different types of people."

Indeed, Rockefeller and Kendall are as unlike as two businessmen could be. Kendall is brash, abrasive, outspoken, and nouveau riche. He is also a staunch Republican who defended Richard Nixon in good times and bad. Rockefeller had been born wealthy and privileged; by American standards, he belongs to the old money class. He is also cautiously apolitical, supporting whoever happens to occupy the White House.

While most businessmen who know Rockefeller find him considerate and, as Michael Forrestal insists, "terribly nice," there were many among both the Nixon Republican new-money clan or the band of dedicated Kendall supporters who found Rockefeller waspish and vindictive when crossed. Surrounded from birth by servants, aides, and lackeys, Rockefeller is used to having his way. When he does not, he occasionally does battle from behind his swaddling of staff members. One friend of Kendall's on the Trade Council board describes Rockefeller as "a miniature State Department, with all the politics and backbiting."

The slighting of Rockefeller—which virtually nobody knew was Nixon's doing and not Kendall's—added to the tension within the Council that already existed among a few of its leading members, who subtly and quietly sought the prestige of unrivaled favor by the Soviet leadership. The strains were to erupt a few years later, after Nixon resigned; for the time being, however, under Kendall's masterful stewardship, the Council functioned as smoothly as could be expected.

One of its first orders of business was to select an American president to manage the day-to-day activities. Realizing that it would help to select someone friendly with Nixon, Kendall proposed one of the Nixon administration's most forceful proponents of East-West trade, the former Assistant Secretary of Commerce for Domestic and International Business, Harold B. Scott. An amiable, intelligent, and soft-spoken man who had contributed generously to Nixon's political campaigns, Hal Scott had been promised a position in Nixon's second-term Cabinet. Because the growing Watergate scandal had created hostility toward the President in Congress, however, Nixon realized he might be unable to have such an obvious partisan confirmed. As a sort of consolation prize, Nixon named Scott as president of the new Trade Council instead.

But Scott was not told, for the Soviets wanted to size him up first. One day Scott received a call from Foreign Trade Minister Patolichev, inviting him to visit the Soviet Union as a guest of the government for a month. Would August be convenient, Patolichev asked. A bit puzzled, Scott said such a tour would be agreeable.

He traveled around Russia, staying in each city with privileged Soviet families. Although he knew that all of his hosts were Party officials, he was unaware that they had been assigned to get to know him well. When he returned to Moscow after the jaunt, he was contacted by the American Embassy, enlightened as to the purpose of his trip, and offered the presidency of the U.S.–U.S.S.R. Trade and Economic Council, which he accepted.

At the same time, Kendall received a remarkable invitation from Brezhnev to spend an entire day, August 28, 1973, at Brezhnev's dacha in Yalta to discuss the Trade Council. This was an unprecedented honor. Although Armand Hammer was to spend a few hours at Brezhnev's dacha in 1978, no other private citizen had even spent a full day there. By 1973, not even Nixon or Kissinger had been invited to the dacha; the rarity of the privilege served to underscore the supreme importance Brezhnev attached to the success of the Trade Council.

Set on a cliff above the Black Sea, Brezhnev's stately villa included an Olympic-size swimming pool enclosed in glass walls that could be opened with the push of a button. Strictly speaking, the villa was located not in Yalta proper but in a suburb, Oreanda—as Nixon and Kissinger emphasized at their 1974 meeting there, since Yalta was the site of Franklin Roosevelt's much maligned conference with Stalin in 1945.

Kendall had brought the Pepsi vice-president for Europe, Mike Lvoff, as translator. They discussed not only the organization of the Trade Council but also specific projects in which Brezhnev was interested. He wanted American firms to help build the Soviet tourism, lumber, and natural-gas industries, and he asked Kendall's help in obtaining contracts.

They also spoke of politics. "Brezhnev told me that the Jewish people in the Soviet Union are smart people," Kendall recalls. "He said, 'If they don't want to stay here, fine, but give me time. I'm not going to let out people from the military or people who know something we don't want you to know, until a pretty good time has gone by.' And I think the guy meant it. But, he said, 'Nobody's going to give me a quota. Nobody's going to tell me how many I've got to let out.' You don't do that to a major power—to say that we want so many Jews out or we're not going to play marbles with you. You just don't do that."

Kendall told Brezhnev that he was unhappy with the man the Soviets had named as cochairman of the Trade Council, Boris A. Borisov, who headed similar joint councils with France, Finland, and Italy. Rosy-cheeked, affable, and not a speaker of English, Borisov would not be an effective promoter of trade, Kendall felt. More important, Borisov was not highly enough placed in the Soviet hierarchy. Kendall proposed Vladimir S. Alkhimov, with whom he had negotiated the Pepsi deal. Alkhimov had excellent access to Brezhnev and Kosygin and was well known to American businessmen. He was smooth and "Western-seeming," and he spoke English quite well. Americans talking with him almost forgot he was a Russian. Brezhnev said he would think about replacing Borisov with Alkhimov.

A small notice had appeared in the Yalta newspaper that Brezhnev was entertaining Donald M. Kendall, that American capitalist who understood the importance of peace and trade. When Kendall arrived at his hotel in Yalta at the end of the day, he found a huge crowd of the townspeople waiting and cheering. They surrounded him, Kendall recalls, and a few asked if they could touch him.

The Trade Council was inaugurated on October 1, 1973, at a dinner in the Granovitovaya Palata in the Kremlin. Earlier in the day Treasury Secretary George Shultz had met with Brezhnev to discuss the Nixon administration's strategy for squelching Henry Jackson's amendment. At the dinner, the Council's directors, who had thought Borisov was to be the Soviet cochairman, saw Foreign Trade Minister Patolichev call Borisov over and whisper something in his ear. Borisov's rosy cheeks drained of color. Thus the hapless Borisov was informed of his deposal, and Alkhimov was named in his stead.

The next day, Shultz met for two hours with Kosygin, and Kendall, Alkhimov, and Scott gave a news conference to announce the Council's formation. Most of the conference was taken up with the subject of granting the Soviet Union most-favored-nation (MFN) status. Alkhimov took the podium to declare, a bit threateningly, that if the United States did not normalize its trading relations with Russia, it would have to "accept the consequences." He couched his admonition in a peculiarly Russian aphorism: "Those who prepare beer have to drink beer."

Later, Kendall met with Brezhnev in his Kremlin office for further discussion of the Trade Council. Tass, the Soviet news agency, described the session as "businesslike and constructive."

Hal Scott ran the New York office, staffed by twenty-five Americans and Russians. He was assisted by the Deputy President, V. A. Pekshev. The Moscow office was run by the Council's senior vice-president, John T. Connor, Jr., a Washington lawyer and son of Eisenhower's Commerce Secretary. Connor was treated with great deference. He was given a Chaika limousine and driver, a dacha outside Moscow, and an elegant apartment in a new building in Moscow. The apartment building was so new that the militia box, with which the comings and goings of foreigners are monitored, had not yet been installed. Unused to Moscow, Connor boasted that he was free from the surveillance that plagues most foreigners. Murray Seeger of the *Los Angeles Times* assured him that his apartment was surely wired like everyone else's. Connor was skeptical but asked the American Embassy to check his apartment for listening devices. They found thirty-five active bugs and fifteen that were inactive but in place.

It was revealing of the relations between Russia and America that even the Trade Council, supposedly a bastion of trust and cooperation, was infiltrated by the intelligence agencies of both sides. Kendall had asked Patolichev to guarantee that the KGB would stay out of the Council's operations. "Can you guarantee that you'll keep your side clean, too?" Patolichev asked. Kendall said he could and arranged it with the Nixon administration.

A few weeks after the Council's New York office was set up, George Shultz called one of the Council's officers and told him, "You've been infiltrated." The officer was furious and announced he would go to Moscow and personally register a complaint with the Ministry of Foreign Trade.

"No, it's not the KGB," Shultz said. "It's us—an overzealous FBI man." The FBI had placed an agent on the staff of the Council's New York office. When the agent was fired, the FBI demanded to know who had leaked the information, but the Council officer refused to cooperate in any way. Eventually, of course, the Soviets placed KGB agents in the Council's New York and Moscow offices.

"I well understand the great role that is played—or can be played—by businessmen in establishing peaceful cooperation between states and between peoples," Brezhnev once told the Trade Council. The Council was not a registered lobby, but it was a boosters club on a grand scale, an Elks Club of multinationals that did business with Russia. Although Lenin had predicted that the capitalists would compete to sell Russia the noose with which they would be hanged, he probably did not envision that the capitalists would actually lobby their governments to grant the credits on which Russia could make the purchase.

Obviously, a lobby can operate without registering with the government. Kendall, for example, was interviewed by *Izvestiya* in June 1974 and asked why he had decided to hold a meeting of the Pepsi board of directors in the Soviet Union. "I wanted all our directors—and they include executives of such well-known companies as General Motors, IBM, and the Chase Manhattan Bank—to become as enthusiastic about the new relations between the Soviet Union and the U.S.A. as I am," he replied. "I personally am ready to give all—or, in any case, most—of my time to setting up American-Soviet contacts."

Convincing other businessmen, who are interested in profit, is one thing. Fighting the Jackson forces, who argued on political and even moral grounds, was quite another. The businessmen began to propound a number of lofty benefits of commerce with Russia. They often invoked Benjamin Franklin, who once wrote that trade between nations cannot help but be beneficial. In the 1974 NBC documentary on Hammer's career, Hammer remarked, "I think that these two great nations have to live together, and if they trade together, I think that they'll maintain the peace of the world." Later in the program, he said, "I think if you trade with somebody, it's pretty hard to fight with them."

Malcolm Forbes, editor-in-chief of *Forbes* magazine, disputes this theory by pointing out that one of the United States' major trading partners before the Second World War was Japan. In fact, the most eloquent advocate of the "trade ensures peace" theory was Norman Angell, who argues in *The Great Illusion* that the "elaborate financial interdependence of the modern world" made war senseless. Ironically, or perhaps fittingly, *The Great Illusion* was a best-seller in the United States and Europe just before the outbreak of the First World War.

A variation of this notion is that of trade as "dialogue" or "building bridges." Since businessmen establish personal camaraderie with Soviet trade officials, the claim goes, the Soviet government will assume a more friendly outlook toward the United States. "As trade relations develop, person-to-person contacts build mutual understanding," Kendall once wrote. "The more they know us and the more we know them, the better." William Verity agrees: "One of the principal benefits of trade is that you get to know each other, that you are forced to learn what people are like and what they're doing. As a consequence you develop a different type of relationship that in the long run, historically, has led to more peaceful relations."

But this idea, which seemed so attractive at the time, was never borne out. All of the Soviet officials who played tennis with American businessmen at posh country clubs may have returned to Moscow charmed by the West—or at least by clay tennis courts—but it is extremely unlikely that their fascination for the United States ever filtered up through the Soviet bureaucracy to influence Politburo decisions. Unlike democratic governments, which can be influenced by the urgings of powerful businessmen, the Kremlin, as the events of the last several years have demonstrated, makes decisions on pure self-interest, free of Western-style sentimentalism. A Soviet bureaucrat knows when to keep his mouth shut, if he values his career.

Occasionally, Hammer justified trade with Russia on his assumption that it brings about a convergence between the two systems. He told *The Times* of London in 1972, "In fifty-one years of dealing with the Soviets I've never known a better climate for growth. We're moving towards socialism, they towards capitalism. Between us there's a meeting ground." The basis of this, of course, is the hoary idea that free trade results in the spread of culture and ideas. By doing business with the Soviet Union, Hammer insists, the West will influence—and, implicitly, "moderate"—the Communist world. But the framers of the Declaration of Independence did not imagine a totalitarian (or, in the opinion of some, authoritarian) society occupying one-sixth of the earth's land mass, a closed system that has proven resistant to democratic notions.

In justifying his amendment, Henry Jackson was just as fatuous. He attacked Kendall's advocacy of trade with Russia on the same basis on which Hammer and others defended it. "We are asked to believe that the prospects for peace are enhanced by the flow of Pepsi-Cola to the Soviet Union and the flow of vodka to the United States," he declared in 1974. "In fact, we will move much further along the road to a stable peace when we see the free flow of people and ideas across the barriers that divide East from West." In trying to legislate "the free flow of people and ideas" across Soviet borders, Henry Jackson misunderstood the nature of Soviet Communism, which cannot exist in a state of freedom.

The most persistent defense of East-West trade was that commerce locks nations into a relationship of mutual dependency that can somehow keep peace in the world. "Increased U.S.-Soviet trade will . . . increase the chances for world peace," Kendall has said, because it results in "a web of interlocking relations of mutual value."

The historian Barbara Tuchman also advanced this theory, albeit in different phrasing, in an article in *The New York Times Magazine* in 1982. She urged that we provide our "enemies" with all the "grain and consumer goods they need in such quantities that they become dependent on us and could not risk the domestic turbulence that would follow if they cut off the source of the supply by war."

But the flaw in this reasoning is the assumption that great "domestic turbulence" would necessarily arise in Russia if foodstuffs are suddenly found in short supply. The Russians have learned the art of patience. Accustomed for decades to shortages of bread, fruits and vegetables, and other essentials, the citizens of the Soviet Union tend to be more docile than most Westerners know. Moreover, as the failure of Jimmy Carter's grain embargo so vividly demonstrated, the Soviets can always shop elsewhere for goods denied them by the United States.

As a rule, the West has tended to become more dependent on trade with Russia than has Russia. Soviet citizens can do little more than gripe about the lack of bread in their stores, but American farmers, deprived of the lucrative Soviet market for their grain, face economic devastation when the United States imposes a grain boycott of the Soviet Union. Brezhnev once even hinted at this phenomenon, in a 1975 speech greeting British Prime Minister Harold Wilson. "The Soviet Union's leaders," he said, "are fully resolved to do everything in their power to make historically irreversible . . . mutually advantageous cooperation of states." Wilson was in Moscow to discuss increasing trade between the two nations, and Brezhnev appreciated that détente, as he envisioned it, would become "historically irreversible" only if the West were dependent on its business with the Soviet Union.

Another popular conception was that détente was a liberal policy embraced by Brezhnev but opposed by the "hard-liners" in the Politburo. But even the most hawkish Kremlin leader must have realized the merits of détente—which meant heightened trade with the West, and which helped to strengthen Russia's industrial and military base.

In 1974 Kendall testified before the Senate subcommittee on international finance:

> There is in the Soviet Union today a leadership which wants this relationship [détente]. There is also an element in that country that wants nothing to do with this relationship, that would love to see Brezhnev thrown out of the government so that they could go back to the cold war era where the military would dominate the scene and we would be right back where we started.

Another time he told the *Washington Post* that the failure to grant the Soviet Union most-favored-nation status would unleash "those forces in the Kremlin opposed to détente."

The most important, and most effective, defense of trade with Russia was the old Kissinger principle of "linkage." The term is so abused that no one is quite sure what it means, but here it meant, in part, that the Russians would want our business so badly that they would alter their conduct to please us. The most visible example of this moderation was the dramatic rise in the number of Soviet Jews allowed to emigrate—35,000 in 1973 and later, in

1979, 54,000. Thus it appeared that Russia was becoming liberalized, and this mistaken impression was conveyed by Kendall, Hammer, and the others.

When the Jackson amendment passed and officially became part of the Trade Reform bill in January 1975, the Soviets abruptly cut off the flow of emigrants. They had not changed their policies, although they realized, in part from Jackson's efforts, that the emigration of Soviet Jews was important to many Americans.

The Politburo had seized upon the emigration of Soviet Jews in an obvious effort to bribe the United States, and it has an unsettling precedent. As the Russian émigré writer Lev Navrozov points out, during the Second World War Hitler proposed an exchange of one million Jews held in Nazi captivity for 10,000 Allied trucks. The Allies rejected the offer. The détente-era flush of Jewish emigration was, for the Russians, a much better deal. Navrozov explains that the Soviet government got from the West a giant truck factory—the Kama River plant—with a capacity of 300,000 trucks a year. In exchange, the Soviets allowed 30,000 Jews a year to leave.

The Nixon administration dealt with problems of emigration and Soviet dissidents in a manner it called "quiet diplomacy." This meant that instead of debating the issue in the halls of Congress, a more effective resolution could be reached in secret communication between the leaders of the two countries.

There was, of course, another aspect to "quiet diplomacy"—the Soviets included Hammer, Kendall, and other prominent businessmen in the ranks of American leaders with the right to request help in these sensitive matters. As a result, the businessmen became valuable emissaries to the Kremlin, and their pleas that trade was beneficial were lent great force.

American Jewish leaders realized immediately the power that certain business leaders held, and so they developed what some of them called a "corporate approach." The director of the National Conference on Soviet Jewry, Richard Maass, was an old friend of Donald Kendall's, and early in 1972 he decided to ask Kendall to intercede with the Soviet leaders to obtain the release of several Soviet Jews who had been refused exit visas. Kissinger and Nixon had refused to intervene, but Kendall had admirable success.

Thomas Murphy, the chairman of General Motors, succeeded in arranging the release of a number of Soviet engineers, but William Verity and David Rockefeller refused even to meet with Maass. Another Jewish leader recalls that Rockefeller once received him, accompanied by a Jewish vice-president of Chase—"his Jew at the door," as he puts it. They spoke for a while. Rockefeller protested that he really had little influence with the Soviet leaders. "Rockefeller was very pleasant," the visitor says, "but we never heard from him or from Chase again." In fact, Rockefeller did help in emigration, but always through official channels: the State Department several times presented him with lists of "hardship cases," which Rockefeller obligingly took to Kosygin.

Of all American entrepreneurs, the one most involved in matters of emigration was Armand Hammer. Unlike the others, he had a well-developed organization for dealing with the problem. One of his attorneys for Soviet affairs was Harry Simon Levy, a Russian-born Orthodox Jew with a heavy accent. A Zionist revisionist and fiercely loyal supporter of Menachem Begin, he seemed an unlikely person to represent Occidental Petroleum in Moscow, but he was extremely competent and fluent in Russian. When the National Conference on Soviet Jewry wanted Hammer's help, they would speak with Levy. They were also able to approach Hammer through his friend Guilford Glazer, a California shopping-mall mogul, who urged them "not to sell Hammer short."

With Hammer's assistance, Jewish leaders were able to meet with Ambassador Dobrynin during the Jackson struggle to explain to the Soviet leadership that a guarantee on Soviet emigration policy would quell a segment of the opponents of Soviet-American trade. Hammer also assisted personally by taking lists of hardship cases to the Kremlin, although he does not discuss these efforts. "I tried to help whenever I could," is all he will say.

Some of his efforts have directly benefited his own staff. His personal Russian-language interpreter, for instance, is a woman named Galina Sullivan. She was a Russian Jew living in Moscow, a translator for Intourist, who married a Frenchman and emigrated in 1970, leaving behind her children from a previous marriage. After marrying for a third time, to an American, she settled in Arlington, Virginia, and was hired by Armand Hammer. When she asked his help in getting her family out of Russia, Hammer took care of the matter.

Now Galina accompanies Hammer on all of his visits to Moscow, translating in all negotiating sessions and Kremlin meetings (Hammer is not as fluent in Russian as he lets on). Galina is therefore able to do something unthinkable for most other Russian émigrés—travel freely in and out of the Soviet Union. She refuses, though, to bring messages or gifts into Russia on behalf of her friends in the Washington émigré community. She also will not discuss her work for Hammer. "Could I let down the man who saved the lives of my children?" she asks.

"I trust him as far as I can throw him," Wilbur Mills, chairman of the House Ways and Means Committee said of Hammer in 1973, "and I've got a bad back." Mills had just received a call from Hammer, who urged him not to support the Jackson amendment.

Although Hammer made many calls to Congressmen while the amendment was being debated, twisting the arms of legislators he generously financed, he was not an effective lobbyist, because his reputation has always been tarnished. Members of the U.S.–U.S.S.R. Trade and Economic Council also complain privately that David Rockefeller was often "too busy" during that period to meet with key Senators and urge that the Jackson amendment be killed. So Donald Kendall took charge of the effort. One of his most important power bases was the multinationals' lobbying organization, the Emergency Committee on American Trade (ECAT). In August 1973, he had ECAT publish a booklet, edited by Senator Daniel Patrick Moynihan's brother Michael entitled *The Multinational Corporation: American Mainstay in the World Economy*. The brochure urged the United States to do business with all countries of the world, including Russia. In keeping with the nautical metaphor, it warned, "This is not the time to lower our flag."

Kendall's most ambitious lobbying effort was sabotaged by an ECAT staff member who supported Jackson's crusade. In mid-September 1973 Kendall sent a telegram to all members of ECAT, asking them to pressure the House Ways and Means Committee to do away with the Jackson legislation.

"PRESIDENT NEEDS AUTHORITY FROM BUSINESS COMMUNITY IN ORDER TO WIN THAT AUTHORITY FROM CONGRESS," the cable said in part. " . . . I URGE YOU AND OTHER MEMBERS OF ECAT TO CONTACT BY TELEPHONE OR TELEGRAM EACH MEMBER OF WAYS AND MEANS IN SUPPORT OF MFN AND ITS VITAL RELATIONSHIP TO U.S. AND SOVIET DÉTENTE. . . ."

But before the executives received their copies of the telegram, they could have read it on the front page of the *Washington Post* under the headline, "BIG FIRMS TO PRESS HILL ON SOVIET TRADE BENEFIT." Someone in the ECAT office, paid to help the organization lobby, had pocketed a copy of the telegram before it was sent and read it over the telephone to an assistant to Senator Abraham Ribicoff, who then leaked it to the *Post*.

The *Post* reporter called Kendall at his home in Greenwich, Connecticut, for comment. As it turned out, Kendall was on his tennis court with Vladimir Alkhimov. Both men spoke with the reporter. Kendall said he had just returned from Moscow where he had had a three-hour meeting with Brezhnev. He explained his position on the Jackson amendment and added that the Soviet Union had made, in recent years, "just tremendous progress" in liberalization of its domestic policies. Before, he said, "you wouldn't even have heard about Solzhenitsyn or Sakharov. Now they let them have press conferences and allow their statements to go out." Alkhimov, as distrustful of the *Post* as President Nixon was, would only venture that he agreed with Kendall.

At times it seemed the news media were out to get Kendall, whose campaign on behalf of Soviet trade seemed suspiciously connected to White House policy. Professor Fred Neal of Claremont Men's College in California proposed a counterweight to Jackson's forces that would not be associated with Nixon—a lobbying group of prominent and respectable citizens called the American Committee on U.S.-Soviet Relations. On May 21, 1973, Neal sent a letter to prospective members lamenting the lack of any pro-détente lobby "other than, possibly, something like the American-Soviet Friendship Society, which consists of a few tired old Communists and fellow travelers plus Cyrus Eaton, and has no influence at all or a negative influence."

Thirty-eight people became its founding members, including Thomas Watson, Jr., of IBM; A. W. Clausen, head of the Bank of America; actor Kirk Douglas; and Don Kendall. Conservatives immediately lunged at this organization, which seemed, because of Kendall, tied to Nixon. Syndicated columnists Evans and Novak penned a column revealing that "A ploy by businessmen, hungry for profits from U.S.-Soviet trade, to use pro-détente liberals as a battering ram against the Jackson Amendment, is being foiled by the realities of American politics." While the inspiration for the group was "ostensibly" Professor Neal's, "a veteran soft-liner and cold war revisionist," it was in truth, according to Evans and Novak, Don Kendall's.

The committee, the column continued, was

> a collection of strange bedfellows. Washington attorney Charles W. Rhyne is an old friend of President Nixon. Thomas Watson, Jr., of IBM contributed $25,000 to Mr. Nixon's re-election. The most important businessman on the committee is Donald M. Kendall—longtime Nixon intimate, front man and spear carrier. As chairman of Americans for the Presidency, Kendall is fighting hard against impeachment. Moreover, he represents those businessmen whose one-time ferocious anti-communism has been diluted by the scent of profits. . . . Prof. Neal is regarded as a front man for businessman Kendall. The lesson for Don Kendall, for businessmen and for the White House is clear. They can enlist

> hordes of liberal professors to condemn Scoop Jackson and his hard-line ways. But whether they achieve their goal of enlisting liberal politicians against the Jackson Amendment is doubtful in the extreme.

The last remark, at least, turned out to be accurate.

For it was a battle of emotions, not wits. Although some of the logic Kendall and others put forth was specious, the reasoning of many of the Jackson amendment's supporters was equally sophistical. In some cases, it was more so. Nicholas von Hoffman, for example, declared in the *Washington Post* in August 1973: "If Russians can leave Russia at will, that will be a powerful incentive for the Soviets to run their country in such a way that their people will want to stay there. . . ." The assumption that the Kremlin would—or could—ever permit free emigration brings to mind a joke on the subject popular in the Soviet Union. Two comrades are dreaming aloud about the golden day when Russia would throw open its borders and allow anyone who wished to leave freely.

"What is the first thing you'd do?" one asks the other.

"I'd climb to the top of the tallest tree I could find," the other replies.

"Why?"

"So I'm not trampled in the rush to get out."

Some businessmen, such as Hammer, even maintained that Soviet Jews were not oppressed. When Brezhnev was interviewed by American journalists in June 1973, he unwittingly responded with an American cliché. "There is no Jewish problem, no question here," he said. "Some of my closest friends from school days onward have been Jews."

An assistant to Senator Ribicoff recalls that in late 1972 Hammer requested a meeting with Ribicoff and brought along a few people from Occidental, including Harry Simon Levy. During the one-hour meeting, Hammer urged Ribicoff not to support the Jackson amendment. "It's better to deal quietly with the Soviets," he said. "They're already predisposed to increasing Jewish emigration, and this will only damage things." He made the incredible claim that there was no anti-Semitism in the Soviet Union. Levy agreed.

The Jackson people managed to enlist the sympathies of those who were concerned about the fate of Soviet Jews and who mistakenly believed that the amendment would lock the Soviet Union into its new, high rate of Jewish emigration. Jackson's supporters cannot have foreseen that the victory of the legislation would bring the emigration rate down by almost two-thirds.

But there were many who saw Kendall's battle, despite his private assistance, as expressly opposed to the struggle for Soviet Jewry. In 1974, for example, the Trade Council had a dinner at the River Club in New York. Kendall departed from his prepared remarks to deliver an impromptu attack on the special-interest groups, including the "Jewish lobby," who, he said, were strangling East-West trade. He also criticized American Sovietologists, many of whom, he said, were Russian émigrés with an irrational hatred of the Soviet Union. A minor squabble immediately followed his speech, as members of the Council, both American and Soviet, rose to voice disagreement. John Connor, the senior vice-president in charge of the Moscow office, protested that Kendall did not speak for the Council. Even Alkhimov took exception, saying that he had been saved by a Jew in the Second World War.

A few angry Council members insisted afterward that Kendall's remarks had bordered on the anti-Semitic. Some, however, such as Milton Rosenthal, former chairman of Engelhard Minerals & Chemicals, did not consider the speech at all anti-Semitic. "He's a forceful, skilled marketing man," Rosenthal says. "He was simply selling his point of view."

Some efforts of the businessmen were simply hampered by the political situation. The directors of the Trade Council brought twenty of their Soviet opposite members to New York in February 1974 to meet with local businessmen and attempt to stir up grassroots support. But the effort was badly timed: just the week before, the Soviets had expelled Alexander Solzhenitsyn.

Shortly thereafter, a few of the Soviet officials joined their American counterparts for a small breakfast meeting in Washington with Senators Russell Long, Abraham Ribicoff, Henry Jackson, and others, to discuss working out a compromise on the trade bill problem. Senator Long acted as the "honest broker" in attempting to get a dialogue going, but the Soviets, who lacked the power to make any policy decisions, would not back down from their position that politics was politics and business was business, and the two should never meet. Long excused himself early, because he had to chair a meeting of the Senate Finance Committee, but he urged everyone to ask questions of each other. No one did; the meeting broke up after a few more brief discourses. Senator Ribicoff invited any of the Russians who wanted to talk privately to just come by his office. None of the Russians took him up on the offer. They had come to deliver a message, not to bargain with the Senators. A valuable opportunity was lost.

At times it seemed that the business world preferred to ignore the policymakers in Washington. One prominent member of the

Council remembers meeting after Nixon's resignation with four other industrialists, several admirals, and a member of the Joint Chiefs of Staff late in 1974. One admiral bewailed the military disadvantages U.S. forces suffered because of certain technology transfers. The next day, the same industrialist attended a private dinner in New York given by a major investment banking house. The guest of honor was Dzhermen Gvishiani, the Soviet official whose specialty was buying high technology in the West. One after another, the thirty other businessmen at the dinner rose to boast about the last big transaction they had made with Gvishiani. "The dichotomy between the luncheon in Washington and the dinner in New York was just astounding," the businessman recalled. "These guys were bragging as if they had just sold a ton of frankfurters."

There were also attempts to influence press coverage of the issue, most of which failed. Al Wentworth, Rockefeller's man in Moscow, once drew aside the Moscow correspondents for *Newsweek* and the *Los Angeles Times* at a reception at Spaso House, the American ambassador's residence. He began to berate them for dwelling on the problems of Soviet Jews. "Why are you writing all these stories about Jews?" he demanded. "We're trying to get this trade bill passed, and you guys aren't helping." Of all the Moscow correspondents, the *Business Week* reporter was the only one, Wentworth says, that he really got along with. "Most of those other fellows were political types," Wentworth recalls, "and I'm an economic type."

Kendall, Hammer, and Rockefeller each received a good measure of criticism for their stands on Soviet trade. On October 30, 1973, Kendall was to be honored by the American Jewish Committee for his philanthropy to Jewish charities. He was told a few months earlier that he would receive its annual civic leadership award. But the AJC was divided in its opinion of Kendall. Richard Maass and several others wanted to thank Kendall for his contributions as well as his unrecognized help in obtaining the release of Soviet Jews. At the same time, though, many of the American Jewish Committee's leaders resented Kendall's opposition to the Jackson amendment and managed to have the award rescinded.

Maass called Kendall and told him there would be no award dinner. "We just can't take the heat," he said. Anyway, he explained, if the dinner were held, it would probably be picketed, which would only make for bad digestion all around. Maass and Kendall agreed to postpone the banquet. It was never rescheduled.

Many Jewish groups had long since boycotted Pepsi-Cola because it was sold in Arab countries but not in Israel. But when the Jackson furor began, some Jewish groups decided that a full-scale boycott of Pepsi-Cola was in order. Bumper stickers were distributed that read, "DON'T DRINK PEPSI—PEPSI SELLS TO RUSSIA—RUSSIA SELLS JEWS."

As it is widely available and therefore vulnerable to a boycott, Pepsi became a target for those who wished to express dissatisfaction with all American companies that did business with Russia. "How do you boycott Mack trucks?" a member of the Jewish Defense League asked. "I don't have many friends who buy Mack trucks every week, but I do have a lot of friends who buy Pepsi."

The Jewish Defense League took stronger action against the Chase Manhattan Bank, since boycotting a bank was hardly dramatic. JDL members threw bricks through the windows of two Chase branch offices in New York on December 1, 1974. The JDL's leader, Rabbi Meir Kahane, urged members to hide bombs in Chase offices in New York. Kahane also allegedly sent a letter in 1974 to JDL offices in New York, urging the bombing of the Occidental Petroleum offices (Interore) in New York. This would be a warning to Armand Hammer, Kahane said, to cease trading with Russia.

The last big push of the anti-Jackson forces came in December 1974. Nixon's trade reform bill, with the Jackson amendment attached, had passed in the House on December 11, 1973, and had gone on to the Senate. In the meantime, Watergate reached its crescendo, with Nixon's resignation on August 9, 1974, and an accompanying swell in anti-Soviet sentiment that seemed related—in part because détente was so closely associated with Richard Nixon. In a small but revealing indication of this phenomenon, in the spring of 1974 the three best-selling books were the *Presidential Transcripts, All the President's Men,* and Alexander Solzhenitsyn's eloquent condemnation of the Soviet penal system, *The Gulag Archipelago.*

The congressional debate no longer merely concerned awarding the Russians most-favored-nation standing. At the end of June 1974, the President's authority to grant Export-Import loans to the Soviet Union without congressional approval expired. Senator Adlai Stevenson, Jr., introduced a new amendment, calling for a ceiling of three hundred million dollars over four years on loans to the Communist bloc—in the context of international finance, a niggardly sum.

After Nixon's resignation, Henry Jackson began to negotiate with Gerald Ford and Henry Kissinger to work out a form of the amendment that the Soviets would not reject. On October 18,

1974—exactly two years after Nixon and Gromyko had initialed the trade agreement—a compromise was reached. After secret talks between the White House and the Kremlin, Kissinger told Jackson that, with some alteration, the amendment would be acceptable to the Soviets. Kissinger said he had Brezhnev's assurances.

Then, in what turned out to be a disastrously tactless move, Jackson crowed for the press on the White House lawn, boasting of his "monumental accomplishment." The Russians, he implied loudly and unmistakably, had capitulated. A few days later, when Kissinger went to Moscow, he found Brezhnev livid with rage. Gromyko handed Kissinger a note warning that the Soviet leaders "decline such an interpretation" of an "anticipated increase in the departure of Soviet citizens from the U.S.S.R." as Jackson had announced. Deciding that this protest was merely a face-saving gesture, Kissinger told no one about the letter. This, too, proved to be a mistake.

Just before the Senate vote on the trade bill on December 20, 1974, ECAT and the League of Women Voters coordinated a lobby offensive to get the bill passed—even with the Jackson amendment, which the Soviets seemed to accept—before the end of the congressional session. Twelve hundred corporate stars were brought to Washington to pressure the Senators. The final effort was a giant dinner hosted by Kendall and addressed by Ford. The bill passed, and Ford signed it into law on January 3, 1975.

But the Soviets, after releasing the text of Gromyko's letter to Kissinger, rejected the bill. With the Jackson and Stevenson amendments attached, it did not resemble the Trade Reform Act that Nixon and Gromyko had initialed in 1973. The Russians stopped payment on their Lend-Lease debt—$686 million was outstanding—and the short-lived era of the big Soviet-American deals was over.

What had happened? Why had some of America's most powerful tycoons failed?

Part of the problem was that Kendall, Hammer, and, by this time, even Rockefeller, were unpersuasive spokesmen. Kendall, for example, proudly (and accurately) claimed that "I don't say one thing over there and another thing here, and the Soviets respect that." The Americans did not respect it, though, because anyone who did that appeared to be a Soviet apologist. Indeed, criticism of government policy in a democratic society is taken for granted;

but criticism of Soviet policy is not brooked by the Kremlin, especially in a visitor who wants to maintain his access. Just as Cyrus Eaton refused to point out Russia's shortcomings, Kendall and Hammer unstintingly defended Soviet domestic policy, knowing that if they qualified their praise at all, Brezhnev might be too busy to see them next time.

Another difficulty was that each of these spokesmen for Soviet trade appeared to have a vested interest: each had his own well-heralded deals. This appearance damaged their credibility, although in fact the money interest in each case was minor. Also, it is hard for a few privileged individuals—stars, really—to raise support in a community of businessmen who are not as favored; though today it may seem odd, there was widespread jealousy of these men among their peers. Moreover, even these privileged spokesmen fought each other to plead the case of Soviet trade; their clash of egos further damaged the cause.

The biggest problem, of course, was Watergate. Although détente—whatever it meant—was killed by other, later events, its decline surely began with the weakening of Nixon's authority and the concomitant strengthening of Congress, as both Kissinger and Nixon argue in their memoirs. In the case of these business-lobbyists, it was initially important to the Kremlin that each have access to the Oval Office—that was, after all, much of their attraction. The impetus for many of the big East-West transactions came directly from the White House. Détente, and its vital component, trade, was a Nixon-Kissinger policy. But as Nixon became politically crippled, influence in the White House was no longer as important.

With Nixon out of the White House and the far less powerful Gerald Ford in, to be succeeded by an ambivalent Jimmy Carter, the era of presidentially directed détente—which turned out to have lasted from 1972 to about 1974—was over. Now that Congress had formally legislated trade controls that the Soviets would not accept, the great need for business-lobbyists disappeared. This meant a diminution of Kendall's standing, especially, and also Rockefeller's, in Moscow. Despite a brief optimistic period at the end of the Carter administration, the era of the several ambassadors *manqués* was largely over. Although none of them gave up their enthusiasm for Soviet-American trade, only one remained a bellwether—the man whose life was tied to the Soviet Union, Armand Hammer.

16

HAMMER'S KREMLIN CONNECTION

"HAMMER KNEW LENIN, damn it," a rival American industrialist active in business with Russia once complained. "How the hell were we supposed to compete with that?"

Armand Hammer's acquaintance with Lenin became a legend in the West after 1972. "Hammer has an incredible mystique in Moscow because of his relationship with Lenin," another businessman remarks. "I've seen him lecture groups of Americans and Russians—he'll reminisce about Lenin, and you can see the Russians' mouths hanging open." Sargent Shriver, who accompanied Hammer to Moscow in July 1972, remembers Hammer adverting, in the midst of a negotiating session with Soviet officials, to a portrait of Lenin hanging on the wall. "He was terrific," Shriver says. "He could bring tears to the eyes of a stone. We went into Lenin's study in the Kremlin and there on the desk sits the little object Hammer gave him. Well, there aren't many people alive—Russians or non-Russians, Communists or non-Communists—who have a gift sitting on Lenin's desk."

During the summer of 1972, at a Kremlin reception attended by several top Soviet leaders, several American businessmen remember Hammer trying almost desperately to corner Brezhnev to speak to him. But a minor official would not permit Hammer to approach the General Secretary despite Hammer's loud and angry protests. Until 1973, for mysterious reasons of Soviet policy, Brezhnev would not meet with any American businessman privately.

In an attempt to prove the exception, just as he had done in the matter of flying his Boeing 727 into Moscow, Hammer drew on his Lenin connection. He acquired two handwritten Lenin letters from an American art dealer, in exchange for a few paintings from his collection and, he says, "a substantial amount of cash," and delivered them to Dzhermen Gvishiani at the end of October 1972, along with a letter for Brezhnev. "This offer of Vladimir Ilyich Lenin's personal writings, Mr. General Secretary," the letter said, "is intended to express my goodwill to the leaders and the people of the Soviet Union, and my appreciation of a friendship with a great man whose memory will always remain sacred to me." A few days later Hammer was taken to see Mikhail A. Suslov, the party ideologist and Secretary of the Central Committee, and reputedly the second-most powerful man in the Soviet Union. Hammer was told that Brezhnev was "out of town."

Suslov, rarely seen in public, occupied the office adjacent to Brezhnev's and shared the same secretary. Hammer found him to be "a shy, extremely modest man; very friendly, in spite of what seemed to be an impassive countenance. He is a scholarly-looking individual with a kindly smile and his intelligent face lit up with animation when he spoke of Lenin." On Suslov's desk, Hammer says, were volumes of Lenin's collected works with places marked by slips of paper. Hammer claims that Suslov had been reviewing Lenin's correspondence with Hammer. "Obviously he had been reading this correspondence," Hammer says, "and knew all about me and my early activities in the Soviet Union."

In fact, just as the Central Committee had issued a resolution declaring support of Hammer's ventures in 1922, so fifty years later it passed a resolution thanking Hammer for his gift of the Lenin letters. Suslov gave him an engraved portrait of Lenin made of silver and other metals from the Urals and told him that next time, Brezhnev would thank him personally. An account of Hammer's meeting with Suslov was recorded on the front pages of all Soviet papers.

But is is unlikely that Suslov had to do research on Armand Hammer. If Suslov was as intelligent as Hammer insists he was, he cannot have forgotten about the man with a career of business dealings with the Soviet Union, a man involved for the past eleven years in an uninterrupted attempt to arrange a number of gigantic Soviet-American transactions.

Suslov and the other top Soviet leaders also presumably knew that Hammer was not a good friend of Lenin's, that the two had conferred only once for little over an hour. Why then did the Soviets repeatedly stress Hammer's ties with Lenin? For a time, the popular American interpretation was that moderates in the Politburo wanted to lend legitimacy—Lenin's imprimatur—to the policy of East-West trade by emphasizing that Lenin himself had approved of Hammer's deals. More believable is the explanation that Hammer's Lenin connection was persistently associated with Lenin's theories of "peaceful coexistence" to assure the West that the Lenin-sanctioned concept of Soviet trade with the capitalist world was intended to bring about peace. By disregarding Lenin's other writings, the Soviet press advertised Hammer's "friendship" with Lenin to insist that détente was a policy of peace and mutual benefit.

This suited Hammer's purposes splendidly. Both the White House and the Kremlin heralded the new era of East-West economic cooperation as the end of the Cold War, and Hammer was ready to use the new political line to build a reputation as a statesman, a sort of grandfather of détente.

One of his methods was an exchange of art. After the 1972 summit, Hammer invited Yekaterina Furtseva, the Soviet Minister of Culture, to view the Armand Hammer Collection on display in the Los Angeles County Museum. This was a stunning array of works by such artists as Cézanne, Corot, Degas, Gauguin, Michelangelo, Picasso, Pissarro, Rembrandt, and van Gogh. It was scheduled to be exhibited in London and Dublin; Hammer arranged to have his collection travel throughout the Soviet Union from October 1972, to August 1973—in Leningrad, Moscow, Kiev, Minsk, Riga, and finally Hammer's ancestral city, Odessa.

In return Hammer wanted to bring a show of the best Impressionist and post-Impressionist paintings from Moscow's Pushkin Museum and Leningrad's Hermitage to the United States. He and Victor drew up a list of forty-one of Russia's finest European holdings, including works by Matisse, Gauguin, Picasso, Cézanne, van Gogh, and Monet. Furtseva enthusiastically agreed to the request.

Since December 1971, Hammer has been a co-owner of the United States' oldest and most prestigious private gallery, Knoedler. The Soviet exhibit was displayed at Knoedler in New York and the National Gallery in Washington during April and May 1973. *New York Times* art critic John Canaday found it "superb." The exhibit attracted enormous crowds; it was a great sensation and was hailed by newspapers around the world. "Dr. Hammer, one of the great impresarios of American business, has pulled off another coup with the Russians," the *The Times* of London declared.

A business associate of Hammer's—probably the entrepreneur David Karr—told the Securities and Exchange Commission under oath that Victor Hammer had told him that "Dr. Hammer paid $100,000 in the early 1970s to Yekaterina A. Furtseva, the Soviet Minister of Culture, to facilitate an art exchange." Although Hammer dismissed the charge as "gossip ... trash ... idle rumor," and Victor denied ever having made the admission, Mrs. Furtseva was reprimanded by the Communist Party, shortly before her death in 1974, for "lavish living," which might have meant accepting too many bribes.

On February 15, 1973, Hammer at last secured an interview with Brezhnev. An interpreter was present, he says, "but I found I could keep up with [Brezhnev] in Russian, so I began to answer directly without waiting for the English translation."

They talked for over two hours. Hammer says only that they discussed "a wide range of subjects." A few other Occidental executives had initially been scheduled to join Hammer but at the last minute were disinvited. "In the normal course of events, where corporations are involved in negotiations, you don't do that sort of thing," one of them says privately. "But Hammer preferred to see Brezhnev alone. I suspect he wanted to make arrangements without anyone else listening."

Hammer says he told Brezhnev, "You remind me very much of Lenin, whom I met in this very building fifty-two years ago." Brezhnev's eyes immediately filled with tears, Hammer recalls. This convinced Hammer that Brezhnev "is a very human person who is trying to do good for his people just as Lenin tried. Fifty-two years earlier when I described the wheat deal to Lenin, and the help I was trying to bring to the starving people of the Urals, Lenin's eyes filled with tears as well. Both men were the same kind, human and warmhearted." Brezhnev gave Hammer a gold watch, which Hammer later displayed for reporters, saying, "It keeps very good time, too."

Apparently the meeting was productive. On April 12, American newsmen were summoned to the Ministry of Foreign Trade in Moscow, where Hammer and Nikolai Komarov, the Deputy Minister of Foreign Trade, sat behind a gleaming mahogany desk adorned with Soviet and American flags and signed several documents. It was the largest agreement in the history of Soviet-American trade: a chemical-fertilizer barter deal assessed at $8 billion, in which Occidental Petroleum would construct a fertilizer complex on the Volga River to produce ammonia from natural gas, arrange for a French company to build a pipeline to link the ammonia factory to the seaports of Odessa on the Black Sea and Ventspils on the Baltic Sea, and provide the Soviets with superphosphoric acid. This would all be paid for with Soviet shipments of ammonia, urea (also made from natural gas), and potash.

That evening, Hammer was interviewed on Soviet television. He described the deal as "the breakthrough in Soviet-American trade" that would "set an example for others in America. . . . It shows that deals can be successfully carried out with the Soviet Union, given patience and goodwill." Wall Street was less excited, having heard similar proclamations from Hammer before. Oxy stock dropped a few points.

There was considerable unfavorable reaction in the United States to the announcement. The news had come not from the U.S. government or the American Embassy in Washington but from *Pravda,* which angered many observers already uneasy about the scale of such unsupervised transactions. *New York Times* columnist James Reston criticized what he called "the new Soviet trade war": "This is not precisely the best way to begin a dramatic and historic new trade relationship between Washington and Moscow. . . . Dr. Hammer, whoever he is, may be serving the Republic with his $8-billion deal with Moscow, but we shouldn't have to hear about this 'historic' arrangement from *Pravda.*"

It was indeed a "trade war." Strategically timed—just two months before the 1973 summit—the fanfare that accompanied the announcement was designed to fire up businessmen and other pro-trade forces. *Izvestiya* even billed the contract as "a perceptible blow" to enemies of Soviet-American trade.

There were peculiarities in Hammer's arrangement that were not to come out for some time. The trade was to take place over a twenty-year period, but there was evidence that the United States did not have enough phosphate rock to meet Hammer's requirements. A report by the Bureau of Mines later in the year concluded that if Occidental were to go through with the deal, American supplies of phosphates would be so depleted within a few decades that America would be forced to import the vital mineral, therefore becoming dependent on the nations of North Africa.

Also, the terminals that Occidental eventually built to store and ship the ammonia at Soviet seaports were of unusual depth. They were, according to a Defense Department consultant, adaptable for the docking of nuclear submarines—a function of which Hammer may have been unaware, but of which the Soviets were probably well apprised.

A year later, in May 1974, the Export-Import Bank approved

a loan of $180 million to the Soviet Union at 6 percent interest, the largest it had ever granted to a Communist nation, to help finance Hammer's fertilizer project. The head of the Ex-Im Bank, William Casey, asserted that it was in the national interest, that the United States had phosphates in abundant supply and needed chemicals such as urea and ammonia. There was an uproar in Congress over the 6 percent loan, which was significantly lower than most government loans to Americans. When Senator Henry Jackson heard about it, he said, "You've got to be out of your cotton-pickin' mind to dream up one like that!"

A Los Angeles-based reporter for *The New York Times* wrote a long analytical article for the Sunday, May 20, 1973, business section of the paper. Entitled "Hammer's Kremlin Connection," it was mildly critical of Hammer's wheelings and dealings in Russia, quoting an unnamed Oxy official, who was skeptical about "Dr. Hammer's latest fling." Furious, Hammer called his friend Iphigene Sulzberger, the mother of *Times* publisher Arthur Ochs Sulzberger. He thundered and cajoled, and the next day the *Times* ran an interview with him on its front page.

Hammer used the interview to disclose new information about his Soviet deals. He said that the Soviets insisted on an exchange of letters by the two governments, indicating approval of the fertilizer deal. Hammer denied this was any kind of political pressure, explaining that the Soviets, concerned about the controversy the deal had stirred up in the United States, wanted an official U.S. statement, for

> sophisticated as they are, they still cannot believe that our Government does not have a veto power over such a large international transaction as this even though it is a private deal of a private corporation. Remember, there are many trading organizations in Russia but there is only one chairman of the board, and that is Mr. Brezhnev.

(The letters were exchanged a week later.)

Hammer's most dramatic announcement was the mammoth pipeline Occidental was hoping to build to bring natural gas from the Yakutsk fields of Siberia to Los Angeles. He explained that Oxy was joining in the venture with El Paso Natural Gas.

Hammer admitted that the pipeline would "require political decisions in Moscow and Washington and, undoubtedly, most-favored-nation legislation." This announcement, days before Brezhnev was to come to Washington, was clearly designed to display the gigantic potential riches in store for America as long as President Nixon took the right action at the summit and Congress followed suit.

The interview was followed by a smaller article by Ted Shabad, then the *Times* Moscow correspondent, reporting on a recent story in *Pravda* on Lenin's instructions to the Politburo on Armand Hammer fifty years earlier. "Here we have a small opening into the American business community," *Pravda* had quoted, "and we must make use of that opening in every possible way." Little had changed in fifty years.

A week later, Hammer called a press conference at the Intourist Hotel on Gorky Street in Moscow to announce that he had signed a "letter of intent" with the Soviets for the gas pipeline. Howard Boyd of El Paso Natural Gas was also at the conference; although the undertaking was once all his, Hammer had so overshadowed him that reporters assumed he was merely Hammer's assistant.

Hammer was careful to point out that he had not signed a contract but, rather, an agreement in principle. He was also circumspect about the details, saying only that the two-thousand-mile-long pipeline would require an investment of four billion dollars—half to finance a fleet of twenty tankers, and half to enable the Soviet government to purchase pipeline equipment and liquefaction technology. The financing was to be led by the Bank of America (whose chairman, A. W. Clausen, was a friend of Hammer's) and by the Japanese government.

Within a month, Hammer was in Tokyo to speak with Japanese Prime Minister Kakuei Tanaka about loans for the gas project. Tanaka was quite interested. There were reports that if the Japanese agreed to help fund the pipeline the Soviets would return to the Japanese government four islands occupied by Russia since the Second World War. This was not only an inducement, though; the Russians knew that by establishing a cooperative Japanese and American presence in an area near China, they could "stabilize" the region.

The pipeline itself was to be built by Bechtel, the San Francisco-based construction firm. A few months earlier, in April, Treasury Secretary George Shultz had gone to Moscow to discuss granting U.S. credit for the project. Although the pipeline idea was eventually abandoned—leaving the Soviets to concentrate on the controversial pipeline to Western Europe a few years later—this brought Shultz to the attention of Bechtel, which eventually hired him after he left the Nixon administration.

The Jackson and Stevenson amendments eventually killed any hope of U.S. government involvement—and with it, the interest of most American and European banks. Another problem was that there was no guarantee that the Yakutsk fields actually had sufficient gas reserves to make the project tenable. At the end of 1973, after months of stalling, the Soviet government finally let an El Paso Natural Gas drilling team inspect the area. But the Russians allowed them only two weeks, barely enough time to set up testing equipment, and the arctic temperatures hampered exploration. The Americans were never satisfied that there was enough natural gas there.

Curiously, with several big American companies involved, the proposed pipeline was never subjected to the same scrutiny that the Siberian pipeline to Europe faced during the Reagan administration. Whereas in the early 1980s, the U.S. government considered the European pipeline dangerous because it would create a European dependency on Soviet gas and at the same time allow the Soviets the opportunity to raise billions of dollars in hard currency, in 1973 the debate was different. What if, a *New York Times* editorial asked, after American firms built the pipeline, the Soviets refused to supply the United States with gas? Was such a gamble worth it?

Hammer's pipeline died a slow death. Once a year, from 1974 to 1978, the U.S.-U.S.S.R. Commercial Commission, an official government organization, met to discuss the issue but found, according to a Commerce Department official, that it was "just too big and scary an undertaking for the two governments to come to any agreement on it."

In September, Hammer announced another deal, which actually came to fruition. In sessions with Hammer and Soviet officials in July 1972, Sargent Shriver had proposed a hotel complex in Moscow to accommodate visiting Western businessmen and provide their companies with office space and facilities. "I had been running the Merchandise Mart in Chicago," Shriver recalls, "and when we were talking about trade, it was almost a knee-jerk reaction for me to make the suggestion." Although Hammer and several other East-West entrepreneurs have claimed credit for the World Trade Center in Moscow, Shriver remarks, "As Jack Kennedy said, 'Success has a thousand parents and failure is an orphan.'"

Nevertheless, at a news conference at the Waldorf-Astoria in New York, with champagne freely flowing, Hammer and Boris A. Borisov announced that Occidental Petroleum was to be the general contractor for the 180 million-dollar complex of four buildings, built by Bechtel and with Chase Manhattan as the leading bank for financing. The World Trade Center would have office space for 400 companies, Telex facilities, a 2000-seat conference hall, theater and concert halls, an underground garage for 600 cars, restaurants, shops, 625 apartments for employees, and a 600-room hotel. It was to be completed in time for the 1980 Moscow Olympics. At the end of the press conference, after Hammer plugged most-favored-nation status for the Soviets, one reporter asked Borisov archly whether Occidental was a "most favored company" in the Soviet Union. Borisov dodged the question.

Today, the World Trade Center stands across the Moscow River from the Hotel Ukraine. It resembles a Hyatt Hotel, and looks like nothing else in the Soviet Union. To the chagrin of Occidental employees, who occupy a small office on the fourteenth floor of the office building, it is known as "Hammer's trade center." The center is dominated by a large, spacious atrium, similar to New York's Citicorp Center, at the center of which is a tall metallic rooster that crows with a prerecorded squawk every hour. Russian prostitutes, having bribed their way past the guards, gather in the hotel lobby by the bar every evening. The World Trade Center is a peculiar island of capitalist decadence surrounded by the mud and debris of sluggardly socialist construction. Barely two years after it was completed, its elevators and escalators were out of commission. While the complex was built by Americans and Europeans, it is maintained by the Russians, who do not understand the sophisticated American equipment. It appears to be falling apart.

At the end of November 1973, Hammer announced that he would make a gift to the trade center: an eighteen-hole championship golf course, designed by the master golf-course architect Robert Trent Jones. James Reston reacted to the announcement with gentle sarcasm, warning that a golf course might be a dangerous thing to introduce to Communists. "Golf is an addiction, like vodka," he wrote. "You can either conquer the world or learn to play golf, but . . . you can't do both." Brezhnev accepted the offer, although the Soviet Embassy in London noted dourly, "Mr. Brezhnev certainly does not play golf." In fact, Hammer eventually gave up the idea, perhaps because of lack of interest on the part of the Soviets.

After years of involvement with the Soviet Union, much of which he had concealed, Hammer had finally become the

American businessman most favored by the Kremlin—and, because it was the time of détente, his special status was extremely visible. After Jacob Beam retired as Ambassador to the Soviet Union in early 1973 and there were rumors that Nixon would name either David Rockefeller or Armand Hammer, Hammer invited Soviet Ambassador Anatoly Dobrynin and his family to spend a weekend with him and Victor in Palm Beach, Florida. The Occidental jet picked up the Dobrynins in Washington in late August and flew them south.

There Hammer and Dobrynin went deep-sea fishing off the Florida coast and later attended a dinner, at which Dobrynin proposed a toast endorsing Hammer as the next ambassador to Moscow. "I'm one hundred percent behind him," Dobrynin said. "He's my candidate." Hammer immediately demurred. "My first duty I owe is to my stockholders."

It is unlikely that Nixon ever seriously considered nominating Hammer, and even more unlikely that the Soviets would have wanted that. Hammer was far more useful to them as a corporate tycoon. By this time, he had become more beloved to the Soviets than even John Reed, the American who is buried in the Kremlin Wall. But whereas Reed was really a dilettante who embraced Communism, Armand Hammer, far more important, advanced not only the cause of trade with the West but also the image of the Soviet Union as a peaceful state. In December 1973, Progress Press in Moscow published a book by Hammer entitled *Russia Seen Twice,* consisting half of excerpts from *Quest of the Romanoff Treasure* and half of recent observations on Russia and politics. *Literaturnaya Gazeta* ("Literary Gazette," the organ of the Soviet Writers' Union) published an interview with him on December 26.

"I am immeasurably happy that I was able to meet and converse with the great founder of your state, Vladimir Ilyich Lenin," Hammer told his interviewer. "I am happy that I met and spoke with General Secretary of the Central Committee of the Communist Party, Leonid Ilyich Brezhnev."

Another time Hammer was interviewed in *Pravda,* similarly comparing Brezhnev to Lenin. "I consider Brezhnev a remarkable leader," he said. "His bold policies have greatly helped the relaxation of tensions between East and West. In this sense, L. I. Brezhnev is directly following the path begun by the great Lenin."

Soviet Life, the glossy English-language magazine published in Moscow for distribution abroad, featured a two-page spread on Hammer in May 1973. The text, which recounted the standard legend about how Hammer came to Russia in 1921 and brought tears to Lenin's eyes, was accompanied by photographs of Lenin's study in the Kremlin adorned with Hammer's bronze monkey, photos of Hammer, Dave Karr, and Sargent Shriver negotiating with Patolichev, and of Hammer with Dzhermen Gvishiani. The article quoted Hammer: "I am proud of having met Lenin and shall never forget his charming personality and cordiality, his words to the effect that our planet is small and the different countries must learn to live in peace with one another."

In November 1973, producer Lucy Jarvis led a film crew from NBC on a trip to Moscow to make a documentary on Armand Hammer's life called "The Russian Connection." Hammer, flattered by the attention, was cooperative and took Jarvis and her crew from London to Moscow on his jet.

On board, Hammer put on his Gucci slippers and smoking jacket, ordered champagne, caviar, and black bread served to his guests, and then announced, "I'll see you in twelve minutes." Sitting in his chair, he stared into space for a few moments. Suddenly, his head slumped on his shoulder. He awoke, deeply refreshed, twelve minutes later and explained that he was skilled in the art of self-hypnosis.

When the plane landed in Moscow, a red carpet was rolled out for Hammer and his wife, his associates, and the NBC crew. Everyone was put up at Moscow's finest old hotel, the National. Jarvis shot footage of Hammer walking in Moscow, wearing a Russian sable hat, and posing in front of the British Embassy—once the Government Guest House, in which Hammer lived before his parents came over to Russia in 1923.

Jarvis, who had produced a landmark documentary in 1962 on the Kremlin, wanted to film Hammer walking into the Kremlin and meeting with Brezhnev. Every Soviet official she spoke with told her that it was forbidden to film the interior of Kremlin buildings; Jarvis, who had done it in 1962, knew better. One official even remarked that some American woman had done a documentary on the Kremlin years before and offered to sell Jarvis the very footage she had compiled earlier. Finally, she went to Hammer and told him that Edwin Newman, her narrator and assistant, was coming to Moscow the next day, specifically to be filmed with Hammer and Brezhnev. She threatened to create a furor if he did not help.

The next morning it was arranged: NBC cameras photographed Newman and Hammer entering the Kremlin and the Council of Ministers Building, walking through the corridors, being greeted by the General Secretary's staff in the outer office, and finally meeting Brezhnev himself. NBC was not allowed to bring in a sound man, because the Soviets are suspicious of any outside listening devices in the Kremlin; Brezhnev's office supplied a Soviet technician.

Brezhnev spent an hour with Hammer, Jarvis, and Newman, proudly showing them around his office and explaining the significance of various devices and sculptures, rhapsodizing about Dr. Hammer and how he had come to Russia in 1921 when the Bolsheviks needed his help, and inscribing photographs of himself for Jarvis and Newman. When the cameras were rolling he became even more genial and outgoing. "I would like to give my warmest greetings to the American people," he said through his interpreter, while standing beside Hammer. "My advice and good wishes to President Nixon. We have formed a very solid basis for good relations between our two peoples. Armand Hammer has expended considerable effort. I help him, he helps me. It is mutual. We do not discuss secrets—just business."

The rest of the Western news corps in Moscow, many of whom had tried unsuccessfully for years to arrange a meeting with Brezhnev, were flabbergasted. Edwin Newman, who had never been to Russia before, had flown in one day, spoken with Brezhnev in the Kremlin the next, and then left the country, with Jarvis and the NBC team, on Armand Hammer's private jet. Such were the privileges of dealing with Dr. Hammer.

Jarvis's crew had spent much time in Moscow searching for the mansion in which the Hammer family had spent more than ten years—the so-called Brown House—but were unable to find it. Hammer had told them that the address of the house was Petrovsky Pereulok 8, but no such address existed in Moscow any longer. Petrovsky Pereulok was the narrow alley perpendicular to the main thoroughfare, Sadovo-Samotechnaya, on which the Brown House stands. The alley was filled in with apartment buildings during the boom in construction of the Stalin years.

After the Hammers left, the Brown House became the headquarters for the *Moscow Daily News* and later the Australian Embassy. In 1962 it became the chancellery and residence of the Lebanese ambassador to the Soviet Union. In 1978, shortly after being posted in Moscow, the Lebanese Ambassador Antoine Yazbek and his wife, Mary, were invited to a state dinner at which they were seated on either side of Armand Hammer. At one point in the dinner, Hammer turned to Mrs. Yazbek and said, "So, how's my house?" Mrs. Yazbek did not know what he was talking about. "You're living in what used to be my house," he said. "That house saw a lot of wine, women, and song."

He reminisced briefly about his life in Moscow in the early days, explaining that "after the war" he received an apartment in the nine-story building at Kutuzov Prospekt 26, the same building in which Brezhnev lived (and in which Brezhnev's successor as General Secretary, Yuri Andropov, has long resided). He returned to the subject of the Brown House, describing the festive dinner parties in the banquet room with singers and actresses from the Moscow Art Theatre. "Is the secret passage still there?" he asked. The Yazbeks had not realized that the passage was there, until they returned that evening and pried open the concealed panel at the side of the marble stairway.

Whether Hammer did in fact have a special apartment in Moscow after the war, he stayed at the Lenin Suite in the National on business trips to Moscow in the early seventies, always taking with him a few favorite paintings to hang on the wall. But Frances, who always accompanied him, grew tired of the traffic noise in the hotel room, Hammer says, and decided that she would not return to Moscow unless they were given better accommodations. Whether on Frances's insistence or out of a desire for more luxurious lodgings, Hammer reportedly told Brezhnev that he would not be coming to Moscow—throughout the seventies he flew to Russia on the average of once a month—if he could not live someplace nicer.

So, in 1976 the Soviets gave him an apartment on the sixth floor of the building in which Russia's literary elite live, across from the Tretyakov Gallery, in the Zamoskvorechye District. The Russians provided the space—really, the space of several apartments—and Occidental, hiring German and Swiss firms, provided the renovation and equipment. The new five-room apartment has two bedrooms, a living room, dining room, and kitchen, a dishwasher, and a deep freeze for Hammer's flash-frozen American steaks. When Hammer found that the district's electrical system was inadequate, the Soviets tore up the streets, creating a traffic snarl, and installed a new system. There are chandeliers and mirrored panels and a Russian maid to prepare the apartment for the Hammers' arrival and look after them while they are there. The walls are hung with masterpieces, all of which Hammer has deeded to the Soviet government after his death, by some of Russia's greatest artists. Above the couch in the living room is Bogdanov-Byelski's *Peasant Girl at the Piano.* The painting over the mantelpiece, N. A. Kasatkin's *Newly Born—Recuperating,* had been sold to an American at the Louisiana Purchase Exhibition in St. Louis in 1904; Hammer acquired it in 1975 after the Soviet Consul General in San Francisco, Alexander Zinchuk, told him that it was being offered for sale in Beverly Hills.

When the apartment was ready in 1976, Hammer threw a huge housewarming party for high-ranking Soviets and Western diplomats and businessmen. By American standards, Hammer's Moscow apartment is not gigantic, but it is, as Hammer brags, "the finest in Moscow." Several other foreigners maintain apartments in Moscow. One is Ara Oztemel, founder and president of an American firm, Satra, Inc., which deals in Soviet exports and imports. Oztemel, however, spends at least as much time in Moscow as he does in the United States, while Hammer, as the chief executive of a company with dealings all over the world, comes to Moscow frequently but for short periods of time.

Details about Hammer's Moscow apartment have been reported widely in the Western press, but there are aspects of his personal dealings in Moscow that he prefers to conceal. There is, for instance, a Soviet citizen, probably a KGB operative, named Mikhail Bruk, who for several years ran the Occidental office in Moscow.

When Lucy Jarvis first went to Moscow in 1962, Eleanor Roosevelt suggested that she look up Bruk, then one of the few Russians who spoke English fluently. Mrs. Roosevelt explained that Bruk had translated for her on her several trips to the Soviet Union. As an old friend of the Hammer family, Bruk may have been recommended to Mrs. Roosevelt by Victor Hammer.

Jarvis was astounded to find that Bruk spoke English with a perfect British accent. When they met, he regaled her with stories about Eleanor Roosevelt. Later she heard that he had gone through training in a British-replica town outside Moscow, set up by the KGB to accustom its agents to all aspects of British life, from movies and shops to colloquial speech. When she returned to Russia in 1973, she found that Bruk had a private office in the Occidental suite on the top floor of the National hotel, directing all of Occidental's Soviet operations.

In the early 1950s, Bruk studied at the Institute of Foreign Languages in Moscow. Because he is Jewish, he was not permitted to study in the English-language faculty but only in the teacher-training department. There, presumably, the KGB took notice of this ambitious student and hired him to organize the Soviet delegations to the Pugwash conferences.

In a society in which being Jewish is normally a severe handicap, Bruk managed to create a successful career in the business of dealing with foreigners and reporting on their activities. He was hired ostensibly as a journalist for the Novosti Press Agency, the arm of the Soviet press that is most directly responsible for disseminating propaganda. His position was in the "Department of Books and Pamphlets," the unimaginatively named section that coordinates liaison with the KGB.

Victor Hammer's son, Armand Victorovich, recalls that in 1961 he recommended Bruk—"whom I had known practically since birth"—to his uncle Armand as an interpreter. From then on, Bruk worked for Hammer, and Hammer found his access to the inner reaches of the Soviet government invaluable. "Now Misha [Bruk] is always with Hammer, always in the center of things, a very, very important person in Moscow," Armand Victorovich says. "It makes me proud."

Bruk explains, "I have known Armand Hammer for thirty-five years, through his nephew, through Victor, and by working with the doctor himself. I am an old family friend. In 1964 I was the first Soviet journalist to write about Dr. Hammer, in *Nedelya,* the weekly news magazine of the official government newspaper, *Izvestiya.*" Bruk denies having worked for Hammer in the sixties. "I began working for him in 1972 and served for four years on the Occidental staff. I quit in 1976. I am no longer associated with Occidental in any capacity. The only help I give the doctor is personal help, as one would help a relative." In fact, although he did resign as chief of the Moscow office in 1976, complaining that he could not get along with Hammer, he is still associated with Occidental. The present Occidental Moscow representative, Terry Riley, concedes that Bruk is kept on as a "special consultant." Riley will not discuss Bruk's association with the "Kiev Gas Board" (as he calls the KGB). "Let us just say that he is well connected," Riley says. "He is extremely helpful."

Although all American companies in Moscow are monitored by the KGB through Russian national employees, who are regularly called into the KGB Lubyanka headquarters for debriefing, only Occidental Petroleum has worked hand in hand with the KGB. Understandably, neither Hammer nor Bruk cares to make this fact public.

Bruk works at his dacha outside Moscow, a rare privilege, as he freely admits. Besides acting as a "facilitator" for visiting celebrities, he also writes occasional articles for the Soviet English-language press. In March 1982, for example, Bruk published an interview with Hammer in the *Moscow News.* Describing Hammer as "a dignified grey-haired bespectacled elderly gentleman," he quotes Hammer's observations on Russia: "The Soviet Union became strong due to the fact that its leadership has led the country all these years along the trail blazed by Lenin. Lenin's policy of peaceful coexistence between the two different social systems is especially vital today in the nuclear age." While Bruk's prose is inelegant, he makes his propaganda points in unmistakable terms.

Bruk frequently travels to the United States with Hammer, and from time to time takes the opportunity to do some work for Novosti. With his fluent English and his British accent, he was able to convince several American newspapers of large circulation that he was a free-lance British journalist who could provide them with news articles on the Soviet Union free of the bias of most Western correspondents. "These big-city American reporters in Moscow are all biased," he told newspaper editors. "I can supply you with articles telling you how it really is."

The *Chicago Sun-Times* fell for Bruk's pitch and printed several articles by "special correspondent Mike Burke," containing the Novosti Press Agency's subtly crafted propaganda line. The *Sun-Times* stopped running Bruk's articles only when Murray Seeger of the *Los Angeles Times* explained who the "special correspondent" really was.

When Lucy Jarvis arrived at the National Hotel in November 1973 to begin filming her documentary on Armand Hammer, she dropped by the Occidental office late one night, having heard that it was still open. There she found a full-fledged vodka party in progress. As she walked in the room, she was introduced to a man of around fifty years named Armand Hammer. For an instant she was taken aback, until he explained that he was Victor Hammer's son. Victor later told her that his son had grown up in the Soviet Union because his ex-wife "insisted" on staying there.

Armand Victorovich had some sort of unspecified job with Occidental, although it was never entirely explained. Jarvis recalls: "He was *everywhere.* If you went to the Bolshoi or embassy parties, young Armand would be there without fail, accompanied by his jazzy wife in a beehive hairdo."

From his small apartment in the workers' district, on Krasnopresnenskaya, in which he lived during the 1950s, Armand Victorovich moved to a large, luxurious apartment in the center of Moscow in the early seventies, with a dacha in the countryside.

His station in Moscow society was apparently improved by his uncle's rise to worldwide prominence. In the early sixties he had an unimpressive job editing a technical journal on vending machines, which were then being introduced to the Soviet Union for the first time; by the seventies, however, he had the cushy position of verification editor at Progress Publishers.

From his first marriage he has a daughter, born in 1956; a second daughter, of a second marriage, was born in 1968. He is now married for a third time, to an attractive co-worker at Progress. "I have had a very unhappy life," he says. "I have lived through so much, suffered so much. Only now, so late in life, am I happy."

During the time of Armand Hammer's much-heralded deals in the seventies, Armand Victorovich rose to great social prominence because of his connection to his famous uncle. He could get whatever he or his friends wanted from abroad simply by asking his uncle or his father. Suddenly he was rich and had the prominence of a Politburo member.

The most treasured privilege in the Soviet Union, enjoyed by extremely few people, is the ability to travel at will, and Armand Victorovich now has a special passport with which he travels around the world. He says that he has been to the United States ten times so far, visiting New York and Los Angeles, and regularly visits Spain, where he can practice the language he studied at the Institute of Foreign Languages.

But he does not travel entirely freely. His wife and two daughters are not permitted to travel with him. In this way he is kept from defecting, as he admits he once considered doing. If Armand Hammer is able to demand a fancy apartment in Moscow, one must assume he could just as easily demand that his nephew be allowed to live in the United States. Evidently, though, Hammer is not that influential.

This is an intriguing and possibly important matter. There are indications that Armand Victorovich was kept in the Soviet Union as a hostage when the rest of the Hammers left in the 1930s, perhaps to ensure that they continued to aid the Soviet government. Similarly, although Armand Victorovich may have entertained the notion of defecting on his first visit to New York in 1960, his daughter was kept in Moscow, perhaps to discourage this plan. Even today, although Victor's son can travel out of the country at will and enjoys the status of an eminent Soviet official, he is kept from defecting because his wife and daughter remain behind as hostages.

While there are no indications that this peculiar situation has any bearing on his uncle's business dealings, it is nevertheless strange that Armand Hammer neither acknowledges nor publicly associates with his Soviet nephew. His aides explain that Hammer dislikes Victor's son, although Armand Victorovich denies any bad feeling between them.

Mikhail Bruk explains that "Dr. Hammer dislikes his nephew. They simply are not close. It's not a warm relationship. You know, sometimes you have a relative you happen to dislike—that's the way it is between the Doctor and his nephew. Dr. Hammer is a self-made man; he pulled himself up by his own bootstraps. But Armand Victorovich has lived all his life on money provided by his father. And Dr. Hammer disapproves of people like that."

Whether Hammer really does not like his nephew or, more likely, for whatever reason does not wish to be identified with him, he refuses to discuss him. Even when Armand Victorovich was working for the Occidental Petroleum office in Moscow, Hammer let it be known that he did not want to appear in public with his nephew. Ambassador Jacob Beam recalls attending the opening of the Armand Hammer Collection at the Hermitage in October 1972. Hammer's nephew, who had not been invited, was present. When Hammer saw that Armand Victorovich was there, he became visibly displeased.

From a child prince in the Hammers' mansion in the late twenties, to a well-to-do but "second-class" citizen living on sufferance, to a prominent hostage—if indeed he is one—in a gilded cage, Armand Victorovich Hammer—a Russian with an American surname—is a living testament to the permutations of the Hammers' relationship with the Soviet Union. Although he frankly appreciates the benefits that his uncle's business dealings have conferred upon him, he is amused by the myth that has grown up concerning Armand Hammer's onetime, one-hour meeting with Lenin. "There was a time," he says archly, "when my uncle's friendship with Lenin was not quite the big thing it is now."

17

THE BEST OF BOTH WORLDS

AFTER JIMMY CARTER became President in 1977, many businessmen thought the old Kendall-Nixon Republicans should turn the U.S.-U.S.S.R. Trade and Economic Council leadership over to Carter people. At least that was the thinking at Coca-Cola headquarters in Atlanta, Georgia. Armand Hammer, who had once again begun to call himself a Roosevelt Democrat and to reminisce about FDR, shared this point of view, and J. Paul Austin, the chairman of Coca-Cola, was only too glad to help Hammer unseat Don Kendall.

In the last days of the Nixon administration, Kendall had climbed aboard the sinking ship by forming the "Americans for the Presidency" committee to defend Nixon. He drew up ads calling for the "preserving of this nation." Many of the prominent Americans he asked to join the committee refused; the final list included such loyal Nixon supporters as Mamie Eisenhower, the Reverend Norman Vincent Peale, and Bob Hope. Later he admitted, "I had no idea what the hell was on those tapes."

Kendall remained influential in Gerald Ford's administration, although he continued to be identified with Richard Nixon. To be sure, he saw Nixon more often out of office than during presidential days. He recalls flying out to visit Nixon at San Clemente during the months after the resignation. He would bring a bottle of Stolichnaya vodka and the Cuban cigars to which Nixon is partial; Nixon would bring out some excellent caviar he had been given by the Shah of Iran; and together they would indulge, in the tower of the compound, after Pat had gone to bed.

The drawback to being loyal to a now unpopular man was that, with Carter in, many thought it was time for Kendall to be out. J. Paul Austin had carefully cultivated Carter, supplying him, as Governor of Georgia, with free rides around the world on Coca-Cola planes. Governor Carter even began calling Coke "my own State Department."

After the 1976 election, Austin introduced Armand Hammer to President-elect Carter. Hammer later told Austin that he too would like to see Kendall removed as chairman of the Trade Council. He intimated that he thought Kendall's exclusive Pepsi deal in the Soviet Union might even be a violation of U.S. antitrust laws and called an antitrust lawyer at Harvard Law School for advice. Hammer was disappointed to learn that no such laws had been broken, but this did not stop him from doing some campaigning against Kendall within the Council at the 1976 meeting in Moscow.

With some people, however, Hammer and Austin did not have to do much convincing. A few influential directors, such as Reginald Jones, the chairman of General Electric, thought Kendall's overly "personal" role in East-West relations amounted to interference with U.S. foreign policy. The squabble in Moscow grew fierce, and the embarrassed Soviet officials asked the Americans to delay the struggle until they were on American soil.

Some of the Russians took sides, though. As much as they appreciated Kendall's efforts, they realized that he no longer had the necessary access to the White House; and they now made it clear that they favored replacing Kendall with Hammer. A Kendall supporter in the Council recalls that Ambassador Dobrynin actually said as much.

The clamor for Kendall's resignation continued into the next year. David Rockefeller, chairman of the Council's Nominating Committee, was assigned to approach Kendall and ask him gently what his "plans" were. Kendall decided that at last it was time to step down from the Council he had done so much to create. Hammer, unpopular among his colleagues in the Council, had very little chance of being elected chairman; in fact, the Soviets' support of him only served to damage his cause further. Instead, G. William Miller, president of Textron, Inc., and a leading Carter supporter, was chosen. Carter's admiration for Miller was so great that he named him, a few months later, as head of the Federal Reserve Board.

In 1978 C. William Verity, chairman of Armco Steel, was elected chairman of the Trade Council. He had the vocal support of David Rockefeller; Verity was a member of the Chase Manhattan board. Rockefeller had wanted Verity as chairman since the initial struggle of 1976. Several Trade Council members report that Rockefeller, who still felt slighted because he was not at first named as a Council director, was a bit too obvious in his disregard for Kendall. Indeed, a few years later, when Kendall ran for the chairmanship of the U.S. Chamber of Commerce, Rockefeller reportedly spoke to a big wheel at the Chamber, Clifton Garvin, the chairman of Exxon, and warned him that Kendall should not be chosen. Kendall was too much of a maverick, Rockefeller warned, too controversial and unpopular. Rockefeller recommended his friend Verity, and Verity was selected. In 1981, when Verity's term was completed, Kendall eventually succeeded in becoming chairman of the Chamber of Commerce.

Now that Kendall was merely a director of the Council, the Soviets realized they could please President Carter, indirectly at least, by allowing Coca-Cola entry to the Soviet market. The problem was that they had guaranteed Pepsi exclusive rights. The agreement covered only cola drinks, however; in March 1978 they agreed to sell Fanta, Coke's orange soda, in the Soviet Union. As a beverage both American and vaguely reminiscent of the fruit drinks with which Russians are more familiar, Fanta enjoyed instant success, although it too was distributed only in "showcase" cities—Moscow, Leningrad, and the resorts of the Crimea.

Later in the year the Soviet government announced that Coke would receive the concession to supply its cola at the 1980 Summer Olympic Games. Coca-Cola had been the Olympics supplier for decades, but the arrangement had been complicated by the Pepsi contract. Kendall insists that "We could have sold at the Olympics if we wanted to, but we questioned its promotional value." The Soviets, he says, asked him to write a letter formally relieving them of their contractual obligations to Pepsi; he adds that he even helped the Soviets get more money from Coca-Cola for the rights by submitting bids that they used as bargaining chips. PepsiCo also probably received a substantial cash settlement. Coke wanted to sell in Russia, and the Russians wanted them in as well, for political reasons. Unlike most American companies, Coke did not abide by Carter's decision to boycott the Moscow Olympics. Carter's boycott, which significantly reduced the attendance at the games, hurt Coke's sales in the Soviet Union. But Coke executives were pleased nonetheless: they had finally invaded Kendall's territory.

The Soviet invasion of Afghanistan affected PepsiCo as well. Until then, Stolichnaya vodka had been selling well in the United States; although, as a "deluxe" vodka, it captured less than one percent of the large American vodka market. After Afghanistan, Stolichnaya sales plummeted. New York City longshoremen refused to unload crates of Stolichnaya at the docks; bartenders refused to serve it. Tsingtao vodka, imported from China, took advantage of Stolichnaya's newfound unpopularity, waging a proxy Sino-Soviet conflict in the American marketplace. "DID THE RUSSIANS MISCALCULATE?" Tsingtao's advertisements blared. "AMERICA'S LOVE AFFAIR WITH RUSSIAN VODKA APPEARS TO BE ON THE ROCKS."

Since the number of bottles of Pepsi sold in Russia depended on the number of bottles of Stolichnaya sold in the United States, Kendall was forced to renegotiate his Soviet contract. Although the Russians allowed him to include Soviet champagne in his sales figures, Kendall's Soviet deal began to lose money.

At the same time, Kendall had rapidly come into disfavor with the more conservative elements of Carter's factious administration. Malcolm Toon, U.S. Ambassador to the Soviet Union, began to send regular dispatches to Washington from Moscow, angrily quoting praise of Kendall in the Soviet press.

Once, Carter's National Security Adviser, Zbigniew Brzezinski, fired off a cable to Toon's successor, Thomas Watson, instructing him to call in a particular Soviet official and deliver a message of consternation of some kind. The Russian arrived at Watson's office at the American Embassy, sat down at the conference table, and promptly shot his cuffs, exposing a large and flashy set of cuff links that Kendall had given him, made of miniature Soviet and American flags back to back. "I just couldn't be too rough on him," Watson lamented later, "with his damn Kendall cuff links staring me in the face."

"People say behind my back," Kendall once commented, "that I dip my fingers too much in politics. And I say, 'Hell, if I could wedge my whole body in, I'd do it.'" When the Republicans returned to Washington in 1981, Kendall, a major contributor to Reagan's campaign, was somewhat restored to influence. As chairman of the U.S. Chamber of Commerce, he spoke often in favor of Reagan's budget plans. Since he had not seen Brezhnev since Nixon's fall, he was no longer in a position to act as unofficial emissary between the Kremlin and the White House as he had in the early seventies.

Kendall has maintained his interest in Russia, although no longer with the high-level contacts he once enjoyed. As chairman of the board of the American Ballet Theatre since 1977, he arranged to bring in Mikhail Baryshnikov as artistic director.

Kendall offered Baryshnikov the position over dinner. "I

brought out vodka I had flavored with peppers from my own garden," Kendall says, "and we had smoked salmon from Iceland. Give a Russian vodka and smoked salmon and he's happy. I also had some brandy I had brought back from Georgia and Armenia, which Misha [Baryshnikov] hadn't seen since he'd left Russia, and by three o'clock in the morning, everything was settled." Although *New York Times* columnist Flora Lewis reported in August 1982 that President Reagan had "been sending word to the Soviet Union privately" through Kendall that the Reagan administration wanted "businesslike" relations with the Russians, and although Kendall continues to travel to Eastern Europe and Russia on company business, his days of sessions in the Kremlin and at the Kremlin are largely over.

Cyrus Eaton, controversial to the last, gave speeches urging Soviet-American rapprochement even when he was confined to a wheelchair. When the Central Intelligence Agency underwent scrutiny in 1975, Eaton revealed that the CIA had asked him to spy for them when he first went over in 1958. "I told them that under no circumstances would I be part of a spying organization," he recalled. On May 9, 1979, Eaton died at the age of ninety-five. His front-page obituary in *The New York Times,* was written by that paper's premier obituary writer, Alden Whitman. In an adjoining article, the paper called him "a different kind of capitalist."

Though Eaton is largely forgotten in this country, the Soviet Union remembers him fondly. Cyrus, Jr., has seen Soviet textbooks that revere his father as one of the few American capitalists with any sense. In July 1982, thirty-five arms-control specialists and scientists gathered in Pugwash, Nova Scotia, to commemorate the twenty-fifth anniversary of the founding of the Pugwash conferences. Several of the original delegates were there, including Harold Brown of the California Institute of Technology, Iwao Ogawa of Japan, and Sergei Kapitsa of the Soviet Union.

David Rockefeller, too, passed largely by the wayside when the fever of détente had broken in the late seventies. While conceding that Nixon's fall was "somewhat of a blow to détente," he insists that the real cause of the decline of détente was "the Carter administration's rather soft line toward the Soviet . . . which, I think, encouraged the Soviets to do many things which they wouldn't have done had there not been such a soft policy."

His last meeting with a Soviet leader was in June 1975 when, in connection with a Dartmouth Conference meeting in Moscow, he spoke with Kosygin. As America lost interest in Soviet trade, however, so did Rockefeller. Under his stewardship, Chase Manhattan fell from the largest bank in the United States to the third largest, and many blamed it on his incessant globetrotting. His trips to Moscow, however, became less and less frequent. Rockefeller's financial influence was diminished with his retirement from the bank in the spring of 1981, leaving him with only the symbolic role of elder banker-statesman and Rockefeller—which may have been his greatest role anyway.

Although Chase, in April 1974, loaned the Soviet government $150 million to construct the Kama River truck plant 550 miles east of Moscow—the plant that turned out the trucks that invaded Afghanistan in late 1979 and early 1980—he admits that "I suppose in today's climate we might not have done that, because there is more concern about Soviet aggressiveness in the world." Still, he adds a touch defensively, Chase should not be blamed. The U.S. Export-Import bank also helped finance the plant, and so "we didn't see any reason why we shouldn't be a part of it."

In January 1982, when the controversy over the Siberian pipeline to Europe erupted, Rockefeller joined several other powerful American private citizens—John McCloy, George Shultz, Melvin Laird, Henry Kissinger, Paul Nitze, and Gerald Ford—at a dinner at the German Embassy in Washington to hear Helmut Schmidt defend German involvement in the pipeline project. Over a meal of overdone lamb and several bottles of Wehlener Sonnenuhr Kabinett '77, they discussed the pipeline until past midnight. Rockefeller did not openly take issue with Schmidt's reasoning; separately, he dismissed the arguments against the project by saying "it's a question of degree." He after all had an interest in the undertaking. Ruhrgas A.G., the West German energy company that made the arrangement with the Kremlin, is partly owned by Exxon, Mobil, and Texaco, all Rockefeller interests.

Averell Harriman, who had negotiated the limited test ban treaty of 1963 with the Russians during the Kennedy administration, later served as unofficial ambassador to the Kremlin for the Democratic Party (for presidential candidates Edmund Muskie in 1972 and Jimmy Carter in 1976). When Marshall Shulman, director of the Columbia University Russian Institute, was named by Carter to head the Soviet desk at the State Department, he lived for a time in the majestic Harriman town house in Georgetown. Shulman appreciated both the first-class lodgings and the advice from Harriman that came with dinner, and Harriman did not mind the opportunity to have a little influence on U.S. policy once again. A few years later, in October 1982, Harriman gave $11.5 million to the Columbia Russian Institute, which was then renamed the W. Averell Harriman Institute for the Advanced Study of the Soviet Union. "It is absolutely essential that this country know what is going on in the Soviet Union," the ninety-year-old Harriman said at the presentation ceremony. "There is so much misinformation, beginning with those in the highest authority in government. To base policy on ignorance and illusion is very dangerous. It should be based on knowledge and understanding."

Yet only one man—Armand Hammer—was left by the 1980s, as indubitably the Kremlin's favorite capitalist. Apparently, the Soviets didn't care that he was unpopular in his own country, for he managed to achieve many of the deals he sought to make.

The Russians seemed to favor Hammer in all business dealings, to the consternation of his American competitors. In September 1977 Dave Karr, who had broken with Hammer in 1973, teamed up with him for one last time to capture the worldwide rights to distribute the coins and medals for the 1980 Moscow Olympics, a project worth as much as three hundred million dollars. It was the sort of undertaking to which American Express was naturally suited; indeed, Howard Clark, the chairman of American Express, was reportedly assured by Alkhimov that he would receive the rights. Clark's company already possessed the requisite billing machinery and credit-card subscriber lists for the United States, France, and England. Somehow, though, Hammer and Karr were awarded the coin deal. "That was the perfect thing for American Express," one Council member said. "There was no excuse for Hammer going in there and taking it." But the Soviet government evidently preferred dealing with Armand Hammer.

There were even times when the Soviets acted in concert with Hammer to make him seem more influential in Moscow than he might really have been. In the spring of 1978, in an elaborate "sting" operation, the FBI apprehended three Soviet U.N. officials involved in espionage. A few months later, in retaliation, the Soviets arrested a Moscow-based executive for International Harvester, F. Jay Crawford, on charges of black-market currency speculation and "illicit" affairs with Soviet women.

Crawford, and not some other American businessman, was singled out probably because he was not influential within his own company, and the Russians knew it. He was the number-two man in International Harvester's Moscow office, and when his boss was reassigned, Crawford Telexed company headquarters, requesting promotion to the top spot. His request was denied. One State Department official believes the Soviets, who routinely monitor Telex communications, concluded that since Crawford was not especially trusted by International Harvester, he would make a good, safe target.

At first, none of the American companies dealing with Russia would register a complaint with the Soviet government for fear of damaging their business relations. Diplomats in the American embassy in Moscow tried in vain to persuade influential corporate executives to demand Crawford's release.

Early in the summer, Treasury Secretary Michael Blumenthal met with Kosygin and, against the advice of the State Department, who urged him to bring up the incendiary topic at the end of his conversation, he complained at the start. He and Kosygin spent two hours arguing about the matter, to no result.

Enraged by their inability to resolve the dispute, certain members of the Carter administration began to pressure the Trade Council. In mid-July, Zbigniew Brzezinski sat down with Hal Scott on a tree stump at the Bohemian Grove (the annual conclave in California for the rich and powerful) and railed about the Crawford incident. If it were not settled in ten days, Brzezinski said, he would have the government stop issuing visas for Soviet officials. He demanded that Scott close the Trade Council as a protest.

The State Department was in a peculiar situation, because, while highly placed officials privately admitted that Crawford was probably guilty of at least some of the charges the Soviets were making, publicly State was required to insist that Crawford was innocent. At this point, in August 1978, Hammer became involved.

The Carter administration appreciated any assistance, but Hammer insists that Secretary of State Cyrus Vance personally asked him to talk with Brezhnev about the Crawford affair. Vance does not recall making such a request. What happened was that Hammer stopped by the office of Marshall Shulman, Carter's Soviet expert at the State Department, said that he was en route for a meeting with Brezhnev, and asked whether he should request that Crawford be released. Shulman agreed that he should and briefed Hammer on the American perspective on the case.

On August 23, 1978, Hammer and the president of the Washington-based Occidental International, Bill McSweeny, arrived in Moscow, telling the Associated Press that Brezhnev had invited them to fly to Yalta on the 25th and visit him at his dacha.

For Hammer, the privilege of meeting for a few hours with Brezhnev at the dacha—only Donald Kendall had done this—was supremely important as a badge of status. "I said to Brezhnev, 'let Crawford out of the country,'" Hammer recalls. "'It's not worth creating such bad blood with the United States over him.' And Brezhnev said, 'Well, we have evidence against him that he unquestionably engaged in currency speculation on the black market.' And I said, 'Well, supposing he did. It certainly isn't worthwhile creating friction with the United States government over that, and it's going to hurt you with American businessmen.'"

The meeting received major attention in *Pravda* the next day. Brezhnev had received Hammer, "the eminent representative of American business circles," in "a friendly atmosphere," the account read. While not referring to Crawford by name, the article made it clear that the contretemps was the major topic of discussion and stressed that the United States had no right to use trade to pressure the Soviets:

> It was emphasized with all clarity that relations between the two countries . . . can be built and developed successfully only on the basis of complete equality and noninterference in the internal affairs of each other. The Soviet Union decisively rejects any attempts of the administration of the U.S.A. to use trade to exert political pressures. Similar attempts shall yield nothing for their initiator and can further complicate Soviet-American relations. . . . A. Hammer thanked L. I. Brezhnev for the visit. . . .

As if to emphasize that Hammer had been instrumental in the matter, Crawford's trial was scheduled for three days later, with Western spectators admitted. To demonstrate the charge of "illicit" relations with Russian women, a key witness was brought in: a woman in heavy makeup and a feather boa, allegedly once involved with Crawford, slinked into the courtroom like a vamp. The Americans present had to bite their tongues to keep from laughing.

Crawford was, unsurprisingly, found guilty as charged, and then the judge suspended the sentence and ordered him to leave the country. He explained his leniency by saying, "Your company is a very good friend of the Soviet Union."

"I think I was largely instrumental in getting them to send him out of the country," Hammer says. When he returned to the United States and was "debriefed" by Shulman, he agreed to keep his role in the affair, whatever it was, a secret. He did not keep his vow for long, though; shortly thereafter he addressed a group of businessmen in California and boasted of his importance in solving the problem.

"We could not be certain whether Dr. Hammer's intervention was the decisive factor in resolving the Crawford affair," Shulman comments, "or whether other considerations at the time moved the Soviet leadership to want to get this and other irritants to the relationship out of the way. Perhaps they proved mutually reinforcing." Ambassador Toon disagrees. "If Hammer says he was instrumental in getting Crawford out, he's lying in his teeth. I pounded the tables, convincing the American business community to take a tough line on the matter. The Soviets hint that Hammer was influential, and that's designed to impress the U.S. government with Hammer's importance. And it *has* impressed the government."

"Hammer's a different person when he's dealing with the Russians than when he's dealing with anybody else," a former high-level Occidental executive says. And the Russians, in return, shower him with tribute. On Hammer's eightieth birthday, on May 24, 1978, he was invited to a banquet in his honor at the Kremlin. There, Vasily V. Kuznetsov, the First Deputy Chairman of the Presidium of the Supreme Soviet, read a birthday greeting from Leonid Brezhnev and pinned a bright red-and-gold medal on his lapel. It was the Lenin Order of Friendship Among the Peoples, usually awarded to foreign Communists, and never before to a businessman.

On another birthday, his eighty-fourth, in 1982, Hammer celebrated by reserving the Kennedy Center in Washington for a concert by the National Symphony Orchestra. He bought all the boxes and many of the orchestra seats and gave them to his friends. There was a wine party at intermission and a cake-and-liqueur reception after the performance, at which he announced that he was contributing half a million dollars to the orchestra and $250,000 to Carnegie Hall. The orchestra played his favorite songs: "The 1812 Overture," "The Stars and Stripes Forever," and, oddly, "I Got Plenty O' Nothin'."

This was Hammer's ostentatious philanthropy at its best. He has acquired a deserved reputation for making charitable donations in flamboyant style. A few months earlier, in September

1981, he was the guest of honor at the Century Plaza Hotel in Los Angeles for the presentation of the annual Armand Hammer Businessman of the Year Award. More than a thousand businessmen and politicians were in the audience to hear Bob Hope introduce the eighty-three-year-old entrepreneur as the "epitome of success" of American capitalism: "an industrialist, an art collector, a diplomat, and a philanthropist."

He gave twenty thousand dollars to Nancy Reagan's White House redecoration fund in March 1981, and in October President Reagan named him chairman of the President's Cancer Panel. At the ceremony, Hammer bubbled, "I was so honored to be asked to do this by the President. I've been a man of dreams, many dreams, and have had the privilege of seeing a great deal of them come true. And now my dream, my greatest dream, is to help free mankind from the ravages of cancer."

Mother Jones magazine responded to Hammer's new position with sarcasm, pointing out that Occidental Petroleum owned Hooker Chemical, which created the Love Canal poison dump. Actually, though, the jibe was unfair: Hooker had discontinued the dumping before Hammer acquired it in 1968. Calling him "the New Mr. Cancer," *Mother Jones* remarked that naming Hammer to the Cancer Panel was like "making Colonel Khadafy director of the Jewish Relief Fund."

In December, Hammer announced that he would give a million dollars to the scientist who cures cancer within the next decade with a method "similar to that discovered by Dr. Jonas Salk with polio vaccine." Also, starting in 1982, he said he would give one hundred thousand dollars each year to the scientist who does the most that year to further efforts to find such a cure.

This was only the latest in a series of extraordinarily generous contributions to the cause. In 1970 he gave $5 million to the Salk Institute in San Diego; six years later he gave the Salk Institute another million to establish the Armand Hammer Cancer Conference and Prize Fund. In 1977 he gave his alma mater, Columbia University, $5 million to help found the Columbia Health Sciences Center, in which cancer research would be done. After a struggle, in which several prominent Columbia alumni protested accepting Hammer's money, the building was renamed the Armand and Julius Hammer Health Sciences Center.

His other major cause is art. The Armand Hammer Collection is now worth an estimated $56 million, and he has deeded part of it to the Los Angeles County Museum (which already features an Armand and Frances Hammer Wing) and part to the National

Gallery. He is a major benefactor of Washington's Corcoran Gallery, a status that has earned him numerous political rewards. In March 1981, he sponsored a supper at the Corcoran before a gala at Ford's Theatre; as one of the event's principal contributors, he sat in the theater, with Frances, alongside Senator Howard Baker, House Speaker Tip O'Neill, and President and Mrs. Reagan.

When the Codex Leicester, a sixteenth-century Leonardo da Vinci manuscript, went up for auction in December 1980, Hammer bought it for $5.8 million. He renamed it, immodestly, the Codex Hammer, and displayed it prominently at the Corcoran during Reagan's inauguration festivities a month later.

Hammer's genius in business is his mastery of the art of promotion, and at self-promotion he is most skilled. His entry in the 1982–83 *Who's Who in America,* for instance, is remarkably long, listing every charitable organization to which he has ever contributed, six honorary degrees, countless honorary positions, awards he has received, and awards in his name. It is, at first glance, astounding.

But for all of his philanthropy, there remains considerable uncertainty about his connections with the Soviet Union. Early in 1981, a memorandum circulated in the Reagan administration warning that Hammer had been in his early days in the employ of the KGB. The memo, dated February 13, 1981, and typed on paper without a letterhead, discusses Julius, the early Communist ties, references to the Hammers in Lenin's works, and so on. "Hammer was reported by a former Soviet intelligence officer, now dead, to be an agent of Soviet intelligence in the 1920s," the memo states. "Since the 1920s, Hammer has consistently supported Soviet interests, however, never in the typical communist or left-radical manner."

Hammer angrily denied all of the memo's charges. Bill McSweeny, Hammer's man in Washington, remarks that "It looks like it was done by the John Birch Society," and adds, "if Dr. Hammer really had anything funny in his background, he wouldn't have passed the security check before he was named to the President's Cancer Panel."

Ambassador Jacob Beam recalls that while many in the embassy in Moscow were "suspicious" of Hammer, "there were no grounds for suspicion." Malcolm Toon, however, says, "I am always uneasy about people who have close, warm relations with the Soviet leadership. There is no doubt that anybody who moves in and out of Russia the way Hammer does has KGB clearance."

One way of dealing with a peculiar background is to commission a biography. This Hammer did in 1973. On Bill McSweeny's suggestion, he contacted Bob Considine, an award-winning sportswriter who had written a long string of popular biographies, from *MacArthur the Magnificent* to *Dempsey—By the Man Himself.* Considine was also the author of *The Red Plot Against America* (1949), which called the House Un-American Activities Committee "the most misunderstood and maligned committee in the history of the Congress."

Considine signed a contract with Cass Canfield at Harper & Row for the book, entitled *The Remarkable Life of Dr. Armand Hammer.* Although McSweeny denies that Considine was paid to write the book, Cass Canfield confirms that Hammer "hired him, so to speak," and that Occidental arranged to buy a number of copies of the book.

Matthew Josephson, in his landmark study *The Robber Barons,* describes the "official biographers" of some of the nineteenth-century's renowned millionaires as lawyers pleading for their clients "before the judgment of posterity." But in *The Remarkable Life of Dr. Armand Hammer,* Considine is more—or perhaps less—than an advocate; he more closely resembles a stenographer. The version is entirely Hammer's.

Omitting entirely Julius Hammer's leadership of the family business, Considine asserts that Armand was a self-made millionaire while in medical school; Julius's role in Allied American is so concealed that Julius becomes "Armand's diligent employee." Julius and Rose, the proprietors of the family's mansion, are reduced to occasional visitors. There is, significantly, no mention of Victor's Russian wife or son. The glaring omissions in the Hammer story are too numerous to list.

With Hammer's darker side obscured, Considine's biography is upbeat and adulatory. It tells the story of a man of amazing ability and creativity, who made his fortune entirely without the peculiar political connections that in reality underlie the Hammer saga. This is no doubt how Armand Hammer prefers to be remembered.

The Remarkable Life of Dr. Armand Hammer made a handy gift to Occidental shareholders at the annual meeting on Hammer's seventy-eighth birthday in May 1976. As shareholders arrived, they were handed autographed copies of the book, along with American flags, small boxes of fertilizer, and other gifts. The public-address system continuously played "America the Beautiful."

Hammer had prepared well for a meeting that he knew would

be arduous. Not only had Oxy stock hit a new low of $13.50, but the company was in trouble with the Securities and Exchange Commission for making illegal domestic and foreign payoffs. Also, many stockholders were angry that company money had paid for Hammer's defense at his Nixon-contribution trial a few months before.

Hammer was greeted by persistent loud boos and hostile questions. There were repeated calls for his resignation amid criticism of his Russian deals and his involvement in bribes at home and abroad. The complimentary copies of his biography did little to quell the hostility of some of his stockholders, but in time at least it came to be accepted as a reliable account of his life, which it is not.

Considine's book was subsequently published in London, as *Larger Than Life*. In 1981 it was published by Progress Publishers in Moscow, in a Russian translation by Hammer's personal interpreter, Galina Sullivan. Its Russian title was *Bol'she Chem Zhizn* (Larger Than Life), and it was of course revised to meet the demands of the Soviet censor: all references to Trotsky and Khrushchev were purged. Hammer even provided the Russian edition with a special foreword, in which he discusses his love for Russia:

> As Russians say, "You can't take the words out of a song." And in the song of my life the word "Russia" means and has meant a great deal. Is it not symbolic that in May 1978, in connection with my eightieth birthday, I was awarded the Soviet Order of Friendship Among the Peoples? . . . I can add with pride that I was not simply a detached onlooker of this progress [of the young Soviet state]. My first steps in business pursuits in Russia were taken under the guidance of V. I. Lenin, and the last were with the direct participation of L. I. Brezhnev.

"From Ilyich to Ilyich," as Russians also say.

The first printing of the Russian edition—fifty thousand copies—sold out within a few hours. This is not only because Hammer is well known in the Soviet Union, but also because many Russians are fascinated with stories about American millionaires.

At the end of November 1981, an article appeared in *The New York Times Magazine* by Edward Jay Epstein entitled "The Riddle of Armand Hammer." Epstein explains the real nature of the Hammer family's involvement with Russia in the 1920s, sketches Hammer's subsequent Soviet dealings, and raises the question:

"Does Hammer merely take advantage of his contacts with the Russians to advance his business interests? Or does Hammer take advantage of his business contacts to serve Moscow's interests?"

The magazine staff carefully checked the accuracy of Epstein's statements and had the article reviewed by *The New York Times*'s lawyers for possible charges of libel. The day after the magazine was published, Hammer submitted a seven-thousand-word response, longer than the article itself. He called his friends, the Sulzbergers, as he had done several times before, and demanded that his rebuttal be printed in its entirety.

Clifford May, Epstein's editor at the magazine, went over Hammer's submission point by point and found that not a single one of Epstein's charges had been refuted. Where Epstein discusses Hammer's connections to the Communist leadership in the twenties, Hammer invoked Considine's biography as an authoritative source. After spending several days reviewing Hammer's response, May concluded in a memo to the magazine's editor, Ed Klein, that they should do no more than publish a letter from Hammer in their Letters to the Editor column.

Hammer's letter, which he condensed from the full-length rebuttal, delicately skirted Epstein's charges. "There are some misrepresentations which go beyond the levels of tolerance," he wrote. "These are the ones that by a pen stroke attempt to denigrate or destroy the very meaning of one's life. This I cannot tolerate in silence." Hammer recited the words of his standard biography: "I went to the Soviet Union to fight typhus. . . . Overtaken by events, I found the role of businessman thrust upon me. . . . This brought me to the attention of Lenin." He continued, "There was nothing hidden about these arrangements."

He also argued that his relations with the Soviet leaders were not continuous over five decades. "In 1930, I left Moscow, never having met Stalin, and did not return until 1961, when President John F. Kennedy asked me to serve as emissary to Nikita S. Khrushchev. . . . Throughout my life," he concluded, "I have been an American capitalist proud to carry its symbol around the world. As the record clearly demonstrates, Occidental and Armand Hammer are dedicated to this great country and its purposes. I hope this letter solves 'The Riddle of Armand Hammer.'"

On July 14, 1982, a letter from President Reagan appeared in Ann Landers's syndicated advice column. Reagan was responding to a deluge of copies of an earlier Ann Landers column on the horrors of nuclear war, a column that Ann had asked her readers to send to the White House. Reagan suggested that they send the nuclear-war column to Leonid Brezhnev instead. Landers agreed with Reagan's suggestion, adding:

> I have asked our mutual friend, Dr. Armand Hammer, chairman of Occidental Petroleum, to see that my column of May 17 is delivered to President Brezhnev, his close personal friend. He has agreed to do so. If I hear from Brezhnev, Mr. President, I'll call you. If YOU hear from him, please call me. It would make my day.

Clearly, if Ann Landers is any indication, Hammer had achieved the status of a kind of statesman.

On the weekend of July 11, 1982, Hammer figured prominently at a wreath-laying ceremony at Franklin D. Roosevelt's grave in Hyde Park, New York. The occasion was the fifth annual "Armand Hammer Conference on Peace and Human Rights—Human Rights and Peace"—its title demonstrating, Hammer once explained, that peace and human rights are inextricably linked.

Sponsored entirely by Hammer and organized by the International Institute of Human Rights (of which Hammer is president), the conference first met in Los Angeles in 1978; subsequent meetings were held in Warsaw and at Campobello. The 1982 conference, which featured such star delegates as Austrian Foreign Minister Willibald P. Pahr, former French Prime Minister Edgar Faure, Senator Jennings Randolph, and Jimmy Roosevelt, was billed by Hammer, in his speech to the closing session, as "a small United Nations." In addition to the ceremonies at the graves of Franklin and Eleanor, reminders of Hammer's reputed friendship with the Roosevelts were abundant. A press conference was held in front of FDR's Oval Office desk in the Roosevelt museum. Hammer declared that Hyde Park was an appropriate site for the conference because "Franklin and Eleanor Roosevelt spent their lives in a selfless quest for peace and human rights, not only for their fellow Americans but for all mankind."

Hammer reveled in the art of private diplomacy, escalating it to a new level with his talents of self-promotion. If he was to be hounded by allegations of corporate impropriety and even questionable connections to the Soviet leadership, at least he would make a concerted effort to create the image of a statesman. In an address to the Foreign Policy Association at the Plaza Hotel in

New York on May 4, 1981, he repeatedly compared himself to two giants of East-West diplomacy, "my friend Averell Harriman" and "that other Young Turk, George Kennan." He has also appeared repeatedly on television to relay messages from Brezhnev.

Many of Hammer's efforts were designed to convince his listeners that the Soviet leaders were men of peace. In late 1979 he appeared on "Meet the Press" to say, "I still think the Soviets want peace and I believe they want peace badly enough that they will not do anything to involve us in a war." He told the Foreign Policy Association in 1981, "I know that Mr. Brezhnev wants to avoid nuclear confrontation, for he more than any of the Soviet leadership has personally experienced war." Later that year he told John Callaway, in an interview on the Public Broadcasting Service, "I think we're lucky that Brezhnev is in Russia. . . . And he is decisive and is a man of peace." Even the day after Brezhnev's death, Hammer appeared on the CBS Morning News to recall that Brezhnev's policies had been essentially peaceful in nature. In an article in *People* magazine a few weeks later, he reminisced about Brezhnev: "One night we had dinner together—and of course lots of vodka. I couldn't keep up with him. He could drink glass after glass. He got very mellow and we talked about peace. . . . He said he would gladly give his life for peace. His eyes filled with tears, and I knew he meant it."

When a reporter for the London *Observer* took issue with Hammer's comparing Lenin to Christ in *Quest of the Romanoff Treasure,* and suggested that to Solzhenitsyn and others Lenin was the architect of the Gulag, Hammer bristled. "I can only tell you what I saw," he replied. "I know that to many he seemed cruel and cold. Solzhenitsyn would be a child in Lenin's day. I'm one of the few people alive now who knew him well."

A few days after Soviet troops invaded Afghanistan at the end of December 1979, Hammer met with Ambassador Dobrynin in Washington. Afterward, he told the press that he was convinced that the Soviet presence in Afghanistan was only temporary. "Mr. Dobrynin has never lied to me," he said.

After Jimmy Carter, in response to the Soviet incursion, imposed an embargo on shipments of both American grain and superphosphoric acid, Hammer flew to Moscow on February 27, 1980, to discuss with Brezhnev a political strategy for removing the embargo. Brezhnev gave Hammer a note to deliver to Carter. After the meeting, Hammer called a news conference in Moscow and said that Brezhnev "felt that Afghanistan's problems could be solved if the United States and the countries surrounding Afghanistan would guarantee that they would use their influence to see that there was no interference from outside in the internal affairs of Afghanistan."

A few days later, Hammer reported that American accusations of a Soviet design to advance to the Persian Gulf and threaten oil supplies were "sheer nonsense." He added Brezhnev's remarkable assertion that "Afghanistan was in the sphere of Soviet influence." In relaying this notion without objection, Hammer seemed to accept it. Even more startling, Hammer urged Americans to "take Mr. Brezhnev at his word." "I have a feeling—and I believe—Mr. Brezhnev was telling the truth."

Realizing that it was not enough to act as Brezhnev's character witness, Hammer then launched his own political initiative, tied, as usual, to Occidental's operations. In August 1980, Occidental announced it had signed a contract with the government of Pakistan to drill for oil in the Potwar Basin, near Islamabad. Though many oil-company executives doubted there was enough oil in the sands of Pakistan to merit an exploration program, there were obvious political considerations: Pakistan is a neighbor of Afghanistan.

One of the Soviets' biggest problems in their Afghan war was the Pakistani border, across which anti-Soviet troops were able to obtain supplies and ammunition, probably furnished by the Chinese and the Americans. Hammer may have used the lure of an oil discovery to pressure Pakistan to seal its border. "I have had some frank discussions with President Zia-ul-Haq of Pakistan," he announced a few months later. "President Zia is confident that the Afghanistan problem can be solved if Pakistan is left alone to resolve the matter with its neighbor, Afghanistan. . . . We should find out if the Russians really mean what they say about moving their troops out as soon as they have guarantees of non-interference in the internal affairs of Afghanistan." One senior member of the State Department during the Reagan administration confirms that "Hammer was always in here with one plan or another to solve the Afghanistan problem. I presume he was also in touch with the President about it. We listened, and listened respectfully, but his ideas were unworkable."

Hammer may have even received advance notice from the Reagan White House when the phosphate embargo was finally lifted. On April 24, 1981, he happened to be in Moscow when the news was made public. He immediately dictated a letter to the President, congratulating him on his "courageous decision," and began talks with Soviet officials to resume the barter.

Seventy percent of Occidental's superphosphoric acid output

goes to the Soviet Union each year—the equivalent of 3.5 million metric tons of phosphate rock, or 6 percent of total U.S. production—which is bartered for Soviet chemicals such as ammonia. But when Carter's embargo interrupted the flow, Occidental had to find a non-American market for some of the Soviet ammonia for which it had contracted. Although the ammonia was supposed to have been brought into the United States, Hammer arranged in early 1981 with ENI, the Italian national energy concern, to provide it with American coal. It was never made clear what ENI did in return. A former Occidental executive believes it off-loaded some of the Russian ammonia.

Occidental does business in Poland, too. In 1973 Oxy supplied the Polish government with the technology to construct a metal-finishing plant, and in 1978 Oxy traded a million tons of phosphate rock for five hundred tons of molten sulphur, after having financed the construction of a new sulphur mine in Poland. Hammer declared that economic aid would eliminate the possibility of a Soviet invasion of Poland. "This is a time in the history of that nation when an American multinational corporation can be of assistance and show confidence to bolster the economy by furthering trade," he said. "Occidental intends to continue to play such a role."

Finally, and most perplexing of all, there was China. Despite the Sino-Soviet rift, China has recently begun a small-scale trade with the Soviet Union with Hammer as broker. In 1979, Hammer recalls, he was at a barbecue with 150 top oil-company executives in Houston. The guest of honor was the vice-chairman of the People's Republic of China, Deng Xiaoping. Hammer says that when the two were introduced, Deng exclaimed, "No introduction is necessary for Dr. Hammer. We know him in China as the American who helped Lenin. Why don't you come to China and help us as well?"

"I told him I could be happy to do so," Hammer recalls, "but it would be difficult at my age unless I could fly in on my own corporate jet. I understood that private jets were not allowed to fly into China." That was swiftly arranged, and two months later Hammer and his aides flew into Peking. They began discussions of the development of the Pingshuo mine in the Shanxi Province, the world's largest coal mine. In 1982 Occidental was awarded preliminary approval for the project. Occidental was also granted the right to bid on oil concessions in the South China Sea. Also, in 1980 the Chinese purchased fifty thousand tons of Soviet urea through Occidental. "The Chinese knew it was coming from Russia," he said, "so I think that bodes well for the future." At a time when the Soviet Union had begun to make at least token efforts toward a rapprochement with China, it was perhaps fitting that they were done through Russia's Western sales agent, Armand Hammer.

Marlon Brando played a character modeled after Armand Hammer in a 1980 film called *The Formula* that was about a cutthroat oil tycoon. Brando's character is a paunchy, ruthless old man. When Hammer heard that Brando received $2.75 million for eleven days' work on the film, he said, "For that kind of money, I would have played the part myself."

Hammer is not embarrassed by his "Captain Queeg" image. He has built Occidental from a rickety company with three dry oil wells into one of the largest corporations in the United States. After merging with Cities Service in August 1982, Occidental expected it would become the eighth-largest U.S. oil company. Occidental Petroleum is now a multinational behemoth with operations in Abu Dhabi, Argentina, Australia, Bolivia, Canada, China, Colombia, much of Europe, Libya, Morocco, the North Sea, Pakistan, Peru, Poland, Rumania, the Soviet Union, Tunisia, and Venezuela.

He follows a "modified" Dr. Atkins diet, he says, though he occasionally allows himself a glass of wine. When he is in Los Angeles, he does most of his work out of his Westwood home, the same one he moved into after marrying Frances in 1956. He gets up early, descending from his bedroom via a winding staircase to an indoor pool in which he swims naked for half an hour each morning in a sort of breast stroke, his head above water so he can listen to the news on the radio. His home telephone is connected to a WATS line, and he makes calls around the world late into the night. He estimates his personal phone bill at a million dollars a year.

On land, he is chauffeured about in one of his two white Rolls-Royces with red carpeting, although he and Frances seem to spend most of their time in their flying luxury suite. He sustains his energy, while his associates tire, by means of self-hypnosis (he once bragged to a reporter, "Napoleon could do it, too."). At the age of eighty-four he keeps up a pace that would ravage many younger men. When an interviewer once asked him about his age, he replied, "I still have all my marbles," and also remarked that his mother "had lived to the ripe old age of eighty-nine." In fact, Rose Hammer died in 1960 at the age of eighty-four.

In his $1.5-million executive suite on the sixteenth floor of Occidental's Los Angeles office, his desk is surrounded by signed photographs of world leaders past and present, ranging from a reproduction of his now-lost Lenin portrait to a picture of Ronald and Nancy Reagan. A photograph of him with Brezhnev at Yalta is always at the front of his portrait gallery.

When Oxy makes money, his shareholders adore him; when it loses money, they revile him. The company's annual meetings, always on his birthday, are, as one angry stockholder charged, "a cult of personality." Gifts such as memo pads, sun visors, art posters, lumps of coal, and Considine's biography of him, are given out, and there is always a large birthday cake. Sometimes, at more festive meetings, the shareholders even sing "Happy Birthday" to him.

Occidental is, to an unprecedented degree, a one-man company. At least four former directors testified under oath before the Securities and Exchange Commission that Hammer made them sign undated letters of resignation. Faced with these charges, Hammer further admitted that eight to ten former directors had signed such letters. One former business associate told the SEC that Hammer had his entire board of directors "in his pocket." This has in fact always been his method of operation: except during the twenties, when he was his father's employee, he has never had to answer to another corporate officer. His company is his personal wealth. *Forbes* magazine estimated in 1982 that Hammer's fortune is "over $150 million." But several Occidental officials believe that Hammer's *personal* assets do not greatly exceed his 1.2 million shares of Oxy stock, worth around thirty million dollars—in multimillionaire terms, relatively modest.

In the last ten years, Hammer has fired or forced into retirement some half dozen company presidents, each of whom had understood he was Hammer's heir apparent. These people comprise an exclusive club known as "Hammer's Other Collection." Hammer brooks no challenge to his one-man rule. Several of his top executives resigned in protest in 1972, when he began negotiating his multibillion-dollar deals with Russia. "I told him his big Russian deals would lose money," one recalls, "and he refused to listen."

Hammer is a loner, and he is extremely secretive about his past. One of his oldest friends (and his lawyer), Louis Nizer, is apparently unaware of the true nature of Hammer's early involvement with the Soviet Union. Nizer's memoir, *Reflections Without Mirrors,* relates Hammer's public, fictionalized version. Armand's brother Victor is forbidden to discuss the family's relations with the Russians.

What drives Hammer? Unlike Howard Hughes or J. Paul Getty, the more typical twentieth-century tycoons, Hammer is not amassing a vast personal empire. When he is gone, Occidental Petroleum will pass to others. He has few heirs: his only son, Julian, who has been convicted of manslaughter and of receiving stolen goods, and who has several times tried to kill himself, will not inherit his mantle. Julian's two children, Casey and Michael, who are interested in business, will probably go to work for Occidental, but their grandfather does not own the company over which he holds sway.

And what impels him to Russia? He insists that he goes purely for the sake of profit, but his Soviet deals have in fact lost Occidental a good deal of money, though for reasons beyond his control. "Business is business, but Russia is romance," he wrote in *Quest of the Romanoff Treasure*; some of his associates say privately that Hammer is drawn by nostalgia or sentiment.

But Armand Hammer is not a sentimental man. No one else involved in doing business with Russia—not Eaton, Rockefeller, or Kendall—has committed so much time and corporate resources to trading with the Soviet Union. He has amassed a corporate empire eminently suited to trading with Russia, though he had made all of his money in other lands.

Perhaps it is the "ambassador manqué" urge that drives tycoons such as Eaton, Rockefeller, and Kendall—the diplomatic prestige that is automatically conferred upon the powerful international businessman who has access to the inaccessible corridors of power, the most cloistered of all being the Kremlin. If there is any other reason, it will probably not come out until Hammer has passed away, and maybe not even then.

In March 1982, Hammer flew to Moscow to see a play at the new Moscow Art Theatre. It was called *Tak Pobyedim,* or "Thus We Shall Triumph," a drama in two parts by Mikhail Shatrov that featured music by Wagner, Chopin, and Beethoven. The play concerned the last years of Lenin's life.

As Hammer watched from the special government box, he saw himself portrayed in his now-legendary meeting with Lenin. Yevgeny Kindinov, who played the twenty-three-year-old Hammer, is at least a head taller than his character is in real life, but, despite the nonresemblance, Hammer praised Kindinov's acting as "quite good." The *Moscow News* printed a photograph of Hammer meeting the cast of the play backstage. It is amusing to see him being fawned over by the actors, including someone who looks a great deal like Lenin.

About the same time, a joke about Hammer was making its way around Moscow: Armand Hammer goes to Red Square to visit Lenin's mausoleum but finds, as tourists so often do, that it is "closed for repair." Undaunted, he approaches one of the guards and demands entry.

"It's closed for repair," the guard snaps. "You can't go in."

Hammer is furious. "Do you know who I am?" he asks. "I'm Armand Hammer."

"I said, the mausoleum is closed for repair."

At last, Hammer angrily draws from his pocket a wrinkled, yellowed piece of paper. "This is a personal letter to me from Vladimir Ilyich himself," Hammer intones. "It says, 'Come visit me anytime.'"

EPILOGUE

THERE IS A MANSION in Moscow to which only the most privileged tourists are invited. It is a private home of stunning opulence owned by an American journalist, Edmund W. Stevens, and his Russian wife, Nina. Just as the tourists of the 1920s carried back tales of the splendor in which the Hammer family lived, so VIPs today relate with amazement the sumptuousness of this peculiar island of cosmopolitan luxury in the gray, bleak Soviet world.

One of the reasons why this household is tolerated—indeed, encouraged—by the Soviet authorities is that it is practically the only place where the "jet-setters" of the United States and the Soviet Union can meet. Long black Chaika limousines regularly pull up outside the Stevens palazzo on Ryleeva Street, and Central Committee members in sable hats and their wives in sleek mink coats enter the stately, icon-filled residence. There they join famous Soviet scientists, writers, movie stars, and even dissidents for splendid gourmet dinners replete with Beluga caviar and plenty of Western liquor. In addition to the Russians, there is certain to be an array of American and European celebrities. Anyone of note visiting Moscow receives at the airport an engraved invitation to dinner at the Stevens home. Averell Harriman, David Rockefeller, the Hammers, Jack Valenti, Charles G. Bluhdorn of Gulf & Western, Sargent Shriver, and Hubert Humphrey have all signed their names in the Stevenses' guest book.

The Soviet elite love to mingle with the rich and the powerful of the West, but more important to the Soviet authorities is that these Western visitors leave Moscow with a favorable impression. For this, the Stevenses' dinners are invaluable. While one is enjoying the sparkling company of Soviet luminaries, it is easy to forget the unpleasant consequences of Soviet foreign or domestic policy. The Russia viewed from the Stevenses' palazzo seems entirely different from the Russia of Alexander Solzhenitsyn.

In the heyday of the Nixon-Brezhnev détente, this confluence of Western and Soviet elites—whether at the Stevenses' home or at meetings of the Trade Council or elsewhere—had precisely the effect the Soviet leaders were after. Many Westerners were convinced that the increased personal contact brought about by East-

West trade would introduce some liberalizations into the previously impenetrable and rigid Soviet Union.

The idea of confluence, which goes by several other names, has gained particular acceptance among those in the West who want it to work. In 1974, Joseph Kraft observed in *The New Yorker* "a kind of interpenetration, a hidden harmony . . . the sense of sympathetic harmony that increasingly binds certain Russians and certain Americans, independent of governments and leaders." Similarly, Samuel Pisar, the international lawyer, has recently written of "the web of relationships" between "human beings immersed in the process of creation, indifferent to the dogmatic pretensions of Marxism-Leninism." Pisar asserts, a bit vaguely, that "this human dimension of détente is bound to increase pressures within the Soviet system for the satisfaction of the other aspirations that have been sacrificed thus far."

But as much as officials in the middle or even upper Soviet hierarchy may enjoy staying at the Ritz in New York, dining at the 21 Club, flying in private corporate jets, or playing tennis at the Greenwich Country Club—as alluring as the life of the West's upper crust may be—Soviet policy is not determined by such sentiments. The hopes of so many American businessmen and politicians that a taste of capitalism would turn the old men of the Politburo from increasing military stockpiles to improving the Russian way of life have been disappointed. All other political considerations aside, the Kremlin's decisions are made by a tiny group of leaders who are largely undeterred by the aspirations of their subordinates.

The Soviet Union has made a high art of the custom of extending regal hospitality to distinguished visitors. A classic example is George Bernard Shaw's visit to Russia in the early thirties amid a devastating famine. He was fed generously. "Starvation?" he remarked when he returned. "Why, I've never eaten so wonderfully!" The most notorious instance of late is the Reverend Billy Graham's trip to Moscow in May 1982. He was chauffeured about the city in a Chaika and treated with great deference. Unfortunately, he did not realize that what he was experiencing was not everyday Soviet life. After a few days he decided—and was impolitic enough to declare publicly—that he had seen no evidence of religious oppression, a pronouncement with which Soviet Jews and Pentacostalists were quick to take issue. Even more remarkably, he proclaimed, "the meals I have had are among the finest I have ever eaten. In the United States you have to be a millionaire to have caviar, but I have had caviar with almost every meal." No one told him that caviar is a luxury available only to Russia's most privileged.

Writers and clergymen are important to the Soviets because they help mold public opinion. Far more consequential, though, are America's business leaders, who command corporate empires and usually have access to the White House. Yet they also tend to be more taken in by the red-carpet treatment than other dignitaries. They are, as Henry Kissinger notes in *White House Years,* "especially susceptible to the bonhomie with which Soviet officials flatter those whom they wish to influence—a style of slightly inebriated good fellowship not totally unknown in some of the reunions of capitalist trade associations."

Accustomed to obeisance in their corporate empires and in the nation at large, they find it hard to resist the lure of respectful attention from some of the most sequestered leaders in the world. Anyone who is admitted to the Kremlin's inner sanctum instantly acquires a tremendous prestige in America; he has become an emissary of the highest rank.

Bertrand Russell observes, "Of the infinite desires of man, the chief are the desires for power and glory." When one has achieved the power of heading a giant corporation, the urge for glory often becomes overwhelming. The glory of being one of the Kremlin's favorite capitalists is so beguiling, in fact, that one does not want to risk losing it. Bill Moyers once asked David Rockefeller why he did not criticize the Shah of Iran, whom Rockefeller saw frequently. Rockefeller replied that if he did, "it probably would have meant that the next time I wanted to see him, he wouldn't have been available." Just as a banker dislikes losing an important client, so these ambassadors without portfolio speak out against Soviet policy at the risk of not being invited back.

There was a tense moment at the 1975 Dartmouth Conference in Moscow when the American delegates produced a disturbing article from a Soviet ideological journal that explained détente as a tactic to weaken American capitalism. The article, by A. I. Sobolev in *The Working Class and the Contemporary World,* asserted that détente follows the precepts of Marxism because it causes America to "lower its guard." The Soviet delegates, hearing of this article, professed astonishment.

Whether this was really the Soviet intent in détente, the recent détente did indeed lull the United States, and persuade America's powers-that-be that Soviet intentions were purer than in fact they were. One of the ways this was accomplished was to enlist a few influential American advocates.

The Soviets have not wined and dined Eaton, Hammer, Kendall, Rockefeller, and Harriman out of some perverse love of American big shots. To be sure, Soviet-American trade, for which each of these men has lobbied long and hard, is vitally important to the Politburo. But just as significant to them is to convince the United States that the Soviet Union is essentially a peace-loving nation, and in some of the outstanding capitalists of the West the Soviets have found convincing spokesmen.

George Kennan has described two very different views of the Soviet leaders. One is of "a terrible and forbidding group of men—monsters of sorts, really." Another is of "a group of quite ordinary men . . . whose motivation is essentially defensive." As oversimplified as this dichotomy is, it accurately depicts the West's inability to decide how to view the Soviet Union. When Brezhnev came to the United States in 1973, *Time* described him as a man just like American politicians—and thus implied that he was really quite benevolent:

> At 66, Brezhnev is not exactly a reluctant star. He does everything with gusto, exuding an earthiness and nervous energy that sometimes evoke comparisons with Lyndon Johnson. He is a natty dresser, tending to dark suits for day and blue suede jackets for informal wear. He can also be vain and demanding; he is the only Soviet leader to wear TV make up. "He has a keen eye for that little red light on the TV camera," observes a U.S. official.

Donald Kendall has made similar observations of these Politburo members in their blue suede jackets. "I've always thought that if Kosygin were in this country he'd be the head of some big corporation," he says. "And if Brezhnev were here, he'd be the ringmaster of Barnum and Bailey's circus. I don't mean that literally, but he is a fantastic showman. . . . Some people can walk into a room and take the place over. That's Brezhnev. Like Nixon." Cyrus Eaton, David Rockefeller, Armand Hammer, and even Averell Harriman have all made similar appraisals of the Soviet leaders they have known.

Although each has suffered opprobrium for his views of the Soviet Union, each has nevertheless been in many ways convincing because of who he was. As outstanding practitioners of free enterprise, they seemed unimpeachable advocates of capitalism. They were almost the perfect spokesmen, and they helped advance a cause—détente—that was dear not only to them but also to the Soviet leaders. Depending on the extent of their involvement in Soviet politics—from Rockefeller, who never met with Brezhnev, to Hammer, who sees Brezhnev on a regular basis and has traveled to Moscow more than 150 times—they speak with an unreserved optimism that has probably done more harm than good to American foreign policy.

This is not to say that they have not, at the same time, accomplished valuable results. Not only have they pleaded a moderation that is often necessary, but some of them have made important contributions. Eaton's Pugwash advanced the arms control movement. Rockefeller's participation in the Dartmouth conferences has increased communication between Soviet and American officials—communication that, if free of false hopes that the friendships formed can moderate Soviet behavior, is a healthy thing. Harriman, as a government official and an elder statesman, has always been an intelligent observer of Soviet policy. Kendall and Hammer both promoted the policy of the White House in the early seventies.

The trouble starts, though, when they venture into the world of personal diplomacy. The ego becomes involved. A pitfall of many men of great wealth and influence is the desire to seek their glory in the realm of foreign affairs, and it is a peculiarly American fault. America, the land founded with a President instead of a king, the country that rejected monarchy for democracy, has nevertheless developed its own form of nobility out of the tradition of the Yankee trader. Nineteenth-century America saw the rise of the merchant princes, men like John Jacob Astor and Cornelius Vanderbilt, poor sons of immigrants whose heirs were grandees and lived in palaces. The twentieth century, an age of world commerce, spawned another breed of merchant prince, the business-statesman: men like the young Averell Harriman now could command audiences with Winston Churchill and Benito Mussolini.

Between the two great superpowers of the modern era, both established in reaction against monarchy, there has arisen yet another class of prince, who, having achieved vast wealth and power under Western capitalism, turns to the exclusive blandishments of the Kremlin. Mere bankers or industrialists in the United States, all literally have the red carpet rolled out for them upon arrival in Moscow. Paradoxically, in the land of socialism more than anywhere else in the world, American capitalists are treated like royalty.

NOTES

This book is based on the author's interviews with businessmen, government officials, and others (a List of Interviews follows the Notes); on newspaper and magazine accounts; on publicly available records; and on documents declassified under the Freedom of Information Act.

The sources include:

The National Archives, Washington, D.C.: State Department General Records. New York State Archives: Lusk Committee. The Federal Bureau of Investigation: files on Cyrus Eaton and Julius Hammer, declassified by author's request under the Freedom of Information Act.

Henry Ford Library, The Edison Institute, Dearborn, Michigan: files on the Hammers. Harvard Russian Research Center Library clippings file on East-West trade. Rockefeller Archive Center, North Tarrytown, New York: files on Cyrus Eaton from selected archives. Bertrand Russell Archives, McMaster University, Hamilton, Ontario. Yale University Sterling Memorial Library, Manuscripts and Archives: the papers of Chester Bowles and Walter Lippmann.

Radio Liberty/Radio Free Europe (New York) clippings files on East-West trade. PepsiCo, Inc., archives (Purchase, New York). The archives of W. Averell Harriman, Washington, D.C. Columbia University Oral History Project, New York. George Arents Research Library, Syracuse University, Syracuse, New York: recorded Mike Wallace interview with Cyrus Eaton (the author thanks Mike Wallace for permission to quote from the 1959 interview).

Dwight D. Eisenhower Library, Abilene, Kansas. Herbert Hoover Presidential Library, West Branch, Iowa. Lyndon Baines Johnson Library, Austin, Texas. John F. Kennedy Presidential Library, Boston, Massachusetts. Franklin D. Roosevelt Library, Hyde Park, New York. Harry S. Truman Library, Independence, Missouri.

In certain instances, when a magazine article has been drawn from one of the archives listed above, the page reference has been omitted.

In the Notes, the abbreviation *NYT* denotes *The New York Times.*

For reasons of style, the word "Russia" is often used interchangeably with "Soviet Union." In several instances, quotations are unattributed, at the request of sources who preferred to be unnamed.

INTRODUCTION: A BANQUET IN THE KREMLIN

Page

Information on the meeting and the background politics is based on interviews with Michael Forrestal, James Giffen, Averell Harriman, Milton Rosenthal, Harold B. Scott, C. William Verity, and others in the Trade Council.

6 "Sitting next to each other . . .": *The Memoirs of Richard Nixon* (New York: Grosset & Dunlap, 1978), p. 610.

8 "The capitalists of the world . . .": Iurii Annenkov, *A Diary of My Meetings,* vol. 2 (New York: International Literary Collaboration, 1966), p. 280.

8 " . . . Businessmen handle unique equipment . . .": Lev Navrozov, *The Education of Lev Navrozov* (New York: Harper's Magazine Press, 1975), p. 320.

PART ONE: THE EARLY YEARS

" . . . this capitalist shark . . .": V. I. Lenin in a speech to the Russian Communist Party at the Eighth All-Russia Congress of Soviets, December 24, 1920. He refers to Washington Vanderlip, who visited him a few weeks earlier in an attempt to obtain a concession for the Kamchatka oil fields, while pretending to be a member of the Vanderlip family that owned the First National City Bank. As he left Lenin's office he befuddled Lenin by joking, "Yes, it is true that Mr. Lenin has no horns and I must tell that to my friends in America." *Lenin on the United States of America* (Moscow: Progress Publishers, 1980), p. 491.

1: A MISSION TO MOSCOW

Page

12 Armand Hammer did present: L. Kunetskaya and K. Mashtakova, *Lenin—Great and Human* (Moscow: Progress Publishers, 1979), p. 151.

12 Armand's grandparents: 1900 Census, Immigration Records, National Archives, Washington, D.C. In a speech to the Foreign Policy Association in 1981, Hammer said, "My father came to the United States when he was one year old."

12 The family settled: Bob Considine, *Larger Than Life: A Biography of the Remarkable Dr. Armand Hammer* (London: W. H. Allen, 1976), p. 1.

12 named for the official emblem: Bertram D. Wolfe, *A Life in Two Centuries* (New York: Stein and Day, 1981), p. 168.

A friend of the Hammer children, Irwin Hymes of New York, provides an interesting and rare glimpse of Armand's childhood in the Bronx. In a letter to *The New York Times* in August 1982, Hymes recounts:

> It was a few years ago, 1907 or 1908, in the Washington Avenue area of the farmland that was the Bronx of those days, that we were harassed by the Maguire brothers—all four of them. "We" consisted of my older brother, Sydney, and me and Harry Hammer, older brother of Armand Hammer, now a noted world figure but then just a pudgy kid who was a no-no because he was a few years younger than the rest of us, who had ripened to the mature ages of 13 or 14. I can still see Armand's lower lip quivering when he tried to join us on our rambles and was told to "g'wan home, kid." [Armand was then about nine.]

> Well, one day in exasperation, Harry, a sallow-complexioned, skinny kid, the oldest of us by a few months, took on the oldest Maguire brother, who was about his age, in the lot behind the frame house of Dr. Hammer, father of the Hammer boys. To our amazement, he whupped him and we were bothered no more. [*NYT,* August 8, 1982]

13 In August 1907: Wolfe, *A Life,* p. 167.

13 The Hammer family: *NYT,* November 6, 1921.

13–14 On the Left Wing Section: Benjamin Gitlow, *I Confess* (New York: E. P. Dutton, 1940), p. 59; Wolfe, *A Life,* p. 168.

14 " . . . a feeling of oppression . . .": Nathan Glazer, *The Social Basis of American Communism* (New York: Harcourt, Brace, 1961), p. 187.

14 "To this day I smile . . .": Leon Trotsky, *My Life* (New York: Scribner's, 1931), p. 274.

15 On Ludwig Martens: Gitlow, *I Confess,* p. 28; Wolfe, *A Life,* p. 164.

15 as his commercial attaché: New York State Legislature, Joint Legislative Committee to Investigate Seditious Activities (Lusk Committee), New York State Archives, State Education Department, Albany, New York, Box 4, Folder 14.

16 sixty diamonds: Theodore Draper, *The Roots of American Communism* (New York: Viking, 1957), p. 202.

16 Julius also traveled: *NYT,* November 6, 1921.

16 "a message sent to the gathering . . ." Lusk files, Box 17, Folder 11.

16 "Comrade Hammer be expelled . . .": Ibid.

17 " . . . always expecting to be attacked . . .": Gitlow, *I Confess,* p. 59.

17 On Julius's abortion trial: *NYT,* June 30, 1920; July 20, 1920; September 21, 1920.

17 donated by Dr. Hammer: Gitlow, *I Confess,* p. 59.

18 Liberty Bonds: Ibid.

18 "a black sheep . . ." *NYT,* September 21, 1920.

18 " . . . 'worth a million dollars'": Ibid., September 19, 1920, II.

18 "In Sing Sing . . .": Wolfe, *A Life,* p. 170.

19 On Armand's upbringing: Considine, *Larger Than Life,* p. 5.

19 " . . . in fairly close touch . . .": Armand Hammer, *Quest of the Romanoff Treasure* (New York: W. F. Payson, 1932), p. 3.

20 His passport application: Edward Jay Epstein, "The Riddle of Armand Hammer," *NYT Magazine,* November 29, 1981, p. 114.

20 British intelligence: Hammer, *Quest,* pp. 4–9.

20 " . . . messages for Martens . . .": Robert C. Williams, *Russian Art and American Money* (Cambridge: Harvard University Press, 1980), p. 203.

20 half owned by Martens: Ibid.

20 Mercedes Benz: Considine, *Larger Than Life,* p. 34.

20 Gregory Weinstein: Edwin Ware Hullinger, *The Reforging of Russia* (New York: E. P. Dutton, 1925), p. 128.

21 Boris Reinstein: Albert Rhys Williams, *Journey Into Revolution: Petrograd 1917–1918* (Chicago: Quadrangle, 1969), pp. 46–47, 153. See also Branko M. Lazitch, *Biographical Dictionary of the Comintern* (Stanford, Cal.: Hoover Institution Press, 1973), p. 336.

21 Wolff: Hammer, *Quest,* p. 27.
21 "Never in my life . . .": Ibid., p. 32.
22 " . . . a private letter to Vladimir Ilyich . . .": *Krasnaya Gazeta,* January 21, 1926.
22 " . . . the boredom of Moscow": Hammer, *Quest,* p. 42.
22 Abraham Heller: Gitlow, *I Confess,* p. 305; Williams, *Russian Art,* p. 197. Heller came to the Soviet Union in May 1921 and became a member of the Supreme Council on the National Economy. A few years later he founded International Publishers, which publishes Communist books and pamphlets for dissemination within the United States.
23 On September 25: A. A. Heller, *The Industrial Revival in Soviet Russia* (New York: T. Seltzer, 1922), p. 59. Heller describes touring factories and metallurgical plants with "our enterprising doctor," as he calls Hammer. While Hammer describes his distress at the "heartbreaking," pitiable conditions of the peasants they came across, Heller tells a different story. When the car in which they were riding developed engine trouble, Hammer seized the wheel and started off at high speed. "He did not mind the bumps or turns of the road or the peasant carts loaded with grain and hay which kept getting in our path," Heller writes, "and we should have gone on splendidly if one of the tires had not burst while we were passing through a village."
23 "We must conclude with *Hammer* . . .": V. I. Lenin, *Complete Collected Works* (Moscow: Political Literature Press, 1978), vol. 53, p. 302.
23 "He greeted me quite cordially . . .": Hammer, *Quest,* p. 90.
24 "Reinstein informed me . . .": Lenin, *Complete Collected Works,* vol. 53, p. 267.
24 the development of the Urals: Ibid., p. 272.
24 "equals electrification . . .": Harrison Salisbury, ed., *The Soviet Union: The Fifty Years* (New York: Harcourt, Brace & World, 1967), p. 12.
24 " . . . just so much hot air": Lenin, *Complete Collected Works,* vol. 53, p. 282.
24 " . . . We almost have something with *Hammer*": Ibid., p. 299.
25 "smaller than I expected . . .": Hammer, *Quest,* p. 60.
25 On Reinstein as "translator": Epstein, "Riddle of Armand Hammer," p. 114. Hammer is careful to point out in *Quest of the Romanoff Treasure* that Lenin's English was good enough for them to conduct the conversation entirely in English (p. 61).
25 "Well, he had known, I suppose . . .": "The Russian Connection—Dr. Armand Hammer," produced by Lucy Jarvis. Broadcast on NBC, June 18, 1974.
25 "I was completely absorbed . . .": Hammer, *Quest,* p. 61. Hammer writes, "To talk with Lenin was like talking with a friend one knew and trusted, a friend who understood" (p. 67).
25 "We conversed for an hour . . .": *Krasnaya Gazeta,* January 21, 1926, p. 5.

26 "Lenin has been called ruthless . . .": Hammer, *Quest,* p. 68.
26 Karl Fabergé and Company: Williams, *Russian Art,* p. 213.
26 the wheat contract: *Documents of Soviet Foreign Policy,* vol. 4 (Moscow: Gospolitizdat, 1957), p. 442.
26 " . . . no reliance on orders! . . .": Lenin, *Complete Collected Works,* vol. 53, p. 310.
26 "We must make a special effort . . .": Lenin, *Complete Collected Works,* vol. 53, pp. 310–11.
27 " . . . the magic of Lenin's name": Hammer, *Quest,* p. 71.
27 " . . . the ceremony of a peace treaty": Ibid., p. 81.
27 On details of the asbestos contract: V. K. Furayev, *U.S.S.R.-U.S.A. Economic Relations* (Moscow: Mysl', 1976), pp. 256–57.
27 " . . . I went to see Mr. Shineman": Hammer, *Quest,* pp. 168–69.
28 "SOVIET GIVES AMERICANS . . .": NYT, November 4, 1921.
28 " . . . Dr. Julius Hammer . . .": Ibid., November 6, 1921.
28 "I am certain that nobody . . .": Ibid.
28 "Dear Mr. Armand Hammer . . .": Lenin, *Complete Collected Works,* vol. 53, p. 324.

2: A LETTER TO STALIN

Page
30 "Uncle Sasha": Bob Considine, *Larger Than Life* (London: W. H. Allen, 1976), p. 41.
30–31 On Alexander Gumberg: James K. Libbey, *Alexander Gumberg and Soviet-American Relations, 1917–1933* (Lexington: University of Kentucky Press, 1977), pp. 12, 14, 57, 75, 122; Albert Rhys Williams, *Journey Into Revolution: Petrograd 1917–1918* (Chicago: Quadrangle, 1969), p. 140.
31–32 On Henry Ford: Armand Hammer, *Quest of the Romanoff Treasure* (New York: W. F. Payson, 1932), pp. 102–09; V. A. Shishkin, *The Soviet State and the West, 1917–23* (Leningrad: Nauka Publishers, 1969), p. 134; Unpublished recorded reminiscences of Charles Sorensen, courtesy of the Ford Archives, Edison Institute, Dearborn, Michigan.
32 If it were a business meeting: interview with David R. Crippen, Ford Archives.
33 "Fate was now beckoning . . .": Hammer, *Quest,* p. 110.
33 "Please pay attention . . .": *Lenin on the United States of America* (Moscow: Progress Publishers, 1980), p. 583.
33 " . . . two Soviet directors . . .": V. K. Furayev, *U.S.S.R.-U.S.A. Economic Relations* (Moscow: Mysl', 1976), p. 73.
33 "I made all the decisions . . .": Edward Jay Epstein, "The Riddle of Armand Hammer," *NYT Magazine,* November 29, 1981, p. 116.
34 Hammer met several local officials: Hammer, *Quest,* p. 120.
34 "Excuse me please . . ." Lenin, *Collected Works,* vol. 45 (Moscow: Progress Publishers, 1970), letter 722.
34 "Make note of *Armand Hammer* . . .": Ibid., letter 723.
35 "Today I wrote . . .": Ibid., letter 724.

35 "I had declined . . .": *Lenin on the United States,* p. 482.

35 a railroad official: Hammer, *Quest,* p.113.

36 "*. . . to the contrary*!!": *Lenin on the United States,* p. 587.

36 "a report of B. I. Reinstein . . .": V. I. Lenin, *Complete Collected Works,* vol. 54 (Russian) (Moscow: Political Literature Press, 1965), p. 652.

36 "To *Comrade Stalin* . . .": *Lenin on the United States,* p. 588.

37 " . . . I told them that I was a capitalist . . .": *NYT* June 14, 1922.

37 "The Allied American Company is to be distinguished . . .": cited in Bob Considine, *Larger Than Life,* p. 255.

37 "A rich slice . . .": Cited by Rep. John Ashbrook in remarks in the House of Representatives, October 17, 1973. *Congressional Record,* 93rd Congress, vol. 119, part 26, pp. 34492–96. In his report, based on research by Herbert Romerstein of the Permanent Select Committee on Intelligence, Ashbrook stated that Hammer "was not a capitalist but at least a Communist sympathizer" (p. 34494).

38 "One personality involved . . .": National Archives, State Department General Records 661.1116/54. Mishell worked for Allied American in Russia and Europe until 1932, when he returned to the United States. He served for a time as Secretary and Treasurer of the National Yarn Company in Cleveland and died in 1943 at the age of sixty-one. (Obituary, *NYT,* July 20, 1943.)

38 " . . . negotiable securities from Trotsky . . .": FBI file on Julius Hammer, declassified under author's Freedom of Information Act request, May 4, 1982.

38 "The greatest actors are in Moscow": Daniel Yergin, "The One-Man, Flying Multinational," *Atlantic,* June 1975, p. 37.

38 fifth anniversary of the Bolshevik Revolution: Ashbrook report, *Congressional Record,* p. 34495.

39 On Julius Hammer and Henry Ford: Ford Archives, Accession 38, Box 47.

39 Borrowing the passport: Because Julius apparently borrowed Heiman's passport—which enabled him to travel freely around Europe until his U.S. citizenship was restored—all federal records on Hammer are filed under Heiman's name. Throughout the twenties, federal agents were confused. Heiman, a sales manager for Patchogue Plymouth Mills in New York, was later described by Benjamin Gitlow in his second volume of memoirs, *The Whole of Their Lives* (New York: Scribner's, 1948), as "a secret member of the Communist party, in charge of receiving the diamonds and jewelry and then converting them to good American dollars. . . ." (p. 46).

3: AMERICAN ROYALTY

Page

40 "a sort of center of social life . . .": Eugene Lyons, *Assignment in Utopia* (New York: Harcourt, Brace, 1937), p. 67. In order to downplay his father's central role, Armand Hammer has long insisted that he and Victor were the sole masters of their mansion in Moscow.

Lyons, however, describes "the Hammer family, father, mother, and sons" as the lords of the manor. Significantly, the house was not provided until Julius came to Russia. Although only Armand Hammer calls their home "the Brown House," the name is used here for ease of reference.

40 "The vodka flowed . . .": Ibid., p. 251.

41 "Reindeer heads . . .": Ibid., pp. 296–97.

41 "Shura and her glowering ways . . .": Ibid., p. 418.

42 " . . . the wonder-windows": Ibid., p. 417.

42 "Drawn to Russia . . .": Ibid., p. 67.

42 Will Rogers: Geoffrey T. Hellman, "The Innocents Abroad," *The New Yorker,* December 23, 1933, p. 20.

42 " . . . a cereal drink": Bob Considine, *Larger Than Life* (London: W. H. Allen, 1976), p. 59.

42 the evils of capitalism: Hellman, "Innocents Abroad," p. 20.

43–44 On Cummings about the Hammers: E. E. Cummings, *Eimi* (New York: Covici, Friede, 1933), pp. 55, 118–23, 192. Although Cummings, as noted, does not refer to the Hammers by name, Eugene Lyons provides a key for interpreting *Eimi.* See Eugene Lyons, *Assignment in Utopia,* p. 418.

44 "Chinesy": E. E. Cummings, Ibid., pp. 55, 118–23, 192.

44 On Julius's correspondence with Ford: Ford Archives, Edison Institute, Dearborn, Michigan: Accession 38, Box 47.

45 "No true Marxist . . .": Bob Considine, *Larger Than Life* (London: W. H. Allen, 1976), p. 59.

45 "On July 14": V. K. Furayev, *U.S.S.R.-U.S.A. Economic Relations* (Moscow: Mysl', 1976), p. 73.

45 "a pretty rotten bunch": J. H. Wilson, *Ideology and Economics: U.S. Relations with the Soviet Union 1918–1933* (Columbia, Mo.: University of Missouri Press, 1974), p. 75.

46 packages to Boris Reinstein: Robert C. Williams, *Russian Art and American Money* (Cambridge: Harvard University Press, 1980), p. 209.

46 On the congressional junket: Armand Hammer, *Quest of the Romanoff Treasure* (New York: W. F. Payson, 1932), p. 176; James K. Libbey, *Alexander Gumberg and Soviet-American Relations, 1917–1933* (Lexington: University of Kentucky Press, 1977), p. 111.

46 "keen and watchful": Hammer, *Quest,* p. 132.

47 Gumberg resigned: Williams, *Russian Art,* p. 211.

47 " . . . considerable apprehension . . .": Williams, Ibid., 210. A Justice Department report at the time advanced the theory that "the Moscow authorities might have advanced part or all of the funds to purchase the bank to obtain a means of transferring funds abroad surreptitiously." ("Dr. Julius Hammer and His Russian Enterprises," State Department General Records, 800.00B)

48 " . . . a regular little city": Hammer, *Quest,* p. 207.

48 coat of arms: Hellman, "Innocents Abroad," p. 20.

49 "Professors, authors, generals . . .": E. Ashmead-Bartlett, *The Riddle of Russia* (London: Cassell, 1929), p. 260.

49 By the end of 1924: Hammer, *Quest,* p. 207.
50 " . . . you have to be the goat": Hammer, *Quest,* p. 209.
50 In 1928, Armand submitted: Wilson, *Ideology and Economics,* p. 155.

4: TROTSKY AND THE YALIE

Page

51 "The Russian people have a right . . .": Jordan A. Schwarz, *The Speculator: Bernard M. Baruch in Washington, 1917–1965* (Chapel Hill: University of North Carolina Press, 1981), p. 485.
52 "Abandon any theory . . .": Peter G. Filene, *Americans and the Soviet Experiment, 1917–1933* (Cambridge: Harvard University Press, 1967), pp. 120–23.
52 " . . . Ford is its St. Peter": Ibid., p. 125.
52–53 On Harriman's upbringing: E. J. Kahn, Jr., "Plenipotentiary—I," *The New Yorker,* May 3, 1952, and "Plenipotentiary—II," May 10, 1952 (two-part profile of Harriman: hereafter, Kahn I and Kahn II). Also, Elie Abel and W. Averell Harriman, *Special Envoy To Churchill and Stalin, 1941–1946* (New York: Random House, 1975), pp. 48–55.
53 " . . . someone I taught rowing to . . .": David Halberstam, *The Best and the Brightest* (New York: Random House, 1972), p. 238.
53 "on a handcar . . .": Abel and Harriman, *Special Envoy,* p. 45. College friends also called him Bill, having decided that "Averell" was too prissy a name. But he preferred Averell and has been Averell throughout his life. Similarly, Nelson and Laurance Rockefeller, in childhood, considered their names unmanly and called each other "Bill."
54 psychological compensation: Kahn II, p. 43.
54 "it is as indefensible . . .": Kahn II, p. 48.
55 "I was very anxious . . .": Interview with W. Averell Harriman, 1981.
55 "Harriman's entry": V. I. Lenin, *Collected Works,* vol. 45 (Moscow: Progress Publishers, 1970), p. 448.
55 " . . . a permanent affair": Interview with Harriman, 1981.
55 enough to supply the world: Filene, *Soviet Experiment,* p. 117.
55 "Everything looks good . . .": From the archives of W. Averell Harriman.
55–56 Concession contract: Harriman archives.
57 "wanted to establish a monopoly . . .": V. K. Furayev, *U.S.S.R.-U.S.A. Economic Relations* (Moscow: Mysl', 1976), p. 147.
57 "smart-dealer": Ibid., p. 148.
58 " . . . a tragic spectacle": Unpublished reminiscences, 1953; from the Harriman archives.
58 "I was one of the few . . .": Interview with Harriman, 1981.
58 " . . . no one believed that": Harriman reminiscences, 1953; interview with Harriman, 1981.
59 On the conversation with Trotsky: Harriman reminiscences, 1953; interview with Harriman, 1981.

60 On the Krassin incident: Harriman reminiscences, 1953.
60 On trip to Baku and Chiatura: Abel and Harriman, *Special Envoy,* p. 50; Harriman reminiscences, 1953.
61 On meetings with Mussolini and Churchill: Harriman reminiscences, 1953.
61 " . . . in a fair spirit": *NYT,* July 9, 1927.
61 " . . . never was a healthy child . . .": Ibid., June 19, 1928.
62 " . . . doing business with the Russians . . .": Interview with Harriman, 1981.
62 "Essential!": Harriman archives.
62 "Harriman came out of the period . . .": Kahn II, p. 51.

5: HOUSEHOLD EFFECTS

Page
63 On American Communists in Moscow, 1928: Interview with Jay Lovestone.
63 The names of the KGB's forerunners: See John Barron, *KGB: The Secret Work of Soviet Secret Agents* (New York: Bantam Books, 1974), pp. 457–62.
64–65 On 1929 visit to Moscow: Bertram D. Wolfe, *A Life in Two Centuries* (New York: Stein and Day, 1981), p. 525; Benjamin Gitlow, *I Confess* (New York: E. P. Dutton, 1940), p. 563.
66 " . . . Comintern organization was improved . . .": Gitlow, *I Confess,* p. 388.
66 On the Arcos raid: Ibid., p. 389.
66 "a political agent": Confidential memorandum, April 12, 1940, compiled when an exit permit was issued in London to Victor Hammer, who went on to France and Italy. State Department General Records, 800.00B.
66 " . . . the money was cabled . . .": Gitlow, *I Confess,* p. 389.
67 Walter Duranty was involved: In *Without Fear or Favor* (New York: Times Books, 1980), his excellent history of *The New York Times,* Harrison Salisbury discusses the charge that Walter Duranty was, as Joseph Alsop said in 1979, "a great KGB agent." Duranty was a staunch defender of the Soviet Union and of Stalin. Salisbury doubts Duranty was in the employ of Soviet intelligence but concedes he "saw Soviet Russia through lenses which, if not rosy, were certainly soft focus" (p. 462).
67 Julius went to New York: *NYT,* November 22, 1927. Julius was described as the "Head of A. Hammer, Inc."
67 state-controlled pencil concern: The head of Mezhdunarodnaya Kniga, Alexander Barmine, describes in his memoirs his "war against capitalist competition, personified for me in Dr. Hammer." See Barmine's *One Who Survived: The Life Story of a Russian Under the Soviets* (New York: G. P. Putnam's Sons, 1945), p. 158.
67 "It is admitted . . .": *NYT,* December 22, 1929.
67 "It would be interesting . . .": Robert C. Williams, *Russian Art and American Money* (Cambridge: Harvard University Press, 1980), p. 211.

67 ". . . several million dollars paid in rubles . . .": *Economic Review of the Soviet Union,* April 15, 1930, p. 156.

68 offered the Hammers a commission of 10 percent: Williams, *Russian Art,* p. 216.

68 syndicate of New York art dealers: Ibid., p. 216. Williams writes further that after the Duveen syndicate's offer was rejected, a bid from Andrew Mellon was accepted. Under a cloak of great secrecy, Mellon purchased, in the fall of 1931, several Hermitage treasures for $6,400,000. See Harvey O'Connor, *Mellon's Millions: The Biography of a Fortune* (New York: John Day, 1933), p. 239. Paul Mellon states that his father had no help from the Hammers in arranging the deal (letter to the author, January 30, 1982).

68 "What do they think we are? . . .": John Walker, *Self-Portrait with Donors* (Boston: Little, Brown, 1969), p. 105.

69 ". . . several warehouses": Bob Considine, *Larger Than Life* (London: W. A. Allen, 1976), p. 75.

69 ". . . Sakho himself left no trace . . .": Williams, *Russian Art,* p. 215.

69 ". . . directly from the Winter Palace": Considine, *Larger Than Life,* p. 78.

69–70 On Lyons's recollections: Eugene Lyons, *Assignment in Utopia* (New York: Harcourt, Brace, 1937), p. 510.

70 "We were married . . .": Considine, *Larger Than Life,* p. 76. They were married on March 14, 1927, according to Hammer's entry in the 1982–83 *Who's Who in America.*

71 purchase of Soviet promissory notes: Hammer told Considine that "Several of Averell Harriman's partners in a manganese concession which they sold back to the Soviets were so eager to unload what they considered little more than pieces of paper that they turned over their three-year notes to Hammer at a whopping 72 percent discount" (Considine, p. 77). Averell Harriman has no recollection of this; moreover, his notes were paid in full by the Soviets. Also, not many people then held Soviet bonds. It does not seem a terribly profitable way for Hammer to have spent a year, if indeed he did.

71–72 The story of Victor's Russian marriage: Personal communication with the author.

72 Victor was denied a visa: Interview with Armand Victorovich Hammer.

72 on September 27, 1931: State Department General Records, 800.00B.

72 "settling the affairs . . .": Ibid.

72 Julius was arrested: Williams, *Russian Art,* p. 218.

73 "worthy political movement": Ibid., pp. 219–20.

73 "Hammer's modesty . . .": Williams, *Russian Art,* p. 220.

73 ". . . secret missions for the Soviet government . . .": State Department General Records, 800.00B.

74 "Is it known to you . . .": Ibid.

74 ". . . no longer interested in any concessions . . .": Ibid.

75 "the debris of Russian hotels . . .": Williams, *Russian Art,* p. 221.

75 "the failing ruble . . .": Considine, *Larger Than Life,* p. 78.

75–76 On Armand Hammer: Geoffrey T. Hellman, "The Innocents Abroad," *The New Yorker,* December 23, 1933, p. 18.

76 Prince Michael: Interview with James R. Graham of Graham Galleries, a longtime acquaintance of the Hammers.

77 On the stolen sword: *NYT,* March 26, 1934.

77 " . . . a true and faithful record": Ibid., November 20, 1932.

78 " . . . the least revolutionary of countries": Armand Hammer, *Quest of the Romanoff Treasure* (New York: W. F. Payson, 1932), pp. 230–33.

78 President Roosevelt: Some Hammer-watchers, misled by a perhaps intentionally confusing passage in Considine's book (*Larger Than Life,* p. 148), have erroneously reported that Armand (or Julius) thanked FDR for recognizing Russia diplomatically by giving him, in the presence of Ambassador Maxim Litvinov, a Fabergé model of a Volga steamboat. See Williams, *Russian Art,* p. 224, or, more recently, Nikolai Tolstoy, *Stalin's Secret War* (New York: Holt, Rinehart and Winston, 1981), p. 339. Actually, the Hammers sold the boat to an ex-convict, Charles Ward, who then had it delivered to Roosevelt in 1943.

79 Alexander Schaffer: Williams, *Russian Art,* p. 225.

79 "Victor Julius Hammer . . .": State Department General Records, 800.00B.

79 "In his Manhattan galleries . . .": *Time,* June 17, 1935, p. 30.

79 more than eleven million dollars: Edward Jay Epstein, "The Riddle of Armand Hammer," *NYT Magazine,* November 29, 1981, p. 118.

6: "A VERY UNUSUAL KNOWLEDGE"

Page

80 On selling the Hearst Collection: Bob Considine, *Larger Than Life* (London: W. H. Allen, 1976), pp. 80–89.

80 " . . . great social implications . . .": Franklin D. Roosevelt Presidential Library.

81 confidant and influential adviser: Considine, *Larger Than Life,* p. 82.

81 Jackson Day address: FDR Library.

81 "What a grand thing . . .": FDR Library.

82 " . . . strong supporter of the free world": Interview with Armand Hammer.

82–83 On Hammer and Lend-Lease: FDR Library.

83 On FDR on Hammer: Based on transcript at FDR Library.

84 On the Russian War Relief benefit: FDR Library.

84 Julius's medical license: Considine, *Larger Than Life,* p. 258.

84–85 On Julius's Communist activities: *Congressional Record,* 93rd Congress, vol. 119, part 26, October 17, 1973, p. 34493.

85 His *New York Times* obituary: *NYT,* October 20, 1948.

86 a rich divorcée: After several years in Hollywood, Hammer's first wife, Olga Vadina, moved with their son to South Laguna, where she died of lung and brain cancer on June 28, 1967. (Orange County records, book 121, p. 378.)

86 On Angela's background and their marriage: From testimony submitted in their divorce trial: Superior Court of New Jersey, Chancery Division, Monmouth County, Docket No. M-1075-54.

86–87 United Distillers: Ibid.

87–88 On Hartnett about Wicker: Hearings before the Committee on Un-American Activities, House of Representatives, 84th Congress, second session, July 12, 1956, pp. 5304–05.

88 "PLEASE BE ASSURED . . .": From the Harry S. Truman Presidential Library.

88 "to augment the supply . . .": Ibid.

88 made *The New York Times: NYT,* April 29, 1946.

88 Drew Pearson: telegram from Helen Wilcox, Hammer's public-relations aide, in Truman Library.

88 " . . . a very unusual knowledge . . ." June 24, 1946, Herbert Hoover Presidential Library. Brewster's letter seems to indicate that Hammer might be useful precisely because of his knowledge.

88 On the Truman interview: Friday, July 19, 1946, 11:30 A.M. Hammer said he was "very anxious to meet the President"; they spoke for no more than fifteen minutes. Truman Library.

89 " . . . first-hand view . . .": *NYT,* July 20, 1946. Hammer said he planned to spend ten days in Europe. Ever since going to Russia, he told reporters, he had "been concerned with the world food problem."

89 "Having observed carefully . . .": Washington National Records Center, Foreign Post Records: Moscow Embassy, 1945.

89 a bitter memorandum: Hoover edited the three-page memo; the author is unknown. Hoover Library.

PART TWO: THE THAW

"The rotten capitalist world . . .": From a speech to Arab ambassadors during the visit of French Premier Guy Mollet, June 26, 1956. Quoted in N. H. Mager and Jacques Katel, eds., *Conquest Without War* (New York: Simon and Schuster, 1961), p. 50. The word "capitalist" appears in brackets in the original citation.

7: "JOHN FOSTER DULLES FIRING AT US FROM UNDER THE TABLE"

Page

93 "The most fearsome living incarnation . . .": *National Review,* January 6, 1959, p. 107.

94 His son came back: Interview with Cyrus Eaton, Jr.

94–95 On Adzhubei's visit: E. J. Kahn, Jr., "Communists' Capitalist—I," *The New Yorker,* October 10, 1977, p. 67. This is the first part of a two-part profile of Eaton; the second appeared on October 17. (Hereafter, Profile I and Profile II.)

95 " . . . the epitome of a capitalist . . .": Profile I, p. 55.

96 "Isn't there something . . .": Robert Sheehan, "The Man from Pugwash," *Fortune,* March 1961, p. 230.

96 "There's never been . . ." Profile II, p. 55.

96–97 On Eaton's business career: Ibid., pp. 55–76.

97 "a colorless fraternity": Ibid., p. 66.

97 crusade against Wall Street: John Chamberlain, "Cyrus Eaton: An Old Man Goes East," *National Review,* January 6, 1959, p. 108.

98 On Eaton's nemesis, Robert A. Taft: Sheehan, "The Man from Pugwash," p. 230.

98 On Acadia Farms and Deep Cove Farms: Profile II, pp. 60–65.

99 "I found pleasure . . .": Profile I, p. 60.

99 " . . . academic pastures": Ian Sclanders, "Cyrus Eaton's Hideaway for Brains," *MacLean's,* October 27, 1956.

99 "Sam's enthusiasm": Profile I, p. 67.

100 " . . . collects thinkers . . .": Sclanders, "Eaton's Hideaway."

100 Alexander Samarin: Ibid.

100 Dr. Chien Tuan-Sheng: Interestingly, Eaton arranged to invite Chien Tuang-Sheng through the Chinese embassy in Moscow. Interview with John Marshall, Rockefeller Foundation Archives.

100 "I make steel . . .": Sclanders, "Eaton's Hideaway."

100 "utterly unlike the Cyrus Eaton . . .": Ibid.

101 " . . . looks like a cardinal": *Cleveland Plain Dealer,* October 25, 1956, "The Breakfast Commentator."

101 "the Greek historians": Ibid., October 26, 1956, "The Breakfast Commentator."

101 " . . . Anti-Reds' Voice": *NYT,* August 31, 1956.

101 Aristotle Onassis: *The Autobiography of Bertrand Russell,* vol. 3 (New York: Simon and Schuster, 1969), p. 83.

102 Eaton converted a schoolroom: *NYT,* July 10, 1957.

102 The Russian delegates: Ibid., July 12, 1957.

102 "There is nothing we can tell . . .": Ibid.

102 "our views represent . . .": Ibid.

103 " . . . if anyone brought a soapbox . . .": "Atomic Powwow in Pugwash," *Life,* July 22, 1957.

103 Leo Szilard: "The statement issued by the meeting is not very exciting," Szilard wrote to Warren Weaver of the Rockefeller Foundation on August 15, 1957. "I did not sign it because it advocated the stopping of bomb tests in a somewhat misleading, even though very meek, fashion." From the archives of the Rockefeller Foundation.

103 Statement of the Pugwash Scientists: Rockefeller Foundation Archives.

103 "war is obsolete": *Washington Evening Star,* July 13, 1957.

103 "never before . . .": *Nature,* August 24, 1957, pp. 358–59.

103 "The Millionaire Philosopher": *NYT,* July 11, 1957.

104 Eaton's Letters to Eisenhower: Dwight D. Eisenhower Presidential Library.

104 " . . . Business Leaders of America": *NYT,* November 8, 1957.
105 " . . . stout defender of democracy . . .": *Financial Post,* November 16, 1957.
105 "I conclude . . .": *New York Herald Tribune,* November 13, 1957.
105 " . . . Hand of Friendship": Ibid., November 8, 1957.
105 " . . . other *sane* men!": Ibid., November 13, 1957.
105 "No one can accuse me . . .": *NYT,* December 3, 1957.
105 Union League: Philadelphia *Inquirer,* January 17, 1958.
106 " . . . Soviet-hate-monger . . .": *Financial Post,* February 15, 1958.
106 "I always worry . . .": Profile I, p. 82.
106 " . . . contribution to the Soviet cause": *NYT,* May 8, 1958.
107 " . . . campaign of vilification . . .": Ibid., May 20, 1958.
107 On Humphrey and Douglas: Walter Goodman, *The Committee: The Extraordinary Career of the House Committee on Un-American Activities* (New York: Farrar, Straus & Giroux, 1968), p. 419.
107 "harassment": *NYT,* May 21, 1958.
107 Which side would Eaton be on: Profile I, p. 82.
108 his stomach could not take it: Goodman, *The Committee,* p. 419.
108 "No useful purpose . . .": Ibid.
108 "Cyrus and I had decided . . .": Interview with Anne Kinder Eaton.
109 "But of course": Ibid.
109 " . . . an absolutely hilarious time": Profile I, p. 68.
109 *Pravda* article: *Pravda,* September 2, 1958, p. 1.
109 Radio Moscow: *NYT,* September 2, 1958.
110 "KHRUSHCHEV TELLS EATON . . .": Ibid., September 3, 1958.
110 *American Mercury*: September 1960.
110 Two correspondents interviewed him: Profile I, p. 78.
110 " . . . time to drop the bomb": Profile II, p. 77.
111 " . . . insane fanatic": Profile I, p. 70.
111 "There is no use having . . .": *Kansas City Times,* November 5, 1958.
111 " . . . you could hear a pin drop": *Cleveland Plain Dealer,* October 23, 1958.
111 the *Nation* waxed exuberant: John Barden, "Cyrus Eaton: Merchant of Peace," *Nation,* January 31, 1959, p. 85.
111 "towering figure . . .": John Chamberlain, "Cyrus Eaton: An Old Man Goes East," *National Review,* June 6, 1959, p. 107.
112 On the troika: *NYT,* January 1, 1959; January 6, 1959.
112 *"Mik-o-yan—murderer!"* Ibid., January 8, 1959.
112 " . . . not a normal capitalist": Profile I, p. 51.

8: THE RULING CIRCLES

Page

113 " . . . the earth had opened . . .": Interview with Senator Daniel Patrick Moynihan.
114 "I've seen Stalin . . .": E. J. Kahn, Jr., "Plenipotentiary—I," *The New Yorker,* May 3, 1952, p. 41. This is the first part of a two-part profile of Harriman; the second appeared on May 10, 1952.

114 the greatest: C. L. Sulzberger, *A Long Row of Candles* (New York: Macmillan, 1969), p. 494.

114 On Bernard Baruch's opinion: *Harold Ickes's Diary* (in the Library of Congress), 1941: p. 5269; 1943: pp. 8175, 8241.

114 "you are our friend": Interview with W. Averell Harriman.

114 George Kennan: *George Kennan, Memoirs, 1925–1950* (Boston: Little, Brown, 1967), p. 264.

115 ". . . never apologized to anyone": Interview with Harriman.

115 resembled Al Capone: *Krokodil,* August 10, 1951, p. 16.

115 ". . . Warmonger": *Ogonyok,* December 1951, pp. 14–15.

116 ". . . the man with the most money . . .": *Current Digest of the Soviet Press,* vol. 10, no. 45, p. 5.

117 "Friendship should not be forgotten . . .": *Pravda,* January 25, 1959, p. 5.

117 ". . . everything from a bear hunt . . .": *NYT,* June 1, 1959.

118 "No American in recent times . . .": Ibid., June 24, 1959.

118–19 Meeting with Khrushchev: Charles Thayer's report of conversation, Harriman archives.

119 Khrushchev ridiculed Harriman's idea: Khrushchev speech to the Central Committee of the Communist Party of the Soviet Union, October 18, 1961. Harriman archives.

120 On Khrushchev's education: Interview with Harriman.

120 "I am a miner by origin": Memorandum of Charles Thayer in the Harriman archives.

121 On Harriman's attempts to leave: Interview with Harriman.

122 On Harriman's news conference: *NYT,* June 26, 1959.

122 On leaks: Associated Press, July 3, 1959. *NYT,* July 2, 1959, p. 1. Time, Inc., telexes in Harriman archives.

122 "My Alarming Interview . . .": *Life,* July 13, 1959, p. 33.

123 "wampum": David Halberstam, *The Best and the Brightest* (New York: Random House, 1972; paperback edition: Fawcett Crest, 1973), p. 93.

123–24 Harriman's letters to Kennedy: John F. Kennedy Library.

124–28 Khrushchev meets the Establishment: Harriman archives; *NYT,* September 18, 1959; *Life,* September 28, 1959, "Exclusive Report: Mr. K Meets U.S. 'Ruling Class,'" pp. 38–39; *Izvestiya,* October 9, 1959, p. 6; "The Day Nikita Khrushchev Visited the Establishment" in John Kenneth Galbraith, *Economics, Peace and Laughter* (Boston: Houghton Mifflin, 1971), pp. 257–67.

125 Donut Institute: Harriman Archives.

128 "The Star-Spangled Banner": *NYT,* September 18, 1959.

9: THE RETURN OF THE "PRODIGAL SON"

Page

131–33 On Angela's divorce from Armand: From testimony submitted in their divorce trial: Superior Court of New Jersey, Chancery division, Monmouth County, Docket No. M-1075-54.

133 the Lenin letters disappeared: An attorney involved in the case recalls that Hammer's attempt to force Angela to acknowledge taking the letters was one of the great sensations of the trial. In 1979 Hammer placed a notice in the July issue of the *National Register of Lost or Stolen Archival Materials,* which listed the three letters and inscribed photograph he had received from Lenin. To date they have not been returned to him.

134 Frances Barrett Tolman: Bob Considine (*Larger Than Life,* London: W. H. Allen, 1976, p. 121) relates that Armand met Frances at Marshall Field's in Chicago. But Lucy Jarvis, while working on the documentary on his life for NBC, found that Frances's late husband had been a major investor in one of Hammer's enterprises in the thirties or forties.

134 tax shelter: Hammer has always insisted (Considine, *Larger Than Life,* p. 121) that he went to California in 1956 to retire: "he had enough . . . and settled down to a life that was intended to be as placid as the Pacific at sunset." This is an unconvincing story. As Hammer continues, even in his eighties, to run Occidental, it seems more likely that he actually planned to embark upon a new career. As 1956 marked the beginning of de-Stalinization in Russia and a Soviet policy of expanded trade with the West, it is reasonable to suppose that the Soviet Union figured in his plans.

134–35 On the Khrushchev interview incident: Roosevelt Library.

136 "Your father tells me . . .": Roosevelt Library.

136 " . . . second-class citizen": Interview with Armand Victorovich Hammer.

137 On the reunion at the Savoy: *NYT,* July 24, 1956. The *Times* article states that Victor had not seen his son "for thirty years," which, if accurate, means he was in Moscow in 1926.

138 On Khrushchev at Hyde Park: A David Gurewitsch, *Eleanor Roosevelt: Her Day* (New York: Quadrangle, 1974), p. 67; interview with Armand V. Hammer.

139–40 On Armand Victorovich in the United States: Interview with Armand V. Hammer, 1982.

140 " . . . no connection with the Russians . . .": James Cook, "The Capitalist Connection" (cover story), *Forbes,* April 28, 1980, p. 48.

141 On Occidental's net losses, 1959 and 1960: Occidental annual reports.

141 discovered gas: Considine, *Larger Than Life,* p. 124.

142 " . . . my friendship with Jack Kennedy . . .": Speech before the Foreign Policy Association, Plaza Hotel, New York, May 4, 1981.

142 On arranging the 1961 trip to Moscow: Kennedy and Roosevelt libraries.

143 "brushed up": Hammer's report on conversations with Mikoyan and Khrushchev, Kennedy Library.

143 " . . . kind of sentimental": *The New Yorker,* December 1, 1962, "Hammer and Khrushchev," p. 52.

144 " . . . more like a capitalist than a Communist": Ibid.

144–45 On the meeting with Khrushchev: Hammer's report, Kennedy Library.

145 " . . . most romantic setting . . .": Considine, *Larger Than Life,* p. 166.
145 "Since they already knew . . .": Hammer's report, Kennedy Library.
145 "What have you been doing . . .": *The New Yorker,* December 1, 1962, "Hammer and Khrushchev," p. 52.
146 "Old timers remember that": *Pravda,* June 30, 1962, pp. 1–2.
146 " . . . I have no power . . .": Joseph Lash, *Eleanor: The Years Alone* (New York: Norton, 1972), p. 273.
146–47 On Hammer and Kennedy: Kennedy Library.
148 "I believe our organization . . .": Ibid.
148 On Hammer's correspondence with Johnson: Johnson Library.
148 "He formerly owned . . .": Memorandum of telephone conversation with Rep. James Roosevelt, Lyndon B. Johnson Library, Austin, Texas.
149 On the 1964 trip to Moscow: Hammer's memoranda of conversations, Johnson Library.
149 the woman wept: Spencer Klaw, "Man With the Golden Touch," *Saturday Evening Post,* March 12, 1966, p. 91.
149 "What should the President do . . .": Johnson Library.
150 press conference: *NYT,* September 27, 1964.
151 "I didn't see Khrushchev . . .": Interview with Hammer.

10: THE LAST OF THE GREAT TYCOONS

Page
152 On the Paris summit: Charles E. Bohlen, *Witness to History: 1929–1969* (New York: Norton, 1973), p. 469; E. J. Kahn, Jr., "Communists' Capitalist—I," *New Yorker,* October 10, 1977, p. 72. This is the first part of a two-part profile of Eaton; the second appeared on October 17 (hereafter, Profile I and Profile II); interview with Anne Kinder Eaton.
153 "When Communism has triumphed . . .": Profile I, p. 72.
153 "must never permit its foreign policies . . .": *NYT,* May 20, 1960.
153 " . . . violating the law": Ibid.
154 "strange aberrations": Ibid.
154 On Mrs. Eaton's luncheon: Ibid., September 27, 1959.
154 " . . . most urgent task . . .": Ibid., December 28, 1959.
154 "a classic example . . .": FBI file on Cyrus Eaton, declassified April 12, 1982, under Freedom of Information Act request.
155 "Eaton greeted Khrushchev . . .": Ibid.
155 Eisenhower believed: Dwight D. Eisenhower, *Waging Peace* (Garden City, N.Y.: Doubleday, 1965), p. 559.
155 Great dachas all across Russia: Interview with Anne Kinder Eaton.
155 " . . . in control of his feelings . . .": Toronto *Globe and Mail,* June 20, 1960.
156 "impressed me right from the start . . .": *London Evening Standard,* June 8, 1960, p. 7.
156 Lenin Peace Prize: *NYT,* May 4, 1960; Ibid., July 2, 1960; Profile I, p. 74.

156 *American Mercury*: September 1960.
157 On Biltmore lunch: Profile I, p. 77.
157 "organized and paid for . . .": Ibid.
157 On Rabinowitch article: Ibid., pp. 74–77. Rabinowitch was correct. Eaton's sponsorship of Pugwash motivated the FBI to investigate each American participant and conclude that all were "liberal in views. . . . Investigations revealed communist front membership on part of some, and associations with CP members; however, no information developed that any were members of CP or were definitely pro-Russian" (FBI Eaton file).
157–58 Eaton goes to Moscow: *Pravda,* December 1, 1960, p. 1; *Moscow News,* December 3, 1960; *Cleveland Plain Dealer,* December 10, 1960.
158 Duke of Windsor: Profile I, p. 51.
158–59 On the Lippmann correspondence: Lippmann Papers, Sterling Memorial Library, Yale University.
159 Eaton's letters to Kennedy: Kennedy Library.
160 "Adlai thought . . .": Profile II, p. 78.
160 " . . . a serious mistake . . .": Chester Bowles Papers, Sterling Memorial Library, Yale University.
160 "It is abundantly clear . . .": Ibid.
161 "propaganda device": Reprinted in the *Milwaukee Journal,* June 22, 1961.
161 " . . . angels weep . . .": Ibid.
161 " . . . a very odd lot . . .": Warren Weaver Reminiscences, Columbia University Oral History Project. Reprinted with permission.
161 "didn't work": Reminiscences of Sir Robert Watson-Watt, Part II, 1964; Columbia University Oral History Project. Reprinted with permission.
161 a specialized jargon: Richard J. Barnet, *The Giants: Russia and America* (New York: Simon and Schuster, 1977), p. 101.
161 " . . . repugnant to my ears": Quoted by Watson-Watt.
161 " . . . difference is fundamental": Barnet, *Giants,* p. 101.
162 " . . . most obvious achievement . . .": *The Autobiography of Bertrand Russell,* vol. 3 (New York: Simon and Schuster, 1969), p. 85.
162 Eaton's office: Profile I, p. 50; Profile II, p. 60.
162 *Pageant:* Profile I, p. 52.
162 " . . . that *Communist*!": Interview with Kay Halle.
163 On Eaton and Baruch: *NYT,* October 6, 1961.
163 On Eaton's 1964 trip to Moscow: Ibid., February 16, 1954.
163 interviewed . . . on Soviet television: Ibid., February 19, 1964.
163 " . . . Soviet Union is moving!": Chester Bowles Papers
163 "'Your people call me a dictator'": Profile I, p. 80.
163 in fine shape: Ibid.
163 eighty-first birthday: *NYT,* December 27, 1964.
164–66 On the Wallace interview: From the Mike Wallace Collection at the George Arents Research Library, Syracuse University; courtesy of Mike Wallace.
165 On Mikoyan, Khrushchev, and the purges: Robert Conquest, *The Great Terror* (New York: Collier Books, 1973), pp. 372, 265, 367.

167 "With my record . . .": Profile I, p. 56.
167 " . . . one of the best-kept secrets . . .": Interview with Cyrus Eaton, Jr., 1982.
167 cattle: *NYT,* September 15, 1971.
168 " . . . his position was correct": Interview with Cyrus Eaton, Jr.
168 North Vietnam: Profile II, pp. 79–80.
169–70 On Eaton in Moscow, 1965: *NYT,* May 25, 1965. The Eatons had also made a brief stop in Moscow in February 1964, at which time Cyrus met with Patolichev, Gromyko, Mikoyan, and Khrushchev: Ibid., February 15, 1964; February 16, 1964; February 18, 1964.
170 "undue devotion . . .": Profile II, p. 79.
171 " . . . my life is a failure . . .": Ibid.

11: THE PRINCE OF CAPITALISM

Page
172 . . . *Knee-Deep in Blood* . . . : Moscow: Pravda Press, 1957.
173–74 On David Rockefeller's upbringing: Joseph E. Persico, *The Imperial Rockefeller: A Biography of Nelson A. Rockefeller* (New York: Simon and Schuster, 1982), pp. 23–26; Tom Pyle and Beth Day, *Pocantico: Fifty Years on the Rockefeller Domain* (New York: Duell, Sloan and Pearce, 1964), pp. 85, 183; E. J. Kahn, Jr., "Resources and Responsibilities" (two-part profile of David Rockefeller), *The New Yorker,* January 9 and 16, 1965 (hereafter: Resources I and Resources II).
175 " . . . the unique power he wielded . . .": Persico, *Imperial Rockefeller,* p. 52.
175 "I can't imagine . . .": Resources I, p. 38.
175 " . . . what movie star is approaching": Ibid., p. 46.
176 Room 5600: Persico, *Imperial Rockefeller,* pp. 116–18.
176 Bilderberg Conference: Resources I, p. 66.
176 Dartmouth Conference: Maureen R. Berman and Joseph E. Johnson, eds., *Unofficial Diplomats* (New York: Columbia University Press, 1977), p. 46.
177 "kingpin": Interview with Norman Cousins.
177 "Nothing impresses . . .": Berman and Johnson, *Unofficial Diplomats,* p. 52.
177 "The Russians respect power": Ibid.
178 On Chase National Bank: Anthony Sutton: *Western Technology and Soviet Economic Development,* vol. 1 (Stanford: Hoover Institution, 1968), pp. 278, 289.
178 " . . . punctiliousness . . .": David Rockefeller, "Chase Manhattan's Transactions in the U.S.S.R.," *Journal of the U.S.-U.S.S.R. Trade and Economic Council,* 1977, p. 14.
178 On Standard Oil: Peter G. Filene, *Americans and the Soviet Experiment, 1917–33* (Cambridge, Harvard University Press, 1967), pp. 117–18; Anthony Sampson, *The Seven Sisters* (New York: Bantam, 1976), pp. 83–84.
179 *Prospect for America:* Cited in Henry Kissinger, *White House Years*

(Boston: Little, Brown, 1979), p. 4; Myer Kutz, *Rockefeller Power* (New York: Simon and Schuster, 1974), pp. 207–10.

179 Ever since World War II: Quoted in Myer Kutz, *Rockefeller Power,* p. 208.

180 " . . . Rockefeller Doctrine . . .": *Pravda,* January 12, 1958, p. 5.

180 " . . . Rockefeller Dynasty": *New Times,* no. 30, pp. 10–13.

180 the spread of abstract art: *Nedelya* (*Izvestiya*'s weekly news magazine), December 29, 1963, p. 6.

180 " . . . do what's appropriate": Resources I, p. 52.

181 On Cousins and Bundy: Lyndon Johnson Library.

181 Cousins had been scheduled: Interview with Norman Cousins.

181 "So this is Mr. Rockefeller . . .": *Khrushchev Remembers* (New York: Bantam Books, 1971), p. 436.

181–82 On Khrushchev and Nelson Rockefeller at the Waldorf: Persico, *Imperial Rockefeller,* p. 86; *NYT,* January 12, 1962.

182–86 On David Rockefeller's meeting with Khrushchev: Rockefeller's memorandum of conversation, Johnson Library; interview with David Rockefeller; interview with Neva Rockefeller Kaiser.

184 On Bill Knox: William E. Knox had been in charge of all of Westinghouse's Russian business from the late twenties on, dealing entirely through Amtorg in New York. After World War II, when he was president of Westinghouse International, he made his first visit to the Soviet Union. He returned to Moscow on October 24, 1962, on business again. The Cuban Missile Crisis had just broken out, and he was amazed to receive a phone call informing him that Khrushchev would like to see him. They spoke for three hours in the Kremlin, and Knox duly reported the substance of the conversation to the State Department. Evidently, Khrushchev had wanted a backchannel to explain his point of view to the United States. Knox died in 1978. (*NYT,* October 26, 1962; October 27, 1962; author's correspondence with Mrs. William E. Knox.)

186 " . . . I sort of brought it to a close . . .": Interview with David Rockefeller.

186 "Khrushchev assumed . . .": Interview with Neva Rockefeller Kaiser.

186 "The guest told N. S. Khrushchev . . .": *Pravda,* August 1, 1964, p. 4.

187 On Rockefeller correspondence with White House: Johnson Library.

187 "interesting": *NYT,* September 12, 1964.

188 " . . . excellent proving around": Ibid., October 22, 1964.

188 back in Moscow: Ibid., November 19, 1964.

188 Senate Foreign Relations Committee: Marshall Goldman, *Détente and Dollars* (New York: Basic Books, 1975), p. 71.

188 survey of economics professors: Louis Budenz, *The Bolshevik Invasion of the West* (Linden, N.J.: Bookmailer, 1966), p. 47.

188 "a direct result . . .": William Hoffman, *David* (New York: Lyle Stuart, 1971), p. 20.

189 " . . . certainly contributed to my knowledge . . .": Interview with Rockefeller.

PART THREE: THE RISE AND FALL OF DÉTENTE

"... a little pregnant": Richard Nixon, *The Memoirs of Richard Nixon* (New York: Grosset & Dunlap, 1978), p. 1027.

12: THE PEPSI GENERATION

Page

201 On Kissinger and Stans: Interview with Harold B. Scott; interview with Maurice Stans.

202 On Stans mission: *NYT*, November 18, 1971; November 21, 1971.

202 On Business International: Ibid., November 28, 1971; November 30, 1971.

202 "I am a Republican": *Business Week*, July 31, 1971, p. 52.

202–03 On Kendall's upbringing and early career: Robert Scheer, "The Doctrine of Multinational Sell," *Esquire*, April 1975, pp. 124–64; *NYT*, July 25, 1976.

203 Joan Crawford: Bob Thomas, *Joan Crawford* (New York: Simon and Schuster, 1978), p. 251.

204–06 On Kendall and Nixon in Moscow: Interview with Donald Kendall; Herbert Klein, *Making It Perfectly Clear* (New York: Doubleday, 1980), pp. 244–47; *NYT*, July 27, 1959.

205 "Do you think ...": *NYT*, July 27, 1959.

206 Elmer Bobst: *Business Week*, July 31, 1971, p. 54.

207 "... my New York law practice ...": Richard Nixon, *The Memoirs of Richard Nixon* (New York: Grosset & Dunlap, 1978), p. 256.

207 On Nixon as Pepsi lawyer: Jules Witcover, *The Resurrection of Richard Nixon* (New York: Putnam's, 1970), pp. 76–77; Earl Mazo and Stephen Hess, *Nixon: A Political Portrait* (New York: Harper & Row, 1968), p. 288.

207 one of his earliest contributors: Maurice Stans, *The Terrors of Justice* (New York: Everest House, 1978), pp. 130–33.

207 ECAT: *NYT*, January 3, 1969. In fact, as it turned out, Kendall unwittingly contributed to Nixon's downfall. It was he who urged the President to install a taping system in the Oval Office. As a trustee of the Richard Nixon Foundation, he and four others—Ross Perot of Electronic Data Systems, Taft Schreiber of MCA, Leonard Firestone of Firestone Tire & Rubber Company, and John Ehrlichman—were charged with planning the Nixon Presidential Library. Kendall went to see Lyndon Johnson at the LBJ Farm to ask about the Johnson Library in Austin. Johnson told Kendall his White House taping system had been "invaluable" in preparing his memoirs. Kendall told Nixon, in September 1969, about this idea. Nixon thought it was a good one, although he did not get around to having the tape recorders installed until more than a year later. See *NYT*, May 13, 1969; Theodore H. White, *Breach of Faith* (New York: Atheneum, 1975), p. 191; Nixon, *Memoirs*, p. 501.

208 Nixon's inner circle: *Business Week,* July 31, 1971, p. 52; *NYT,* January 17, 1970; Bruce Mazlish, *In Search of Nixon: A Psychohistorical Inquiry* (New York: Basic Books, 1972), p. 40.

208 "Town House" fund: J. Anthony Lukas, *Nightmare* (New York: Viking, 1976), p. 111.

208 Allende: Nixon, *Memoirs,* p. 489; *NYT,* July 25, 1976; Henry Kissinger, *White House Years* (Boston: Little, Brown, 1979), p. 673; Scheer, "Multinational Sell," p. 162.

208–09 Llewellyn Thompson: Interview with Kendall.

209–10 On Kendall's pitch to Kosygin: Interview with Kendall.

211 Monsieur Henri Wines: *NYT,* April 6, 1972.

212 "émigré vodka": Kissinger, *White House Years,* p. 1212.

212 Pepsi deal announced: *NYT,* November 17, 1972; *Wall Street Journal,* November 17, 1972.

213 "A swallow of cold Pepsi . . .": J. C. Louis and H. Z. Yazijian, *The Cola Wars* (New York: Everest House, 1980), p. 205.

213 "But don't forget . . .": *Izvestiya,* June 7, 1974, p. 3.

213 *The New Yorker* cartoon: December 16, 1972, p. 43.

213 full-page advertisement: *NYT,* February 5, 1973.

213 Soviet Tupolev Tu95: London *Daily Telegraph,* May 30, 1977.

213 Coke . . . not pleased: *NYT,* November 18, 1972.

214 Kendall on Nixon friendship: *Wall Street Journal,* November 17, 1972.

214 "the first time in our history . . .": Frank Mankiewicz, *Perfectly Clear* (New York: Quadrangle, 1973), p. 15.

214 On the *Post* story: May 13, 1927. The source was probably David Karr (see chapter Thirteen).

214 Jack Anderson: *Washington Post,* December 31, 1972.

214–15 Stevenson: Hearings before the Subcommittee on Europe of the Committee on Foreign Affairs, House of Representatives, 93rd Congress, second session, May 22, 1974 ("Détente"), p. 118.

215 " . . . a lot of things the Soviets do . . .": Interview with Donald Kendall, 1981.

217 "Détente at the St. Regis": *The New Yorker,* June 30, 1975, p. 25.

218 On board meeting in Russia: "To Russia with Pepsi" (a portfolio) *Fortune,* August 1974, pp. 191–93.

13: "THE BIGGEST DEAL IN HISTORY"

Page

219 On Hammer's jet: Edward Jay Epstein, "The Riddle of Armand Hammer," *NYT Magazine,* November 29, 1981, p. 71.

219 On Hammer's meeting with the Eatons: Interview with Anne Kinder Eaton; interview with Cyrus Eaton, Jr.

220–21 Libya: Daniel Yergin, "The One-Man, Flying Multinational" Part 2, *Atlantic,* July 1975, pp. 56–57; Anthony Sampson, *The Seven Sisters* (New York: Bantam, 1976), pp. 170, 252–53.

221 Bechtel: Mark Dowie, "The Bechtel File," *Mother Jones,* September/October 1978, p. 11.

221 ". . . Central Intelligence Agency . . .": Epstein, "Riddle of Armand Hammer," p. 120.

222 ". . . none of the rumors were borne out": Interview with G. Henry M. Schuler.

222 "a terrible price . . .": Quoted in William Scobie, "The Kremlin's Favourite Capitalist," London *Observer,* August 9, 1981, p. 32.

223–24 Hammer correspondence with Johnson White House: Johnson Library.

223 "Lyndon was unsure of himself . . .": Interview with Myer Feldman.

224 ". . . the President is uneasy . . .": Johnson Library. Memo declassified February 10, 1982. Rostow's memo to the President, however, remains classified under the donor's deed restrictions. Presumably the memo contains remarks unfavorable to Hammer that would embarrass Rostow or Johnson if released.

225–26 On Hammer and the Eatons in Cleveland: Interview with Cyrus Eaton, Jr.

226 ". . . presiding over a disaster": *Business Week,* December 18, 1971, p. 79.

226 "I know you wonder . . ." *Oxy Today,* September 1972.

227 David Karr: Roy Rowan, "The Death of Dave Karr and Other Mysteries," *Fortune,* December 3, 1979; *NYT,* October 5, 1979. Karr died on July 7, 1979, having just opened the Cosmos Hotel in Moscow that he had built. His widow charged that he was poisoned by the Russians. Sargeant Shriver doubts this: Karr's physician in Paris—also Shriver's—performed the autopsy and was satisfied that Karr died of a heart attack.

227 ". . . we organized it": Rowan, "Dave Karr." Because he was in Moscow with Hammer, Shriver was bypassed as George McGovern's running mate the first time around. At the time, McGovern, having just received the Democratic nomination, was casting about for a Vice-Presidential nominee. His aide, Frank Mankiewicz, suggested Shriver, and McGovern said, "Get Shriver on the phone." When McGovern learned that Shriver was in Moscow and unreachable, he decided to go ahead and name Thomas Eagleton. (Interviews with Shriver and Mankiewicz.)

228 On the Lenin letters: See Yergin II, p. 63.

228–29 July 18, 1972, announcement: Yergin II, p. 64; *NYT,* July 18, 1972; July 19, 1972; July 21, 1972.

230 On Hammer's meeting with Nixon: *NYT,* July 21, 1972.

230 ". . . a memorable day in my life . . .": E. J. Kahn, Jr., "Communists' Capitalist—II," *The New Yorker,* October 10, 1977, p. 80.

230 ". . . dissolve our relationship": Interview with Cyrus Eaton, Jr.

231 On Hammer and Kosygin: *NYT,* September 15, 1972.

231 On gas pipeline: Ibid., October 30, 1972.

231 "He told us": Yergin II, p. 66.

231–32 Eaton welcomed the reporter: Personal communication with the author.

232–34 On Hammer's trial: *NYT,* December 11, 1974; December 13, 1975; January 30, 1976; March 5, 1976; *Wall Street Journal,* March 5,

1976; *NYT,* October 2, 1976; Louis Nizer, *Reflections Without Mirrors* (New York: Doubleday, 1978), pp. 431–46; interview with Robert Pack; interview with Myer Feldman.

234 " . . . $50,000 is not enough . . .": "John Callaway Interviews Armand Hammer" (aired October 8, 1981, WTTW Chicago. Distributed nationally on PBS).

235 " . . . absolutely no connection": *NYT,* April 18, 1976.

14: ONE KARL MARX SQUARE

Page

236–37 On Rockefeller in Red Square: Interview with Peter Bakstansky.

237 " . . . the big leagues": Interview with Joseph V. Reed, Jr.

237 press conference: Interview with Murray Seeger; interview with Bakstansky; *NYT,* May 22, 1973; interview with David Rockefeller.

238 " . . . broader vision of peaceful engagement": Henry Kissinger, *White House Years* (Boston: Little, Brown, 1979), p. 152.

238 "EATON JOINS ROCKEFELLER . . .": *NYT,* January 16, 1967.

238 IBEC: *NYT,* January 16, 1967; interview with Cyrus Eaton, Jr.

239 " . . . Two-Way Traffic": *NYT,* January 16, 1967.

239 On Sorensen and Ball: Kissinger, *White House Years,* p. 152. Of the report, Sorensen says, "I was surprised by that, and so was George Ball" (interview with Sorensen).

239 After the 1968 election: Peter Collier and David Horowitz, *The Rockefellers: An American Dynasty* (New York: Holt, Rinehart and Winston, 1976), p. 428.

239 Rumania: Kissinger, *White House Years,* 153–55; Collier and Horowitz, *The Rockefellers,* p. 428.

240 Rome: *NYT,* March 6, 1971.

240 Dartmouth Conference, 1971: *NYT,* July 17, 1971.

240 "shook the world": Kissinger, *White House Years,* p. 755.

240 "stiff and formal . . .": Interview with David Rockefeller.

240 trade unit in Vienna: *NYT,* August 11, 1972.

240 Soviet TV: *NYT,* August 31, 1972.

240 Chase announces Moscow office: Interview with Joseph Reed.

240–41 Alfred Wentworth: *NYT,* December 27, 1972; interview with Alfred Wentworth.

241–42 On flying into Moscow: Interview with Joseph Reed; interview with David Rockefeller.

242 Kosygin: *NYT,* May 22, 1973; *Los Angeles Times,* May 29, 1973; interview with Reed.

243 " . . . red carpet had rolled up . . .": Interview with Reed.

243 Soviet press attacks Rockefeller: *Los Angeles Times,* May 29, 1973; "Bill Moyers' Journal: The World of David Rockefeller," PBS, February 7, 1980.

243 "The most farsighted . . .": *Pravda,* February 27, 1973, p. 4.

244 Soviets on Nelson Rockefeller: *Pravda,* August 22, 1974, p. 4.

244 " . . . walk on water": Interview with General James Gavin.

244 " . . . most powerful business-statesman . . .": Interview with Reed.

244 "The Marxist propaganda . . .": Interview with David Rockefeller.

245 Moyers on Rockefeller: "Bill Moyers' Journal."
245 secret of this power: Interview with Murray Seeger.
246 his wealth: *NYT,* September 26, 1974; December 4, 1974.
247 On power of Rockefeller Foundations: Myer Kutz, *Rockefeller Power* (New York: Simon and Schuster, 1974), pp. 207–10.
247 " . . . a very strange way . . .": Leonard Silk and Mark Silk, *The American Establishment* (New York: Basic Books, 1980), p. 207.
247 "I have contacts . . .": Interview with David Rockefeller.
248 " . . . Chase is there": Interview with Jacob Beam.
248 "dubious banking": *NYT,* May 31, 1973. Citibank closed its Moscow office in 1980.
249 "would amount to aid . . .": Ibid., October 22, 1964.
249 Russians want Rockefeller as ambassador: *NYT,* April 17, 1973; *Washington Post,* August 27, 1973. After Beam's retirement in January 1973, the post was kept vacant. Beam explains, "Kissinger came to Moscow very frequently, and as far as he was concerned an ambassador there would have only been an encumbrance. His personal channel of communication was Anatoly Dobrynin." As he was not named Secretary of State until August 1973, Kissinger sought to circumvent Secretary William Rogers. (Interview with Jacob Beam)
249 "They do roll out the red carpet . . .": Interview with David Rockefeller.
250 " . . . Curious psychological twist": "Multinational Corporations and United States Foreign Policy," Hearings before the Subcommittee on Multinational Corporations of the Committee on Foreign Relations, U.S. Senate, 93rd Congress, second session, July 18, 1974.
250 " . . . they compartmentalize . . .": Interview with Joseph Reed.
251 *"Rokfyeller!"*: Interview with Norman Cousins.
251 " . . . revere, blandish, and exalt . . .": Collier and Horowitz, *The Rockefellers,* p. 428.

15: THE CLASH OF EGOS

Page
252–53 Brezhnev in Washington: *NYT,* June 21, 1973; *Washington Post,* June 20, 1973; Ibid., June 23, 1973; Richard Nixon, *The Memoirs of Richard Nixon* (New York: Grosset & Dunlap, 1978), pp. 877–84.
253 Eaton: E. J. Kahn, Jr., "Communists' Capitalist—II," *New Yorker,* October 10, 1977, p. 83.
253 " . . . believing congregation": *Washington Post,* June 23, 1973.
254 On the Jackson amendment: Joseph Albright, "The Pact of the Two Henrys," *NYT Magazine,* January 5, 1975, pp. 16–26; Paula Stern, *Water's Edge* (Westport, Conn.: Greenwood Press, 1979).
254–57 On the formation of the Trade Council: Based on interviews with members of the Council.
258 On Kendall at Yalta: Interview with Donald Kendall. Also *Pravda,* August 29, 1973, p. 1.

259 On the Trade Council in Moscow: *NYT,* October 3, 1973; interviews with members of the Council; *Washington Post,* October 3, 1973.

259 John T. Connor, Jr.: Interview with Connor; interview with Murray Seeger.

260 "I well understand . . .": *Pravda,* December 1, 1976, pp. 1–2.

260 the noose: Experts on Lenin generally agree that it is unlikely he ever wrote such a thing. That he *said* it is certainly conceivable. Alexander Solzhenitsyn tells an anecdote about Lenin and Karl Radek at a Party meeting in Moscow. "Comrades," he is supposed to have said, "don't panic, when things go very hard for us, we will give a rope to the bourgeoisie, and the bourgeoisie will hang itself." Radek then asked, "Vladimir Ilyich, but where are we going to get enough rope to hang the whole bourgeoisie?" To which Lenin replied, "They'll supply us with it." (Quoted in Carl Gershman, "Selling Them the Rope: Business and the Soviets," *Commentary,* April 1979, p. 35.) Professor Donald Carlisle of the Harvard Russian Research Center has found a different but related citation in the works of Lenin. In *Left-Wing Communism—An Infantile Disorder,* Lenin speaks of supporting Arthur Henderson, the Labour member of the British War Cabinet in 1920, "in the same way as the rope supports a hanged man."

260 "I wanted all our directors . . .": *Izvestiya,* June 7, 1974, p. 3.

261 Malcolm Forbes: Interview with Malcolm Forbes.

261 "elaborate financial interdependence . . .": Norman Angell, *The Great Illusion* (New York: Putnam's, 1913), p. 76.

261 " . . . person-to-person contacts . . .": Donald Kendall, "Is the U.S.S.R. a Good Trading Partner?" in "Common Sense in U.S.-Soviet Trade" (Washington: American Committee on East-West Accord, October 1979), p. 12.

262 " . . . We're moving towards socialism . . .": London *Times,* July 19, 1972, p. 16.

262 "We are asked to believe . . .": Robert Scheer, "The Doctrine of Multinational Sell," *Esquire,* April 1975, p. 163.

262 " . . . web of interlocking relations . . .": Kendall, "Common Sense in U.S.-Soviet Trade" (April 1978), p. 38.

262 " . . . domestic turbulence . . .": *NYT Magazine,* April 18, 1982, p. 44.

263 " . . . historically irreversible . . .": *Pravda,* February 15, 1975, p. 1.

263 "hard-liners": The American misperception of Politburo hard-liners opposing a liberal Soviet leader was prevalent, remarkably enough, even in Stalin's time. Ambassador Joseph E. Davies observed in 1941 that Stalin "insisted upon liberalism of the Constitution even though it hazarded his power and party control." See *Mission to Moscow* (New York: Simon and Schuster, 1941), p. 106.

263 " . . . in the Soviet Union today . . .": "The Role of the Export-Import Bank and Export Controls in U.S. International Economic Policy," Hearings before the Subcommittee on International Finance of the Committee on Banking, Housing and Urban Affairs, U.S. Senate, April 23, 1974, p. 284.

263 "those forces in the Kremlin . . .": *Washington Post,* September 16, 1973.
264 On Hitler's offer: Lev Navrozov, *New York News-World,* March 15, 1982.
264 "corporate approach": Interview with Richard Maass.
266 " . . . I've got a bad back": Stern, *Water's Edge,* p. 72.
266 ECAT lobbying thwarted: *Washington Post,* September 16, 1973.
267 Fred Neal: *NYT,* July 11, 1974.
267–68 Evans and Novak: *Washington Post,* July 17, 1974.
268 "If Russians can leave Russia at will . . .": *Washington Post,* August 27, 1973.
268 " . . . Some of my closest friends . . .": *Time,* June 25, 1973, p. 32.
269 " . . . selling his point of view": Interview with Milton Rosenthal, 1982.
270 "Why are you writing . . .": Interview with Murray Seeger, 1982.
270 On Kendall and American Jewish Committee: *NYT,* September 20, 1973; interview with Richard Maass.
271 "DON'T DRINK PEPSI . . .": *NYT,* December 10, 1972.
271 "How do you boycott Mack trucks?" Hackensack, N.J., *Record,* December 20, 1972.
271 Jewish Defense League: *NYT,* March 11, 1974; December 2, 1974; February 8, 1975; March 31, 1975.
271 1974 best-sellers: *NYT Book Review,* July 14, 1974, p. 45.
272 " . . . such an interpretation": Stern, *Water's Edge,* p. 170.
272 ECAT lobbying offensive: Russell W. Howe and Sarah H. Trott, *The Power Peddlers* (Garden City, N.Y.: Doubleday, 1977), p. 231.
272 "I don't say one thing . . .": Interview with Donald Kendall.

16: HAMMER'S KREMLIN CONNECTION

Page
274 "He was terrific . . .": Interview with Sargent Shriver.
275 " . . . substantial amount of cash": Bob Considine, *Larger Than Life* (London: W. H. Allen, 1976), p. 177.
275 Hammer on Suslov: Ibid., p. 178.
276 1973 art exchange: Ibid., pp. 170–75; *NYT,* February 6, 1973, p. 1; May 3, 1973, p. 50.
277 hints of bribery: Quoted in *NYT,* February 13, 1979, "How is Occidental Run?"
277 On Hammer's meeting with Brezhnev: Considine, *Larger Than Life,* p. 180.
277–78 chemical-fertilizer barter deal: *NYT,* April 10, 1973; April 13, 1973; May 22, 1974; June 4, 1974.
278 Reston: Ibid., April 15, 1973.
278 "a perceptible blow": Ibid., April 19, 1973.
278 did not have enough phosphate: Lee Smith, "Armand Hammer and the Phosphate Puzzle," *Fortune,* April 7, 1980.
279 "Hammer's Kremlin Connection": *NYT,* May 20, 1973.
279 "sophisticated as they are . . .": Ibid., May 21, 1973.

279–81 Gas pipeline: *NYT,* June 9, 1973; June 15, 1973; *Washington Post,* July 31, 1973; *NYT,* December 4, 1973; Mark Dowie, "The Bechtel File," *Mother Jones,* September/October 1978, p. 11; interviews with U.S. Commerce Department officials; "Businessmen in the News: Armand Hammer & Sickle Co.," *Fortune,* July 1973, p. 25.

281–82 Trade Center: Interview with Sargent Shriver; *NYT,* September 19, 1973; April 20, 1974; September 2, 1975. Maurice Stans remembers that Kosygin suggested the idea in November 1971 (interview with Maurice Stans).

282 Golf course: *NYT,* November 18, 1973; June 4, 1974. James Reston, "Moscow's Fatal Mistake." Daniel Yergin, "The One-Man Flying Multinational," Part 2, *Atlantic,* July 1975, p. 65.

283 ". . . He's my candidate": *NYT,* August 28, 1973; *Washington Post,* August 27, 1973.

283 ". . . immeasurably happy . . .": *Literaturnaya Gazeta,* December 26, 1973.

283 ". . . a remarkable leader": *Pravda,* September 23, 1973.

284–85 NBC documentary: Interviews with Edwin Newman and Lucy Jarvis.

285–86 Brown House: Interview with Mary Yazbek, 1982.

286–87 The Moscow apartment: Interview with Bill McSweeny; *NYT,* November 22, 1976; Considine, *Bol'she Chem Zhizn* (Moscow: Progress Publishers, 1981); Williams, *Russian Art,* p. 191.

288 ". . . It makes me proud": Interview with Armand V. Hammer.

288 ". . . as one would help a relative": Interview with Mikhail Bruk.

289 *Chicago Sun-Times:* Interview with Murray Seeger.

289–90 On Armand Victorovich's rise: Interview with Armand V. Hammer; interview with Lucy Jarvis.

291 "Dr. Hammer dislikes his nephew": Interview with Mikhail Bruk.

291 Ambassador Jacob Beam: Interview with Ambassador Jacob Beam.

17: THE BEST OF BOTH WORLDS

Page

292–93 Kendall replaced: Interviews with members of the Trade Council. Kendall became chairman of the Chamber of Commerce in April 1981.

294 On Coke in Russia: *NYT,* April 9, 1978; interview with Donald Kendall.

294–95 On Pepsi and Afghanistan: *NYT,* January 24, 1980; February 24, 1980; January 23, 1980.

295 "I just couldn't be . . .": Interview with Ambassador Jacob Beam.

295 ". . . too much in politics . . .": Kendall, speech at Babson College commencement exercises, Wellesley, Massachusetts, May 17, 1980.

295–96 Baryshnikov: *NYT Magazine,* April 11, 1982, p. 28.

296 On Flora Lewis's report: *NYT,* August 27, 1982.

296 Eaton and CIA: *NYT,* June 17, 1975.

296 Eaton's obituary: Ibid., May 13, 1979.

296 Pugwash reunion: Ibid., July 19, 1982.

296 "somewhat of a blow . . .": Interview with David Rockefeller.

297 Dartmouth Conference 1975: Rockefeller remains a faithful Dartmouth participant.

297 incessant globetrotting: "David was always off playing the head of state," one Chase official privately complains, "while Walter Wriston at Citicorp stayed in New York beating his brains out."

297 "we didn't see any reason . . .": Interview with David Rockefeller. Loans to the Eastern-bloc nations have always been a tiny percentage of Chase's total international exposure. The Chase 1980 annual report lists $499 million in loans to Eastern Europe—no separate figures for the Soviet Union are available—which is less than 2 percent of all overseas lending.

297 Helmut Schmidt: William Safire, "Helmut's Dinner Party," *NYT,* January 10, 1982; interview with David Rockefeller, 1981.

298 "It is absolutely essential . . .": *NYT,* October 22, 1982.

298 On the Olympics coin deal: *NYT,* September 9, 1977; interviews with Trade Council members.

298–301 F. Jay Crawford: Interviews with Trade Council members, including Hammer; *NYT,* June 28, 1978; August 24, 1978; *Pravda,* August 26, 1978; interviews with State Department officials; interview with Marshall Shulman; interview with Malcolm Toon.

301 Lenin Order: *NYT,* May 26, 1978; interview with Armand Hammer. A Soviet interviewer, in a profile in *Soviet Russia* (December 1981, p. 3) noticed in Hammer's buttonhole the bar of the Lenin Order. Evidently, he wears it only in the Soviet Union.

301 On Hammer's eighty-fourth birthday: *NYT,* May 26, 1982.

302 Bob Hope: Edward Jay Epstein, "The Riddle of Armand Hammer," *NYT Magazine,* November 29, 1981, p. 69.

302 Redecoration fund: *NYT,* March 20, 1981.

302 "I was so honored . . .": Ibid., October 6, 1981.

302 "the New Mr. Cancer": "Meet the New Mr. Cancer," *Mother Jones,* January 1982, p.10.

302 Million-dollar prize: *NYT,* December 4, 1981.

302 Other cancer awards: Ibid., February 1, 1976; July 19, 1977.

303 Ford's Theatre: *Washington Post,* March 24, 1981.

303 " . . . The John Birch Society": Interview with Bill McSweeny.

304 "hired him, so to speak": Interview with Cass Canfield.

304 " . . . judgment of posterity": Matthew Josephson, *The Robber Barons* (New York: Harcourt, Brace: 1934), p. 455.

304–05 May 1976 shareholders meeting: *Wall Street Journal,* May 24, 1976; *NYT,* May 22, 1976; *Business Week,* January 10, 1977, p. 36.

305 "As Russians say . . .": Bob Considine, *Bol'she Chem Zhizn* (Moscow: Progress Publishers, 1981), p. 5.

305–06 "The Riddle of Armand Hammer": *NYT Magazine,* November 29, 1981, p. 68; December 20, 1981, p. 110; interview with Clifford May of the *NYT Magazine.*

307 " . . . Conference on Peace and Human Rights . . .": *NYT,* July 12, 1982.

308 "I still think the Soviets want peace . . .": Milton Moskowitz, et al., *Everybody's Business* (New York: Harper & Row, 1980), p. 518.

308 "I think we're lucky . . .": "John Callaway Interviews Armand Hammer" (aired October 8, 1981, WTTW Chicago. Distributed nationally by PBS).

308 In an article: *People,* November 29, 1982, p. 91.

308 " . . . Solzhenitsyn would be a child . . .": London *Observer,* August 9, 1981, p. 31.

308–09 On Afghanistan: *NYT,* January 31, 1980; February 28, 1980; UPI interview, March 6, 1980.

309 On Pakistan: *NYT,* August 9, 1980; speech before Foreign Policy Association, May 4, 1981.

309 happened to be in Moscow: *NYT,* June 26, 1981.

310 Superphosphate: *NYT,* May 10, 1982.

310 ENI: *Wall Street Journal,* October 30, 1981. ENI is Ente Nazionale Idrocarburi.

310 Poland: *NYT,* November 19, 1973; May 29, 1978; speech before Foreign Policy Association.

310 China: *NYT,* April 11, 1982; Radio Liberty interview, April 20, 1979; *NYT,* March 26, 1982. Also, in the fall of 1981, Hammer acquired Iowa Beef Processors to sell the Soviet Union desperately needed beef. The acquisition was expedited by Hammer's buying for David Murdoch, who owned the company, an Arabian stallion worth fifteen million dollars. (Epstein, "Riddle of Armand Hammer," p. 72; *NYT,* December 17, 1981.)

311–12 Hammer's personal life: Daniel Yergin, "The One-Man Flying Multinational," Part 2, *Atlantic,* July 1975, p. 60; Susie Gharib Nazem, "Occidental Petroleum's Odd Couple," *Fortune,* November 19, 1979, p. 71; Epstein, "Riddle of Armand Hammer," p. 71; James Cook, "The Capitalist Connection" (cover story), *Forbes,* April 28, 1980, p. 48; *Wall Street Journal,* December 7, 1981; May 12, 1978.

312 " . . . cult of personality": *Wall Street Journal,* May 18, 1981.

312 Directors sign letters of resignation: *NYT,* February 13, 1979, based on leaked testimony from SEC hearing on Occidental's attempted takeover of Mead, Inc. Other former Oxy officials also confirm that Hammer offered them directorships with the condition that they sign undated letters of resignation. In addition—and a great obstruction to journalists, naturally—Hammer pays many of the executives he fires a "consultant's fee," which can be revoked if they reveal any information to the press.

312 "Over $150 million": "The Forbes Four Hundred," *Forbes,* September 13, 1982, p. 136.

313–14 *Tak Pobyedim: Moscow News,* no. 13, 1982.

EPILOGUE

Page

316 Joseph Kraft: "Letter from Moscow," *The New Yorker,* July 29, 1974, p. 75.

316 Samuel Pisar: "Let's Put Détente Back on the Rails," *Common Sense in U.S.-Soviet Relations* (Washington: American Committee on East-West Accord, April 1978), p. 8.

316 George Bernard Shaw: cited in *NYT,* May 15, 1982.

316 Billy Graham: *NYT,* May 13, 1982.

317 Henry Kissinger: *White House Years* (Boston: Little, Brown, 1979), p. 153.

317 Bertrand Russell: *Power* (New York: Norton, 1938), p. 11.

317 ". . . he wouldn't have been available": From "Bill Moyers' Journal: The World of David Rockefeller," PBS, February 7, 1980.

317 "lower its guard": Norman Cousins, "Dartmouth IX," *Saturday Review,* July 12, 1975, p. 4. The journal's Russian title is: *Rabochiy Klass i Sovremenniy Mir.*

318 George Kennan: "Needed: A New American View of the U.S.S.R.," *Common Sense in U.S.-Soviet Relations* (Washington: American Committee on East-West Accord, April 1978), pp. 31–32. From remarks presented to the Council on Foreign Relations and published in the *Washington Post* on December 11, 1977.

318 *Time:* June 25, 1973, p. 37.

318 ". . . ringmaster of Barnum and Bailey's . . .": Interview with Donald Kendall.

319 the red carpet. Although the red carpet is an age-old tradition of European royalty, the term "red carpet" did not enter the popular vocabulary until the legendary train, the Twentieth Century Limited, began to roll out a red carpet for its passengers upon boarding at Grand Central in the early twenties. According to Ben Hall's *The Best Remaining Seats: The Story of the Golden Age of the Movie Palace* (New York: C. N. Potter, 1961), the showman S. L. (Roxy) Rothafel suggested the red carpet treatment to the train's management, the New York Central, and received in payment a lifetime railroad pass. Lucius Beebe proposes in his *The Twentieth Century Limited: The Greatest Train in the World* (Berkeley, Calif.: Howell-North, 1962) another, not necessarily contradictory version: that the Century's use of the red carpet was "inspired by the red carpets footmen in the various Vanderbilt homes along Fifth Avenue were accustomed to spread across the sidewalk whenever a member of the family entered his carriage or automobile, a custom which only came to an end in 1942 when the last Vanderbilt mansion disappeared and Mrs. Cornelius Vanderbilt moved into an apartment. The Vanderbilt tie-in with the lofty *ton* of The Century was a natural."

LIST OF INTERVIEWS

Much of the material in this book is based on personal and telephone interviews, conducted between January 1981 and July 1982, with more than one hundred people in business, government, and journalism; with friends, acquaintances, relatives, and close associates of the major figures; and, with the exception of the late Cyrus Eaton, with the major figures themselves.

Apart from those listed below, many who agreed to be interviewed prefer to remain unnamed.

The Principal Figures

Armand Hammer
Averell Harriman
Donald Kendall
David Rockefeller

Relatives

Fox Butterfield
Anne Kinder Eaton
Cyrus Eaton, Jr.
Armand Victorovich Hammer
Michael Hammer
Neva Rockefeller Kaiser

Associates

Peter Bakstansky
Mikhail Bruk
Norman R. Comiskey
Cartha DeLoach
Myer Feldman
William F. McSweeny
Joseph V. Reed, Jr.
John Reuther
Terry Riley
Roger Robinson
Sargent Shriver
Galina Sullivan
George D. Taylor, Jr.
Alfred Wentworth

Businessmen and Others Involved in East-West Trade

Howard L. Clark
Benjamin F. Crane
Michael V. Forrestal
James Giffen
Carl Marcy
Ara Oztemel
Milton F. Rosenthal
Harold B. Scott
C. William Verity, Jr.

Friends and Acquaintances

Norman Cousins
Malcolm Forbes
George Franklin
General James Gavin
Celia Gould
James R. Graham
Edna Gurewitsch
Kay Murphy Halle

Professor Milton Katz
Jay Lovestone
Gerald Stein
Ella Wolfe
Mary Yazbek

Government Officials, Past and Present

Morris Amitai
Jacob Beam
Eli Bergman
Lawrence F. Brady
William Farrand
Gerald Hamilton
Charles Horner
Thomas Hoya
Tal Lindstrom
John Maury
Senator Daniel Patrick Moynihan
Tom Niles
Herbert Romerstein
Professor Marshall Shulman
Maurice Stans
Walter Stoessel
Mrs. Llewellyn Thompson
Malcolm Toon
Cyrus Vance
Valentin Zabijaka

Journalists

Edward Jay Epstein
Fred Friendly, Jr.
Dave Hamilton
Yuri Handler
Joseph Harsch
Lucy Jarvis
Robert Kaiser
Vladimir Kozlovsky
Lawrence Leamar
David C. Martin
Clifford May
Lev Navrozov
Edwin Newman
Robert Pack
Harrison Salisbury
Murray Seeger
Henry Shapiro
Hedrick Smith

Others

Richard Barnet
Paige Bryan
Cass Canfield
William Gill
Nathan Glazer
Jerry Goodman
Pavel Litvinov
Richard Maass
Frank Mankiewicz
Arthur Schlesinger, Jr.

INDEX